WORK, YOUTH, AND SCHOOLING

Contributors

James D. Anderson

Geraldine Jonçich Clifford

Larry Cuban

W. Norton Grubb

David Hogan

Harvey Kantor

Joseph F. Kett

Marvin Lazerson

Daniel T. Rodgers

David B. Tyack

Work, Youth, and Schooling

HISTORICAL PERSPECTIVES

ON VOCATIONALISM IN AMERICAN

EDUCATION

Edited by Harvey Kantor and David B. Tyack

Stanford University Press, Stanford, California 1982

Stanford University Press
Stanford, California
©1982 by the Board of Trustees of the
Leland Stanford Junior University
Printed in the United States of America
ISBN 0-8047-1121-6
LC 81-50788

ACKNOWLEDGMENTS

This book is the product of a conference sponsored by the National Institute of Education (under contract number 400-78-0042) and held at the Boys Town Center for the Study of Youth Development, Stanford University, on August 17–18, 1979. We are deeply grateful to the Institute for this support and to the Boys Town Center for its fiscal and collegial support of the work leading up to and stemming from the conference. Naturally this report does not necessarily reflect the views of either agency. Dr. Lana Muraskin of the Institute played a crucial role in the planning of the conference and the editing of the report. We are much indebted to her for her scholarly and administrative expertise and her interest in the entire project from beginning to completion.

At the conference the authors and editors benefited from penetrating and wide-ranging criticism of the initial papers by participants, and in particular by the assigned discussants: C. H. Edson, Paula Fass, Patricia Graham, Herbert Gutman, Carl Kaestle, Daniel Rodgers, and Arthur Wirth.

H.K.
D.B.T.

CONTENTS

CONTRIBUTORS

JAMES D. ANDERSON is Associate Professor of History of Education at the University of Illinois, where he teaches history of American education, history of black education, and institutional racism. His M.Ed. and Ph.D. degrees were taken at the University of Illinois. His research interest focuses on black educational and social history, desegregation, and institutional racism. His contribution in this volume derives in part from a larger study of the formation and development of black education in the South, 1865 to 1940.

GERALDINE JONÇICH CLIFFORD is Professor of Education at the University of California, Berkeley. Author of *The Sane Positivist: A Biography of Edward L. Thorndike* and studies of the impact of educational research upon schooling, she has turned to the examination of the private papers of "ordinary" Americans. Professor Clifford is preparing a history of school and college life in nineteenth-century America, as perceived and experienced "at the grass roots."

LARRY CUBAN is Associate Professor of Education at Stanford University. Between 1974 and 1981 he served as superintendent of schools in Arlington County, Virginia. He is the author of *To Make a Difference: Teaching in the Inner City* (1970) and *Urban School Chiefs Under Fire* (1976). He is currently completing a study of how teachers have taught since 1900.

W. NORTON GRUBB teaches economics, statistics, and research courses in social and economic policy areas at the Lyndon B.

Johnson School of Public Affairs, the University of Texas at Austin. He is coauthor, with Marvin Lazerson, of *American Education and Vocationalism* (1974) and *Broken Promises: The State, Children, and Families in Post-War America* (1982).

DAVID HOGAN is Assistant Professor in the Education, Culture and Society Division of the Graduate School of Education at the University of Pennsylvania. He was educated at the University of Sydney, Australia, and the University of Illinois. He has recently finished a manuscript, *Education and Progressive Reform in Chicago,* and is currently Associate Director of the Philadelphia History of Education Research Project.

HARVEY KANTOR is a graduate student in the history of education at Stanford University. He is currently working on a dissertation on the origins of vocational schooling in California, 1900–1930.

JOSEPH F. KETT is Professor of History at the University of Virginia, where he teaches American cultural and intellectual history. He is the author of *The Formation of the American Medical Profession: The Role of Institutions, 1780–1860* (1968) and *Rites of Passage: Adolescence in America, 1790–Present* (1977).

MARVIN LAZERSON is Professor of Education at the University of British Columbia. He is the author of *Origins of the Urban School* (1971), and coauthor, with W. Norton Grubb, of *American Education and Vocationalism* (1974) and *Broken Promises: The State, Children, and Families in Post-War America* (1982). He has written extensively on the history of education and on the relationship of history to social policy.

DANIEL T. RODGERS teaches American intellectual and cultural history at Princeton University. He is the author of *The Work Ethic in Industrial America, 1850–1920* (1978). He is currently engaged in a study of political ideas in nineteenth-century Britain and America.

DAVID B. TYACK is Vida Jacks Professor of Education and History, Stanford University. His publications include *The One Best System* and *Managers of Virtue* (forthcoming).

WORK, YOUTH, AND SCHOOLING

Introduction: Historical Perspectives on Vocationalism in American Education

HARVEY KANTOR AND DAVID B. TYACK

I

At the turn of the twentieth century, the idea of using schools to train young people for work captured the imagination of American reformers. Convinced that schools had failed to keep pace with changes in the nature and meaning of industrial life, they proposed a radical reorientation of purpose and curriculum in American education. The central task of the school, they argued, was to integrate youth into the occupational structure. To accomplish this required not only differentiated programs' and courses, but also a new spirit of vocationalism. As one advocate remarked, school life should be permeated with "the idea that school is to prepare for a vocation and that vocation is to be wisely selected."[1]

Both contemporary observers and later scholars generally agree that this movement marked a significant turning point in the social history of American education. Indeed, one of the most striking features of the turn-of-the-century ferment has been the permanence of the changes that were introduced. Over the years the idea that school should prepare youth for work has become a common rationale for schooling and has provided support for numerous vocationally oriented programs, many of which continue to attract a good deal of financial support from state legislatures and Congress and to employ large numbers of teachers and administrators. They enroll students in a variety of courses, ranging from career awareness in elementary grades to specific skill training in high schools.[2]

There is little evidence, however, that these reforms have actually eliminated the conditions they sought to address. Early advocates promised that vocational education and guidance would solve a host of economic and social ills. Vocational schooling, they claimed, would integrate immigrants into the labor force, slash worker turnover, lessen labor conflict and social alienation, reduce unemployment, and increase occupational opportunities for poor and working-class youth. Yet during the last fifty years, major evaluations of vocational programs have repeatedly questioned the benefits of vocational training. Although some studies have found that vocational graduates have lower unemployment and receive higher wages than other comparable students, the majority of studies have concluded that there is little economic advantage to vocational training, as opposed to non-vocational, at the high school level.[3]

Even allowing for the rhetorical oversell that usually accompanies educational reforms, the hopes for vocational education appear to have been misplaced. As several scholars have recently pointed out, the sources of poverty, unemployment, and economic inequality are primarily rooted not in the nature of schooling but in the organization of the economy. Consequently, by focusing on educational reform rather than on the structure of work and the labor market, vocational reformers attacked the symptoms rather than the sources of the conditions they hoped to eliminate.[4]

What then accounts for the rise and persistence of vocationalism in American education? Why did turn-of-the-century reformers turn to schools to ameliorate the social and economic ills plaguing American society? How did these initial efforts shape the subsequent relationship between school and work? Until recently, these questions provoked little debate. Historians of education, following the lead of Ellwood Cubberley, generally applauded the rise of vocational schooling, viewing it a democratic movement to liberate the educational system from outmoded practices. Only by adding practical, relevant courses, it was ar-

gued, could the high school meet the diverse needs of an expanding clientele without abandoning public education's commitment
to equal opportunity for all members of American society. Indeed, house historians of vocational education and guidance,
eager to promote their cause and celebrate its democratic promise, have portrayed the rise of vocationalism as an almost inevitable development in a democratic and heterogeneous society.[5]

In the last fifteen years, however, a number of scholars have
reexamined the history of vocational reform and have painted a
different picture of these events. Revisionist historians have argued that vocational education was part of a middle- and upper-
class movement for social control and order in a corporate state.
Vocational education, they say, was hardly the product of democratic sentiments, but was shaped by businessmen and efficiency-minded educators interested in using schools to adapt young
people to the unjust nature of the corporate-industrial society
emerging at the turn of the twentieth century.[6] In a similar vein,
neo-Marxist writers on the history of education have contended
that vocational programs were designed to turn out docile, efficient workers who were well adjusted to the demands of large-
scale industrial production. Vocational education, they argue, operated not to liberalize opportunity, but to teach working-class
youth their proper place in the expanding capitalist division of
labor.[7]

Criticism has come from other sources too. Today there is once
again considerable concern about youth unemployment and the
connection between school and work. Numerous reports and
studies have identified the transition from school to work as a
major social problem, and have advanced a variety of programs to
bridge what is believed to be a major gap between the classroom
and the workplace. Yet contemporary policy analysts often differ
markedly from reformers at the turn of the century. Whereas
child labor was seen by earlier advocates of vocational education
as a problem to be solved by additional schooling, some analysts
now see compulsory schooling as a problem to be solved by
exposure to the workplace. The Coleman panel's *Youth: Transition to Adulthood* (1974), for instance, argues that secondary
schools segregate youth by age and shelter them from work and
useful contact with adults. The panel proposes that much of the

responsibility for socializing young people to work be shifted from the school to the workplace itself. Work, the panel maintains, is a preparation for life; school only reinforces an irresponsible youth culture.[8]

In retrospect, it is puzzling that vocationalism in education appealed to such a wide spectrum of groups, including some—such as business and labor—that generally regarded each other as adversaries. As Harvey Kantor indicates in his essay, people of widely differing ideologies and interests agreed that vocational training might bring schools into better alignment with the economy. To be sure, advocates of vocational training often differed among themselves over who should control the new programs and what should be their form and purpose. John Dewey, for example, challenged proposals for a separate system of vocational schools, arguing as some radicals do today that such a plan would create a stratified school system. Some reformers called for highly specific skill training; others were more interested in a "life-career motive" that would permeate all instruction. Some wanted to turn out docile employees willing to adapt to routine factory labor; others questioned the whole notion of a profit economy and wanted to restore, in Helen Marot's words, the "creative impulse in industry."[9] But whatever their ideologies or specific plans or interests, a wide spectrum of leaders agreed that vocationalism in education was a key to the restructuring of American society.

II

The essays in this collection explore these and other related issues. Larry Cuban suggests that one explanation for the rise and persistent popularity of vocational education lies in an analysis of interest group politics, especially the lobbying power of the National Society for the Promotion of Industrial Education (NSPIE) and its successor, the American Vocational Association (AVA). Founded in 1906, the NSPIE lobbied vigorously for over a decade to win federal support for vocational education. In 1917 it played the decisive role in securing congressional and presidential approval of the Smith-Hughes bill, which mandated federal aid for vocational training in home economics, agriculture, and trade and industrial subjects. But the group's influence did not stop there. When the Federal Board of Vocational Education (FBVE) was established in 1917, its members were drawn largely from the ranks of the NSPIE. Moreover, by 1926 the NSPIE had been transformed from a single-purpose but broad-based reform coalition into an active professional association (the AVA) dedicated to maintaining the victory achieved in 1917. This task has since been performed with only minor setbacks.

Indeed the power of this group, Cuban argues, has extended far beyond "what one would predict from the size of its staff or membership." Using lobbying techniques honed in the decade-long struggle to win approval of Smith-Hughes, the AVA has for over fifty years thwarted opposition to vocational education legislation and consistently won higher federal appropriations for vocational programs. Even in the face of persistent criticism from blue-ribbon panels, federal studies, and academic evaluations, the AVA influence in Congress remained exceptionally strong. In fact, one recent study ranked the AVA fourth among the most effective Washington education lobbies.

Legislative victories, however, did not guarantee that vocational programs would be implemented effectively. At best, Cuban suggests, the evidence on implementation is mixed. Although state-level implementation appears to have been successful—by 1918 all states had submitted vocational plans to the FBVE and had begun to receive federal funds—the picture at the local level is much less conclusive. Although some early studies indicated that high school offerings in home economics, agriculture, and trade and industrial subjects increased dramatically after the passage of Smith-Hughes, other studies showed that the time students spent in vocational courses was quite limited. A 1931 study, for instance, revealed that in some urban school districts vocational courses constituted as little as 1 percent of the time students spent in school.

What accounts for the apparently limited impact of federal vocational education legislation? Cuban suggests that federal efforts were impeded by a variety of organizational factors within local and state school bureaucracies, such as the diversity of local school districts and the traditional resistance by teachers to outside meddling in the classroom. Joseph Kett, however, suggests that we search elsewhere for an explanation. Like Cuban, Kett seeks to understand how a movement that generated such high expectations could have produced such meager results. Where Cuban finds clues to this puzzle in how laws were passed and implemented, Kett suggests that we look at the ideas of the first generation of vocational educators, particularly those who led the drive that culminated in the passage of Smith-Hughes. By analyzing their ideas about work, unemployment, and economic mobility, Kett argues, it is possible to gain a clearer conception of why vocational education seemed so plausible to its early advocates, as well as how many educators may have misunderstood the economic conditions they confronted.

Most vocational educators, according to Kett, combined recent ideas about science and professionalism with traditional ideas about work and the work ethic to forge a powerful intellectual justification for vocational education. Eventually this ideology blinded them to the nature of work and the labor market in the early twentieth century. They shared with Frederick Winslow Taylor the idea that skill meant the application of organized knowledge, and were influenced by emerging conceptions of professionalism that linked jobs to one another in a smooth, steady career ladder, from lower to higher occupational rungs. Thus many vocational reformers ignored accumulating evidence that work was requiring less and less skill, and they did not perceive that many "blind-alley" jobs were probably only temporary youth jobs, rather than permanent barriers to occupational mobility. They hoped to reform work and eliminate "dead-end" jobs by shaping all occupations to professional models. By misperceiving the nature of the conditions they faced, vocational reformers, according to Kett, often proposed educational solutions when other responses might have been more appropriate.

Did the turn-of-the-century furor about youth and work, then, reflect changing cultural perceptions more than it reflected changes in actual labor market conditions? Perhaps. Although evidence on nineteenth- and early twentieth-century labor markets is scant, most working youth in the United States have probably always been concentrated in the least desirable occupations. In addition, as Burton Bledstein and others have shown, in the late nineteenth and early twentieth centuries the culture of professionalism was beginning to exert a powerful influence on middle-class social thought.[10] Yet as the essay by Norton Grubb and Marvin Lazerson and that by David Hogan point out, the early twentieth-century concern about youth, work, and schooling involved more than faulty perceptions of work and labor market conditions.

According to Grubb and Lazerson, in the first decades of the twentieth century the relationship between work and schooling was fundamentally transformed. Rooted in changes in labor markets, stemming largely from changes in the organization of work, this transformation inextricably linked education to employment and altered the primary purposes of public education. For the first time, Grubb and Lazerson assert, school became the primary route to employment; and preparation for a place in the labor market became the "raison d'être of public education." Only by examining these institutional changes—which involve considerably more than the growth of federally assisted vocational courses—is it possible to understand the impact of vocationalism on American education.

Indeed, the consequences of these changes were enormous for youth, schooling, and social policy. First, as schools increasingly became a major path to employment, young people withdrew from the labor market and went to school. Between 1900 and 1920, the percentage of fourteen- to eighteen-year-old males at work dropped from 43 to 23 percent, and females from 18 to 11 percent. At the same time, the high school enrollment of fourteen- to seventeen-year-olds rose from approximately 8 percent in 1900 to over 44 percent in 1930, and the proportion of high school graduates increased from 6.4 percent of seventeen-year-olds in 1900 to 16.8 percent in 1920 and to 29 percent in 1930. During the depression the ratio of graduates almost doubled. Second, schools themselves were transformed in order to prepare youth for entry into the labor market. Differentiated curricula, vocational courses in the trades and business, guidance, and testing were introduced as schools assumed responsibility for integrating youth into the occupational structure, often sorting students according to class, race, and sex. Finally, by removing young people from the labor market and certifying them for future occupational roles, this transformation has defined the character of twentieth-century American youth policy (with some notable exceptions in the 1930's and more recently in the 1970's). It has reinforced tendencies to rely on educational solutions to labor market problems and blocked other more direct intervention, such as job creation and employment programs.

Thus, whereas Cuban locates the roots of vocationalism in interest group politics and Kett in changing cultural and intellectual values, Grubb and Lazerson conclude that an analysis of the rise of vocationalism must focus on the evolution of institutional relationships between school and work. It was this shift, in their view, that defined educational responses to problems of work and the labor market and that transformed schooling into a mechanism of occupational training, selection, and certification.

David Hogan examines theoretical perspectives on work and schooling that shed light on how and why this shift occurred. According to Hogan, the most common explanation of the economic functions of education—that is, human capital theory—suggests that the development of links between school and work reflected the increasing demand for skilled labor generated by technological change. This neoclassical analysis is based on the dual assumptions that technological change increases the complexity of jobs (by replacing low-skill jobs with high-skill jobs and by upgrading the skill requirements of remaining jobs) and that education produces the cognitive and technical skills to perform more difficult tasks. Yet there is, Hogan points out, a considerable body of historical and contemporary evidence, some of it outlined in Kantor's essay, indicating that technological change has not increased the skill requirements of many jobs. Beyond minimal levels, the impact of additional education on job skills is difficult to discern in a wide range of occupations.

What then links education to work? In particular, what accounts for the steady expansion and escalation of educational requirements for work—that is, credentialism—in the United States in the twentieth century? There are a number of alternative theories, most of which suggest that employers use education as a measure of general personal traits such as discipline, perseverance, and trainability rather than as a measure of specific technical or cognitive skills. But any analysis, according to Hogan, must contain three elements: a description of the structure of labor markets, a specification of the processes in schools that link schools to the labor market, and an account of the forces that sustain these structural linkages.

First, Hogan contends, the labor market is not unitary, as human capital theory generally assumes, but is segmented into three major divisions: an independent primary market, a subordinate primary market, and a secondary market. Each of these corresponds to a different type of control on the job and each, in turn, requires different behavior and personality traits of its workers. Second, schools have been linked to these labor markets through organizational processes within schools that socialize students to work norms and sort them among different curricula. Eventually the process distributes graduates to different labor markets. Finally, these structures have not been shaped and sustained by market mechanisms expressing a generalized popular demand for schooling, but have been shaped by political struggles between groups with different goals and interests, as in the case of vocational education.

What has been the outcome of these struggles? Some researchers have concluded that educational expansion is linked closely to economic opportunity, since, it is argued, as education has become the criterion of access to more and more occupations, the importance of class, race, and sex has declined. According to Hogan, Grubb and Lazerson, and several other recent critics, however, educational expansion in the twentieth century has not led to greater economic opportunity. Instead, they argue, it has diverted attention from fundamental economic problems and has contributed to the reproduction of the class structure by differentiating among students on the basis of class, sex, and race. Thus working-class students have been channeled into vocational tracks, young women into traditional female courses such as cooking and sewing, and middle-class students into academic courses.

Only recently have historians begun to investigate systematically the relationship between education and jobs for immigrants, blacks, and women; many issues remain unresolved.[11] How, for example, did the development of links between school and work influence the educational behavior and labor market participation of immigrant, black, and women workers? Did educational achievement have equal payoffs for all groups, or did some benefit more than others from additional schooling? By what standards, moreover, should economic returns to education be evaluated? The essays by James Anderson and Geraldine Clifford address these issues.

Perhaps nowhere has there been a greater gap between rhetoric and reality than in the history of black vocational education. Few groups have placed greater faith in the equalizing power of schooling yet received such meager economic returns for their additional education. Since the nineteenth century, black educational leaders have responded to this situation in a variety of ways, but according to Anderson three strategies have dominated the history of black vocationalism. One strategy was to adapt black vocational schooling to those occupations in which large numbers of blacks were employed and to encourage black youth to make "realistic" decisions about future careers. This tactic characterized the educational ideas and practices of the post-Civil War normal schools such as Hampton and the "black land-grant institutions" chartered by the second Morrill Act in 1890, both of which emphasized black teacher training through a manual labor process.

The second strategy, which flourished in the black vocational guidance movement during the 1930's, questioned the philosophy of advising black youth to pursue racially defined occupations. Instead, black vocational leaders—much like their white colleagues in the movement—proposed to increase black occupational opportunities by using well-developed school guidance programs. They argued that this would not only widen occupational choices for black youth, many of whom had a limited knowledge of the job market, but it would also help to reduce unemployment among black youth by diversifying their occupational options and teaching them about the problems of living in a modern industrial economy.

Vocational guidance, however, did little to expand occupational opportunities for black youth. After the Second World War black leaders stressed a third strategy: obtaining equality of opportunity in academic secondary schools and colleges. Since 1950, Anderson points out, this strategy has produced dramatic educational gains for black Americans, and in 1976 the median number of years of schooling completed by blacks equaled that by whites. Yet, as in the past, educational achievements rarely produced commensurate gains in job opportunities and income, except for black professionals. From 1952 to 1968, though the mean education of black male workers rose from 67 to 87 percent of that of white male workers, the median wage and salary incomes of black workers rose only from 58 percent to 66 percent of white incomes. Most of this increase, moreover, was largely due to black emigration from the South.[12]

Despite this disparity, Anderson concludes, increases in educational attainment may bear economic fruit for black Americans, although not in ways commonly expected. Rather, he suggests, by sharpening the contradictions between blacks' educational attainment and their occupational achievement, educational success may illuminate the shortcomings of educational panaceas for labor market conditions. This may serve to direct attention toward remedies that directly combat labor market discrimination.

For women, as for black Americans, the economic payoff of additional schooling has been less than for white males. Yet women too have consistently sought more schooling. In fact, in the late nineteenth and early twentieth centuries, female high school graduates consistently outnumbered male graduates by approximately three to two. According to Geraldine Clifford, part of the reason for these female enrollment patterns may be found in the ways that sex has shaped women's participation in the work force and in the ways that schooling has influenced the occupations women could enter.

Historians have only recently begun to investigate how class, race, ethnicity, region, and family have influenced women's labor force participation, but as Clifford notes, at least three patterns stand out.[13] First, the women's share of the labor force has increased steadily since the late nineteenth century, rising from 18.3 percent in 1900, to 20.4 percent in 1920, to 27.9 percent in 1950, and to 46 percent in 1978. Second, sex has always circumscribed the occupations considered appropriate to women. Although the percentage of women in nonmanual work increased from 28 percent of working women in 1900 to 45 percent in 1940, almost all women worked in sex-segregated occupations that were popularly viewed as "women's work." In 1940 more than 75 percent of all women workers were in jobs that employed less than 1 percent of all male workers.[14] Third, the average woman worker rarely received more than 50 to 55 percent of the wages men received for their work. Even where men and women held the same job, the pay gap remained substantial.[15]

Vocational reformers were uneasy about these trends, concerned that having a job was undermining women's traditional roles as wives and mothers. Reformers also recognized that many women only remained in the work force for a short time, which made vocational education seem wasteful. Accordingly, where vocational training was given, it usually focused on traditional female occupations, such as dressmaking, sewing, and, after 1900, secretarial skills, and centered as much as possible on home economics and domestic science. Such courses might be beneficial in women's occupations, but more importantly, they also prepare women for their expected "careers" as wives, mothers, and housekeepers.

It is difficult, however, to assess the impact of vocational education for women on their labor force participation. Although vocational reformers differentiated vocational training by sex, Clifford questions the degree to which "the sometimes obligatory course in home economics" actually influenced women's work. More important, she concludes, since the late nineteenth century a woman's position among workers came to be broadly defined more by the amount than the type of education she possessed. Increasingly, the girl who left school after the eighth grade was limited to factory labor, whereas the growing number of female high school graduates could find jobs in the expanding white-collar sector of the economy. Thus, although a gap remained between women's educational achievement and the reality of a sex-segregated labor market, staying in school may have given a woman occupational options that were unavailable to less-educated women.

III

Many of the early debates about the connection between school and work have obvious echoes in our own time. Indeed, as noted earlier, during the last decade the relationship between school and work has once again become one of the foremost topics of educational discussion. Concern about "the decline of the work ethic," the phenomenon of "over-education," and spiraling rates of youth unemployment—especially among minority youth—has created a public preoccupation with the vocational purposes of schooling and has stimulated a flurry of proposals to make school more relevant to adult life and the world of work. Some reformers propose a dramatic reorientation of the educational system so that all phases of school experience will be job-oriented. Others have advanced plans to alternate periods of school with periods of work so that young people will have work experience while they remain in school. Still others—James Coleman is perhaps the best known—question the utility of school-based vocational training and wish to transfer the responsibility for socializing young people for work from school to the workplace itself.[16]

Historical analysis cannot provide tidy lists of lessons from the past by which to evaluate these policies. To be successful, remedies must be specific to time and place, and they must be sensitive to context. Some of the current proposals for vocationalism in education, however, give a feeling of *déjà vu,* a sense that some policymakers may be recycling old solutions to problems that have proven resistant to purely educational correction. In these essays we have sought to provide perspectives on changing contexts, attitudes, and institutions, and to open a window to the past through which one may view the assumptions and policies that shape current debates about youth, work, and schooling.

Vocationalism in American Education:

The Economic and Political Context, 1880-1930

HARVEY KANTOR

In the opening decades of the twentieth century the idea of using schools to prepare young people for work grew into a major campaign to integrate the school more closely with the economy. Across a wide spectrum of opinion, reformers became convinced that the school should mediate between youth and the workplace, or as one proponent stated, "act as a transmitter between human supply and industrial demand."[1] It was the central task of the school, reformers argued, to train youth for jobs and to guide them into occupations that suited their talents and interests and matched the economic needs of their communities.

This contrasted with attitudes and practices common earlier. Although schools had long sought to teach steady work habits and to instill respect for manual labor, for most of the nineteenth century formal education played a relatively minor role in specific occupational preparation. Most urban youth went to school for five or six years, usually leaving at age twelve or thirteen to receive vocational training by means of apprenticeship or informal on-the-job training. In rural areas, young people went to school in seasons when they were not needed for work on the farm, which lowered the opportunity costs of attending school to nearly zero. They generally attended school for a few months at a time for a span of several years.[2]

This essay was originally drafted with David Tyack, whose assistance I gratefully acknowledge. Needless to say, errors in judgment are my own.

Certain youth from middle-class families, bound for white-collar positions or the professions, might find a good deal that was of practical value in nineteenth-century classrooms, at least in such things as grammar, penmanship, and ciphering. Yet prior to 1880, schools were seldom seen as mechanisms to prepare youth for jobs. Nor, by and large, did people expect that schooling beyond the elementary and grammar grades would influence one's chances for employment. Nationwide, as late as 1890, only 3.5 percent of seventeen-year-olds graduated from high school. In fact, many nineteenth-century Americans warned against the economic consequences of prolonged schooling. As one Portland, Oregon, newspaper editor remarked in 1879, too much education might "graduate whole regiments of sickly sentimentalists: young gentlemen unused and unfit for work."[3]

As the turn of the century approached, however, the pressure for change became intense. Beginning in the 1880's, schools were charged with being irrelevant to the economy, with failing to teach the skills needed for occupational mobility, and with ignoring the social consequences of modern industrial life. Groups from outside and inside the educational system—including businessmen, labor leaders, farm spokesmen, social reformers, and many educators—demanded that schools abandon the traditional classical curriculum in favor of specific, vocationally oriented courses. It was the job of the school, they argued, to train youth for work and to integrate them smoothly into the occupational structure.[4]

What prompted this outburst? Why did so many reformers join the campaign to vocationalize the schools? Although reformers often differed widely in their interests and ideologies, almost all agreed that changes stemming from the spread of industrial capitalism—particularly changes in the organization of work—made school reform imperative. This essay examines those changes and describes the political forces that shaped educational policies and programs.

Changes in Work, 1880–1920

Between 1880 and 1920 the scope and character of the American economy underwent drastic change. As Robert Wiebe and Samuel Hays have shown, during these years a fragmented, regionally oriented economy characterized by small workshops and farms was transformed into a national urban-industrial network increasingly dominated by large corporations.[5] Industrial output expanded rapidly, quadrupling between 1870 and 1900 and doubling again in the next twenty years. At the same time, wealth was increasingly concentrated in the leading sectors of the economy, until by 1920 the largest 5 percent of all industries earned 70 percent of total corporate net income.[6]

The changes in these years, however, involved more than rapid increases in output and the development of national markets. Corporate growth and consolidation also laid the foundation for an organizational transformation in American business. Most mid-nineteenth-century firms, according to Alfred Chandler, were single-unit enterprises that relied on market mechanisms to coordinate the activities of the economy and to allocate its resources. Operating in a limited geographic area, generally engaged in a single economic activity (for instance, production but not distribution, or vice versa), and dealing in a single product line, these firms were relatively simple organizations. Indeed, in such enterprises management barely existed as a separate function. Office and floor were closely linked and usually located in the same building; and the owner, with the help of a few trusted assistants, could personally supervise the firm's operations as well as coordinate other necessary business activities.[7]

By contrast, the corporate giants of the early twentieth century brought a wide range of economic activities under their control, taking over functions formerly left to the market. Leading businesses added a host of new activities—including marketing, sales, and advertising—differentiated their product lines, and expanded their operations nationwide and worldwide. In these enterprises, management became a vital concern. Once relatively simple in hierarchy and function, businesses developed multilevel, functionally differentiated systems of organization to coordinate their various activities. They introduced elaborate statistical and budgetary procedures to plan future operations. And finally, in place of the owner and his few trusted assistants, they increasingly turned to new schools of business and engineering for professionally trained managers to oversee corporate operations.[8]

But the drive to centralize the control of economic activity did not stop with new managerial and marketing arrangements. As managers began to rationalize the production and distribution of economic resources, they also turned their attention to the production process itself, altering the organization of work and the nature of the work process. The pace of these changes varied substantially from one industry to another and from place to place. In some industries, such as textiles and shoe manufacturing, they were well under way by the 1860's and 1870's. In others, older methods of work lingered into the first decades of the twentieth century. But by 1920 most observers agreed that in the leading sectors of the economy the workplace bore little resemblance to the craftsmen's shops and farms characteristic of the mid-nineteenth-century economy.

The physical growth of the workplace was the most apparent change. When the factory replaced the small workshop as the dominant mode of production, the scale of the workplace increased dramatically. As late as the 1850's, most workers were employed in shops with fewer than ten employees, and factories with over 100 employees—concentrated in the textile industry—ranked as manufacturing giants. By 1900, however, the four largest manufacturing plants in the United States each employed over 8,000 workers, and even these were modest by later standards. In 1909, for example, Cambria Steel had nearly 20,000 employees at its Johnstown, Pennsylvania, plant; General Electric had 15,000 at Schenectady, New York, and 11,000 at its plant in Lynn, Massachusetts; Pullman had 15,000 at its Chicago plant in 1913; and by 1916 the Ford plant at Highland Park, Michigan, employed 33,000 workers.[9] Small workshops persisted alongside these colossal enterprises, but they employed a decreasing proportion of the labor force. Daniel Rodgers has calculated that in 1919, in the northern states east of the Mississippi River, three-fourths of the wage earners in manufacturing were employed in factories with more than 100 employees, and 30 percent in factories with over 1,000.[10]

As the scale of production expanded, employers and managers sought to systematize and centralize the control of factory operations. In earlier manufacturing enterprises, skilled workers had retained wide discretion in the direction of their own work, defining the timing and manner of production, determining the pace of work, ascertaining its cost and quality, and hiring and firing their own helpers. After 1880, however, employers increasingly sought to remove the control of production from the shop floor and centralize it in the hands of management. By 1900, for example, production control systems in many factories included the specification of parts, instructions for production procedures, the direction of the movement of materials, and methods for controlling and recording the direct costs of operations. In each case, the objective was to increase management's control of the production process, largely at the expense of the craftsman's autonomy, by shifting the control and knowledge of the production process from the shop floor to the office. Under this system of scientific management, wrote Frederick Winslow Taylor, its most prominent advocate, "the managers assume . . . the burden of gathering together all of the traditional knowledge which in the past has been possessed by the workmen and then of classifying, tabulating, and reducing this knowledge to rules, laws, and formulae." [11]

Similarly, as the control of production was centralized, occupations became more specialized and the subdivision of labor became more minute. Increasingly, in the 1880's and 1890's, factory managers split the work process into smaller and smaller tasks, rendering many of the skilled trades obsolete. In the clothing industry, for example, where it had been common practice for a tailor to make an entire garment, coat manufacture was divided into thirty-nine separate occupations and each garment passed through the hands of fifty to a hundred workers.[12] A similar multiplication of occupations occurred in slaughtering and meat packing. Prior to the 1890's, slaughtering and butchering had been a highly skilled craft; as Walter Weyl and A. M. Sakolski remarked, the cattle butcher knew "the butchering business in all its details" and was able "to perform his craft with one or two helpers." During the 1890's, however, managers of large packing houses introduced an extensive division of labor, fracturing the labor process into over thirty occupations with twenty rates of pay.[13] These were only the most conspicuous examples of the subdivision of tasks. Between 1880 and 1920, the specialization of labor spread to many industries; not only tailors and meat packers, but glassblowers, furniture and cabinet makers, iron molders and puddlers, carriage makers, and other skilled craftsmen saw their work divided and subdivided.[14]

In most industries, moreover, the subdivision of labor was accompanied and stimulated by the mechanization of the production process. As the Lynds wrote, in numerous industries "the muscle and cunning of the master craftsman" were replaced by "batteries of tireless iron men."[15] Nowhere, however, was the twin impact of specialization and mechanization more evident than in the newly emerging automobile industry. When the Ford Motor Company was founded in 1903, building automobiles was a task reserved for skilled craftsmen who had received their training in bicycle and carriage shops. According to Keith Sward, at the beginning of the twentieth century automobile making "revolved around the versatile mechanic, who was compelled to move about in order to do his work. Ford's assemblers were still all-around men."[16] By 1908, the job had been partially split up and there were several assemblers, each one responsible for fewer operations. But these changes were minor compared with what was to come. As the Lynds described the auto part plant in Muncie, Indiana, in the 1920's, the worker "stands all day in front of his multiple drill press, undrilled rings being brought constantly to his elbow and his product carried away." Over and over he performed the same operation, "three times each minute, nine hours a day."[17]

These changes dramatically altered the nature and meaning of work, for by undermining the craftsman's control of production, they greatly reduced the need for appreciable skills on the factory floor. In numerous industries where mechanization and the specialization of labor were extensive, the relative importance of the skilled worker declined and the relative importance of the semiskilled increased. For example, prior to the 1880's in the steel industry, according to David Brody, the "rolling mills had required highly skilled men to catch and pass hot steel through the rolls . . . men of long experience and at a premium in America." By the first decade of the twentieth century, however, the steel mills were to a great extent manned by semiskilled operatives "adept at routine mechanical duties which were not comparable to the virtuosity of the hand rollers."[18] In many other industries as well, both old and new, the relative importance of the all-around skilled worker decreased. In such industries as shoes, textiles, glass, furniture, automobiles, and steel, the necessity for all-around skill declined and a monotonous repetition of movements came to dominate the production process.[19]

The transformation of work deeply eroded the apprenticeship system, for the notion of training a young worker in all the elements of a trade on the shop floor no longer made sense. In many trades that prior to the 1880's had required years of training and experience, operative jobs were so subdivided that they could be learned within a matter of weeks. According to the Lynds, for example, all the castings in a Muncie foundry in the 1890's had been made by highly skilled molders with years of experience, but by the 1920's over 60 percent were made by semiskilled machine molders who needed only a "fortnight or so of training."[20] Likewise, in the meat-packing industry, Weyl and Sakolski reported in 1906 that any ordinary laborer could be trained in most meat-packing operations in less than a week.[21] Perhaps the most striking example of how little time was needed to learn a trade came from the experience of the Emergency Fleet Corporation during the First World War, when the shipyards had to call for unskilled workers to meet their increased demand for labor. It was reported that the training periods for occupations from bolters to ship fitters averaged nineteen days.[22] In short, as many contemporaries pointed out, it was no longer necessary for every worker to have a thorough knowledge of all the processes of a trade; generally, learning one branch or subdivision of a trade would suffice.

To be sure, the industrial transformation of work did not eliminate all skill. As Paul Douglas found in his investigation of the skilled trades in 1921, highly skilled workers with a "thorough knowledge of the whole mechanism" were still prized in machine repair and maintenance. In fact, many corporations complained about the shortage of highly skilled machinists that resulted from the erosion of the old apprenticeship system, and they often established their own schools to recruit and train workers to repair and service the machines that were transforming the labor process. But these skilled workers, Douglas reported, were "distinctly in the minority." More and more, he concluded, the typical factory job stripped the individual of the skill and judgment that had once been a necessity.[23]

On the other hand, if the need for all-around skill declined, the importance of supervisory and managerial functions increased. As the barriers distinguishing skilled and unskilled work gradually disintegrated, a hierarchical social division of labor—based not so much on skills as on wages, status, and authority—replaced them. In the steel industry, according to Katherine Stone, the technical division of labor was gradually replaced by "strictly demarcated job ladders, linking each job with the one above and below it in status and pay to make a chain along which workers could progress."[24] These developments were not confined to steel. In many American industries, as David Hogan has documented, the social division of labor expanded.[25] Whereas in 1900 employers hired on the average one foreman for every 89 workers, by 1930 they hired one for every 34. But the foreman was only one link in an expanding managerial hierarchy. Increasingly, he too took orders from the college-trained engineers and technicians who staffed the ranks of lower and middle management.[26]

Even the office was not immune from the drive to rationalize and centralize work. After 1900, as the clerical labor force expanded rapidly, employers applied the principles of scientific management and the subdivision of labor to the office, fracturing office work into numerous occupations—typist, stenographer, bookkeeper, copyist, file clerk—and routinizing the operations of each job. In the process, most office work was also sexually segregated. Whereas the typical mid-nineteenth-century clerk had been a male, working, as Harry Braverman has written, at a "total occupation," by 1920 offices were staffed largely by women working at subdivided, strictly supervised tasks that more and more resembled work on the factory floor.[27]

By 1920, then, work in America had been substantially reorganized. Mechanization had replaced hand production, the minute specialization of labor was splintering the skilled trades, and the control and knowledge of production was increasingly removed from the shop floor and centralized in management. Historians have debated how widespread these changes were. In many smaller firms, no doubt, older modes of production persisted. But in leading manufacturing industries at the center of the American economy, few contemporary observers doubted that work had undergone dramatic change.

Responses to Changes in Work and the Workplace

The transformation of industry sharply challenged mid-nineteenth-century beliefs in the moral preeminence of work. As Daniel Rodgers and James Gilbert have shown, for many middle-class Americans in the mid-nineteenth century a belief in the value of work had formed the moral core of life. Work, many believed, built character, ingrained self-restraint, provided the chance for self-expression, and opened the path to deserved status and reward. Yet as the century progressed and as factories grew larger and work more subdivided, it became difficult to justify the belief that hard work would build moral character or lead to economic success. Where, many middle-class Americans asked, was the opportunity for the semiskilled to learn the skills that would lead up the economic ladder? Amid the routine of the factory, where was the opportunity for self-fulfilling labor? Even in farming, which had been glorified as an occupation that built character through hard work, success seemed to depend more and more on fluctuations in world markets, on the manipulation of the currency, and on scientific knowledge and mechanical invention.[28]

If the new patterns of work challenged middle-class assumptions about the moral benefits of work, on the factory floor they often produced opposition and conflict. As Herbert Gutman and others have shown, industrial capitalism often clashed sharply with working people's values and expectations, work habits, and sense of time. Clinging to traditional irregular, task-oriented approaches, working people often opposed strenuously and at times successfully the tightly controlled, relentless pace of factory labor. Even in the highly disciplined shoe factories and textile mills, irregular work patterns persisted. Indeed, for many workers in industrial America—skilled and unskilled, native and immigrant—the adjustment to the regular, clock-disciplined labor of the factory came slowly if at all.[29]

Resistance to the new patterns of work took many forms, but

one of the most astonishing responses was the rate of labor turnover. Data gathered between 1905 and 1917 indicated that the majority of industrial workers switched jobs at least once every three years. Systematic studies of textile mills, automobile factories, steel plants, and machine works found that the yearly turnover often exceeded 100 percent. In one month alone— December 1912—the Ford Motor Company reported that 48 percent of its employees left their jobs. Not all of this shifting from job to job was voluntary. Although employers did not keep systematic records until just prior to the First World War, many workers were probably fired or laid off. Though factory managers placed a premium on discipline and regularity, the industrial economy itself was highly unstable. In many industries—including textiles, boot and shoe making, glassmaking, canning, meat packing, and foundry work—periods of intense activity were followed by weeks of idleness. Moreover, much of the turnover was concentrated among the young, unskilled, and newly hired. Yet most studies of turnover in the work force concluded that well over half of those workers who left their jobs did so voluntarily.[30]

Many workers, particularly second- and third-generation craftsmen, also resisted assaults on their control of production. According to David Montgomery, as employers intensified their efforts to centralize control, highly skilled craftsmen continually struggled to protect their autonomy. Perhaps the most common strategy in both unionized and non-unionized trades was the "stint," an output quota fixed by workers themselves. (Taylor called this "soldiering.") Among some groups of workers— glassblowers, potters, iron molders, and puddlers in steel mills— these limits were openly acknowledged, but as the 1904 Commission of Labor survey on output restriction indicated, stints flourished throughout factories and were far more common than many investigators had suspected.[31]

Struggles also became increasingly militant. Between 1881 and 1905, Montgomery points out, control strikes (strikes over union rules and recognition) and sympathy strikes (where different unions lent each other support in their battles to enforce union rule) became more common, especially in older industries where craft traditions were strong or craft unions dominated. Strike activity was not, however, limited to skilled craftsmen with long traditions of union organization and worker control of production. In the first two decades of the twentieth century, first-generation immigrant laborers and machine tenders also engaged in numerous strikes. With little job control to defend, they usually struck for better working conditions or higher wages, or against wage reductions. Many immigrant workers were attracted to the International Workers of the World (IWW), which conducted radical strikes over wages and working conditions from the textile mills of Lawrence, Massachusetts, to the migrant labor camps of California.[32]

In the political arena, too, there were signs of discontent and unrest during these years. Between 1900 and 1920 the Socialist Party scored many local electoral victories. In 1912 Socialists were elected to public office in more than 340 cities, and in the presidential elections of 1912 and 1920 the Socialist candidate, Eugene V. Debs, won over 900,000 votes.[33]

In the face of this varied opposition, manufacturers, businessmen, and social reformers proposed a variety of programs to integrate workers into the altered system of production and to make the new forms of work more palatable. Beginning in the 1890's, many firms—eventually including U.S. Steel, General Electric, and other large manufacturers—introduced profit sharing plans, stock purchase options, and wage incentive schemes, hoping to ameliorate the rigors of factory labor by giving workers a "stake" in production. Other efforts, known as welfare work, aimed at promoting workers' loyalty by improving plant safety, providing company pension plans, and sponsoring social services such as relief associations, libraries, clubs, and classes. For example, the H. J. Heinz Company of Pittsburgh, a pioneer in this kind of activity, added a "recreation room, a relief association, annual outings, and perhaps the first of the welfare secretaries, a 'Mother Dunn' who was charged with hiring and firing as well as checking on absentees and counseling those in need."[34]

By no means did all employers adopt these sorts of corporate policies. Although a few farsighted industrialists, like H. J. Heinz and Edward Filene, systematically did so, others insisted that productivity and profits would be boosted only by limiting costs. They only reluctantly abandoned old labor policies, often under the pressure of strikes, continued high turnover, and efforts of social reformers and labor unions to pass legislation mandating improvements in plant safety, workmen's compensation, and the abolition of child labor. Yet by 1914 one report found that 2,000 firms had already introduced welfare plans for their 1.5 million workers.[35] One manufacturer pointed out that welfare work was not simply a result of humanitarian sentiments, but was "conducting business on business principles."[36]

Concern about labor unrest and turnover also led to the creation of employment and personnel departments to select and hire employees for jobs. Where hiring and firing had once been the prerogative of skilled workers or foremen on the factory floor, by the second decade of the twentieth century it was being systematized in centralized personnel departments staffed by professionally trained personnel managers. Turning to professional psychology and sociology, personnel managers experimented with systematic procedures for matching employees with jobs, including job analysis to determine the component skills of different jobs and batteries of vocational tests to determine whether a particular worker possessed the physical and mental traits appropriate for a given job.[37] These early experiments with job analysis and vocational tests were less successful than their proponents had hoped, but personnel work continued to flourish, particularly in large firms such as Ford, Goodyear, General Electric, and Westinghouse. In 1911, fifty company officials met to form the Employment Managers Association, and by 1918 the association had nine hundred members at its convention.[38]

Welfare and personnel work was one response to the tensions and conflicts produced by the spreading industrial capitalism. State labor legislation was another. Between 1890 and 1920, for example, several states enacted laws regulating the physical environment of the factory and restricting the labor of women and children. States also established a number of administrative bodies, including factory inspection bureaus, to enforce these laws. There were other responses too. In the aftermath of the First World War, there was even a brief flurry of interest in plans for "industrial democracy." Some employers introduced "employee representation plans" and set up "works committees" where workers and managers could meet to discuss problems of production and to consider grievances.[39] Yet few of these plans attracted as much attention or were as widely discussed as educational reform. Increasingly, as James Gilbert has noted, it was to education, and particularly vocational education, that Americans turned for a response to industrial conflict and social alienation.[40]

The Rise of Vocationalism in Public Education, 1890–1920

The idea of using schools to train youth for work was not entirely new in the early twentieth century. From the mid-nineteenth century on, social critics had attacked the narrowly academic curriculum of the grammar schools for overstocking the nation with clerks and ladies of leisure disdainful of manual labor. After 1890, however, what had been a loosely articulated desire to use schools to prepare youth for the workplace blossomed into a major movement, attracting almost every group in the nation that had an interest in education. Businessmen, manufacturers, farm leaders, labor spokesmen, social reformers, intellectuals, and many educators joined the campaign to vocationalize the schools. These groups often differed about the form and purpose these new programs should have. But across a wide range of ideologies, reformers agreed that vocationalism in education promised to teach young people the attitudes, values, and skills necessary for adapting to the altered structure of production.

One of the loudest advocates of vocational education was the National Association of Manufacturers (NAM), which began in the 1890's to ask how schools could assist in the growing international competition for markets. Alarmed by Germany's rapid rise to international economic power and impressed with the German system of vocational schools—which provided finely calibrated skills needed in specialized commerce and industry—the NAM pressed hard for two decades to introduce trade schools, continuation schools (part-time schools), and vocational guidance into American education. Initially, many industrial and commercial employers created such schools in their own companies. Several large manufacturers, including General Electric, Westinghouse, American Telephone and Telegraph, and U.S. Steel, created their own "corporation schools" as part of their personnel and welfare work. It was the task of these schools to recruit and train workers to repair machines; to teach lower-level managers; and to train workers for the white-collar positions, such as clerk, salesman, and typist, that multiplied rapidly after 1880. Eager to have the costs of such instruction borne by public funding, employers joined with others in the coalition that successfully lobbied for the Smith-Hughes Act.[41]

How could vocational education aid American business in international competition? The NAM advanced several arguments, of which three stand out. First, NAM leaders argued that modern industry suffered from a shortage of highly skilled workers. Mechanization and specialization had undermined the old apprenticeship system and made informal on-the-job training inefficient; consequently, the shortage of skilled workers could only be filled by skill training in specialized vocational schools. Second, the NAM hoped that vocational education would help stabilize the work force. Better socialized workers, they argued, would understand their role in the specialized industrial economy and adapt more readily to the nature of industrial work; hence absenteeism and turnover would decline, and efficiency and output would increase. Finally, NAM leaders expected vocational education to weaken union control of job entry, and thereby to help establish management's prerogatives in the administration of the factory. As one businessman put it, it was time to snatch workers' education from "the hands of the trade unions, . . . the Industrial Workers of the World, and the Socialist Party."[42]

Labor leaders were understandably reluctant to join a movement with such an anti-union bias. Earlier experiences with private trade schools that had been created by manufacturers to bypass, union-controlled apprenticeship programs—and had in some cases provided students as strike breakers—reinforced labor's doubts about vocational education. In addition, labor leaders were often suspicious of business influence in the public schools, and believed that many teachers were hostile to organized labor. By 1910, however, the AFL's Committee on Industrial Education expressed support for industrial training in the public schools.

Why the AFL shifted its position is not entirely clear, but historians have suggested at least three reasons. First, as Arthur

Wirth has observed, union people shared with businessmen the conviction that schools were boring, abstract places, irrelevant to the needs of children. "The pupils," it was reported at the 1909 AFL convention, "become tired of the work they have in hand, and see nothing more inviting in the grades ahead. They are conscious of powers, passions, and tastes which the school does not recognize. They long to grasp things with their own hands and test the strength of materials and the magnitude of forces."[43]

Second, as Norton Grubb and Marvin Lazerson have stressed, by 1910 union leaders recognized that the vocational movement was gaining widespread support and acted to counter business domination of it. They believed that unions should insist on public rather than private sponsorship of vocational training, on the participation of labor in educational decision making, and on the avoidance of extreme specialization in training. As one AFL member stated in 1912, "We cannot stop the trend in the direction of this kind of education in the school; but, we can, if we cooperate with the educators, have it come our way."[44]

Third, the AFL position on vocational education reflected uncertainty within the labor movement about the kind of future that workers should hope for within the capitalist division of labor. On one side were those who believed their children likely to remain workers, and therefore thought the children could benefit from practical training that would lead to better pay and a higher standard of living. On the other side were those who hoped that their children might rise to become foremen or salaried white-collar workers, and therefore feared vocational training would create a stratified school system that would deny their children education leading to economic mobility. The way these views shaped organized labor's position on vocational education is not entirely certain. But the debate underlines how the transformation of the labor process and the erosion of apprenticeship forced workers to look increasingly to education in order to ensure their children's economic future.[45]

Another source of support for vocational education, besides business and labor, was middle-class activists and social scientists, many of whom were involved in other social reforms during these years. Among the supporters of vocational education were, for example, Jane Addams, Edith Abbott, Frank Parsons, Paul

Douglas, John Dewey, and the child labor reformer Owen Lovejoy. Alarmed that mechanization and specialization had robbed work of its creative potential, these reformers hoped that vocational training would restore meaning to work, promote industrial democracy, and gradually put an end to child labor. By uniting general and practical education, Jane Addams argued, vocational education would help workers see the full dimensions of their labor, and thereby restore meaning and dignity to work that had been fractured and deskilled by the new industrial processes. It would, moreover, teach the value of industrial cooperation and instruct young people how to work together democratically.

Perhaps, some even suggested, vocational education would be the first step in the transformation of the workplace. Owen Lovejoy told a convention of the National Society for the Promotion of Industrial Education (NSPIE) in 1913 that vocational educators must demand jobs worthy of young people. According to Lovejoy, the "captains of industry" ask, " 'Here are the jobs: what kinds of children have you to offer?' " Educators must reply, " 'Here are your children: what kind of industry have you to offer?' " Indeed, Professor Frank Leavitt of the University of Chicago added, "Why should we hesitate to lay hands on industry in the name of education when we have already laid hands on school in the name of industry?"[46] Even the National Education Association (NEA) joined the crusade to transform industry through education. Caught up in the post-First World War fervor for industrial democracy, the association passed a resolution in 1919 that stated:

Industry in this country must be reorganized. All industry must become educational to those who engage in it. The workers must find in their work an opportunity for self-expression and self-development. Human— not commercial—value must be placed first in our great industrial establishments. The rank and file of those who produce the wealth must, through their organization, share in the control of the policy of the institutions for whom they work.[47]

These views contrasted sharply with the vision of employers who hoped that vocational education would provide practical skill training and adjust young people to the fragmented labor of the factory. The views also differed from those of many other vocational educators who stressed the need for industrial efficiency. To vocational leaders such as David Snedden, Massachusetts commissioner of education, and Charles Prosser, executive secretary of the NSPIE, the vision of Addams and her colleagues was vague and impractical. Vocational education, they contended, should be geared to the needs of industry—to the immediate practical skills that might help workers fit smoothly into industrial occupations and perhaps move up a notch or two on the economic ladder. Vocational education and guidance, Prosser told the NEA in 1912, must fit "the great mass of our people for useful employment." It was time, he added, to establish separate vocational programs—college preparatory, commercial, industrial arts, and domestic science—to impart specific vocational skills and to match young people with jobs that suited their interests and capabilities:

More and more, in our theory of the American public school system, we are swinging around to the idea that it is to be the mission of the schools of the future to select by testing and training—to adjust boys and girls for life by having them undergo varied experiences in order to uncover their varied tastes and aptitudes and to direct and to train them in the avenues for which they display the most capacity. Such a program would require a differentiation of the course of study for pupils between 12 and 14 years of age.[48]

This vision of practical, differentiated schooling also appealed to many social reformers, educators, and social investigators who were beginning to worry about high dropout rates, especially among immigrant working-class youth. Beginning in the early twentieth century, numerous studies indicated that tens of thousands of urban youth between the ages of fourteen and sixteen were leaving school without completing the eighth grade.[49] Study after study arrived at similar explanations for early school leaving: the children disliked school and preferred to work; and the children's wages were needed to supplement family income. Indeed, many children disliked school intensely. Helen Todd, a factory inspector in Chicago, interviewed 500 working children in 1908; 412, she reported, stated that they preferred to work in a factory rather than go to school, even if their families did not need the additional income.[50] In Milwaukee, in 1922, the school system offered working children 75 cents a day—comparable to a young worker's average wage—to attend full-time public school; out of 8,000 youth only sixteen accepted this offer.[51]

The studies generally agreed on the kinds of jobs these children found. Unskilled, poorly paid, often seasonal, with high turnover, poor working conditions, and few opportunities for advancement—these jobs were what the investigators labeled "dead-end" or "blind-alley" jobs and what economists today often call the secondary labor market. One study of 14,000 working children in Philadelphia in 1912 reported that only 3 percent were in skilled trades; the others entered jobs with "little or no opportunity for improvement and no competence at maturity."[52] Surveys of working children in New York, Chicago, St. Louis, and other cities reported similar conclusions. In Chicago, for example, a study of working youth between fourteen and seventeen reported that only 7 percent were in occupations where they received any training in a skill; in New York, only 5.2 percent were in such occupations; and in St. Louis, 88 percent entered unskilled jobs.[53]

In addition, surveys indicated that most young people remained at jobs only for a few months. In Rochester, New York, for instance, young people aged fourteen to sixteen changed jobs about three times a year; in New York City about one-third of working youth changed jobs six times a year; and in Maryland over 50 percent reported that they had held their present job for less than two months. The investigators uniformly labeled these youth as victims and losers—children whose health was poor, whose parents exploited them, who were in many cases mentally subnormal, and who faced bleak economic futures. Summarizing the findings of numerous studies and surveys, Paul Douglas described these youth as drifting "from job to job, from industry to industry, still unskilled and exposed to all the social and industrial evils which threaten adolescence." When the child becomes an adult, Douglas concluded, he "finds himself one of the class of the permanently unskilled with the attendant low wages and unemployment of his class."[54]

Some investigators, including Douglas, recognized that leaving school early was often an economic necessity for youth, but many others labeled poverty an excuse and looked elsewhere for explanations. Some blamed parents, especially immigrant parents, who, they argued, did not recognize the importance of additional schooling or were greedy for the extra income their children brought home. Yet many blamed the schools. The traditional curriculum, they asserted, was irrelevant to the needs of these working-class youth. "The great lack," a Massachusetts commission stated in 1906, "is in the system, which fails to offer the child of fourteen continued schooling of a practical character."[55] What these immigrant children wanted and needed, this report stated, as did many others like it, was an education adapted to their economic futures—in short, a curriculum specifically directed at future employment.

Would additional vocational training until age sixteen eliminate low-paying, unskilled factory labor for working-class youth? Most evidence suggested otherwise. Several studies of working children showed little or no difference between the wages of children who had completed elementary school and those who had not; and in most jobs open to youth, even some high school attendance appeared to make little difference in income.[56] Yet few vocational reformers confronted this reality. Mostly middle-class professionals—who had come to think of occupations as careers requiring extensive training and preparation—they hoped that all work might be reformed by shaping it to professional models. Just as professional school paved the way for a well-rewarded career in medicine, law, and other professions, vocational training might lead to a well-rewarded "career" in the factory. Yet the earnings of factory workers in Philadelphia peaked at age 25. Working-class families probably had a more accurate picture of the real labor market than the middle-class reformers who wanted them to have a "life-career motive."[57]

The Politics of Vocationalism

By 1910 these diverse groups were agreed that some form of vocational education was needed, but they often battled vigorously over who should control vocational training and for what purposes. On one side were proponents of separate vocational schools, who included businessmen, manufacturers, and a wing of vocational reformers led by Snedden and Prosser. They stressed the need for close cooperation between vocational programs and local industry and for narrow vocational training to teach specific skills for particular jobs. Only in separate schools, they argued, scorning the cultural claims of academic educators, would this training be successful. On the other side were those who wished to integrate vocational education into the public school system. Supporting this position were many educators, labor leaders, and social reformers. They opposed separate schools for a variety of reasons. Most importantly, they argued, separate vocational schools would violate fundamental principles of democracy in education by channeling working-class students into predetermined occupational slots, which would allow little opportunity to pursue an education leading to other occupations.[58]

One of the sharpest conflicts concerning these issues arose over the Cooley Bill in Illinois.[59] This bill, sponsored by the Chicago Association of Commerce and drafted by Edwin G. Cooley, a former superintendent of Chicago schools, proposed to establish a separate State Commission of Education to administer vocational education for youth over fourteen. Support came from an educational-industrial complex composed of businessmen and "social efficiency" advocates. This coalition wanted vocational schools to impart practical occupational skills and feared that academic educators were incapable of providing this training.

First introduced before the Illinois state legislature in 1913, the Cooley Bill aroused bitter opposition and was finally defeated. Ella Flagg Young, Chicago's innovative superintendent of schools and a strong supporter of vocational education, voiced her opposition, claiming that the bill threatened to make the classroom into a "mere factory workroom."[60] John Dewey also fought this legislation, arguing that a dual school system, such as the one proposed by the Cooley Bill, would duplicate school administration, create arbitrary distinctions between different groups of pupils, and unnecessarily narrow the scope of vocational education. And above all, Dewey contended, a dual school system would undermine democracy and turn vocational schooling into the handmaiden of industry. "The kind of vocational education in which I am interested," he wrote in 1915, "is not one which will 'adapt' workers to the existing regime; I am not sufficiently in love with the regime for that. It seems to me that the business of all who would not be educational time servers is . . . to strive for a kind of vocational education which will first alter the existing industrial system, and ultimately transform it."[61] The Chicago Federation of Labor joined in the opposition,

claiming the Cooley Bill would create a "caste system of education which would shunt the children of the laboring classes at an
early age first into vocational courses and then into factories."[62]
These groups gathered widespread support, and despite repeated
efforts by powerful backers, the Cooley Bill failed to pass.*

In other states too the idea of a dual school system became a
source of political controversy. Yet despite such disagreements,
by 1910 the diverse vocationalist groups, with the addition of
reformers who advocated agricultural education, had joined in an
uneasy but powerful national political coalition and launched a
concerted drive to win federal support for vocational schooling.
Their efforts began to pay off in 1914, when Congress appointed
the commission on National Aid to Vocational Education. The
commission was dominated by members active in the NSPIE—
including the society's secretary, Charles Prosser. Not surprisingly, then, the commission's report restated many of the familiar
arguments for vocational education: the need to ensure the nation's competitive position in world markets, to increase economic returns to workers, to eliminate dead-end jobs and increase occupational mobility for working-class youth, to reduce
industrial and social unrest, and to democratize education. In
addition, the commission presented a case for federal assistance
for vocational education. In a highly mobile national labor mar-

---

*Similar controversies in other states were also resolved in favor of a unitary
system of control. But the defeat of proposals for a dual school system by no
means eliminated criticism that vocational education fostered a school system
stratified on the basis of class, race, ethnicity, and sex. George Counts, in *The
Selective Character of American Secondary Education* (Chicago, 1922), demonstrated that high schools were perpetuating glaring inequalities. Counts's study
indicated not only that working-class, immigrant, and black children were under-
represented in high school, but that those who did attend were much more likely
to be enrolled in one- or two-year vocational programs than in academic programs. Other studies, though less skeptical of vocational education, were also
critical of its class implications. In 1938, for example, the government-sponsored
Russell Report on vocational education reaffirmed the need for vocational training
but strongly criticized the social-class aspects of vocational education. The federal
program in vocational education, the report stated, has disregarded "the American ideal of a single system of schools and has encouraged the creation of a dual or
separate school system for the education of workers. Stated in plainest terms, the
concept behind the program of vocational education would segregate the young
people who are to become industrial workers from those who are to go into the
professions and other scholarly pursuits and would provide separate facilities for
these two groups." See John D. Russell et al., *Vocational Education*, Staff Study
no. 8, Advisory Committee on Education (Washington, D.C., 1938), p. 129.

ket, the commission said, states and localities could not be expected to tax themselves to train youth who might work elsewhere; consequently, the country must think of national policies "not only in the making and selling of products, but also in the education and employment of labor."[63] In short, training for a national labor market required federal support.

Finally, in 1917, Congress passed the Smith-Hughes Act, allocating federal funds for vocational training "of less than college grade," in trade and industrial subjects, home economics, and agriculture, for students over fourteen enrolled in public schools. In addition, the Act specified three types of schools eligible for federal funds: all-day trade schools, continuation schools for young workers, and vocational evening schools. The Act also established a Federal Board of Vocational Education to administer the allocation of funds—granted on a matching basis—to the states.

Smith-Hughes did not provide support for many of the vocationally oriented courses that had already been introduced into American high schools early in the twentieth century. And there appears to have been a bias against white-collar work. For example, practical training in commercial and business subjects had become commonplace—and very popular with students—in many urban high schools, but the Act did not provide aid for these courses. It would also be erroneous to assume that trade and industrial training originated with the passage of this federal legislation. On the contrary, vocational training in these areas had already become a part of the high school curriculum in many states prior to Smith-Hughes. One 1910 study conducted by the NSPIE found that 29 states already had some form of vocational education in trade and industrial subjects, home economics, manual training, and agriculture.* Nevertheless, the passage of Smith-Hughes was not simply an empty gesture. As the essays in

---

*Even after the passage of Smith-Hughes, federal aid was not crucial to the existence of vocational education. In 1925–26, for example, the total federal allotment of $7,184,902 represented only 24 percent of the expenditure on vocational education and 23 percent of the expenditure on trade and industrial education. See Marvin Lazerson and W. Norton Grubb, *American Education and Vocationalism: Documents in Vocational Education, 1870–1970* (New York, 1974). In 1938 the Russell Report (p. 112) estimated that non-federally aided vocational education was "at least equal to" and "possibly in excess" of the federal program.

this collection demonstrate, it helped legitimize the idea- that school was a way to prepare youth for entry into the labor market; and by assuming that job training in school required federal intervention, it constituted a major step in the use of education as a tool of federal social policy.

Rhetoric and Reality in Vocational Schooling

Educational reformers promised that vocational schooling would solve a number of pressing economic and social problems. It would, they said, lessen youth unemployment, increase economic mobility for poor and working-class youth, reduce high rates of labor turnover, restore meaning to routine factory labor, and offer a practical, relevant education to thousands of youth bored by the classical curriculum. Indeed, the rhetoric surrounding the vocational education movement was little short of millennial. Yet, in hindsight, vocational education appears to have been an illusory solution for the economic, social, and educational ills that accompanied the industrial transformation of work. This is strikingly illustrated in the history of three vocational programs: continuation schools for young workers, vocational guidance, and vocational education for girls.

Mandated by Smith-Hughes, continuation schools were the largest sector of federally aided vocational education. These schools enrolled many more students than federally assisted evening schools or all-day trade schools, and they declined only when the depression of the 1930's reduced the demand for young workers.[64] The clientele was, of course, predominantly working class. These were the young people who were already working at the dead-end jobs in factories, shops, and businesses and who so alarmed social investigators. Typically, these young people were compelled by law to attend part-time classes four to eight hours a week from age fourteen to sixteen or in some cases eighteen. The curriculum in such schools varied, from stress on job-related skills to remedial instruction in basic skills and training in citizenship and health. Usually, some combination of these subjects was offered, with teaching adapted to the work experience of the pupils (as in business English, business arithmetic, or the history of industry). There is abundant evidence that high school educators were relieved not to have "ne'er-do-wells" and "hand-minded'' working-class children—mostly second-generation immigrants—in their regular classes.[65] The continuation school, however, enabled educators who saw education as a kind of panacea to relieve their consciences and at the same time permitted youth to earn wages, which they and their parents wanted. Employers in the secondary labor market could still hire youth as a force of cheap, unskilled workers, easily laid off during periods of slack demand. Not only the NAM, however, but also the AFL endorsed part-time schools, as did many liberal legislators and social workers.

The claims made for the efficacy of a few hours of continuation school instruction were grandiose. Continuation educators argued that the schools would make students good citizens, effective parents, efficient workers, and healthy individuals who would know how to make good use of their leisure time. The New York commissioner of education termed the state's continuation school law the ''children's charter.''[66] According to Paul Douglas, continuation schools would make it possible for working children ''to rise from the bottom,'' and hence would help ''break down class stratification.''[67] Few reformers then claimed—as many policymakers do today—that participation in the work force was genuinely educative for youth. Rather, they argued that industrial work had become miseducative, and that part-time instruction could offset the disadvantages working children faced. It could give them the sort of training and guidance, as both workers and potential citizens, that would enable them to rise on the economic ladder.

How would continuation schools foster occupational mobility? Paul Douglas, in his study of industrial education, offered an explanation. Likening the occupational structure to a ''multi-storied house''—the first story composed of the unskilled jobs, the second of the semiskilled, the third of the skilled, the fourth of clerical work, and the top of managerial and engineering positions—Douglas suggested that opportunity for mobility depended on which system of industrial education was provided. One system, the all-day trade school, offered an ''outside staircase'' from the bottom to the top floors. Although this system would give mobility to some workers, its impact would be slight, since it was outside the industrial system and would therefore benefit only those able to forgo earnings while being trained. The continuation school, however, provided an "inside stairway" that enabled workers to earn while learning. By this means, children of the poorest classes could have the opportunity to rise on the occupational ladder.[68]

This was hardly a satisfactory plan for lessening economic inequality. By concentrating on the character of industrial education rather than the structure of work and the labor market, it attacked the symptoms rather than the sources of the conditions it hoped to eliminate. Douglas seems to have understood this; he astutely analyzed changes in the organization of work, and chided vocational educators for their failure to recognize that most factory labor no longer required extensive all-around training in technical skills. Yet he nonetheless concluded, as did many others, that the worker needed "perhaps more education than he ever did before" and that the continuation school was "the best single system of industrial education" available.[69]

Like the advocates of the continuation school, early advocates of vocational guidance were a diverse group, spanning a wide spectrum of ideologies and interests. In general, however, they agreed on a number of points: that the way people found jobs was "inefficient and wasteful"; that laissez-faire economics and nineteenth-century individualism were ill-adapted to early twentieth-century industrial society; and that schools must, therefore, aid young people in the "intelligent choice of a vocation" and "help children make their start in life with purpose, preparation, and insight."[70] If schools did this, not only would it benefit the economy and society by efficiently matching workers to jobs. It would also help the individual, since, they argued, workers properly fitted to tasks at which they could succeed would be happier, more fulfilled people.[71]

The advocates of guidance combined inspirational rhetoric with new ideas about careers and science. Appalled by the "aimless drifting" and "job-hopping" of working-class youth, they wished to share their vision of a rewarding career with all segments of American society. Proper attention to the "life-career motive," they proclaimed, would make school more lively and interesting, instill the "right attitude toward work," and lead to a lifetime of fulfilling labor.[72] The life-career motive, Charles William Eliot told the NEA in 1910, impels adults to "do our best work in the world." It leads people to "greater serviceableness and greater happiness—to greater serviceableness, because the power and scope of individual productiveness are thereby increased; to greater happiness, because achievement will become more frequent and more considerable, and to old and young adults alike happiness in work comes through achievement."[73]

Less inspirational but just as influential were the social scientists who believed that an improved technology of occupational analysis and assessment could eliminate much of the uncertainty in "choosing a vocation." As educational psychology and sociology grew apace, and as social scientists surveyed the relationship of industry and commerce to education in many cities, hopes grew that vocational guidance could become a science capable of determining the abilities of students and finding the appropriate niches for them in the economy. Having much in common with the new personnel managers in American industry, guidance pioneers like Meyer Bloomfield collaborated closely with businessmen, hoping to develop precise job specifications by task analysis and to devise ways to match human abilities with job needs. E. L. Thorndike was optimistic about the prospects of this collaboration. "Through the knowledge of the science of human nature and its work in the industries, professions, and trades," he wrote in 1913, "the average graduate of Teachers College in 1950 ought to be able to give better advice to a high school boy about the choice of an occupation than Solomon, Socrates, and Benjamin Franklin all together could give."[74]

Scholarly criticism of these techniques cast doubt on their utility; but it failed to dampen enthusiasm for the idea of using scientific guidance to aid youth, not only in their choice of occupation but in all life decisions. "Vocational guidance," wrote a superintendent in 1915, "seeks the largest realization of the possibilities of every child and youth, measured in terms of worthy service; vocational guidance seeks this not through the school alone, but through the upbuilding influences that work and life beyond school ought to afford every human being."[75]

What, however, did "work and life beyond school" afford? Some vocational reformers were less than sanguine about these future prospects. After completing a survey of young workers in

Cincinnati in 1912, Helen Woolley, the director of the city's Vocational Guidance Bureau, stated: "The facts we have presented seem to me to throw serious doubt upon the wisdom of allowing the public school to undertake the placing in industry of children under sixteen. There is no work open to them worth advising them to take."[76] Alice Barrows, director of the Vocational Guidance Bureau in New York City, also doubted the wisdom of much that passed for vocational guidance. She questioned whether "anyone has the right to guide children systematically into vocations." All too often, she said, this meant providing cheap labor to employers in "a more subtle and indefinable exploitation of children than the world has ever seen—subtle and indefinable because all would be done in the name of 'the good of the society and the child.'" Sensitive to the gap between the reality and the rhetoric of the vocational guidance movement, she concluded: "To arouse the ambition and interest of a child of fourteen by promising him 'trade training' the value of which is dubious, and then a job where he 'can work up' when we have no facts to prove that he can work up, and a distinctly uncomfortable feeling that he probably cannot, is after all even worse than stunting a child by premature labor so that you cannot arouse his ambition at all."[77]

Yet Barrows and Woolley, like their more optimistic colleagues, also endorsed educational remedies for dead-end jobs. Indeed, their chief strategy was to make the classroom more attractive in order to keep students in school longer—usually until sixteen—and thereby to postpone, but hardly to eliminate, the enervating experience of dead-end work. "If the school," Helen Woolley suggested, "could lend all its energies to readjusting its system of instruction to meet the needs of the children who are now leaving, and thus hold them in school, it would be rendering a far greater service than it could in finding for them jobs, which, at best, are of no advantage to the child."[78] Here lay perhaps the most positive contribution of the new vocational classes. These classes, although they probably did little to improve students' life chances when they left school, may well have made schools more lively and interesting places for those young people who found the traditional curriculum ill adapted to their tastes and needs.

If the reality of blind-alley employment troubled some advocates of vocational guidance, the rising rate of female participation in the labor force posed equally disturbing dilemmas to reformers interested in vocational training for girls. Between 1890 and 1920, wage work became increasingly common for both middle-class and working-class women, particularly young, single women in their late teens and early twenties. Middle-class girls entered fields such as office and clerical work, retail sales, nursing, and teaching. Working-class girls took factory jobs, making clothes, processing food, laundering, and doing other work commonly considered extensions of their tasks at home. In 1920, two out of every five girls fifteen to twenty years old worked outside the home.[79]

Vocational reformers differed among themselves over how to respond to these trends. Concerned that having jobs threatened women's traditional roles as wives, mothers, and homemakers, the great majority of educators stressed the importance of home economics and domestic science for all girls. Few doubted that wage work was only temporary for girls. Most female wage earners, educators argued, would leave the labor force to marry and raise children. Moreover, they added, even if a woman remained at work after marriage, it was important for her to learn how to manage a home. Indeed, many advocates of home economics maintained that managing a "modern home" had become a "scientific" task, requiring special instruction and training. "The upbuilding of a modern home," one California educator wrote in 1911, was characterized by "applied art, applied science, and applied economics." "In all this work," he stated, "women must lead and direct, and the schools must provide them for their work."[80]

Training in home economics promised little relief from the long hours and low pay of women's work in factories and department stores. And not every educator embraced this vision of vocational training for girls. Some educators questioned the relevance of home economics, charging that it ignored the reality of changing industrial conditions and robbed girls of the opportunity to prepare for the labor market. "We have idealized about girls too long," wrote Florence Marshall, principal of the Manhattan Trade School for Girls. "We should like so much to see them taught a little domestic science and art, hygiene and home nursing, and a few other things . . .'' But, she added, ''accepting the fact that under present conditions girls are and must be wage earners, must we not insist that they be trained for wage-earning occupations?''[81] Willystine Goodsell echoed these convictions. The problem of women's ''dual vocation''—as homemaker and wage earner—did indeed pose perplexing difficulties for vocational educators, she said; but reality demanded that girls be prepared for wage-earning occupations. Though training for homemaking should ''unquestionably be furnished such women as need it,'' it would seem ''the better part of wisdom to accept a situation in which millions of girls and women are employed in gainful occupations for varying periods of years and see to it that before entering upon their vocation they be given as thorough and all-round preparation for work as is given to their brothers.''[82]

Goodsell's vision of vocational training for girls may have helped counter the prevailing ideology that a woman's place was in the home. For some middle-class girls, at least, high school training in clerical skills or office work probably provided a route into one of the growing number of white-collar occupations, many of which were beginning to require at least some high school attendance. But for the most part vocational training in the high school rarely challenged traditional stereotypes of women's (or men's) work. Nor did it question sex discrimination in the labor market, which sharply limited women's occupational opportunities. In contrast to the academic subjects, vocational courses in high school were typically segregated by sex. Boys were often required to take manual training, girls home economics. In the more specialized skill courses, boys were concentrated in trade and industrial subjects such as printing, carpentry, auto repair, and sheet metal work; girls took clerical and office skills, dressmaking, and millinery, and normal classes to prepare teachers. If vocational training offered girls a doorway out of the home, at the same time it reinforced the sexual stereotypes that girls would face in the outside economy.

Conclusion

The early advocates of continuation schools, vocational guidance, and vocational training for girls were by no means unique in the contrast between their rhetoric and reality; such a contrast has pervaded the history of educational reform in the United States. From the mid-nineteenth century on, leaders from many segments of American society have turned to education as a way to eliminate the social dislocations and economic conflicts generated by the spread of industrial capitalism. Rarely, however, have these reforms actually solved structural problems. In fact, many of the conditions that educational reform claimed to be able to solve—such as poverty, unemployment, economic inequality, crime, and social alienation—remain as pressing as ever.[83]

Yet the rise of vocationalism early in the twentieth century marked a significant turning point, one that transformed the purpose and practice of education. By the 1920's the idea of using school to train youth for jobs had become a primary rationale for education and had stimulated a flurry of reforms to integrate the school more closely with the economy. Assuming functions that formerly had taken place outside the classroom, schools added classes to teach job-related attitudes and skills, introduced new programs to convince students and parents of the value of the new courses, and created new structures to sort and select students for the new curricula. The president of the Muncie school board succinctly summarized these trends. "For a long time," he told the Lynds, "all boys were trained to be President. Then for a while we trained them all to be professional men. Now we are training boys to get jobs."[84]

The impact of vocationalism was felt beyond the classroom, too. By focusing on educational remedies for problems rooted in the structure of work and the labor market, vocationalism also reshaped the debate about education and work. How to adjust young people to industrial labor, not economic reorganization, became the central focus of discussion; how to foster individual mobility by means of schooling, not economic equality, became the guiding principle of twentieth-century social policy. Vocationalism in education transformed conflicts over the organization of the economy and the nature of American society into policies aimed at proper socialization; and this narrowed debate about the nature and meaning of work, as well as altered educational practices.

Few educational movements have exerted such an influence. Today the ideology of vocationalism continues to shape conceptions of education and work. In recent years, as the concern about youth unemployment and job dissatisfaction has intensified, policymakers have once again turned to education for solutions, proposing a variety of plans to adapt school to the needs of the workplace. Yet the history of vocationalism provides little evidence that vocational education in its various forms can actually eliminate the conditions it seeks to deal with. Indeed, by attacking symptoms rather than causes, current policies, much like their predecessors, may dim rather than brighten the prospects for economic equality and satisfying work.

Enduring Resiliency: Enacting and Implementing Federal Vocational Education Legislation

LARRY CUBAN

Consider the following items carefully:

1. In the last half-century, during boom and bust, war and peace, vocational education bills have regularly and overwhelmingly been approved in both houses of Congress. Most senators and congressmen have embraced the legislation with unqualified enthusiasm.

2. At the depth of the depression, when federal aid in many areas was cut back, Congress appropriated $10 million more than President Roosevelt had requested for vocational education. The president condemned the "active lobby of vocational teachers, supervisors, and administrative officers in the field of vocational education who are interested in the emoluments paid in part from federal funds."[1]

3. In Atlanta, in what must be a first, a high school was named after a law: the Smith-Hughes Vocational High School.[2]

4. One vocational education appropriation was approved in perpetuity. Yes, forever.[3]

The triumph of vocational education as a federal priority is nicely captured in six decades of legislation that has shipped increasing amounts of federal money to 50 states for distribution. Annual appropriations totaled over $600 million in 1978.[4] The evident popularity of vocational schooling with lawmakers rivals that of dams, river projects, and defense installations.

But the popularity is not universal. Friendly and hostile critics, government investigations, and informed citizens have pointed out serious flaws in vocational education's conception, organization, operation, and results. A few studies have even stressed the dangers of overzealous lobbying. All vocational legislation, according to a former executive director of the American Vocational Association (AVA), "has been imposed on national administrators almost entirely as a result of the articulated demands of business, industry, and agriculture and the legislative leadership of the Congress." The enthusiasm of Congress in the face of ample evidence of defects in the vocational education enterprise is one of a number of puzzles and contradictions buried within the history of federally funded vocational education in the twentieth century.[5]

There are other puzzles as well. One is the small enrollment in vocational education despite the presumed victory of its advocates in the first two decades after 1900. After a half-century of federal support, no more than one-quarter of all high school youth were actually enrolled in vocational curricula or in separate vocational schools.[6] Another puzzle is the way the AVA, a small Washington-based professional organization, has had its fingerprints all over each piece of vocational education legislation. How could such a small organization wield such clout with Congress? Finally, even though one-quarter of high school students were enrolled in vocational curricula in the 1970's, virtually no information is generally available describing what actually goes on in these schools and classrooms. Thus it is very difficult to confirm whether or not learning by doing—the very basis of vocational education as promoted by its partisans—occurs and actually holds students in school longer. These are only a few of the puzzles and contradictions that emerge from an analysis of the literature on the politics and implementation of federal legislation.

The perspective of this paper differs from that of others in this book. Joseph Kett concentrates on the ideology of vocational educators and the power of these ideas; Marvin Lazerson, Norton Grubb, and David Hogan view the triumph of vocationalism in the context of the intersection between economic forces, social class structure, and the political process. I have chosen to tell how particular laws were passed, and have tried to capture in detail the complicated texture of a political process at work. Of one thing I am certain: no comprehensive explanation of the apparent success in getting the federal government to take responsibility for subsidizing vocational education in public schools can ignore how these laws were passed and how the congressional mandates were executed.

The balance of this paper is divided into three sections. First, I review the major legislation and what has been written about each law's origins, enactment, implementation, and results. Next I deal with two questions that emerge from this review: the paradox of the popularity of vocational education with Congress despite persistent criticism, and the puzzle of an apparently faulty process of implementation. The answers to each of these questions, which complete the paper, are often tentative or speculative; as I make clear, much research remains to be done.

Federal Legislation on Vocational Education

Since 1900, over fifty federal laws have dealt with vocational education in public schools. Of these laws, two significantly influenced the directions vocational schooling has taken: the Smith-Hughes Act (1917) and the Vocational Education Act (1963). Few researchers have investigated these laws in all their aspects.*

Smith-Hughes Act. This piece of legislation has attracted the most attention from students of vocational education. They generally agree on the statute's origins, enactment, and initial implementation by the federal agency charged with executing the law. They disagree, however, over the law's impact.

*The Smith-Hughes Act (1917) was extended and expanded by the following laws: George-Reed Act (1929); George-Ellzey Act (1934); George-Deen Act (1936); George-Barden Act (1946). In addition, there were amendments to these laws and other legislation that included vocational education, such as the National Defense Education Act (1958), the Area Redevelopment Act (1961), and the Manpower Development Training Act (1962). The Vocational Education Act (1963) departed significantly from the Smith-Hughes pattern, and subsequent amendments to the VEA in 1968, 1972, and 1976 enlarged and further defined the 1963 organic act. See J. Chester Swanson, *Development of Federal Legislation for Vocational Education* (Chicago, 1966).

For the most part, writers locate the roots of the legislation in the desire of Progressive reformers to deal with the worst excesses of industrialism by vocationalizing public schools. Efforts in such states as Massachusetts to introduce and spread vocational schooling helped create a national reform lobby called the National Society for the Promotion of Industrial Education (NSPIE), an uneasy but effective coalition of businessmen, unionists, educators, and professional reformers. Each interest group viewed vocational education as a panacea for the economic, social, and schooling problems of the day. The NSPIE promoted vocationalism as a solution whose time had come.

Writers are unanimous in crediting the NSPIE and an interlocking network of educators, businessmen, legislators, public officials, ad hoc committees, and blue-chip business coalitions for brokering the bill, first through the National Commission on Vocational Education, appointed by President Wilson in 1914, and then through Congress.[7] The details of the effective, decade-long lobbying by the NSPIE to get a federal subsidy for vocational education are captured in a number of studies. Though these studies differ on a few points, they generally agree on the NSPIE's decisive role in moving the bill through both houses of Congress and securing the president's signature.[8]

Signed on the eve of the nation's entry into the First World War, the Smith-Hughes Act provided for the "promotion of vocational education," whose subjects it defined as agriculture, trade and industry, and home economics. The major aim of such schooling "shall be to fit for useful employment public school students fourteen years of age or older." The subjects to be taught, the number of hours to be spent in instruction, and the amount of time for supervised work in the field were all prescribed in the law. Funds could be used for paying the salaries of vocational teachers in the targeted occupations named in the law. Finally, each state had to prepare a plan for review by the Federal Board of Vocational Education (FBVE), a body expressly established by the law. The Federal Board could "withhold the allotment of monies" if the plan or subsequent regulations went unheeded by a state.[9]

Between 1917 and 1933 the Federal Board, the first and only national school board, allocated funds to the states, approved staff-written regulations, and gave general oversight to the law's implementation. An executive director and regional agents carried out the FBVE's policy directives, reviewed state plans, wrote bulletins, held conferences, and distributed money to the states. Though the law's language called for a federal-state partnership, the FBVE exerted much influence over how states used Smith-Hughes funds. The only other federal grant-in-aid program that had a greater influence, according to a 1938 study of vocational education, was the National Guard. In 1933, as an economy measure, Congress stripped the FBVE of its authority and funds and transferred it to the Office of Education. There it served as an advisory committee until 1946, when it was abolished.[10]

The implementation of the 1917 law—a half-century of federal, state, and local operations between 1917 and 1963, when the second Vocational Education Act was passed—has gone largely unnoticed by historians. Yet the law was effectively carried out by the FBVE, and it did affect school organization, administration, curriculum, and instruction. How much is difficult to assess.

There are two major early sources of data (and judgments) on the implementation and impact of the law. One is the writings of Charles Prosser, an ex-superintendent of schools, the top staff man for the NSPIE, and the chief architect of the 1917 law.[11] Prosser—"the master craftsman of vocational education"—was appointed the first executive director at the FBVE. In less than a year, he had prodded every state into accepting the law and producing a vocational education plan as called for in the statute. In his brief tenure there, his passion for separate vocational schools and the specific-task training of students for existing jobs produced policy directives, articles, and advice to thousands of like-minded advocates across the country. His descriptions of the FBVE's work remain the only detailed narrative of the early federal implementation of vocational education. Historians and textbook writers have drawn liberally from Prosser's data and conclusions.[12]

Prosser's conclusions on the first federal subsidy of secondary-school curricula are straightforward. With legislatively mandated state plans, a uniformity in vocational education finally developed; the number of separate vocational schools and the total high school enrollment in vocational courses climbed; qualified state supervisors and teachers were hired; and federal subsidies stimulated larger state and local contributions to vocational schooling. Charts, graphs, and warm testimonials to vocational education stud his writings, supporting his view that the 1917 Act had made a lasting and beneficial imprint on public schools across the nation.[13]

The second major source on the execution and impact of the law is the Russell Report. This study was published in 1938 by the Advisory Committee on Education, which was appointed by President Roosevelt after a congressional debate over the extension of the 1917 law in the midst of the depression. The author was John Dale Russell, a University of Chicago professor and former assistant commissioner for higher education at the Office of Education. The report was sharply critical of vocational education, with particular emphasis on the negative impact of the Smith-Hughes Act on public schools.

Analyzing the two decades of the law's influence, Russell concluded that the rigid allocation of funds for specific instructional categories had converted a program originally intended to stimulate vocational education into a "federally dictated program in many states." Consequently, local experimentation was stifled. And the federal government, instead of drawing out state and local support as intended, was simply subsidizing existing programs. Also, because Smith-Hughes funds went to schools that scheduled vocational classes of two to three consecutive hours, unlike the conventional high school classes of one hour or less, and because money went to clubs such as Future Farmers of America, he concluded that the gap between general and vocational schooling had widened.[14] The net result, said Russell, was a "program that has not greatly changed since it was first introduced."[15]

In making these points, Russell attacked both the lack of reliable statistics and the absence of information on programs. He said, for example, that enrollment figures, the very centerpiece of every true believer's faith in vocational education, were unreliable. A person who went to an evening class only twice was counted as one enrollment in the published reports, the same as a student who spent the entire year in an occupational class in a full-time secondary school. Thus the citing of increased enrollments as a sign of a significant impact was, he concluded, misleading.[16]

In general, the few writers since 1938 who have examined the Smith-Hughes Act differ in their views in the same way as Prosser and Russell. That is, most agree that the act influenced the development of vocational education, but they disagree over whether the act helped or hindered public education.[17] For example, the views of Melvin Barlow, official historian of the AVA, parallel those of Prosser, who Barlow said "above all others . . . understood what vocational education was all about." Barlow, like Prosser, cited the rapid growth of enrollment in the four traditional occupations and the leadership of the Federal Board. "It is clear," Barlow and AVA Executive Secretary M. D. Mobley wrote in 1965, "that the vocational education program of the nation has advanced more rapidly with federal funds than would have been the case without them." And more important, they argued, were certain other consequences of the Act: the creation of state boards of vocational education, the development of standards, and the improvement of supervision.[18]

No recent writers outside the AVA orbit, however, have assessed the law's impact as optimistically as Barlow; his judgment remains a minority one. Most writers emphasize the law's narrowness, specificity, and inflexibility, all of which were identified in the 1938 Russell Report.* Typical of the majority opinion is the work of Grant Venn, a former agriculture teacher, school superintendent, and professor of education. Prior to his 1966–70 tenure as head of the vocational division of the U.S. Office of Education, Venn wrote a study of vocational education that in part focused on the effects of the 1917 legislation.

Stressing the historical context of the Smith-Hughes Act, Venn argued that pre-First World War assumptions about vocational programs, high school, instruction, and available jobs were deeply embedded in the law. These assumptions, he said, remained largely unaltered until 1963. And Congress, Venn concluded, by surrounding these assumptions with a legal barbed wire of details and prescriptions, legislated vocational schooling into grooves that became ruts. He pointed to inflexible unifor-

---

*Rupert Evans underscored the obvious result of the law, that no significant vocational education was developed below the ninth grade, or age fourteen. See his *Foundations of Vocational Education* (Columbus, Ohio, 1971), p. 165.

mity, a lack of experimentation, dual programs and administration, instruction tailored too closely to the existing high school organization, an outdated emphasis on farming and crafts, and a narrow outlook that equated job training with a lifetime vocation.[19] Like Russell and others, Venn saw negative consequences in a law that froze the structure and practice of vocational education. As Arthur Wirth wrote, "Such specificity handicapped vocational education from attaining the flexibility required to meet the demands of fast-moving technical and social change."[20]

A somewhat different position on the Smith-Hughes Act is taken by Marvin Lazerson and Norton Grubb. They see the Federal Board as a weak body, only advisory and administrative, and one severely hampered in its discretion by the details of the statute. This conflicts with the interpretation of Prosser, Barlow, Russell, and Venn, who offered abundant data to support the view that the FBVE was aggressive, that it exceeded its legal mandate in some instances, and that it saw its mission as propagating the doctrine of a one best vocational education system. All these writers, in short, saw the FBVE as an effort by reformers to force compliance with the law in order to spread their version of the vocational gospel.*

Another point that Grubb and Lazerson contest is that of increased enrollment. Wisely, they look at the percentage of high school students enrolled in industrial and trade courses, rather than at the total numbers, which Russell and others called misleading. Comparing high school enrollments in 1912–13, before federal aid, and in 1924, five years after federal subsidies to the states began, they find about the same percentage of high school students were enrolled, 7 percent. Furthermore, they point out, enrollment in part-time schooling shot up, one clear result of the 1917 Act.[21]

On the impact of the Smith-Hughes Act, Lazerson and Grubb

---

*Russell (p. 40) pointed to two instances of regulations that exceeded the letter of the law. First, the requirement that three consecutive clock hours a day be devoted to vocational subjects was not in the law. Second, the diverting of funds from teacher training to administration and supervision was not mentioned in the legislation. Michael Imber, in "Compulsory Continuation Schools for Young Workers: An Early Attempt to Combine Schooling and Work" (Stanford University, Boys Town Center for the Study of Youth Development, n.d.), examines the impact of the Federal Board on schooling.

concur with the dominant interpretation. "The structure of vocational education," they state flatly, "has remained largely unchanged since the passage of the 1917 Smith-Hughes Act." They, however, extend the lack of real change beyond 1963, despite subsequent amendments to the law. Their stress on "persistent failures" and continuities in vocational education after 1963 sets them apart from other writers.[22]

Whatever the differences in historical interpretation, the operations of the only national school board, which touched thousands of localities and tens of thousands of schools, remains a largely unexamined chapter in federal education policy. It deserves full investigation.

Vocational Education Act (VEA). Called the second Magna Charta (Smith-Hughes was the first) and a "new day" for vocational education, the apparently tradition-breaking legislation of 1963 has attracted even fewer scholars to explore its origins, enactment, implementation, and effects.[23] This act, writers generally agree, originated in the perceived shifting manpower needs of the late 1950's and early 1960's. High unemployment among untrained workers and changes in technology brought demands for the training of workers in occupations not covered in the American high school curriculum. Continuing criticism of the schools, together with a growing awareness of minority and youth problems, led President Kennedy to propose that a Panel of Consultants on Vocational Education review and evaluate existing programs and recommend improvements.[24]

This panel, just as critical of vocational education as the Russell Report (although restrained in its language), established clearly the need for expanded vocational education. Eight of ten youths would not complete college, the panel found, and only 18 percent of the high school students surveyed by the panel staff were taking a predominately vocational curriculum. Existing programs, the panel concluded, were insufficient to meet shifting national manpower needs or to integrate large numbers of unemployed, disadvantaged youth into the economy. Moreover, the amount of vocational education that was available varied dramatically by region and socioeconomic status.[25]

The panel criticized the uniformity in vocational curricula, insufficient planning, substantial data gaps, and fragmentary evidence of accomplishment. It called for the expansion of occupational programs for high school youth, for much more federal support for post-high school adults, and for more training for the unemployed, particularly the disadvantaged. By increasing federal subsidies and abolishing the rigid formulas inherited from Smith-Hughes legislation, all of these recommendations could be financed.[26] The panel's report was presented to President Kennedy in November 1962. Thirteen months later, the Vocational Education Act was signed by President Lyndon B. Johnson.

Only a few accounts detail how the report's recommendations passed through both houses. A Princeton University senior thesis on that subject was purchased and published by the AVA. Also, Melvin Barlow's writings trace the course of the legislation through Congress. Both accounts note the substantial influence of the AVA at each stage of the legislative process.[27]

Though the law itself did not embrace the panel's recommendations entirely, it nonetheless departed dramatically from the goals of the Smith-Hughes law and its subsequent extensions. Total appropriations were enlarged. Non-categorical grants were increased, allowing state funds for more program development. States were given more discretion in transferring funds between categories. The law focused clearly on high school and post-secondary training, including the handicapped and disadvantaged, and on upgrading the skills of the underemployed and unemployed. In addition, funds for innovative programs, research, curriculum development, and residential vocational schools were in the omnibus bill. The law, however, did continue the funding of the Smith-Hughes occupational categories, which showed the lobbying strength of the AVA.[28] In effect, the 1963 Act broadened the definition of vocational education to prepare people for many jobs rather than to meet specific market demands. It mandated program flexibility and encouraged experimentation.

Within a few years questions were raised about the implementation and effects of this law, which presumed stunning changes in how states and local school systems would operate their vocational schools and high schools. Garth Mangum for one, an economist and manpower policy analyst, wrote a number of articles and studies on vocational education and its intersection with national manpower demands. In 1968 he concluded that although the reported expenditures for vocational education had tripled and the construction of area vocational schools had jumped, "the extent to which high school students are being prepared for employment after two years of VEA is unimpressive." He blamed the permissiveness of the legislation: "New objectives were prescribed and added resources were provided, but the Act made no necessary connection between the two." Furthermore, the "lack of national leadership from the Office of Education" made any movement at the state level most difficult.[29]

David Rogers, a sociologist leaning heavily on Mangum's data, embraced the same conclusions in a report to a national committee studying high schools. Despite the promising changes stimulated by the law, he felt, many states were "reluctant to follow federally established priorities." He questioned whether many "reforms spelled out in such detail . . . have been implemented."[30]

The 1968 Amendments. The principal study of the implementation and impact of the 1963 law was completed in December 1967 by the National Advisory Council in Vocational Education, a group created by the VEA specifically to report on the subject.* This study, greatly influenced by Venn, then serving as the U.S. commissioner of education's appointee to direct the vocational education division, laid the basis for the substantial amendments that Congress added to the VEA in 1968.[31] Summarizing achievements of the 1963 statute, the Advisory Council also listed a number of "limitations," a euphemism for weaknesses used in many reports. The council recommended strong support for the new directions charted by the VEA. Specifically, they recommended sharper targeting of handicapped and disadvantaged youth, additional funds for post-secondary and adult programs, more flexible allocations, improved planning, research and evaluation by the states, and a reliable reporting system. The emphasis, again, was on improving and providing general job skills for youth and adults, not on preparing them for particular occupations.[32]

---

*The Advisory Council report, *Vocational Education: The Bridge Between Man and His Work* (Washington, D.C., 1968), was cited earlier. Readers should note that Garth Magnum was a member of the council and Melvin Barlow was staff director to the council. Barlow was also a staff member of the 1963 Panel of Consultants.

Many of these recommendations were endorsed by Congress and included in the 1968 Amendments. Harry Summerfield's description of the proposals' progress from the Advisory Council report to the president's desk acknowledges the AVA's decisive role. He also stresses Venn's influence, in shepherding key ideas through the Advisory Council, discreetly briefing congressmen and their assistants on key parts of the bill, and releasing information to supportive legislators in a timely fashion. Whatever the process, the relationship between the Advisory Council recommendations and the various portions of the statute are "too obvious to be accidental."[33]

The 1968 congressional additions to the 1963 law gave America's public schools, in Venn's words, a mandate that was "probably the most challenging in their history." The amendments would bridge national needs with those of youth, and would make "occupational preparation a major responsibility of our schools." Existing occupational programs would be expanded. New ones would be designed "to equip slum youth, disadvantaged adults, and handicapped persons with job skills and to meet the nation's manpower needs."[34]

The impact of the ensuing federal funds on states and localities was assessed in a 1974 report by the General Accounting Office (GAO). The GAO report, based on a seven-state study, found that:

1. In some states the ratio of federal to state-and-local dollars declined rather than increased as intended; in other words, the expected catalytic effect of federal funds on state funds did not materialize.

2. Large amounts of federal funds were retained at the state level for administration.

3. Though vocational opportunities were made available for handicapped and disadvantaged individuals, these groups were not given the high priority Congress intended at state and local sites.

4. Increased federal funding did not produce proportionately higher enrollments.

5. State allocation of funds was made indiscriminately rather than selectively for needs specified in the law.

The GAO report included the response of the Department of Health, Education, and Welfare (HEW) to the identified weaknesses. Except for the one item on the catalytic effect of federal dollars, HEW concurred with the points made by the investigators.[35]

In order to monitor the impact of the 1968 Amendments, the U.S. Office of Education contracted with Northern Arizona University for Project Baseline, a series of vocational education studies. Project Baseline subcontracted with Mary Ellis for her *Report to the Nation on Vocational Education*, which appraised the impact of the amendments over the period 1971–74. Ellis identified fifteen congressional expectations associated with the amendments, such as enrollment growth, increased state and local funding, and the targeting of handicapped and disadvantaged. Repeatedly, Ellis pointed out the paucity or unreliability of data with which one might assess how the expectations were fulfilled.* Where data were available and reliable, they were included. "While there is enough quantitative evidence," she concluded, "to suggest that vocational education programs have indeed been serving greater numbers of persons during the four-year period examined . . . , there is a dearth of qualitative evidence showing the extent to which programs have achieved 'high quality' as specified in the Vocational Education Amendments of 1968."[36]

Mildly dissenting from the GAO report, Ellis gave as her primary evidence of a positive impact an old standby, increased enrollment. After six decades as a measure of impact of vocational education legislation, after serving Prosser and other partisans as the single, clearest test of effectiveness, enrollment figures were the only data Ellis could rely upon in 1975.

The issues of unreliable data and the ambiguous impact of vocational education subsidies continue. Though the 1968 Amendments were renewed with modest changes in 1972 and 1976, Congress narrowed its intent to focus more clearly on handicapped, disadvantaged, and post-secondary students. More requirements for planning, evaluation, and reporting were included. And Congress directed the National Institute of Education (NIE) to study vocational education and produce a policy analysis by 1981.

---

*The unreliability and unavailability of data had been a steady refrain in the Russell Report (1938), Panel Report (1963), Advisory Council (1968), and GAO Report (1974).

In view of the unresolved issues, the criticism, and the unanswered questions since 1917, and in view of the unabated congressional enthusiasm for increased appropriations, a legislative mandate to find some answers to persistent questions is a mild and welcome departure for the Congress in dealing with vocational education.

Congress appropriated four million dollars to discover: 1) how vocational education funds are distributed to state and local school systems; 2) how, and to what degree, states and localities comply with planning, evaluation, and reporting requirements of the 1976 Amendments; 3) how federal legislation is implemented in school districts; and 4) how effective vocational programs are.[37] This brief survey of the literature* on two major pieces of federal legislation on vocational education suggests a few conclusions:

1. Writers generally agree on the origins of these laws but differ greatly over their effects.[38]

2. There are apparent continuities in how the vocational education laws responded to the strong social, economic, and educational criticism of the times. The promise that vocational education would cure unemployment, integrate minorities and immigrants, cut the number of dropouts, and motivate students to stay in school was heard both at the turn of the century and in the 1960's.

3. Federal legislation before and since 1917 was influenced by well-organized lobbying groups.

4. The intent of Congress was that the legislation would move from specific occupational preparation serving the existing labor market toward flexible programs serving both manpower needs and people, particularly the disadvantaged and handicapped.

5. Independent, federally sponsored reports over four decades have criticized federal implementation, state and local practices, and the strong resistance of state and local programs to what Congress expected. These critical reports have not diminished congressional enthusiasm for vocational education; if anything, new legislation has been drafted to renew, expand, and define further the federal interest in vocational education.

*For further bibliographical discussion, see note 38, p. 308.

From these conclusions two questions emerge:

1. In view of persistent, substantial criticism and uncertain success, why has legislation on vocational education been so resilient?

2. How has the implementation of federal legislation led writers to conclude that state and local jurisdictions resisted congressional efforts to improve vocational education?

Resiliency

Any answer to the first question, however speculative, must at some point take into account the influence of the AVA and its predecessors, their background and tactics. First, some genealogy. The National Society for the Promotion of Industrial Education, founded in 1906, achieved its primary goal of securing a federal subsidy for vocational schooling. In 1917 the NSPIE changed its name to the National Society for Vocational Education, and in 1926 it merged with the Vocational Education Association of the Middle West to create the AVA. The current 55,000-member AVA traces its roots directly to the NSPIE. Founded as a lobby and converted into a professional association, the AVA carries the legacy of aggressive lobbying to promote vocationalism by means of federal legislation as surely as a child carries its parents' genes.[39]

Though no history of the NSPIE or the AVA has yet been written, this effective, reform-minded coalition, born in the Progressive years with President Theodore Roosevelt as a charter member and later with President Woodrow Wilson a warm ally, has received some attention from historians. Though the NSPIE was a small national organization (it had less than a thousand members in 1912), it succeeded in midwifing the Smith-Hughes bill into legislation. The reform lobby's decisive role was made evident, Prosser reported, when President Wilson signed the bill with four pens that had been made by boys in a Buffalo vocational school. Three pens went to congressmen who had sponsored various vocational education bills; the fourth pen went to the NSPIE.[40]

After the NSPIE victory, reformers did not leave to chance what would happen to vocational schooling. When the Federal

Board for Vocational Education was established, over half of its members were drawn from NSPIE leaders. The first executive director was Prosser. In effect, the reformers became the implementers. Prosser's successors with the Board maintained close ties with the professional organization. After Congress shifted the Board to the Interior Department's Office of Education, the intimate ties between administrators of the program and the AVA continued, as they have down to the present day.[41]

The conversion of a single-purpose reform coalition into a professional association dedicated to both maintaining and expanding legislative victories captures the essence of the NSPIE-AVA history. From the few accounts that exist, the AVA has apparently been effective far beyond what one would predict from the size of its staff or membership. The word "apparently" is used because the writings that will be cited here are by both supporters and critics of the AVA. A fuller description and analysis might change the general outline sketched here, but such a study has yet to be done.

"I firmly believe," AVA Executive Secretary Lowell Burkett said in 1977, "that AVA has only one reason for existence, and that is to promote and improve vocational education." Scattered evidence suggests that the organization has performed its task well since 1917. Aggressive lobbying tactics and very close ties with Congress, a pattern set by the NSPIE, continued into subsequent decades. And since 1934 the AVA has had only four executive secretaries; this continuity may help explain its effectiveness.[42]

The general strategy used by AVA lobbyists has been to work closely with key congressmen from southern and rural states to draft bills. Whenever opposition to bills arose, techniques refined in the long struggle for the Smith-Hughes Act were used. The AVA would inform its regional, state, and local members of what the issues were and of which congressmen favored or opposed the bill, and then urge individuals to contact their representatives to make the case for vocational education. Lists of congressmen and senators were drawn up; sample telegrams were drafted; key state and local educators were asked to appear at hearings. In uncertain districts, local vocational educators called businessmen, public officials, war veterans, and others to ask them to intercede with the representatives on behalf of vocational schools. Bolstering these tactics were an annual convention and a steady stream of newsletters, bulletins, and copies of the monthly *American Vocational Journal*, all of which were opportunities for the organization to give legislators space and time to make political points with constituents.[43]

Except for unsuccessfully opposing the transfer of the FBVE to the Office of Education in 1933, the AVA has had an exceptionally strong influence with Congress. Venn gave the AVA credit for the legislative successes. Russell, underscoring the AVA's influential tactics, reported a debate in the mid-1930's where an angry senator told his colleagues:

A few moments ago I was advised that 73 telegrams had been received in my office during the last three hours. They read alike and that they are inspired is evident. Somebody has been spending from 60 to 75 cents per telegram to wire me to vote for the proposed increase in the [vocational education] appropriation . . . I do not blame this man for wiring throughout my state, not only to educators, but to the American Legion posts, and labor and farm organizations; but it is the most thorough job that has been done since the days when we received telegrams to oppose the utility holding company bill.[44]

In part because of such lobbying, Congress increased vocational education funds during the depression by $10 million over what President Roosevelt had requested.[45]

The organization's deep involvement in all phases of the legislative process led one writer to state flatly that M. D. Mobley, the AVA's executive secretary, was "consulted on the writing of all federal legislation." Barlow and Kliever detailed AVA activities throughout the year-long process that led to the 1963 legislation. That the Smith-Hughes occupational categories remained untouched (President Kennedy and the Panel Report both recommended the termination of the categories) is another instance of an AVA position written into the law. Barlow's description of Burkett's efforts in 1967–68 suggests intimate ties between the AVA and Representative Roman Pucinski in guiding the 1968 Amendments through the Congress.[46]

An informal acknowledgment of the lobby's role in shaping federal legislation comes from Stephen Bailey's study of Washington education lobbies. He asked high-level federal policymakers and congressional aides to rate the effectiveness of over three hundred educational interest groups. He found the AVA to be rated the fourth most effective lobby.[47]

None of this, of course, is conclusive. These are perceptions and reports. But what cannot be ignored is that since the 1930's every piece of vocational education legislation has authorized and appropriated more funds than the previous law. Nor can it be ignored that increased appropriations have come in the face of blue-ribbon panels and federal reports containing many criticisms.

Much research remains to be done. How does the organization operate internally? What does its staff (ten in 1955; 35 in 1977) do to maintain relationships with Congress and the field of vocational education? The interlocking network between the AVA, Office of Education bureaucrats, congressmen and senators supportive of vocational education, and House and Senate staff has yet to be mapped out. The same is true of the state network of vocational supervisors, AVA leaders, college professors, legislators, and local school officials.[48]

Fragmentary as this review of the AVA is, there is little question that this half-century-old Progressive coalition still employs effective tactics. The small band of shrewd and dedicated lobbyists, housed across the river from the Capitol, probably does not fully explain vocational education legislation, but no explanation for the persistence of this legislation over the years can omit tracing in detail the role of the AVA.[49]

Nor can any answer to the question of resiliency omit the triumph of the idea of vocationalism in the minds of educators, reformers, and parents. By 1918 vocational preparation had already become one of the "Seven Cardinal Principles" of schooling. Subsequent decades saw the hardening of this shared belief. Preparing high school students for jobs if they were not going to college became an essential ingredient of the ideology of public schooling.[50]

This triumph of the vocationalist ideology made federal legislation for improvements in vocational education seem sensible and worthwhile to both lawmakers and constituents. What gave vocationalism its ideological victory was that it, like many other early-twentieth-century reforms, was sold and installed as a school-based solution to national problems. Vocational education promised, according to its pre-1917 promoters, to assimilate immigrants into the labor force, overcome poverty, check migration from farm to city, permit the United States to compete on equal terms with foreign producers, and cut the number of dropouts. In the depression, vocational education would take care of unemployed youth; in the First and Second World Wars, it would equip factory workers for the war effort; in the 1960's, it would give the country technological superiority and train the unemployed; and in the 1970's, it would train the poor, handicapped, and excluded to enter the labor market and find meaningful jobs. Yet there is no body of evidence that points to the fulfillment of these multiple and often contradictory promises.[51]

Does this reflect the traditional public faith in the ability of schools to do pretty much anything they set their minds to? Perhaps. David Cohen and Bella Rosenberg, however, suggest other possible reasons why the public accepts laws that somehow have produced very little.

Some laws, they say, fail miserably to effect what was intended, yet are passed repeatedly for other, equally important reasons. Using mid-nineteenth-century compulsory school attendance laws as an example, they review the promises made for such laws: they would insure equality, curb delinquency, improve morality, and improve schooling. None of these outcomes occurred, Cohen and Rosenberg point out. How to explain the failure? Laws, they say, are rational instruments of social policy but they are more. Laws express "attitudes, values, and states of mind." Laws have sometimes been passed "less for what they produced than for what they promised and preached." Laws can be viewed as declarations of faith, a "form of political theater."[52]

Like plays, laws can be understood in terms of how they shape moral and emotional expression for an audience, not just in terms of their functional impact on a "target population." Like plays, laws can be seen as an encounter between an organized presentation of meaning and an audience. Legislation involves expressive and communicative encounters between those who shape and articulate meaning in the culture and those who listen and respond.[53]

In short, vocational education laws may declare the public faith that schools prepare youth for jobs. The failure to achieve the legislative intent may be less important than the expression of the citizens' deep feelings about what schools should do. And perhaps it may be less important than easing the guilt of elite parents and of educators who have spent most of their time and effort on college-bound students. Work and schooling, it seems, are intuitively associated in people's minds. In a society where work and productivity are so "crucial to an individual's sense of accomplishment," Norton Grubb points out, "it is immediately appealing to turn to work and work experience as the appropriate way to socialize the young."[54]

To summarize, the role of the AVA, the effective selling and reselling of vocational education as a solution to national problems, and the possible symbolic uses of legislation all suggest an enduring resiliency for vocational education. Critiques of vocational education may yield journal citations and dissertation footnotes, but if the record means anything, these paper blasts have led only to increased appropriations, streamlined procedures, and perhaps a more defined federal interest. No criticism, no evaluation has yet diminished the enthusiasm of Congress. Vocational education seems to be politically insulated from serious, comprehensive evaluations, by the government or others, that recommend retrenchment, reorganization, or dismantling.

Implementation

The implementation of vocational education laws is intimately related to the question of resiliency, since failures in vocational education have usually been blamed not on laws themselves, but on how they were carried out. Many writers have reached the conclusion that state and local school systems have resisted congressional efforts to implement and improve vocational education. This, therefore, is the second question I deal with: what is it about the implementation process that has led to this conclusion?

Before answering the question, however, it is necessary to clarify the term implementation and the context in which it is used. Implementation means executing a policy: translating a decision or law into programs. Although the process of converting a law into practice involves how well or poorly the law is drafted and what consequences occur after the bill is signed, this analysis stresses what administrative and political actions take place to achieve the legislative intent. Effective implementation, then, only means that "the program was able to do what it set out to do in the time it set for itself."[55] As for the context, it is important to stress three points: the considerable diversity among the states and localities; the "dynamic conservatism" that often marks local school system responses to mandated changes; and rival conceptions of implementation.[56]

The diversity of the governance, organization, and operation of vocational education is stunning. Donald Gentry identified four different state governance patterns of meeting the federal mandate, in addition to the various ways state boards of education organize themselves with their superintendents, directors of vocational education, and state departments. Structural differences in governance only scratch the surface. The size, wealth, political culture, and many other traits of the states add to the diversity. Of course the assumption here, which remains untested, is that these traits influence organizational and individual behavior.[57]

At the local level, where there are currently about 16,000 school districts, the variety is equally remarkable. School districts are large and small; rich and poor; rural, suburban, small-city, and metropolitan. Some districts are organized to embrace elementary through high school; others only elementary or only high school. Some school systems have appointed boards, most are elected. Some districts have teacher and principal unions, others do not. Variations among and even within local school systems—and those mentioned are only a few—in complex, still unknown ways affect how federally or state-mandated changes are viewed and responded to.

Finally, all of the components within either a local or a state system are only loosely tied to one another. Though paper authority, as shown in organizational charts, makes school systems appear to be tightly controlled, quasi-military organizations, teachers and principals display a great deal of independence in relation to school boards and superintendents. Decentralized, discretionary behavior by groups within a school district only increases diversity in performance.[58]

State and local diversity and loosely linked organizations must be incorporated into any discussion of implementation because they make it a more complex task to translate policy into practice.

If one views implementation as a fragile chain stretching from the lawmaker, through a federal agency with many bureaucratic levels, and finally to the thousands of school districts with their internal variety, only a shadow of the complexity is suggested. This conventional image of a chain suggests the potential for gaps and breaks in implementation once a bill is signed into law.

Another aspect of the context is the stubborn conservatism, the tendency to fight to remain the same, that describes local responses to efforts over the last century to change instruction, the curriculum, and classroom organization. Much has been written about how innovation seldom got past the classroom door; how staffs surrounded and absorbed program changes, leeching them of novelty and transforming them into conventional practices; and how staffs simply sabotaged changes.[59]

None of this is to say that schools have not changed, since they obviously have. Services have been added. Reforms in organization and governance have occurred. The curriculum has expanded. But basic classroom instruction and organization appear to have altered only minimally. If this is so—and far more research needs to be done on this point—it is because public school teachers and administrators in the last century have provided the same limited answers to a fundamental question: What are the different ways to manage and teach in an organization where students are unselected and come involuntarily, where instruction is delivered by an adult isolated from peers to a group of 25 or more students in one or more rooms, from five to seven hours a day, 30 or more weeks a year? The answers to that question, which include graded classrooms, textbooks, teacher-directed instruction, a uniform curriculum, and quiet and orderly classrooms, have persisted for well over a century in the face of repeated, forceful, well-reasoned, and imaginative efforts to change classroom instruction and organization.

Finally, there is the point about the different ways of looking at implementation. David Cohen, John DeSanctis, and Eleanor Farrar have sketched out three distinct views of the process:

Center-to-periphery. This is the familiar view. Programs are conceived by federal officials and carried out by local districts. Federal agencies set goals and make blueprints, and state and local districts passively accept what comes down. From this linear, social-engineering perspective, programs fail either because federal officials expected too much, too quickly, of messy, often irrational state and local organizations; or because of local sabotage and malfeasance.[60] The dominant image from this perspective is the chain stretching from Congress to the local school, with federal officials surefootedly stepping from one link to the next as they achieve one objective after another.

Bilateral Process. A RAND study, cited by Farrar and colleagues, of Office of Education-sponsored innovations found mutual accommodation between local and federal aims in those programs that succeeded. Thus the bilateral perspective casts local districts as active participants, not spectators, in federally designed changes. Federal goals are negotiated in conjunction with local ones. The dominant image is not of a chain, but of a tug-of-war between equally matched participants.

Multilateral Process. This perspective sees a federal program from the local school district's viewpoint. Dozens of local concerns and problems jostle one another, competing with the federal mandate. Budget problems, school closings, principal firings, lawsuits, threatened teacher strikes, and a host of other issues compete for the decision maker's attention; a federal blueprint for a legislatively authorized program can gain only passing notice. This conception is based on organizational research that established how loosely organized, decentralized, and independent the portions of a school system are. Implementation thus becomes problematic. Groups within the system view federal plans differently; attention is erratic; linkages are uncertain and disjointed— the ankle bone is sometimes connected to the thigh bone.

These various perspectives are useful because they supplement the familiar linear, top-to-bottom view of implementation to offer other possibilities. Given this context, let me turn to the initial question on implementing federal legislation. Two periods clearly emerge: 1917 to 1963, and 1963 to the present.

The Federal Board Administers the Law, 1917–33. In the first two decades after the 1917 legislation, implementation by the FBVE was particularly effective at the state level; programs intended by the law were installed in the time set for them. At the local level, the evidence is inconclusive and sparse, though suggestive.

The writings of Prosser, Allen, Wright, and Hawkins—all staff members at various times with the FBVE—describe the hectic, intense, and productive early months of implementation.[61] Within one year, 1917–18, all the states had passed enabling legislation to receive funds, submitted State Plans that complied with the law's requirements, initiated teacher training in colleges, and begun receiving reimbursement. In addition, within a few years after the law was passed, state departments of education and vocational divisions had organized themselves around occupational categories named in the law. This was an impressive achievement in legislative implementation.

The creation of State Plans signed by both state and federal authorities and reviewed by the FBVE, and the promulgation of staff-written regulations that followed, made it possible for the Federal Board to influence state vocational programs directly even though contributing only modest financial support. Federal regulations were encased in Policy Bulletins, the first of which was published in 1917. Each Policy Bulletin and any subsequent revisions appeared in the Federal Register and gave staff-written rules the authority of law. Policy Bulletin No. 1, for instance, was revised five times before 1963, yet it retained basic portions written by Prosser and the staff in 1917. Thirteen of the eighteen topics on which rules were written in 1917 were essentially the same in 1937.[62]

The Policy Bulletin contained specific requirements for State Plans. To ensure that states produced uniform plans consistent with the requirements, topical outlines for a State Plan were written by FBVE staff and given to each state director of vocational education. The staff's close attention to uniform, detailed plans tailored to the legislation was confirmed in the 1938 Russell Report. State officials told Russell that "federal agents participate actively in the drafting of the plan by the state officers." Even before a plan goes before the State Board for approval and submission to the FBVE, "the criticism of the Federal officers has been obtained and the plan may have been substantially revised under their guidance."[63]

Worse yet, according to Russell, was how on occasion federal officials exceeded their authority and state bureaucrats acquiesced. The Smith-Hughes Act, he pointed out, made no mention of devoting three consecutive clock hours each day to strictly vocational subjects. This was only an interpretation of FBVE staff that was included in the requirements; but "most state and local officials apparently believe it to be a provision of the Organic Act itself."[64]

An obvious explanation for the effectiveness of federal-state implementation was that the reformers themselves—Prosser, Allen, and many early members of the FBVE—administered the law. Implementation often breaks down initially when those who have designed the policy have no part, whether or not by choice, in executing it. This was not the case with the Smith-Hughes Act. Moreover, the implementers used a clear-cut systems management or accountability model, which became commonplace as a federal strategy in subsequent decades but was novel for that time. In short, federal implementation of the Smith-Hughes Act worked according to the center-to-periphery model. And the mood of most state educators toward vocational education was receptive; it was an idea whose time had come. Finally, the main body of expertise on vocational education was located at the federal, not the state, level. Since few experienced state supervisors were available, state officials looked to Washington for guidance.

Implementation within the thousands of local school districts is less clear. There is little question that the lure of federal money led to the hiring of more vocational supervisors and teachers in the targeted occupations and to the creation of courses. Enrollment figures, flawed as they are, reveal at the very least a higher number of participants than before 1917, although the proportion of students in vocational education may not have increased dramatically.

In one 1932 study, for example, high school courses in 54 cities were examined before and after the 1917 legislation. The percentage of high schools offering courses in home economics increased from 53 percent in 1915–17 to 95 percent in 1930–31; schools offering agricultural courses increased from 12 to 45 percent; and industrial arts courses from 27 to 82 percent. Another way of gauging implementation at local high schools is to check scheduled class hours. A 1939 study of home economics courses revealed that federally reimbursed schools generally scheduled the mandated requirement of a double period of instruction, and none had less than one period of it.[65]

As suggestive as this limited evidence seems, other data disclose gaps in implementation. In one study of a number of cities, the percentage of student time in 1931 devoted to vocational subjects varied from only 1 percent in New Orleans to 29 percent in Joliet, Illinois, for industrial arts. In another, fourteen-city study, student time in home economics courses was 4.7 percent in 1923–24; seven years later it had declined to 3.8 percent. Similarly, an investigation of small midwestern city high schools before and after the 1917 legislation showed that 13.8 percent of high schools offered industrial arts courses in 1915–18. A decade later it was 13.4 percent.[66]

Also, access to vocational programs seems to have been restricted. In the state of New York in 1935–36, all-day trade and industrial courses were available in only thirteen communities, mostly cities of over 60,000. Of 978 New York cities and towns, 479 did not offer home economics courses in high school. That most vocational studies were confined to urban areas is supported by a national study of home economics showing 43 percent of rural schools without such offerings.[67]

An anthropologist who lived in a midwestern rural community between 1939 and 1941 reported that the first vocational agriculture teacher was hired in 1933, a decade and a half after the federal legislation was passed. Vocational agriculture, the anthropologist said, was "the only subject in the high school curriculum which in content and instructional method is completely appropriate functionally to the needs of the community, and it is the only subject which a large portion of the community opposes and ridicules."[68]

What complicates the local implementation picture even more is that some vocational and regular high schools chose not to take the federal subsidy. Franklin Keller reported that such prominent vocational schools as Milwaukee's Boy's Trade and Technical High School and Detroit's Cass Technical opted out. Cass Tech's principal explained: "We have no Smith-Hughes classes in our day program. There are several reasons for this, but the sufficient one is that the time requirements of a three clock-hour session in shop (or fifteen hours a week) and a three-hour session in 'related work' is not flexible enough for our program."[69]

An additional complication in state-to-local implementation is seen in the state administrators who were expected to carry out the federal mandates. In 1918 the Federal Board determined that Smith-Hughes funds set aside for teacher training could be used to pay the salaries of state vocational education supervisors. This regulation (it is not in the Act) stimulated the growth of supervision. "Many of those appointed to supervisory positions in the early days of the program," wrote Prosser and other former FBVE staff, "had a meager conception of the work." State administrators had to deal with an activist FBVE staff and a maze of complicated federal regulations. Unlike the federal bureaucrats, many of whom had been involved in the lobbying for and drafting of national legislation for vocational education, state directors and supervisors were drawn from vocational education instructors on college staffs simply in order to get the program under way.[70]

Consider further the roles state supervisors were expected to play. "The state supervisor," Prosser wrote, "was a missionary in his state, an itinerant teacher of teachers, and . . . a stimulator of communities." Moreover, the supervisor "had the onerous duty of checking the work of teachers and schools." He or she had to judge whether teachers taught well, whether schools were effective, and whether federal standards within State Plans were being met.[71]

A New York study of vocational education in the 1930's described the business education supervisor's role.

In addition to being responsible for the Regent's Examination, the supervisor is required . . . to inspect and supervise the high school commercial departments, visit registered private business schools, prepare special reports, revise existing syllabi and prepare new ones, to cooperate with Teacher Education and Certification Division, to work with the various teacher training institutions, and to maintain contacts with various organizations concerned with business education.[72]

Few supervisors accomplished such tasks. In home economics, for example, by the end of the first decade after the law was passed 44 states had at least one supervisor for all its teachers; seven of these states had two or more full-time supervisors, and the turnover among these supervisors following the passage of the law ran to 44 percent by 1927. Much later, the supervisor-teacher ratio was still very low. Alabama, for example, in 1947 had nine state department staff members for every thousand vocational teachers. The most supervisory time available was in rural states; in New York, Pennsylvania, and Massachusetts, by contrast, the ratio of state staff per thousand teachers was only 13, 22, and 13 respectively.[73]

How often did supervisors visit teachers? Russell reported one survey that found vocational agriculture teachers being visited three to four times a year. This was probably higher than average; once a year was probably typical. Whether it was one or four, there was very little contact. The hundreds of teachers spread across an entire state were just too large a load for each supervisor to carry, given the other responsibilities these men and women had.[74]

However infrequent such visits were, however well-intentioned and smiling the supervisor was, the occasional arrival of a state official was probably viewed by teachers as an inspection. In the early years of vocational supervision, Prosser wrote, few teachers "welcomed the supervisor into their classrooms, and still fewer 'confessed their weaknesses' and sought professional training in order to do a better job of teaching." None of this is to suggest that annual conferences, summer sessions, bulletins, and classroom visits were trivial or insubstantial services to teachers. They were, however, probably insufficient to make an enduring impact on classroom instruction. The tight managerial ties supervisors were expected to have with school districts and teachers could not develop because of limited personnel and conflicting roles. Slackness, along with the traditional autonomy of schools, prevailed.[75]

All the evidence cited here is, of course, fragmentary. Few intensive, well-documented studies have been made on how widespread vocational course offerings were and how available they were to students in different school systems. The size of classes, the training of teachers, and the nature of the classroom instruction remain unclear without carefully detailed local studies of comprehensive and vocational high schools.

This much is clear: federal implementation of the Smith-Hughes Act was conceived and executed from the center-to-periphery perspective, and this was probably unsuitable for state-to-local implementation. The initial unfamiliarity of state supervisors with the law, the many and conflicting expectations buried within prevailing notions of supervision, and all the other economic, logistic, and psychological problems already discussed probably made state-to-local implementation more of a bilateral or multilateral process, depending on the school district.

Office of Education Administers the Law, 1933–63. The policies, procedures, and functions begun in the first sixteen years under the FBVE remained largely the same after Congress transferred the administration of the law from the FBVE to the Office of Education (OE) in 1933. At this time the FBVE's executive director, J. C. Wright, whom Prosser had hired in 1917 as a trade and industrial education agent, had been chief since 1922. After the transfer he became assistant commissioner for vocational education, remaining in that position until he retired in 1946. The basic organizational structure established under the FBVE, with sections for each occupation—for instance, agricultural education—was adopted by OE and remained intact until 1963, except for the adding of legislatively mandated occupations such as distributive education.

The shift to OE reduced the federal role in vocational education. Prosser saw in the shift a loss by the FBVE of independent authority and influence. At OE, at least two bureaucratic layers separated the assistant commissioner for vocational education from the commissioner. When the commissioner met with his top staff, no vocational education official attended these meetings.[76]

The reduced federal presence in vocational education probably contributed to a hardening of existing patterns. Routine took precedence over initiative; standard operating procedures went unquestioned. The primary OE functions of collecting data, publishing bulletins, and providing technical assistance to state and local school systems became routine chores for the Division of Vocational and Technical Education. Monitoring, inspection, and tough-minded reviews of State Plans were foreign to OE officials at this time.[77]

After the 1933 transfer shrank the federal role, the initial center-to-periphery conception of implementation that was embedded in FBVE's early strategies continued at OE. And OE staff, many of whom had worked under the FBVE, continued to seek compliance with Policy Bulletins. But as Russell reported, there was a considerable mellowing from the Federal Board's aggressive promotion and review of local efforts.

From 1917 to 1963, then, first under FBVE and later OE, the federal implementation of the Smith-Hughes Act and its subsequent modifications was probably effective with the states but less so with local school districts. Recall that effective, as used here, only means that vocational education programs were established to do what was intended in the allotted time. If there was any overt resistance to implementation by states and local districts before 1963, as the initial question posed, the evidence I have seen does not show it. Where implementation did not occur, the reason was probably less conscious resistance than state and local diversity. In the face of grandiose and conflicting roles for state supervisors, persistent and autonomous local practices probably insulated schools and classrooms from mandated changes.

The 1963 Vocational Education Act and the 1968 Amendments. The verdict of most informed observers on how well the Smith-Hughes Act was executed at the state level is clear. Prosser, Russell, Barlow, Venn, and others saw the law as being carried out effectively. The verdict on the implementation of the 1963 law and its amendments is equally clear. Garth Mangum, David Rogers, Michael Kirst and Joel Berke, Mary Ellis, the National Advisory Council, investigators for the GAO, and others have found these laws to be erratically and ineffectively executed at both the state and local levels. State and local school districts, they have generally concluded, have hewed closely to traditional Smith-Hughes practices and resisted new federal efforts; what changes there have been have occurred with the speed of wind eroding rock. Congress seconded this verdict on the 1963 law when they passed the 1968 Amendments and later changes.[78]

The evidence presented in these reports and by these writers is rich in details of ineffectual and hapless implementation:

1. One report concluded that "programs for hardcore unemployed have not been developed in relation to the need. . . . Few programs have been developed to reach the high school dropout. . . . States have not allocated resources for curriculum materials development commensurate with the need."[79]

2. A researcher who investigated New York state vocational education programs in the early 1970's said that "of all the federal school programs in New York, vocational education has been the most free from federal control, the most resistant to urban claims, and the most protective of its long-established autonomy within the N.Y. State Department."[80]

3. The GAO report concluded that "in many instances federal funds have been used to maintain existing activities year after year rather than primarily to initiate new program options." One state assistant commissioner for vocational education told GAO investigators that to end protracted conflict with the state legislature over state funds, "his agency paid the bulk of the state administrative costs with federal funds because these funds did not entail rigorous managerial review and accountability."[81]

4. A 1973 report concluded that "a disproportionate amount of vocational education funds still goes into home economics and agriculture."[82]

5. Though federal spending in vocational education increased 550 percent between 1960 and 1970, state and local spending for the same service increased 700 percent. A researcher concluded: "Although Congress expanded and refocused federal support for vocational education through the 1963 Act and the 1968 amendments, enactment of the legislation did not lead to an increase in the proportion of federal funds in the outlay for vocational education."[83]

These observers laid the blame for ineffective implementation on a Congress that added new, ambiguous goals to vocational education legislation already top-heavy with old, blurred ones; on an encrusted, lethargic OE bureaucracy married in spirit to the AVA; on recalcitrant state officials who took federal dollars with one hand and thumbed their noses at OE requests with the other; and on reluctant local officials who only wanted a continuing federal subsidy to support and expand vocational programs already in operation for decades.[84]

The tone, if not the details, of these writings on implementation assumes that entrenched federal and state bureaucracies or stubborn local educators frustrated the designs of lawmakers. Some researchers do explore the possibility that the law and follow-up regulations themselves were so seriously flawed as to permit any implementation to achieve very little. Most of these works assume a center-to-periphery model of implementation, and few consider alternative models or examine the process from the state or local perspective.

Few also take into consideration the organizational difficulties of changing state administrative practices embedded for decades into loosely linked yet complex bureaucracies. And fewer still investigate the actual process of carrying out federal programs. The Endo and Wirt and the Summerfield analyses of Venn's work at OE in the late 1960's in implementing a special vocational education program are two of just a small number of such studies.

It seems, then, that this is the answer to the question of why writers have seen state and local school systems as resisting congressional efforts to improve vocational education: the notion of resistance derives from a center-to-periphery view of implementation, which dominates writing in the field. The question shifts dramatically if bilateral or multilateral perspectives, which recognize the fact of diversity, are used. To ask what state and local factors are at work that shape federal implementation efforts is a very different question. Any answer to such a question would need to explore organizational processes within local and state bureaucracies, political forces at work both locally and at the state level, and the persistent, dynamic conservatism that marks schools and classrooms.[85]

There are, of course, other explanations than organizational ones for the apparent ineffectiveness of local and state responses to vocational education. Other interpretations stress the impact of continuing low enrollments in vocational programs and the existence of alternative programs (continuation programs, Civilian Conservation Corps, and the like) that drained away students from mainstream, full-time vocational programs; the ebb and flow of worker demand in various labor markets that was often out of phase with school system vocational goals; the stubborn obstacles inherent in using educational solutions to solve economic problems; or the entrenched attitudes of middle-class and working-class parents toward work and education.

Each of these competing explanations, by itself or in concert with others, can make a plausible if not compelling case to explain why state and local systems behaved the way they did in executing the changing federal mandate. Each interpretation, clothed in facts and arguments, could persuade reasonable people to view this issue through a different lens. So the organizational interpretation presented here, admittedly, is only one of a number that could have been used to explain a complicated phenomenon. Why was it chosen? When a writer chooses what weight to give the various factors that explain something, the writer's experience inevitably colors the choice. And so it was with me.

I have served in the public schools for a quarter of a century, both as a teacher and as an administrator. The impact of organizational processes on the initiation of new programs, the rational and irrational elements at work daily in an institution, and the plainly visible shaping of individual and group behavior—these I have seen and felt firsthand. I have entered this experience, along with my research, into an equation in order to explain what happened to programs mandated by law. Readers should be aware, however, that other interpretations are both available and plausible.

Conclusion

Among the many puzzles and contradictions that revealed themselves in this brief study of the politics and implementation of federal legislation on vocational education, I have dealt at length with only two. Because very little has been written by historians and political scientists about the politics and execution of these laws, a short review and analysis rather than a full-scale study has resulted.

To answer the initial question, on the enthusiasm of Congress for vocational education, I focused on the role of the AVA; the effective selling of vocational education as a solution to national problems; and the symbolic importance of laws as expressions of faith in what schools ought to do. This tentative answer suggests that historical, political, and social-psychological analyses might be combined to explore this question further. To answer the second question, on implementation, I tried to show that the Smith-Hughes Act was very effective at the state level, particularly under the aegis of the Federal Board. But for the 1963 legislation and subsequent amendments, state-level implementation was spotty and, where compliance occurred, it may well have been token rather than widespread.

In addition, I suggested other ways of looking at implementation than the traditional linear perspective. Different perspectives might lead researchers to ask different questions, particularly with regard to the political and organizational forces at work locally and in the state. As to the specific areas where research is needed, I reemphasize here that the Federal Board's two-decade-long experiment in directly shaping schooling deserves recapturing by historians. The continuing absence of detailed description and careful analysis of what happened in local school districts will retard any serious interpretation of the extent and effectiveness of vocational schooling. And the lack of serious histories of vocational schools and descriptions of vocational classrooms or teacher and student behavior also prevents the reaching of conclusions that go beyond speculation.

Such research often seems far removed from the decision-making arenas in Washington and the various state capitals. Yet for policymakers who invest public funds in vocational programs, an historical awareness of what has occurred in the enacting and implementing of federal legislation may well illuminate the different choices they must make. Policymakers generally carry in their heads pictures of what they think happened; it is up to historians to see that these pictures are reasonably accurate.

The Adolescence of Vocational Education

JOSEPH F. KETT

In this paper I examine the content and contemporary appeal of the ideas of the first generation of vocational educators in America, those who led the drive for federal support of vocational education that culminated in the Smith-Hughes Act of 1917. Such an examination, I hope, will help us to understand how a movement that has produced so few positive results could have generated such high expectations and such an enduring legacy.

Despite a great deal of the salivating rhetoric that usually accompanies major federal initiatives in education, the enthusiasm of the educators, professional reformers, businessmen, social workers, labor leaders, and farmers who coalesced in the drive for federal support was nonetheless authentic. It was also contagious. In Congress, although there was some disagreement over the wisdom of federal aid to education and over conflicting House and Senate versions of the bill, the idea of vocational education was not seriously challenged.[1]

Alongside the high hopes of the architects of vocational education, one has to set evidence that vocational graduates have generally failed to derive significant vocational advantages from their educational experience. The architects of the Smith-Hughes Act had put forward vocational education, particularly industrial education, as a cure for poverty, unemployment, and national decline. Yet there is little evidence to suggest that vocational education has accomplished any of these goals, or even an alternative set of goals. Occasional studies have indicated, it is true, that graduates of vocational schools have lower unemployment rates and higher earnings than graduates of comprehensive schools who do not go on to college. It is undoubtedly true that some vocational graduates have been able to locate employment quickly after graduation by returning to employers for whom they had worked in cooperative work-study programs or by using the contacts of vocational teachers.[2] But from 1940 to the present, the most carefully constructed studies have usually found that vocational graduates do not enjoy significant advantages. In 1942, for example, Selden C. Menefee published the results of his study of over 3,000 high school graduates in four major cities; he found that, measured by employment and earnings, the vocational graduates did not on balance have any advantages over the comprehensive graduates. And more recently, Charles Brecher's study of occupational upgrading in five industries in New York City pointed to a similar conclusion. New York City had public vocational high schools for four of the five industries that Brecher studied: apparel manufacture, food services, health services, and construction. In each case the jobs open to vocational graduates were no better than the jobs open to any high school graduates.[3]

As evidence has mounted that vocational education has not lived up to expectations, the fundamental assumptions of vocational education have come under increasing attack from academic economists and educators. From Charles Prosser in the early 1900's to U.S. Commissioner of Education Sidney P. Marland, Jr., in the 1970's, vocational educators have argued that increasing the skill of the work force would assuage social problems. To use the language of the 1960's and 1970's, they have been committed to investment in human capital, and their ideas have been assailed for the same reason as human capital theory.[4] The problem with human capital theory, many argue, is that by focusing on the deficiencies of the work force, it neglects those of the workplace. Problems develop not because workers lack skills, but because jobs that require skills are in short supply. At present many economists have abandoned human capital theory for some version of the dual-market hypothesis. Proponents of this hypothesis argue that some businesses, especially those to which youth and the poor have access, do not desire either a skilled or a stable work force. Academic critics of human capital theory have had the initiative during the 1970's, and Marland's career education plan, which rests on human capital assumptions, has been subjected to blistering attacks in educational journals.[5]

Despite these attacks, vocational education has continued to attract support. Between 1965 and 1970, for example, federal expenditures for vocational education doubled. In addition, many of the concepts behind the manpower programs of the 1960's and 1970's, which were represented by acronyms such as WIN, JOBS, and MDTA, were foreshadowed by the ideas of vocational educators between 1900 and 1925. There are, to be sure, some differences between manpower programs and traditional vocational education. The former have not been based primarily in public schools or oriented only toward youth. Yet these differences should not obscure some basic similarities. The architects of the Smith-Hughes Act, no less than the proponents of manpower programs, envisioned a subordinate role for the full-time school in vocational education. Moreover, the very idea of a "manpower policy" was implicit in their notion that labor was a national resource, to be conserved and rendered more efficient through wise public policy. The commencement of draft deferments for skilled workers coincided with the drive to secure federal support for vocational education in the Smith-Hughes Act, and reflected ideas about "human resources" identical to those of vocational reformers.[6] Similarly, the career education launched by Commissioner Marland during the 1970's contains few ideas not to be found in the writings of vocational reformers of the early 1900's.[7]

The ideas of the early vocational reformers, some of which were reincarnated during the 1960's and 1970's, had a potent impact on Congress during its deliberations over the Smith-Hughes bill. Prosser was effectively the author of the Smith-Hughes bill, and the major arguments that he advanced suffused the report of the Commission on National Aid to Vocational Education (1914), as well as the congressional debates over the Smith-Hughes bill. One need not suppose that ideas are self-activating or ignore the presence of interest groups such as vocational teachers, who recognized federal support as a source of expanding professional opportunities for themselves, to see the impact of ideas on the Smith-Hughes bill.[8]

Yet a student of these ideas confronts some immediate problems. The first arises from the diversity of groups that supported federal aid for vocational education. Their platforms ranged from vocational education in agriculture to home economics education and industrial education. The cosponsors of the bill, Hoke Smith and Dudley Hughes, represented an agricultural state, Georgia, and until recently the lion's share of federal funds has gone to vocational agriculture. Home economics has long attracted the largest number of students. But between 1900 and 1925, industrial educators such as Prosser and David Snedden were the most articulate spokesmen for vocational education. Although industrial education has never attracted large numbers of students, industrial educators dominated the Federal Board for Vocational Education, which was established to administer the Smith-Hughes Act.*

The second problem is that industrial educators themselves disagreed on a number of issues. The sharpest dispute was whether vocational education should train young people in specific occupational skills or provide them with a vocational orientation and general concepts relating to industrial processes. This dispute enlisted Prosser, Snedden, and the National Society for the Promotion of Industrial Education (NSPIE) on the side of training in specific skills and John Dewey and other humanitarian Progressives on the side of education in general industrial knowl-

---

*On financing, see Lloyd E. Blauch, *Federal Cooperation in Agricultural Extension Work, Vocational Education, and Vocational Rehabilitation* (New York, 1935, reprint ed. 1969), p. 213. On enrollment trends, see Layton S. Hawkins et al., *Development of Vocational Education* (Chicago, 1951), p. 213. Different authorities tend to give different enrollment estimates and, as Larry Cuban has noted, any estimate of enrollment merits some skepticism. Still, the general picture is clear. In 1930, at the end of a steep rise, the enrollment in federally subsidized industrial education classes was approximately 625,000. In 1949, after recovery from a decline during the Second World War, it stood at 750,000. In the same year, enrollment in federally subsidized home economics classes was over 1.3 million, up from 250,000 in 1930. Enrollment in vocational agriculture classes rose from 200,000 in 1930 to 630,000 in 1949. Between 1949 and 1960 these proportions did not change significantly. With respect to the domination of the Federal Board of Vocational Education by industrial educators, Charles Prosser, the board's first director, had been secretary of the National Society for the Promotion of Industrial Education; and of the six assistant directors, three came from the field of industrial education, one from commercial education, one from agricultural education, and one from home economics. *Ibid.*, pp. 148–55.

edge. This disagreement led to a related dispute over whether vocational education should be administered separately from general education, with Prosser and Snedden taking the side of separate administration. The conflict was intense, and continued long after the Smith-Hughes Act had for the moment settled the issue in favor of Prosser and Snedden.[9]

In addition, there were differences between working assumptions and stated beliefs, between assumptions that entered the movement as a byproduct of the practices of trade schools during the late nineteenth and early twentieth centuries and the ideas of leaders like Prosser and Snedden. Prosser and Snedden, for example, specifically rejected the idea that vocational education was a substitute for apprenticeship. Possessed of a broad vision of the objectives of vocational education, they did not want to restrict it to those trades where apprenticeship had flourished. And yet, they conceded, the assumption that vocational education was a substitute for apprenticeship was at the heart of the movement.[10] Finally, to complicate matters further, during the 1920's Snedden, who had been an enthusiastic supporter of vocational education as commissioner of education in Massachusetts between 1909 and 1916 and as first president of the National Society for Vocational Education (previously the NSPIE), became increasingly critical of the direction taken by vocational education.

It would be misleading to push these qualifications too far. For all the diversity of the movement, the ideas that shaped the Smith-Hughes Act were those of Snedden, Prosser, and the NSPIE. And for all their disagreements with others, Snedden and Prosser were adept at building a consensus.[11] The particular form of vocational education they favored placed far more emphasis on training in entry-level occupational skills than the form espoused by John Dewey, but their analysis of the need for vocational education did not differ greatly from Dewey's. Few vocational educators would have disagreed with the following propositions:

1. The relationship between school and work had become problematic under modern conditions. Rapid industrial change during the late nineteenth century had pitted the once smooth avenue between the classroom and job. The introduction of machinery was turning young workers into mere tenders of machines and thus was wrecking apprenticeship. Deprived of the opportunity,

which apprentices once had, to learn an entire craft, young people who left school between the ages of fourteen and sixteen blindly stumbled into "dead-end" jobs that lacked opportunities for advancement. Without opportunities to learn job skills, they soon became dissatisfied and began to drift from job to job. Some became psychologically attached to drifting. They acquired the mentality of casual laborers and were incapable of sticking to any job for long. The results were industrial unrest, social waste, and individual despair.[12]

2. The solution to these problems lay primarily in public vocational education, which would prompt young people to remain in school longer and would provide them with the occupational skills needed to advance themselves. This generalization about the beliefs of vocational reformers calls for some qualifications. John Dewey, for example, thought that vocational education would prolong schooling, but not because young people would stay in school longer in order to acquire entry-level occupational skills. Rather, Dewey thought that the introduction of occupational studies into the curriculum would enrich education and thus make it more attractive. Prosser and Snedden, in contrast, did not believe that a general prolongation of full-time schooling was either possible or desirable. Snedden ridiculed "cold storage" education, that is, vocational education conducted before one actually started to work. He and Prosser were convinced that effective occupational training could never occur independently of occupational experience.[13]

Yet it would be wrong to make too much of these qualifications. Prosser thought that schools could explain the general principles behind specific occupations, and he wrote disdainfully of "pick up" education, acquired casually and exclusively on the job. But he thought the most promising model for vocational education was the part-time continuation school, which allowed young workers to alternate between schools and occupations. The Smith-Hughes Act stipulated that every state had to devote at least one-third of its federal funds to part-time schools. Here as elsewhere the Act represented a substantial victory for Prosser's views, but he continued to believe that even a one-third allotment was too low. Despite disagreements, then, vocational reformers shared some basic beliefs about the importance of formal education in vocational training.

3. Vocational reformers also believed that vocational education would place the transition from school to work on an efficient and scientific basis. Vocational decisions made as a result of introspection, peer pressure, or family advice were unlikely, they thought, to be the best decisions. As a corollary, many reformers believed that the optimum decision could be made for each youth on the basis of psychological testing, which would guarantee that round pegs would be placed in round holes. Science made it possible to predict the vocational futures of young people by means of interest and aptitude tests, and hence to offer advice that was vastly superior to folksy misinformation passed on through the family or occupational grapevine.[14] But vocational guidance was merely one example of a general preference for the efficient and scientific. Prosser kept his distance from vocational guidance (and the Smith-Hughes Act did not allow federal funds to be spent for guidance counselors), but he thought that in the best of worlds young people would use vocational skills to advance steadily within a single occupation. Few vocational reformers were in sympathy with young people inclined to move through occupations like jackrabbits. They disdained job-hopping and the casual upgrading of skills by means of instruction on the catch-as-catch-can principle. They associated what later economists would call labor mobility with labor turnover and industrial unrest.*

4. Another corollary of these beliefs was that reason rather

---

*These propositions need some qualification. Paul Douglas cited a large number of studies that rested the case for industrial education partly on the proclivity of young people to shift from one low-level job to another. The anxiety over job-hopping updated traditional fears about the vicious character of the street trades. Douglas himself thought that boys in between jobs were the ones most inclined to join gangs. Prosser associated job stability with social contentment, and instability with "parasitism," labor organizers, the IWW, and political disturbances. Only during the 1930's did vocational reformers in number begin to come around to the view that job-hopping in youth was not a sign of vocational failure. See C. Darl Long, *School-Leaving Youth and Employment* (New York, 1941). In recent years there has been a tendency to view job-shifting in youth as a prerequisite for success rather than as a mark of failure. See Eli Ginzberg et al., *Occupational Choice: An Approach to the General Theory* (New York, 1951), p. 214. Yet Snedden believed all along that job-shifting among all age groups would occur in the normal course of events, with or without industrial education. See Snedden, *Vocational Education* (New York, 1920), p. 21. At times, Prosser implied the same; see Prosser and Allen, *Vocational Education in a Democracy* (New York, 1925), p. 63.

than custom would shape the attitudes of members of different social classes in the future. Although the reformers recognized economic and psychological differences between classes, they thought that appeals to reason would overcome many of these differences. Proponents of vocational guidance, for example, were aware that customs played a role in guiding lower-class youths toward dead-end jobs, but they believed that such customs were founded only on ignorance and would yield to reason. Like most Progressives, they had faith in the transforming power of correct information, and they espoused the ideal of social cooperation rather than class conflict.

The Appeal of Vocational Education

Much of the intellectual and social experience of reformers reinforced these beliefs. They lived in an age that was fast discovering the value of statistics, and they were able to point to several contemporary studies that documented the evils of dead-end jobs, drifting, tramping, and labor turnover.[15] Their confidence in education reflected not only the traditional American faith in schooling, but also the apparent success of recent experiments with professional education in fields such as engineering, agriculture, and education. The professional school was one of the models for the vocational high school. Reformers claimed that the Smith-Hughes Act would do for secondary education what the Morrill Act had done for higher education.[16] They believed that, as demands for skill were upgraded, some occupations were becoming more like professions. Meyer Bloomfield argued, for example, that under modern conditions businessmen were less entrepreneurs than "commercial engineers" whose concern was not to haggle over prices but to get merchandise as swiftly and cheaply as possible from wholesalers to consumers.[17] Further, just as the expansion of formal education in law and medicine had heightened the prestige of those professions, even trades requiring few skills would gain in dignity (and hence become more attractive to youth) if they were taught in schools.* Reformers

---

*The U.S. Commissioner of Education noted in 1916 that in order to teach a trade in school the work had to be studied and reduced to principles. As long as there were principles to teach, even the work of salesgirls could be elevated to the status of a skilled trade. See *Report of the Commissioner of Education, 1916* (Washington, D.C., 1916), p. 173.

hoped that the entry into trades would come to resemble the smooth transition from professional school to professional practice. Such a transition was appealing because it was efficient, marked by a minimum of floundering among occupations. The founders of vocational education understood this point better than most, for they were themselves usually products of professional education.*

Their faith in education was tied, in turn, to faith in science, for the new professional schools were imbued with a belief that engineering, agriculture, and education were sciences and that professional men systematically trained in these sciences were superior to inventive or inspired amateurs. Finally, their faith in science was one of the factors that disposed them favorably to the ideal of class cooperation. Characteristically, the influential textbook *Vocational Education in a Democracy* by Prosser and Charles R. Allen dwelled on the increased "social wealth" that resulted from the discovery of ways to control the boll weevil, the potato bug, and black rust.[18]

Supporters of vocational education usually saw themselves as advance agents of modern economic and intellectual forces. They were inclined to radical juxtapositions between the past and present. Once all had been simple; now everything is in turmoil. Once jobs demanded little education; now they call for advanced training. Once the transition from youth to adulthood had been smooth; now it is rough.[19] In their eyes the industrial changes of the 1880's and 1890's had transformed every aspect of American life save education, and now it was education's turn. Yet their

*The first director, Prosser, and most of the first assistant directors of the FBVE had been students or teachers in professional schools. Prosser had attended a business college and had a Ph.D. from Columbia. Layton S. Hawkins had been a student and later head of the Department of Science and Agriculture at Cortland State Normal School in New York. Lewis H. Carris held an M.A. from Columbia and had risen through the ranks from principal to superintendent to assistant commissioner for vocational education in New Jersey. Josephine T. Berry was a graduate of Teachers College, Columbia and had been an assistant in the Department of Household Administration at the University of Chicago. She later became head of the Department of Home Economics at a normal school in Illinois. Frederick G. Nichols had been a student and teacher at a business college. John Calvin Wright was a graduate of both a business college and a normal school. The only assistant director to have entered the field of vocational education after having had an apprenticeship (as a saw filer) and practiced a manual trade was Charles H. Winslow. See Hawkins, *Development of Vocational Education,* pp. 148–56.

thinking was not always as "modern" as they thought. For all their talk about social efficiency and applied science, many of their attitudes derived from values that were entrenched long before the late nineteenth century.

Their tendency to view job-shifting as pathological, for example, had roots in antebellum conduct-of-life books, in which the footloose opportunist never enjoyed a high reputation.[20] True, vocational reformers reversed the traditional relationship between moral qualities and vocations, by substituting the idea that a steady job would produce steady morals for the idea that the development of character would immunize youth against the spirit of drifting. But in this case it was the technique rather than the underlying value that was new.

Perhaps the most time-honored of all of the reformers' values was that of work itself. Far from emerging as a byproduct of the advanced stages of industrial capitalism, their attitudes toward work were embedded in the tradition of middle-class Protestant America. In this tradition, work was not only a guarantor of success, but a form of self-expression, an unveiling of the soul.[21] At the very time when traditional attitudes toward work were coming under attack, vocational reformers sought to revive them. They looked to vocational education and guidance to revitalize work experiences, and thereby to dissuade workers from seeking in amusements morally perilous substitutes for the exhilaration that attended dignified labor. The President of M.I.T. identified the problem:

On every hand we meet with the tragedy of failure or of partial failure and see the dissatisfaction and the misery that is brought about by the placing of square pegs in round holes. In these days men who are to amount to anything must be workers in some field, intellectual or manual. If they are to be happy or moderately happy, they must get their pleasure, or the major portion of it, from work. If they must look elsewhere for such pleasure, they are almost invariably doomed to dissatisfaction if not misery.[22]

Erville Woods described the answer: "Better vocational adjustment will link the real interests and energies of the spirit with productive tasks instead of allowing them to be turned to merely recreational activities, which in the cramped monotony of industrial communities so often verge on the unsocial and criminal."[23]

By advancing honest work as a substitute for perilous amusements and as an anodyne for social unrest, reformers revealed the conservative cast of their minds. Yet the celebration of the work ethic was not without a radical potential. This commitment to work, though not in itself implying a call for social change, could feed criticism of any system that neglected to educate people to work, and by implication any society that sustained such a system. From Robert Owen's utopian experiment at New Harmony in the 1820's to Jonathan Baldwin Turner's call in 1850 for an "industrial university" on the Illinois flatlands, educators had contrasted practical or useful education with the classical humanism of conventional colleges and universities. The kind of practical education praised by Owenites and by Turner, which emphasized the natural sciences, was not the same as the vocational education esteemed by Prosser. Yet the sort of scientific instruction promoted by radical Owenites like William Maclure, who was the moving force behind the New Harmony schools, focused on the conveyance of a few simple precepts that would enable workers to understand the scientific principles behind their trades and thus would elevate the trades themselves. This made it easy to blur the line between scientific and vocational training, and possible for radicals to rally around the flag of "industrial knowledge." Maclure, for example, adapted Pestalozzianism to industrial education by arguing that the principles of mechanics were best taught by the study of machines; and Turner proposed that his industrial university teach all "studies and sciences of whatever sort, which tend to throw light on any art or employment which any student may desire to master."[24] Vocational reformers of the early 1900's laid claim not only to this tradition but, at times, to its explicit radicalism. In 1915, for example, John A. Lapp and Carl H. Mote complained that corporation lawyers were educated at public expense in state universities to help their clients evade the law, yet honest laborers had to struggle for knowledge; they advanced vocational education less as a cure for unrest than as a device to destroy the "bulwarks of class exploitation."[25]

The Problem of Vocational Education

In sum, reformers blended traditional and recent ideas into a powerful synthesis. Yet in retrospect there are a number of points where their thought appears to have been vulnerable to attack and where it did indeed draw criticism from contemporaries. These apparent soft spots involved the relationship between vocational education and (1) industrial demands for skilled labor, (2) unemployment, and (3) occupational mobility. By analyzing the reformers' responses to criticism in these three areas, we can gain a clearer perception of the impulses behind their thought and the reasons why their ideas seemed so plausible to enlightened contemporaries.

Paul Douglas, in his classic study of apprenticeship and industrial education, identified the first of these problems. "The extension of machinery," he wrote, "broke the trades up into many parts. Learning a trade was no longer a difficult affair." In *The Iron Man in Industry* (1922), Arthur Pound made the same observation, and concluded that vocational education was a waste of time and money because the subdivision of tasks had reduced the need for skilled workers. What was the point in teaching skills if fewer and fewer workers needed them?[26]

One possible answer to Pound was to instruct young people in how work was organized within specific industries—in effect to train them to be managers of work rather than workmen. At the very time when demands for industrial education were on the rise, Frederick W. Taylor, the apostle of scientific management, was urging that managers take over from skilled workmen the scheduling of tasks on the factory floor. For a variety of reasons, however, vocational reformers were reluctant to orient the movement toward the education of managers. One reason for this reluctance was that reformers wanted vocational education to uplift vast numbers of young people, not just the fraction of them who were potential managers. A more important reason lies in the suspicion of white-collar work that permeated the movement. Although reformers did not restrict the concept of skill to the attainment of manual dexterity, they usually associated skill with the manual trades. They talked of industrial intelligence, but it was the intelligence of the skilled operative rather than skilled manager that they had in mind.

The reasons behind this suspicion of white-collar work are open to speculation, but an attractive hypothesis can be forged from some bits of circumstantial evidence. Foreign-born laborers increasingly dominated the working class during the late nineteenth century; by 1890 over a third of all workers in "manufacturing and mechanical industries" had been born outside the United States. Throughout the second half of the nineteenth century, educators voiced abundant complaints that native American boys seemed to prefer the lowliest clerkships to honest manual labor. These complaints suffused the manual training movement, which, as Snedden noted, was the staging ground for many vocational educators. These educators argued that, among other benefits, vocational education would reduce American dependence on foreign labor and would quiet industrial unrest (which contemporaries often blamed on foreign-born agitators in the working force). To have emphasized education for managers would have been to compound the problem rather than to provide a solution, since a solution depended on the success of efforts to increase the dignity of the trades and thus to attract native-born youth to manual work.[27]

Having rejected the obvious answers to the argument that the subdivision of tasks reduced the need for skilled workers, vocational educators pursued two other approaches to the problem. First, they drew comfort from a number of signs that industrialization was creating more skilled occupations than it was destroying. The most striking evidence of this tendency was the remarkable growth of correspondence schools between 1890 and 1920.[28] There had been experiments with correspondence schools before 1890, most notably the Chautauqua Literary and Scientific Circle, but Chautauqua's focus had been cultural rather than occupational. The turning point came in 1891 with the establishment of International Correspondence Schools in Scranton. ICS began as an effort to provide Pennsylvania with a supply of trained mine inspectors in the wake of new state mine safety laws. The only available treatises on mine safety had been addressed to the problems of British mines, where conditions were notably different from those in American mines. In subsequent years, ICS expanded its curriculum to include such fields as electricity. By all accounts the demand for its courses came mainly from young men between 23 and 27 who found that they lacked the skills to qualify for what were essentially new occupations. By 1900 the cumulative enrollment of ICS was 250,000; by 1910, 1.3 million. In time, of course, correspondence schools would generate much of their own demand with lavish advertising and would design their offerings to meet occupational aspirations that were fanciful or Mittyesque (magician, private detective). But between 1890 and 1920 demand was both intense and spontaneous.[29]

The growth of correspondence schools was not the only sign of the times that convinced vocational reformers of a rapidly rising demand for skilled workers. Many of the vocational schools that started out between 1890 and 1910 as substitutes for apprenticeship in trades like printing soon found themselves responding to local business pressure by including courses in electric wiring and electroplating. Similarly, the same period witnessed a growth of schools sponsored directly by corporations, especially by corporations, like General Electric and Westinghouse Electric, that were situated in fields marked by burgeoning technology. In such fields the problem with apprenticeship was not that the subdivision of tasks had rendered education of any sort meaningless, but that apprenticeship could not provide the number of skilled workers needed.[30]

Although the spontaneous growth of correspondence schools and vocational schools provided evidence that the demand for skilled workers was rising, vocational reformers recognized that not everyone could expect to find a job calling for complex knowledge. Yet they continued to associate vocational education with increased skill for all workers; in their eyes its dividends were universal. It is easy to dismiss their ideas as wishful thinking, but before doing so it is worthwhile looking more closely at the connotations they gave to the word skill. At times they equated skill with the mastery of complicated manual operations and with the comprehension of sophisticated mechanical concepts. But they also used skill to signify any kind of organized knowledge whose application would yield higher productivity. Snedden and Prosser, for example, often drew their illustrations of the need for a more skilled work force from the ranks of unskilled workers such as night watchmen.[31] In so doing they were not seeking to dazzle their readers with paradoxes, but to reaffirm views that had a wide following among Progressive thinkers during the first two decades of this century.

In the writings of Frederick W. Taylor one can find the clearest statement of the claim that skill was needed to perform apparently unskilled jobs. The illustration Taylor most often presented—indeed, it became famous—to show how an apparently unskilled occupation actually demanded skill was the handling of pig iron. Taylor acknowledged that in the conventional understanding pig iron handling did not call for any skill. Handlers merely picked up a piece of iron, walked a few yards, and dropped it on a pile. Taylor seriously argued that an intelligent gorilla could be trained to do the job better than a man. Why then talk about the need for skill? Because pig iron handling was a science, which Taylor followed the president of M.I.T. in defining as "classified or organized knowledge of any kind."[32] As a supervisor at the Bethlehem Steel Company, Taylor had increased the productivity of pig iron handlers by determining the optimum daily distribution between work and rest periods. Further, Taylor was convinced that some systematic training had to be given to workers if they were to learn to work in accord with scientific laws. Like Prosser, Taylor argued that occupational training by casual observation of veteran workers in the shop had to give way to conscious efforts to transmit organized rules to each generation of workers, even pig iron handlers.*

This brief excursion into Taylorism not only suggests the distinctive connotations that terms like skill and science had for the first generation of vocational educators in America, but also yields some clues to the appeal of vocational education. Between the publication of Taylor's *The Principles of Scientific Management* in 1911 and the Smith-Hughes Act, Henry Ford had given a practical demonstration at his Highland Park plant of the relationship between increased productivity and higher wages. During the First World War, moreover, the massive effort to train workers for war industries provided vocational reformers with evidence that organized vocational instruction was both feasible and effective.

Vocational reformers believed, thus, that virtually any incre-

---

*Taylor, "The Principles of Scientific Management," *ibid.*, pp. 40, 59, 114–115. Daniel Bell has described Taylor's system as a search for a social physics. "Once work was scientifically plotted, Taylor felt, there could be no dispute about how hard one should work or the pay one should receive for labor"; see Bell, "Work in the Life of America," in Haber, *Manpower*.

ment in the skill of workers would yield individual and social benefits. In retrospect, their thinking on this issue appears shallow. A half century of antagonism between capital and labor has provided little support for Taylor's optimistic belief that scientific management would create a harmony of interests in every factory. At the time, however, many saw in Taylor's concepts another illustration of the ways in which science could be a benefactor of society.

The second area in which the thought of the first generation of vocational reformers appears in retrospect to have been especially vulnerable was the relationship between vocational skills and employment. Rising rates of unemployment among teenagers during the last two decades have thrust the issue of unemployment to the forefront of debates over vocational education and manpower training. Critics have launched a twin-pronged attack on vocational education. First, they emphasize, the structure of business in a capitalistic society contributes far more to unemployment than the level of skills in the work force. And second, increasing the skills of individual workers will merely force workers into a game of musical chairs; the more skilled workers will bump the less skilled from low-level jobs, which will replenish the ranks of the unemployed.

For a number of reasons, the early vocational reformers did not draw these conclusions. As noted, they thought the demand for skilled labor was rising and would continue to rise. One can read through their writings without encountering any reference to the "overstocking" of the skilled manual trades. "Overstocking" appeared in their writings only in reference to the unskilled trades.

Yet they did not believe that the issue of unemployment could be put down so simply. At the time when the drive for federal support of vocational education was gaining momentum, evidence was mounting that the causes of unemployment were structural rather than personal. Increasingly, unemployment seemed to be rooted primarily in economic forces that expanded and contracted job opportunities for young people and adults alike, rather than in the decline of apprenticeship and the inadequate training of workers.

Between 1909 and 1925 a number of economists began to describe these forces. In 1909 Sir William Beveridge delivered a seminal report to the Royal Commission on the Poor Laws and Relief of Distress; he later expanded it into a book, *Unemployment: A Problem of Industry*.[33] Studying unemployment among London dockworkers, Beveridge de-emphasized laziness and inadequate training as causes. Unemployment, he argued, resulted from seasonal fluctuations in the demand for labor. He traced these fluctuations to the preference of employers for a "stagnant pool" of laborers who could be called upon from day to day depending on whether ships arrived.

Beveridge shifted attention from the unemployed to unemployment and from human to structural causes of unemployment. In America, similar investigations initiated by the Committee on Women's Work of the Russell Sage Foundation resulted in Mary Van Kleeck's *Women in the Bookbinding Trade* (1913), *Artificial Flower Makers* (1913), and *A Seasonal Industry* (1917), and Louise C. Odencrantz's *Italian Women in Industry* (1919). These studies, all of which underscored seasonal fluctuations in demand as the cause of unemployment, formed the basis for important syntheses published between 1919 and 1925 by Sumner Slichter, Don D. Lescohier, and Herman Feldman.[34]

The implications of the studies of these economists ran counter to the views of the educators. Slichter summarized the basic contention of the economists when he claimed that "it is impossible to understand the transient habits of many workers without knowledge of the industrial conditions, including temporary jobs, out of which these habits in large measure arise."[35] Feldman carried the argument a step further by insisting that, given the structure of industry, increments in vocational training would not increase the general level of job satisfaction, because job satisfaction depended less on the quality of laborers than on the structure of labor markets.[36]

For several reasons, however, the challenge posed by these economists failed to produce a significant reassessment of the premises behind vocational education. In part, it was a matter of timing. Beveridge's ideas did not make a fast crossing of the Atlantic. They received respectful attention from Frederick A. Mills's *Contemporary Theories of Unemployment and of Unemployment Relief* (1917), which noted that American studies of unemployment lacked "the concreteness, the fullness, and the general applicability characteristic of four or five of the standard English works."[37] Detailed studies of poverty among the working poor appeared earlier in Britain than in America. In Britain, for example, Beveridge's work had been foreshadowed by the social investigations of Charles Booth and the Webbs. As early as 1891 Sidney Webb had described "the fearful daily struggle for bread at the Dock gates."[38] Comparable studies not only developed more slowly in America, but tended to lack any uniform theme. American ideas about unemployment were scattered over such areas as the evils of private employment agencies, the need for industrial education and vocational guidance, the role of land monopoly and immigration, and the problems of vagrancy and tramping.[39] In such a climate it was easy to assume that vocational education was only one of a number of ideas that could play useful roles in assuaging unemployment.

American ideas about unemployment, besides being less pointed than British ones, were more colored by moralism. Though Beveridge said that casual labor was demoralizing, he dwelled on its economic causes rather than its moral causes. Americans did not ignore the former, but were more emphatic than Beveridge about the latter. Lescohier, for example, said casual labor was "as dangerous as the tentacles of a devilfish," not because casual laborers suffered economic deprivation, but because the absence of full-time work led them to develop a taste for leisure:

Starting out as common laborers, or even as skilled workers, twenty years before, they worked steadily for a time, then became subject to irregular employment, either because of industrial conditions or because of drink or vice or a taste for traveling. Gradually, they became more and more irregular in their working and life habits, and crystallized into casuals living from day to day and hand to mouth without self-respect or ambition.[40]

Lescohier's views found an echo in the writings of so sophisticated a vocational reformer as Paul Douglas, who wrote:

The period of idleness between positions, which has been shown to be so large, is another evil factor in the child's industrial life. He is neither at work nor in school; he is industrially adrift. Unemployment for adults is bad enough; for children it is positively vicious. It breaks down habits of industry which are slowly forming, and exposes them to all sorts of positive dangers. Loafing about "waiting for something to turn up" does not make strong men and women. For the city child, such idleness is especially dangerous. The "gang spirit" seizes the unemployed boy, and he seeks satisfaction in his group, generally to anti-social ends.[41]

None of this excluded the idea that unemployment had structural causes, but it subtly legitimated the contribution that education could make to the elimination of unemployment. If the problem created by casual labor was the decay of character rather than the loss of wages, then the school, especially the vocational school, could play a role. This was the conclusion drawn by Lescohier and Feldman no less than by Douglas.[42]

The relationship between vocational education and occupational mobility constitutes the third vulnerable area in the thought of early vocational reformers. Although the approaches of reformers to the issues already discussed hint at their approach to this one, this extremely complex area merits separate treatment. The basic assertion of vocational reformers appeared simple and straightforward. Young people taught occupational skills in schools would be able to find jobs with ladders of advancement, and thus would avoid the occupational slag heap represented by dead-end jobs. Several components of this proposition did not elicit serious dissent. No one doubted that dead-end jobs existed or that school dropouts were restricted, at least initially, to dead-end jobs. Both the Douglas Report in 1906 and a similar Massachusetts study during the 1920's indicated that young people who had abandoned full-time schooling before the age of sixteen usually held low-level jobs. In textile mills they were sweepers, oilers, and bobbin boys and girls; in shoe factories they were stitchers of simple seams and helpers on nail machines; in candy factories they carried boxes.[43] Everyone agreed, moreover, that such jobs were dead-end, in the sense that they did not offer significant employment prospects beyond the teen years. There were bobbin boys and girls, but not bobbin men and women.

This line of thought was plausible, but it contained a number of questionable assumptions. First, granting that dead-end jobs did not offer attractive (or any) future employment prospects, was it true that young people who took such jobs could not find attractive work later in some other line? It was possible to view the matter in a different light: so-called dead-end jobs might have been merely temporary youth jobs that did not necessarily foreshadow flat occupational trajectories in maturity. Second, reformers assumed that occupational prospects depended primarily on the possession of skills. Even if we accept their argument that demands for skilled labor were on the upswing, this assumption was problematic. What evidence was there that young people from poor homes, even when taught vocational skills, would choose the kind of employment reformers believed was desirable? Was it not possible that reformers underestimated the impact of social class on occupational choice?

To take up these issues in order, Snedden was the one vocational educator to reject the concept of dead-end jobs. He did not believe that juvenile work in messenger services or textile mills or department stores sentenced young people to bleak occupational futures. As a corollary, he thought that vocational education would never be very effective for those between the ages of fifteen and eighteen. In his view continuation schools were a poor idea because the juveniles who attended them would be unable to see any connection between the principles they learned in school and the low-level occupations to which they were restricted because of their age. Rather than train juveniles for jobs they could not hope to enter until they were older, Snedden came to believe that vocational education should concentrate on people between twenty and thirty, making use of full-time residential schools and drawing workers from a wide geographical area and from many sectors of industry.[44]

Snedden could never persuade others, however, that what appeared to be dead-end jobs were merely temporary youth jobs. It was difficult to settle the issue on the basis of available evidence. The trouble was that most contemporary studies of youth in the labor market failed to distinguish between the grade of school leavers and their age. Hence it was impossible to say whether the manifest economic advantages enjoyed by older youth resulted from their additional schooling or merely from the fact that they were older. Interestingly, the only study (to my knowledge) that distinguished between grade and age raised doubts about the economic value of schooling as such. In a study of 800 Iowa schoolboys, Ervin E. Lewis demonstrated that there was no correlation between the grade and age of school leavers. Boys of the same age leaving different grades received similar beginning wages. Indeed, Lewis's study indicated that seventeen-year-olds who left school after the eighth grade actually averaged slightly higher starting wages than seventeen-year-olds who left either the eleventh or the twelfth grade ($8 against $7 and $6.50). But this was an obscure study, and its implications had no significant impact on the thought of vocational educators.*

In truth, the issue of dead-end jobs was a good deal more complex than anyone realized. Studies conducted during the 1930's by August B. Hollingshead, Percy E. Davidson, and H. Dewey Anderson indicated that Snedden was certainly correct when he said that as young people matured they could move from low-level youth jobs to desirable occupations. Davidson and Anderson's study of male workers in San Jose, California, for example, showed that many who became skilled workers or clerks had started out in messenger services. Yet the same studies indicated that some youth jobs were more likely than others to lead to attractive adult occupations, and that social class determined the kind of youth job one could obtain. Hollingshead observed, for example, that in Elmtown those who worked as pin boys in bowling alleys during their teens usually came from the lower social classes and usually had difficulty finding desirable jobs in factories during young manhood. In contrast, middle-class youth were more likely to start as store clerks and then proceed at eighteen or twenty into well-paid factory positions.[45]

*Ervin E. Lewis, "Work, Wages, and Schooling in Eight Hundred Iowa Boys in Relation to Problems of Vocational Guidance," in Meyer Bloomfield, ed., *Readings in Vocational Guidance* (Cambridge, Mass., 1924), p. 248. Vocational reformers usually rested their case for the cash value of industrial education on the superior earnings of the graduates of a small number of technical high schools established during the late nineteenth century. But these schools were actually preparatory schools for engineering colleges, and attracted children of upper-income families. One study that tended to support Lewis's argument was Edward L. Thorndike et al., *The Prediction of Vocational Success* (New York, 1934). In this longitudinal study of over 2,000 New York City schoolchildren, Thorndike noted that such factors as academic performance in school had no more than a very weak correlation with vocational success, but that a strong correlation existed between physical size at age fourteen and vocational success. This may have been a reflection of the disposition of employers to prefer mature workers, for physical size could be used to make fast judgments about maturity. See *ibid.*, p. 111.

These studies, obviously, were not available to vocational reformers during the first two decades of the century; and in the absence of compelling empirical evidence, underlying moral values shaped the preferences of both sides. Snedden's values, for example, bore a strong resemblance to those of nineteenth-century success ideologists who had urged boys to be willing to start at the bottom of the ladder, never to disdain work as degrading, and to be ready to seize opportunities as they appeared. In effect, success writers had told youth not to expect much from the first job. Implicit in such advice was a certain tolerance of job-hopping. As long as a young man was ambitious, self-disciplined, and possessed of character, job-hopping was a legitimate way to rise in the world. In contrast, Snedden recognized, most vocational reformers were transfixed by an image of an ever-expanding domain of "clean" occupations, those marked by an orderly progression from the lower to higher rungs.[46]

Snedden was correct in stating that most trades did not contain and never had contained such opportunities for smooth advancement. But his antagonists were not talking about the past, and in some respects not even about the present. As Meyer Bloomfield, one of the founders of the vocational guidance movement, wrote in 1917:

In connection with these incessant changes in the character of occupations one general rule should be noticed: the finer, higher types of labor are coming to the fore, while the low-grade and debasing types of toil tend to drop out. It is a higher pursuit, one demanding more intelligence and training, to operate a steam shovel than to dig with a hand shovel in a ditch. . . . This has been called the age of specialists. The observation is true enough, but it does not tell the whole story. Men and women are specialized more and more in the finer, more delicate operations, not simply because they are more interesting, but because machines are performing more and more of the rough, crude forms of labor.[47]

In view of the fact that virtually all vocational reformers were schoolmen, and indeed representatives of the first generation of professionalized school administrators, it is scarcely surprising to see many of them attracted by the argument that all occupations were becoming more like the professions.

This dispute over dead-end jobs contained the seeds of a related issue, the effects of social class. As noted, reformers assumed that workers would make rational vocational decisions. In this context, "rational" meant a decision to maximize economic gain over the long term. Although rarely subjected to critical scrutiny, this assumption certainly needed it. The assumption resembled the belief, later ridiculed by Reynolds and Shister in their *Job Horizons* (1949), that workers shopping for jobs behaved like scientists, "carefully gathering all the relevant facts and then choosing the job which promises the greatest net advantage."[48] The problem with this belief was that it ignored the role of cultural conditioning. Reynolds and Shister noted that many working-class males believed jobs were always scarce and the best policy was to choose the first available job. Business cycles had taught the working class to be pessimistic. Fearing unemployment and privation even in boom times, workers placed little value on locating the job that promised the greatest opportunities for advancement. Instead, they sought jobs that were not physically demanding and that rewarded seniority with job security.[49]

What Reynolds and Shister found among working-class males in New Haven in the 1940's unquestionably also prevailed earlier in the century. Some vocational reformers recognized that class and ethnicity could condition occupational choice. Louise C. Odencrantz noted, for example, that Italian-American girls restricted their own mobility because they feared the moral implications of answering advertisements for jobs or looking on their own.[50] In 1913 Frank Taussig observed that "All the associations of nurture and family, all the force of example and imitation, keep a youth in the range of occupations to which his parents belong. In a highly mobile and democratic society like the United States, environment tells less than in older countries. The gifted and alert may feel ambition to rise, but the mass accept the conditions to which they are habituated."[51] Taussig fully accepted the concept, first advanced in 1874 by the English economist J. E. Cairnes, that competition for jobs in industrial society was not free. The average workman, Cairnes wrote, "finds his power of competition limited for practical purposes to a certain range of occupations, so that, however high the rates of remuneration in those which lie beyond may rise, he is excluded from sharing in them."[52] Cairnes called this the theory of noncompeting groups; it exerted a potent influence on the thinking of American economists from Francis

Amasa Walker in the 1870's to Taussig. Indeed, it also influenced some vocational reformers, most notably Paul Douglas. Douglas compared American occupational structure to a multistoried building in which workers who entered on the ground floor without skills were excluded from rising.[53]

Although interest in social stratification was intensifying during the first two decades of the twentieth century, vocational reformers usually paid little attention to these ideas. For them, lower-class origins were a disadvantage, but not a profound psychosocial deprivation. Douglas was the only vocational reformer to employ the concept of noncompeting groups, and he stripped it of much of its potency by immediately affirming that vocational training would transform noncompetitors into competitors.[54] Thomas Nixon Carver of Harvard expressed the dominant view in his influential *Essays in Social Justice* (1915):

Because vocational guidance and vocational education go at the underlying cause, instead of attacking symptoms, they must appeal to every real progressive. By training the rising generation out of those occupations where labor power is over-abundant and into those where it is under-abundant, you not only increase the productivity of every individual so trained, and therefore society at large, which is very important; but you accomplish the still more important result of tending to equalize incomes in different occupations.[55]

As "real progressives," vocational reformers followed Carver rather than Taussig, but it is still reasonable to ask why they were able to slide around this issue so easily. To phrase the question in these terms admittedly makes any kind of answer problematic. It is intrinsically difficult to understand why someone did not believe something. But it is possible to offer a few clues. First, Taussig's argument was not as compelling at the time as it appears to be in retrospect. No body of empirical evidence existed to support his position. Taussig conceded that there were no studies tracing individuals through their occupational careers. There was little reliable information even about the distribution of wealth in America; for this he was forced to extrapolate from Prussian statistics.[56] Second, Taussig himself did not exclude the possibility that class distinctions would wither under modern conditions. "In modern times and especially in democratic communities," he wrote, "the barriers which separate the groups tend to be broken down, and the passage from one to another becomes more easy."[57] The main reason for this gradual erosion of class barriers, Taussig argued, was the spread of education. Like common school reformers since the 1840's, Taussig thought that public education could break the "thralls of environment," not only by giving poor children the opportunity to learn but also by leveling the airs and pretensions of wealthy children.

This still left the problem of explaining why, despite education, there were so many poor and dispirited workers in America. Taussig and Carver had a ready answer, one that helps to explain why so many American thinkers could express both alarm about the extent of poverty and optimism about its future decline. Although schools opened the way to something better, Taussig wrote, "during a half century or more, ever fresh streams of immigrants have brought new supplies of common laborers, taking the places left vacant as the children of their predecessors have made their way into the higher groups. . . . These constant new arrivals have kept down the wages of the lowest group, and have accentuated also the lines of social demarcation between this group and others."[58] Carver had an identical view, and concluded that immigration restriction was a necessity. Taussig was less certain. Yet whether or not one favored immigration restriction, the implication was clear. Immigration, a factor essentially external to American business enterprise, explained why a nation with so many free schools had so many poor people. Further, a sharp decline in immigration after the outbreak of the First World War suggested to many that the problem might solve itself.*

Granting that contemporary economists and vocational reformers were sensitive to poverty and to class differences, and granting also that their faith in the curative power of education rested on some plausible and widely held beliefs, their thinking about poverty and social class was scarcely profound. One suspects that their knowledge of poverty and the poor came from reading rather than personal experience. As members of the

*The *Report of the Committee on National Aid to Vocational Education* predicted (p. 18) that in the future America would not be able to rely on a limitless supply of foreign laborers. Total immigration in 1914 was 1,218,480; in 1915, 326,000; in 1916, 298,826. In 1918 it was just over 100,000. See U.S. Bureau of the Census, *Historical Statistics of the United States, Colonial Times to 1957* (Washington, D.C., 1975), pt. 1, p. 105.

native-born middle class, they were separated from working-class immigrants by a vast cultural gap, surely a much broader gap than separated Reynolds and Shister from the working-class males whom they studied during the 1940's. Nothing better illustrates the distance between the leaders of the vocational education movement and the working class than the absence, among all the arguments they used to justify vocational education, of the one that would have occurred first to workers. This was the argument that vocational education would remove juveniles from direct competition with working-class adults for low-level jobs.[59]

The Vocationalization of Education

The resolution of these challenges by vocational reformers has some implications for what Grubb and Lazerson call the vocationalization of education. This term signifies more than simply the introduction of vocational education. Grubb and Lazerson view vocational education as one phase of a more general process in which public education came to be bound closely to economic opportunities. At some point in the late nineteenth century, they argue, staying in school began to be positively correlated with occupational opportunities. Grubb and Lazerson suggest that the dramatic increase in school enrollment after 1890 reflected both the fracturing of skill lines as a result of industrialization and the increasing impersonality of workplaces. Industrialization increased the number of unskilled workers and often replaced craft work with semiskilled work. Semiskilled jobs, since they no longer led to positions requiring greater skill and offering greater rewards, became less attractive. In addition, large corporations removed hiring from the shop and delegated it to the personnel department. The upshot was that parents who could afford the opportunity costs prolonged the education of their children in the hope that education would enable the children to bypass unskilled and semiskilled occupations. The value of such prolonged schooling lay not in the occupational skills taught in school, but in the school's inculcation of such skills as literacy and manners, which were more likely to appeal to personnel directors than to shop foremen.[60]

The interpretation advanced by Grubb and Lazerson differs

from that of the early vocational reformers at a number of important points. Where Snedden and Prosser argued that the value of schooling lay in the skills taught by schools, Grubb and Lazerson locate the value primarily in the fact of schooling itself. The longer one stayed in school, the better the job one obtained. Whether one studied Latin or carpentry mattered less than whether one stayed in school. The interpretations differ also in their perceptions of the nature of the problem. The early vocational reformers believed that the decline of apprenticeship made it impossible to meet demands for skilled labor. Lazerson and Grubb argue that a declining demand for skilled labor was destroying the kind of skilled positions to which apprenticeship had once led.

Yet these interpretations agree on one point. Both view the response, whether vocational education or prolonged schooling, as a solution to an objective problem. Something was happening in the occupational market for youth that called for new measures. This approach is questionable for several reasons. First, as Grubb and Lazerson concede, our knowledge of objective conditions in the youth labor market during the late nineteenth century leaves much to be desired. Many of the early vocational reformers, for example, certainly exaggerated the extent to which apprenticeship had ever been the normal entry route into occupations, and hence exaggerated the significance of the alleged decline of apprenticeship. Grubb and Lazerson, for their part, may be exaggerating the extent to which industrialization reduced the opportunity for upward mobility by job-hopping and the casual upgrading of skills through on-the-job training. Davidson and Anderson's study of workers in San Jose in the 1930's found that most adult workers had made several job shifts, acquiring new skills as they moved along. In other words, it is at least possible that there has been more continuity between nineteenth- and twentieth-century ways of entering the labor market than historians have been willing to allow.

A second problem with focusing on objective causes of the vocationalization of education is the tendency to neglect subjective values and cultural norms. As anyone knows, policy decisions have often been based on misperceptions of reality. Those who seek to explain the vocationalization of education are actu-

ally trying to explain a vast range of decisions—to prolong education, to build more secondary schools, to build more vocational
schools. Why should we assume that all or even most of these
decisions were based on an accurate reading of objective conditions, and why, as a corollary, should we then search only for
those objective conditions?

The case of the early vocational reformers provides an apt
illustration of this point. Despite their distorted perceptions of the
labor market, they met with little opposition from contemporaries. In addition, underlying values were at least as important
as objective conditions in shaping their ideas. A growing world of
dead-end jobs (an objective condition) may indeed have been
threatening the economic position of many young people in the
late nineteenth century. Yet contemporary complaints about
dead-end jobs may have reflected the values of reformers as much
as any objective conditions. Unless we indulge ourselves in a
romantic image of preindustrial America as a land of opportunity
for youth, we must recognize that dead-end jobs existed long
before the late nineteenth century. They may have been increasing in number; but what is most clear is that such jobs were unacceptable to reformers who assumed that most jobs should be open-
ended and who associated job-shifting with the world of dead-end
labor.

Objective conditions surely played a role in nurturing the values of reformers. The growth of the professions, for example,
provided some with an attractive occupational model. More important, although the claims of reformers often went beyond
available evidence, they were nevertheless plausible claims. That
is, they at least fit some pieces of evidence, and at the same time
they were not contradicted by any substantial body of evidence.
Finally, the views of reformers harmonized with a host of related
ideas about the need for national efficiency, the superiority of
systematic instruction as compared with the casual acquisition of
skills, and the value of making the manual trades attractive once
again to native-born youth.

The Assimilation of Vocational Education

Figures like Prosser and Snedden, although triumphant in shaping the Smith-Hughes Act to their own objectives, were on the

periphery of American educational thought during the 1920's. Indeed, Snedden's vision of a massive system of state-supported vocational schools for young adults and federally subsidized training for everyone from ticket-takers to door-to-door salesmen increasingly set him apart from vocational education itself. From the perspective of educators in the mainstream, the basic problem with the kind of vocational education advocated by Prosser, and by Snedden in an extreme form, was not that it threatened to sully the pure academic curriculum with vocational studies, but that it bore at best an ambivalent relationship to the ideal of prolonging education. Neither Prosser, Snedden, nor the NSPIE thought that full-time schools were the right place to teach occupational skills. As noted, their ideal was the part-time school and alternation between school and work. In large measure their hope that vocational education would spur upward mobility was tied to their belief in part-time schooling. As Paul Douglas observed, the poor could not afford the opportunity costs of prolonged full-time schooling, and hence would never be able to get from full-time schools the kind of vocational training needed for mobility. In contrast, most educators who advocated the prolongation of education equated it with full-time schooling. The idea of prolonging education was closely related to the belief that occupational choice should not occur during the impressionable years of adolescence, a belief that drew overwhelming support from contemporary psychologists.[61]

Between 1920 and 1940 vocational education underwent an important transformation that led to a decline in the influence of Prosser and the Federal Board for Vocational Education and to the gradual assimilation of vocational education into the mainstream of American education. This transformation had several sources. First, the advocacy of part-time schooling ran counter to many existing practices in vocational schools. The Smith-Hughes Act initiated federal support for secondary vocational education, but it did not initiate vocational education. All sorts of vocational and technical high schools had proliferated in response to local needs during the late nineteenth and early twentieth centuries; most of these were full-time schools that trained young people for a relatively small number of skilled trades in which machinery was undermining apprenticeship. In addition, to gain passage of the Smith-Hughes Act vocational educators had to give state boards of education considerable discretion in the spending of funds. During the 1920's, state boards were less committed to part-time schools than the Federal Board, which complained that state boards were spending too much on all-day secondary schools.[62] The economic collapse of the 1930's, moreover, tended to drive young people out of jobs and into school, which frustrated the objective of using schools to supplement on-the-job training. As events eroded the intellectual position of the Federal Board, a greater emphasis was given to vocational guidance and "industrial arts" programs, which did not attempt to convey occupational skills.[63] In 1933 the Federal Board lost its administrative functions; in 1946 it was abolished. Having won the battle in 1917, Prosser lost the war.

The growing importance of the all-day secondary school in vocational education made it easier for vocational education to move into the mainstream of American public education. As Prosser's influence declined, vocational educators could claim that they were no less committed to the prolongation of education than the proponents of general education. Yet there was a price to pay. The more vocational education came to share the goals of general education, the more it came to share the insularity of general education. Whatever might be said of Snedden and Prosser, at least they were keen students of industrial change. Snedden, with his talk of efficiently trained door-to-door salesmen and street car conductors, often sounded like Gradgrind. But the extreme positions he reached resulted from his refusal to accept easy compromises and from his insistence on following logic wherever it led.

During the 1930's, in contrast, vocational education was falling under the control of educators who had little incentive to pay close attention to industry or to stay abreast of recent developments in the social sciences. Their niche within American education was narrow but comfortable. The American Vocational Association, founded in 1926, formed an increasingly strong lobby; and as Larry Cuban notes in this volume, funds continued to flow into vocational education. From time to time criticisms appeared, but these were quickly turned aside with calls for better implementation of existing programs.[64]

On the whole, the staying power of early vocational education ideas has been remarkable. Although the reputation of vocational education among economists has gradually declined, and although academic psychologists have become increasingly skeptical of the assumptions behind vocational guidance, legislators still take their cues from AVA lobbyists, who present a rosy picture of vocational education and its achievements. Indeed, well into the 1960's congressional hearings on proposed vocational education laws were carried out almost without any recognition at all of the existence of serious academic criticisms of vocational education and guidance.[65]

Education and the Labor Market:

Recycling the Youth Problem

W. NORTON GRUBB AND MARVIN LAZERSON

For much of the post-Second World War period, schooling enjoyed sustained growth. Expanding enrollments, increasing salaries, and booming expenditures all stimulated the size of the educational sector. Economic expansion meant that there was no problem of absorbing the higher numbers of college graduates. Against this background, the contractions of the 1970's and early 1980's seem especially severe. Declining enrollments, taxpayer revolts forcing cutbacks in spending, and problems in placing college graduates in "suitable" jobs have reversed the experiences of the fifties and sixties. Though demographic shifts are partly to blame, the abysmal economic conditions of the seventies—high rates of unemployment and inflation, and a low rate of growth—have been more potent factors in the tribulations of schooling.

In the frantic search to improve macroeconomic conditions, the relationship between schooling and work has come under investi-

Our thanks to Geraldine Jonçich Clifford, Elizabeth Hansot, Harvey Kantor, Lana Muraskin, Daniel Rodgers, and David Tyack for their thoughtful comments. Portions of this paper draw on a forthcoming book on the state, families, and children in post-Second World War America. This work has been supported by grants from the Ford Foundation and the Carnegie Corporation to the Childhood and Government Project, University of California, Berkeley, and by grants from the LBJ Foundation to W. Norton Grubb and from the University of British Columbia Research Grants Committee to Marvin Lazerson.

gation. One major concern has been the declining economic returns to schooling, especially to college. The implication that
many students are "overeducated" relative to the ability of the
labor market to absorb them and that we should reduce the
schooling most individuals receive portends an end to the growth
of education. A second major concern involves the charge that
schooling works not by instilling real skills, but merely by serving
as a "credential" or "signal" in a process of selection that may
be inefficient or inequitable. A third concern is seen in a host of
proposals aimed at reducing youth unemployment by improving
the transition from schooling to work. These proposals implicitly
assume that conventional schooling fails to prepare adolescents
for employment. All of these issues are linked by the charge of the
"irrelevance" of schools, which suggests that reforms are necessary to restore some semblance of rationality to the relationship
between schooling and work.[1]

Though much of the recent discussion implies that these are
new problems, in fact the dilemmas of young people and of
preparing them for employment have been a continuing feature of
public debate. The terms of that debate were set at the turn of the
century, when employment and schooling became inextricably
linked. Since then, school-based and educational reforms have
been proposed whenever the behavior of the young has received
attention. Just as consistently, the reforms have proved unsatisfactory, and then another cycle of concern over shiftless youth,
the sorry state of the work ethic, and the antisocial behavior of
minority and working-class adolescents begins.[2] The recurrence
of the youth problem suggests either that the "resolutions" of the
past have resolved nothing, or that the same kinds of problems
have been generated anew in different periods.

To assess which of these is true, we need to understand why the
youth problem arises, what the nature of the reforms has been,
how successfully the reforms have solved the underlying problems, and what the limits of the proposed solutions have been. We
will have to understand how contradictory pressures within the
state have affected policies toward youth, particularly the pressure to expand individual opportunity, to eliminate inequalities
and the privileges of class, race, and sex, versus the pressure to
retain privileges and to legitimate the inequalities embedded in

public programs. We may then be able to understand the complexities, both historical and current, of the relationship between schooling and work.

This paper is an initial exploration of these questions. First, we examine the dimensions of the current youth problem, with particular attention to the ways this problem is treated as an educational issue and to the limits of treating labor market problems as educational problems. Second, we speculate about which changes in labor markets at the turn of the century affected youth employment and affected schooling as preparation for employment. Third, we examine the nature and consequences of the vocationalization of American education, a process that established the importance of schooling in the occupational hierarchy. Finally, we outline an agenda for research that takes us beyond the tentative hypotheses argued here.

This essay represents an effort to address some issues we consider unresolved and to suggest some hypotheses that seem plausible in the light of what we do know. Implicitly, we are also groping toward a reformulation of several concepts; these include vocationalism, which in the past has been too narrowly construed as vocational education, and human capital theory, which has dominated much of the current research on schooling and earnings. Necessarily, much of what we present is still at the stage of hypothesis, in need of empirical investigation and theoretical refinement. Because of the preliminary nature of our analysis, we slight the variations that preoccupy historians—variations by region of the country, ethnicity, race, class, and sex.

The Educational Solution to "Youth Problems"

To many commentators, American youth are in a terrible state. Pregnancy and venereal disease, alcohol and drug abuse, juvenile crime, illiteracy, unemployment, and disaffection from the workplace—the litany of problems is endless. To a great extent these concerns are rooted in real problems. Youth unemployment has been high and increasing, reaching a postwar high of 19.9 percent in 1975, and unemployment for black youth has been around 40 percent. Though the long-run effects of teenage unemployment are uncertain, for nonwhites especially the lack of work has immediate consequences—in terms of income—that continue into adulthood as lower earnings and higher unemployment.[3] Juvenile delinquency is rising, most alarmingly for crimes of violence and for younger adolescents. Teenage pregnancy represents a critical issue, with serious consequences for both mother and child in terms of schooling completed, economic resources, and health problems. Other forms of pathology among adolescents—suicide, drug abuse, drinking, running away—have been taken as indicators of serious problems, though the evidence in these areas is more difficult to interpret.

But even though the attention youth receives is partly a response to real problems, especially if the consequences of the problems endure into adulthood, we cannot explain the intensity of feelings about youth simply by the reality of these problems or by a concern over the "waste of human resources" they represent. Many "youth problems," like unemployment among young whites, diminish with age; others, like juvenile delinquency, tend to be concentrated among lower-class and minority youth, precisely the groups that have been the most shabbily treated and that have been the easiest to ignore in public policies. Those adolescents who represent a quiet waste of human resources—who fail in school, drop out, or become alienated without demanding any social response—are not usually the target of public programs or private outrage. To some extent, then, the "youth problem" is a set of adult responses to various forms of "acting out" among teenagers, noncriminal behavior that is forbidden only to adolescents: disobedience, status offenses, overt sexuality (especially for women), rowdiness. We also need to recognize the hostility latent in those adult reactions. The idleness of youth, the self-absorption of a period that is a moratorium and a time of decision making, the sexual explorations of adolescents, the indulgences of "youth culture"—all arouse the hostility as well as the envy of adults.*

---

*The process of coping with our ambivalence toward young people by the psychological mechanisms of splitting and projection—of blaming "other people's children" for bad behavior, and accusing them of corrupting one's own children—is particularly active in the case of adolescents, most of all in discussions of the evil effects of youth culture and the dangers of the wrong crowd. See Kenneth Keniston, "Notes on the Role of Children in American History," unpublished (1973).

The "youth policy" that has developed to cope with these problems has been unplanned, but it has nonetheless been consistent. It has largely involved the simultaneous extension of schooling and the elaboration of school and nonschool training programs. The schooling and training resolution has prevented youth either from flooding a labor market unable to absorb them or from remaining unattached to the labor force (or the family) and therefore being potential troublemakers. But the elaboration of educational programs cannot be rationalized merely on the grounds that they warehouse young people. Educational programs have thus been justified by the values they impart, the skills they teach, and the advantages they confer in terms of earnings and occupational status. If we understand the "youth problem" as a dual problem—in part a set of responses to the reality of unemployment, juvenile crime, and other concrete problems, and in part a hostile response to youthful "acting out"—then we can understand the appropriateness of educational solutions to "youth problems." Educational programs that prepare some youth for their adult roles represent a rational response to some "real" dimensions of the youth problem. These programs may also be effective in giving young people a sense of purpose, in providing them with alternatives to acting out, and in giving them the economic and social status necessary for adult roles. But even if programs are ineffective in preparing students for occupations, they may still be appropriate if they merely occupy students and keep them off the streets and out of trouble. Thus we can understand the two functions of schooling—training, or preparing students for the labor market, and warehousing, or keeping them out of the labor market—as responses to different aspects of the youth problem.

The dual role of schooling has been apparent for decades. A broad spectrum of educational programs, including the G.I. Bill, vocational education, two-year colleges, and expanded college enrollment during the 1960's, has kept youth out of the labor market, reducing what would otherwise have been politically unacceptable increases in unemployment.[4] More recently, questions about training and warehousing have become prominent, particularly as the rates and levels of youth unemployment have reached historic highs. But youth have always been victims of high unemployment; their plight in the 1970's represented a deterioration in a chronic problem rather than a new phenomenon.[5] The persistence of high unemployment for youth implies that conventional macroeconomic policies are inadequate to resolve the youth unemployment problem, and suggests that the youth labor market is structurally different from the rest of the labor market.

The labor markets for youth and adults may differ on at least four dimensions: knowledge of the job market, educational attainments, level of racial discrimination, and employer hiring preferences. Though there is some evidence that a lack of knowledge increases unemployment, the evidence is not substantial; after initial entry the information problems of youth appear similar to those of adults. The impact of low educational attainments appears stronger; as educational requirements for most occupations increase, teenagers with limited schooling are prevented from being considered for an ever-increasing proportion of jobs. There is, of course, a large racial component to youth unemployment, although again this parallels the discrimination against nonwhite adults; unemployment rates tend to be twice as high for black youth as for whites, and for Hispanics about 50 percent higher than whites.[6]

But the critical difference between the labor markets that adults and youth face is that employers prefer to hire older workers. For most jobs, especially those with career potential, employers will not seriously consider teenagers except in periods of labor shortage.[7] The reasons vary. Some employers cite child labor and minimum wage laws as barriers to hiring young people, though the evidence is far from clear.[8] More commonly, employers complain that young workers are more unstable than adults. In an economy with low unemployment, such objections might not prevent young people from being hired. But in an economy with chronically high unemployment, where it is usually possible to hire a slightly older worker, there is no reason for employers to run the risks of hiring younger workers. The employment rate of adolescents suffers as a result.

The complex problem of youth unemployment, then, involves a variety of labor market conditions and personal factors, often in ways that cannot be separated. Yet the proposals and programs that have been offered follow a predictable pattern: rather than deal with the labor market aspects of youth unemployment, they seek still more educational solutions. Attention has focused on the "transition from school to work," which in turn has been viewed as a problem of insufficient information about work and of school curricula irrelevant to work. The result has been the expansion of vocational education throughout the 1960's and 1970's, the development of career education, the proliferation of work-experience programs, and the expansion of vocational two-year colleges.[9] Educational solutions to youth employment problems have also moved outside the schools. The manpower programs of the 1960's have been revived as "employment and training programs," most of them contained in the Comprehensive Employment and Training Act of 1973 (CETA) and in the Youth Employment and Demonstration Projects Act (YEDPA), passed in 1977 specifically in response to the high rate of unemployment among youth. These programs encompass a variety of activities, but here again the specific programs for youth focus for the most part on training and warehousing rather than direct employment.* There is little evidence that the training programs work much better than the school programs; perhaps the task of doing in a short time what the schools have failed to do over ten years or more is well-nigh impossible.[10] But if the training function of CETA and YEDPA has been less than overwhelming, their warehousing function appears to work quite well. Simply by enrolling young people, these programs reduced the youth unemployment rate in 1976 by about 3.9 percentage points compared to what it might have been in the absence of such programs.[11] If nothing else, employment and training programs have provided places for

---

*Good summaries of the programs include *CETA: An Analysis of the Issues*, National Commission for Manpower Policy, Special Report no. 23 (May 1978); and *Employment and Training Report of the President, 1978*. Within CETA, only 24 percent of youth are in public employment positions (compared with 43 percent overall); the other 76 percent are enrolled in CETA Title I programs, which provide training, counseling, and other services, but not employment. A large number of those employed are in summer positions, jobs so temporary—and so obviously aimed at "warehousing," or keeping youth off the streets—that it is difficult to consider them serious efforts at either employment or training. YEDPA has also failed to change the thrust of federal policy; the bulk of enrollments are in the Youth Employment and Training Programs, which again provide only training and ancillary employment services. For data, see *CETA: An Analysis of the Issues*, Table 4.

thousands of young people no longer in school and yet with no "adult" positions.

Although educational solutions were reinforced during the 1970's, the youth employment problems rooted in labor markets—in racial discrimination, in discrimination against younger workers, in the inflation of educational requirements, and in the abysmal quality of jobs available to young people—have been completely ignored. The emphasis on education and training as the basic approach to youth issues essentially reflects a political and ideological resistance to incursions into the prerogatives of "private" labor markets and "private" firms; and it also reflects the ambivalence of adults about whether the problems youth face are real or simply a form of acting out. As we will argue in the next section, this form of youth policy emerged earlier in the twentieth century and became institutionalized; its successes have subsequently made it extremely difficult to search for alternative policies. The result has been to narrow the range of possible options in dealing with the problems of youth.

Labor Markets and the Schools: The Progressive Resolution

On one level, the changing relationship between youth, work, and education in the early twentieth century can be simply put: teenagers, especially those between the ages of thirteen and sixteen, withdrew from the labor market and went to school. The gross statistics are striking. The percentage of fourteen- to eighteen-year-old males at work dropped from 43 to 23 percent between 1900 and 1920, and fell further to 12 percent by 1930. For females, the decline was from 18 to 11 to 5 percent. The high school enrollment of fourteen- to seventeen-year-olds between 1900 and 1930 climbed from almost 8 percent to over 44 percent. In 1900, 6.4 percent of all seventeen-year-olds were high school graduates; the figures rose to 16.8 percent in 1920 and 29 percent in 1930.[12] Evidently, not all youth left the labor market and went to school; school attendance varied by region, ethnic and racial group, and sex. Social class and family income continued to exert strong influence over the decision to stay in school or to work. But the trend was clear and powerful: between 1900 and 1930, the regional, ethnic, racial, sexual, and class differences in length of school attendance narrowed considerably. By the late

1920's, thirteen- to sixteen-year-olds tended to be out of the labor market and in school.[13]

Why youth began to withdraw from the labor market and stay in school has never been satisfactorily explained. The traditional argument, that the increased demand for technical skills required more schooling, has proved inadequate, since skill levels may not have increased at the turn of the century.[14] The more rigorous enforcement of child labor and compulsory attendance legislation undoubtedly played some role in making it more difficult for young teenagers to find work, by raising the nuisance to employers in hiring young people.[15] Public concern about the immorality and potential delinquency of youth on the street mushroomed; this provided a justification for institutionalizing young people in adult-controlled settings.[16] New cultural values coalesced around the developing concept of adolescence as a time to be sheltered in preparation for adult responsibilities; this increased the pressure to keep teenagers in school and away from the adult world.[17] Since school attendance had always been closely associated with income and class, higher living standards allowed some youth to stay in school longer.* Changes in schools themselves, such as modifications in the curriculum and the introduction of Progressive pedagogy, might have made schooling interesting enough so that those on the borderline opted to stay in school. There may also have been a kind of snowballing effect,

*The role of income levels in permitting longer stays in school has been advanced as central to the expansion of the schooling at the turn of the century. For example, Modell attributes the greater propensity of Irish households to supplement family income with children's earnings, compared with native-born whites, to differences in the family head's income. Similarly Hogan found, for working-class families in Chicago, that working rather than continuing in school was an economic decision based on the need to survive or, where families were above the poverty line, to assure some economic security by purchasing a house. Of course, these kinds of economic barriers have always kept the poorest children out of school; but as an explanation for changes over time this is a weak argument. During the nineteenth century, both working-class and middle-class youth who could have stayed in school left to enter the job market. And conversely, working-class and immigrant children appear to have entered high school in great numbers after 1900, when the income of their parents may have been deteriorating because of the increasing inequality of income distribution and when immigrants were generally poor. Thus we suspect the role of increasing affluence in the rise of school attendance was distinctly minor. See John Modell, "Patterns of Consumption, Acculturation, and Family Income Strategies in Late Nineteenth-Century

which became more apparent in the 1920's, with youth staying in school in part because their friends were there.

Though the merit of these explanations obviously varies, taken together they do suggest a rationale for the lengthening school attendance. But they also neglect a fundamental component of the withdrawal of youth from labor markets and their continuation in school. Changes in the labor market itself shaped a new relationship between schooling and work in which youth were both pushed out of the market and pulled into school. The changes in the labor market transformed the role of schooling in the occupational structure. Two issues seem especially important. The first has to do with the nature of the youth labor market: what kinds of jobs were available to young people, what difference did age make in entering the labor force, and how much were skills learned on the job the basis for advancement? The second has to do with the relationship between schooling and occupational success: how much did schooling contribute to future adult achievement?

We can only offer speculative answers to these questions; the data are not readily available, and the connections between schooling and work are too poorly understood to be definitive. What follows is a series of hypotheses suggesting how we might begin to understand the changed relationship between school and work in the first decades of the twentieth century and speculating about the impact of that change on the schools and on youth. In brief, we hypothesize that a fundamental transformation of the relationship between schooling and work occurred during the Progressive era, largely in response to changes in labor markets. This transformation, which we refer to as *vocationalism* or the *vocationalization of schooling*, made preparation for a place in the occupational structure the raison d'être of public education. The processes underlying the vocationalization of schooling were

America," in Tamara K. Hareven and Maris Vinovskis, eds., *Family and Population in Nineteenth-Century America* (Princeton, N.J., 1978); and David Hogan, "Capitalism and Schooling: A History of the Political Economy of Education in Chicago, 1880–1930," Ph.D. diss. (Univ. of Illinois, Urbana, 1978), pp. 366–82. On widening wage and income differentials at the turn of the century, see Jeffrey Williamson, "The Sources of American Inequality, 1896–1948," *Review of Economics and Statistics*, 58 (1976): 387–97; and Peter Lindert, *Fertility and Scarcity in America* (Princeton, N.J., 1978), ch. 7.

not fully implemented until after the Second World War, and they were not the only developments to affect schooling and work in the twentieth century. But between 1900 and 1930 the basic elements of vocationalism were established, and they have shaped our educational system and our social responses to the problems of youth ever since.

Much of our argument about the twentieth century is based on assumptions about nineteenth-century youth labor markets—how they differed from twentieth-century markets and how they changed over time. The evidence on the nineteenth century is exceedingly sketchy, however.[18] It appears that nineteenth-century youth, compared to those of the twentieth century, were more actively involved in labor markets. The nineteenth-century youth, moreover, were linked to adult economic roles primarily by the economics of their households, not by the school. Working-class and poor youth left school early, probably whenever they could find employment as unskilled laborers or, in the case of girls, as domestic servants. The work young people had was irregular and insecure, and they moved frequently between jobs, unemployment, and schooling. Going to school was common but not universal. Time spent in the work force before marriage was much longer than it is now, probably ten to twenty years, compared to three to five years in 1970. The contribution of young people to their family's income was often substantial and necessary. Early work experience, in addition to its economic necessity, was valuable to some extent as a means of upward mobility. Even if we recognize how transient and limited in terms of advancement much work for youth was, the high levels of self-employment and the existence of skilled craftwork still suggest that, at least for white males, work was arranged in a hierarchy of skills. What young people learned on the job could have great value in occupational advancement; it could lead to artisanship or self-employment, in ways that became much less likely in the twentieth century. The postponement of work for a few years—a basic tenet of reformers during the Progressive era—had little justification in the mid-nineteenth century. Staying in school for a few additional years probably had only limited and uncertain economic payoffs, and conversely, leaving school early did not have the kind of detrimental impact on subsequent careers that it came to have.*

During the last half of the nineteenth century a number of trends began to change the relationship between schooling and employment. One was the fracturing of vertical skill ladders. Large-scale manufacturing displaced small-scale craft production, as the routinization of production led to labor specialization and deskilling and as craftsmen were replaced by machines and machine operatives. The chances for artisans to start their own shops began to decline. The traditional argument that work would lead to self-employment in a trade had less and less meaning as the artisan shop became an anachronism or a small, specialized exception within manufacturing. In the post-Civil War era the worlds of wage earners and businessmen separated: it became less possible to move upward from the status of worker to that of owner or manager. This did not mean that all jobs suffered skill degradation or that all opportunities to learn skills on the job and to enter the growing middle class were eliminated. But many jobs did lose their craft basis and become mechanized versions of the work of nineteenth-century "laborers." At the same time, a minority of positions were elaborated into a new aristocracy of manual labor based on greater skill requirements and including some supervisory activities.[19] In view of these changes, which

---

*Michael Katz and Ian Davey found that school attendance in Hamilton, Ontario, in 1861 and 1871 "exerted no influence upon the occupation of young men"; see "Youth and Industrialization in a Canadian City," in John Demos and Sarane Boocock, eds., *Turning Points: Historical and Sociological Essays on the Family* (Chicago, 1978). This is not to suggest that schooling in the nineteenth century had absolutely no economic returns. Although access to most professions and commercial occupations could be gained without very extended schooling, it nonetheless required literacy, a skill undoubtedly helped by schooling. The mid-nineteenth-century feminization of teaching, nursing, and librarianship gave women access to occupations for which schooling proved useful and sometimes necessary. Debates over public funds for high schools reveal a concern over the potential vocational role of secondary education; see Bella Rosenberg, "The Search of Equity and Fairness: The Assumptions of Public Responsibility for Secondary Education, 1821–1880," Qualifying paper, Harvard Graduate School of Education, 1975. We hypothesize, however, that in an economy in which many youth learned skills on the job, in which skills learned at one level could secure advancement, and in which there were limited efforts to make schooling an occupational prerequisite, the relationship between schooling and employment was much more tenuous than it became in the twentieth century.

were well under way by mid-century, the early entry of workers into unskilled positions made less economic sense. As a result, more families tried to delay their teenage children's entry into the labor market and keep them in school, where the chance was greater that they could gain access to an occupation with some kind of career and some progression in terms of earnings and status.

A second barrier to mobility among jobs of different skill levels and earnings, which also affected the value of schooling, emerged more fully after 1900 with the growth of large corporations and the development of rationalized hiring policies. With large corporations, the outlines of the "dual economy" began to emerge. In place of an economy with a large number of relatively small firms, many sectors came to be dominated by a few corporate giants; at the same time, a number of small, peripheral, and generally weak firms still existed.[20] Within the corporations, an emphasis on the work-force stability and "scientific management," especially after the First World War, led to personnel policies that dictated the structuring of jobs and advancement among positions. As a consequence of the development of internal labor markets—patterns of upward mobility within a firm, rather than among jobs in different firms—an individual's initial job became more important as a determinant of occupational mobility.[21] In order to obtain most jobs in larger firms, where jobs tended to pay more and to have the prospect of more stability and career mobility than in small firms, it was first necessary to gain access to the internal labor market of a large firm. A consequence of scientific management was that this access increasingly required formal schooling, as personnel policies rationalized hiring. The removal of hiring from the foreman or the shop to the personnel department took employee selection from the people most experienced in the actual job requirements. Surrogate "skills," primarily appearance and literacy, were substituted for job-related skills. Personalistic, family- and kin-oriented hiring practices became less important—though they by no means disappeared—as formal criteria gained greater acceptance.[22]

Among the most important of the formal criteria was educational attainment. The rationality of using schooling as a hiring credential has been widely debated, but it did have some obvious advantages. School attainment was unambiguous, easily verifiable, and cheap to use; it testified to a certain level of persistence and stability; and it could be justified as a reflection of ability even if it proved not to be, since schooling was regarded as a meritocratic institution.[23] The precise reasons why schooling became a credential remain elusive. Nevertheless, its adoption as part of rationalized hiring procedures, together with the development of internal labor markets that put a premium on working for large firms, meant that leaving school early to go to work was likely to lead to a less stable, lower-paying job in a peripheral firm, and to make it difficult to gain access to the better positions in larger firms. These changes occurred at different rates in different regions and sectors of the economy. They may also have occurred later than some of the other changes we describe, since personnel departments existed only in the largest firms well into the 1920's, and most young people continued to get their first job through family and peer-group contacts. But if our hypotheses are correct, then the restructuring of labor markets as large corporations developed and rationalized their hiring procedures reinforced the economic value of staying in school.

The fracturing of skill ladders, the development of internal labor markets, and the rationalization of hiring procedures did not necessarily reduce the number of jobs available to youth who left the high school before graduating. Rather, these changes affected the kinds of jobs dropouts could get and the prospects for mobility from unskilled jobs. Technological developments may also have driven youth out of the labor market, though it is difficult to be sure.[24] Jobs like messenger boy and department store cash runner, typically filled by young people, did indeed disappear with the telephone and cash register; but the development of a pool of unskilled jobs in what has come to be known as the secondary labor market created jobs that both unskilled youth and adults could do. Though there is some evidence of an increased substitution of youth for adult workers within the pool of unskilled jobs,* in many firms employers replaced young people

*Joseph Kett, *Rites of Passage: Adolescence in America, 1790 to the Present* (New York, 1977), pp. 144–50. Using Hamilton data, Katz and Davey, "Youth and Industrialization," found for boys a slight trend toward working earlier, when comparing 1851 and 1871; 41 percent of all fifteen-year-old males were employed in 1851, and 53 percent in 1871. The reverse occurred for girls, however; 34 percent of

with immigrants—older, with family responsibilities, and more stable—who were perceived as more suitable for the technologies coming to dominate large industries.[25] We suspect that discrimination against young people purely on the basis of age may have begun around the turn of the century, for much the same reasons as the discrimination against teenagers today.[26] We also suspect that this was the source of the "wasted years syndrome," the time between fourteen and sixteen when only "dead-end" jobs were available, which added to the economic pressures to stay in school. The way age discrimination arose after the turn of the century is still conjecture that needs to be investigated; but it does suggest why, in an economy that generated so many unskilled jobs, young people who dropped out of school found it so difficult to find decent employment.

Two other changes in the pattern of occupations added to the reasons for staying in school. The first involved the expansion of managerial and office positions in the first decades of the twentieth century.[27] Again, why schooling became such an essential mechanism of access to these jobs remains unclear, but we suspect that many of the skills required in office positions—literacy, computational skills, bookkeeping, and accounting, as well as the behavioral norms deemed appropriate—were effectively taught in school. Like teaching, the new office positions were highly stratified by sex: secretaries, clerks, and bookkeepers were women in low-paid positions; men became managers and accountants, with relatively high pay and status. Given the near-universal assumption that women would stay in the labor market for only a short period, employers undoubtedly preferred already-

---

all fifteen-year-old females were employed in 1851, and 16 percent in 1871. This suggests that the income returns to schooling rose first for girls, then for boys. Walkowitz reports an increase in male youth under fifteen among unskilled iron workers in Troy, New York, between 1860 and 1880. On the growth of unskilled labor, Walkowitz's findings are especially instructive. In terms of actual jobs in the iron mills, the number of unskilled workers increased from 180 to 1,121 in the two decades, the number of skilled molders only from 426 to 762. The job market during the expansion of the iron industry appears to have opened up considerably for unskilled workers, including those under twenty, but only slightly for skilled workers; the percentage of skilled workers under twenty declined from 12.3 to 7.6 percent. Daniel J. Walkowitz, "Statistics and the Writing of Working Class Culture: A Statistical Portrait of the Iron Workers in Troy, New York, 1860–1880," *Labor History*, 15 (1974): 416–60.

trained "office girls" to assuming the training costs themselves. For women, schooling for white-collar occupations brought economic advantages they would not otherwise have had.[28]

The second development that may have changed the relationship between schooling and occupations involved professionals. Particularly for women, the rapid expansion of semiprofessions (like teaching and nursing) that had barely existed before meant that longer school attendance opened up new options. But the expansion per se of professional occupations was not particularly important: between 1900 and 1920 the proportion of the labor force in professions—including technical professions—increased only from 4.25 to 5.40 percent.[29] More significant were the increased visibility and status of professionals during the Progressive era, their higher incomes relative to other occupations, and the fact that increased schooling became necessary for access to professional positions. During the Progressive period, the conception of a professional as having special powers because of special knowledge—and thus long years of schooling—became established. Thus subsequent efforts to professionalize occupations have all involved increasing the schooling requirements as an assured means of attaining greater status, income, legitimacy, and control.* At the same time that other developments were reinforcing schooling as a mechanism of access to specific occupations, the efforts to professionalize by increasing school requirements provided an additional incentive to stay in school, as well as a potent symbol of the social status and economic power that could be gained through education.

In sum, these five changes were at the core of the new relationship between work and schooling: the shattering of mobility through on-the-job skill acquisition because of the deskilling of craft work; the creation of barriers to mobility in the development of internal labor markets and rationalized hiring procedures that

---

*Note that in the connection between years of schooling, professional standing, status, and earnings there is a circularity: since the early twentieth century, the efforts to professionalize occupations have built upon an *assumption* that more schooling merited more status and higher earnings, yet at the same time the development of professionalism helped to *establish* this relationship. On professionalism in the Progressive era, see Magali Sarfatti Larson, *The Rise of Professionalism: A Sociological Analysis* (Berkeley, Calif., 1978), ch. 9; and Collins, *The Credential Society*, ch. 6.

relied on schooling credentials; the growth of discrimination against youth; the expansion of office and managerial positions for which skills and behavior could be readily acquired in schools; and changes in the nature of professionalism. Of course, the pace of change varied: the changes in the leading sectors of the economy left some regions less touched, and the changes obviously did not eliminate all small firms or all self-employment. In many communities—in the South, in farm areas, on the frontier— a few extra years in school probably made little difference in the status one attained as an adult. And where such changes did occur, the extent to which young people recognized those changes and acted accordingly is difficult to know. Evidently, the ability to act on the recognition of changes in the labor market was always constrained by class, race, and sex, since postponing entry into the labor market was a luxury that many could not afford, and since discrimination within labor markets limited the advantages that schooling could confer. Those who entered and stayed in the secondary labor market received little from their schooling. So did most blacks, because many occupations were barred to them. For girls, the value of schooling as a means of access to teaching and other semiprofessions and clerical work was circumscribed by discrimination in a sex-segregated labor market. Finally, noneconomic reasons governed many educational decisions. Among some groups schooling was an end in itself, since individuals gained status from schooling even where economic returns were uncertain. Many ex-slaves, for example, initially flocked to schools for noneconomic reasons; by the early 1900's, however, economic reasons were probably playing an important role in their schooling decisions, despite the discrimination they faced.

Whatever the difficulties in ascribing schooling behavior to perceived changes in labor markets, there is circumstantial evidence to support this link. It seems likely that youth (and their parents) could see which jobs led to higher wages and more security. The segmentation of labor markets—the development of internal labor markets, the growing distinction between unskilled and semiskilled work and that of professionals and managers, the conventional distinction between blue-collar and white-collar work born in the Progressive era—may have made some of the connections between schooling and occupational success more obvious; the growing inequality in wages and income distribution may have heightened the differences. Certainly, educators and reformers of the period preached tirelessly about the economic value of schooling; exhortations to stay in school to increase one's earnings, to "learn to earn," filled volumes. But most of all, it is hard to imagine that young people would have continued to flood into the high schools if the promises that schooling would pay off had been completely wrong. Even though the mechanisms by which changes in the relationship between schooling and work influenced individual behavior remain obscure, by the 1920's a new conception of schooling had become common. The president of the school board in Muncie, Indiana, expressed the idea of vocationalism perfectly in the mid-1920's: "For a long time all boys were trained to be President. Then for a while we trained them all to be professional men. Now we are training boys to get jobs." The working-class parents of Muncie accepted this role for the schools. The Lynds found that working-class families wanted their children to stay in school so that they could get ahead.[30]

The consequences of the changed relationship between schooling and work have been vast, for youth as well as for schooling. The transformation of work helped create the concept of adolescence as a moratorium before adulthood, because it increased the advantages of delaying entry into the labor force. The "discovery" of adolescence in the Progressive era—building on nineteenth-century foundations, to be sure, but novel in the magnitude of the interest—reflected a fast-developing reality in the lives of young people. Staying in school, along with living at home while in school, delayed the shift to full adult responsibilities and created an ambiguous period between childhood and adulthood, a period of anxiety because the decisions seemed momentous and irreversible.*

---

*The irreversibility of adolescent decisions, which was assumed by turn-of-the-century reformers, has not been fully studied, but we suspect that it took on some of the elements of a self-fulfilling prophecy. Believing it, reformers expanded secondary schooling and then college as a way of delaying labor market entry; soon, decisions by 14–18-year-olds about schooling and work tended to become irreversible. On the transition to adulthood, see John Modell, Frank F. Furstenberg, Jr., and Theodore Hershberg, "Social Change and Transitions to Adulthood in Historical Perspective," *Journal of Family History* (1976): 7–32.

The vocationalization of American education has also transformed educational institutions themselves. Though we often think of vocationalism in terms of differentiated curricula and conventional vocational courses, the ideology and practice of vocationalism have been considerably more extensive. Vocationalism narrowed the debate over the purposes of schooling. *How* to prepare youth for jobs in the labor market, rather than *whether* this should be done, became the focus of discussion. The differentiation of the curriculum followed, in response to differentiation within the labor market. Concepts of fairness and equality of opportunity were also transformed by vocationalism. In the prevailing view, a single curriculum that preceded either work or college denied equal opportunity; since one could not move vertically through an occupation or industry, different programs based on varying abilities and interests were the only fair way to prepare people for different roles in the labor market. In reproducing the stratification of the labor market within the schools, vocationalism recognized that "reality."

Another implicit recognition of changing occupations came in the declining discussion of the dichotomy between "head and hand." Advocates of manual training before 1900 complained that "hand" labor and "brain" labor were becoming sharply distinguished, and that the middle-class and working-class worlds were becoming increasingly separated. They challenged this division by calling for a curriculum that trained both hand and brain. Progressive reformers like John Dewey and Jane Addams similarly called for vocational training that would enable even unskilled laborers to think about their work, and would thus narrow the gap between the mental and the manual as much as possible. Implicit in the call to enlarge the responsibilities of education toward work was a recognition that work itself had been degraded. But by the 1920's, the debate over the brain-hand cleavage was all but over. As the labor process had successfully established the separation between skilled and unskilled labor, so too did schools accept it. So drastic had the change been that the criticisms of the labor market that underlay the manual training movement and some forms of vocational education disappeared. Educators now said almost nothing against labor markets; instead, they condemned the schools for not being sufficiently adapted to the market.*

Finally, just as the educational solution to youth problems narrowed the conception of what the schools might do, it also narrowed the range of feasible social policies. Save for the limited experience of the 1930's and the development of youth employment programs in the 1970's, schooling and training rather than job creation and direct employment have defined American youth policy. The coercive power of the solution worked out early in the century, reinforced in the 1920's and 1930's and fully established after the Second World War, has left us with few theoretical alternatives and almost no practical ways to resolve the continuing problem of youth. At base, governmental reluctance to tackle alternatives and to intervene in private labor markets (except under the most adverse conditions) is political, a part of the support of the liberal democratic state for "private" institutions. But the attractiveness of the educational solution has also been a block to formulating other kinds of reforms; policymakers have consistently reasserted the potential of schooling, rather than face its limitations.[31]

In these ways, vocationalism reshaped the conception of the schools and the purpose of going to school. This constitutes the first strand of vocationalism: the access to valued occupations through schooling. In turn, this has also meant that alternative mechanisms of access to various occupations—apprenticeship systems, family ties, and experience, for example—have gradually been eliminated for all but the least rewarding jobs. Vocationalism has thus been part of a significant shift, as yet incomplete, in the mechanisms of allocating social goods like income and status. The new mechanisms have continued to permit limited individual mobility but within a structure of inequality.

*In *The Spirit of Youth and the City Streets* (1909), Addams wrote: "If a child goes into a sewing factory with a knowledge of the work she is doing in relation to the finished product; if she is informed concerning the material she is manipulating and the processes to which it is subjected; if she understands the design she is elaborating in its historic relation to art and decoration, her daily life is lifted from drudgery to one of self-conscious activity, and her pleasure and intelligence [are] registered in her product." See also Marvin Lazerson, *Origins of the Urban School: Public Education in Massachusetts, 1870–1915* (Cambridge, Mass., 1971), chs. 3–7.

The second strand of vocationalism involves the payoffs for attending school. With schooling increasingly serving as a mechanism of access to occupations valued for their earnings, status, or working conditions, schooling began to make a significant economic difference after 1900. The precise roles schooling plays in the labor market remain obscure—whether it operates by passing on cognitive abilities or behavior patterns, whether it is a signal of ability, or whether it is a credential in some irrational sense. But its role in leading to positions with higher earnings and status is relatively unambiguous, and appears to be a corollary of its role in allocating individuals in labor markets; if schooling failed to confer any economic advantage, then it could not be true that schooling served as a mechanism of access—and thus also of limitation of access—to valuable occupations.* The two strands of vocationalism—the use of the schools as an allocation mechanism and the existence of economic returns to schooling—became intertwined after 1900. They have dominated all discussions of education since.

How Has Vocationalism Worked?

The variety of current dilemmas in the relationship between schooling and work poses the question of how well the educational solution—the conception of vocationalism outlined in the previous section—has worked. Based on the available (and sketchy) evidence, our best hypothesis is that historically vocationalism has worked relatively well, for several reasons. First, many of the expanding occupations—particularly office and clerical work—were ones where job skills were clearly teachable;

---

*The tentativeness of our analysis reflects an attempt, as yet incomplete, to rethink human capital models. On the one hand, we suspect that human capital theory is correct in positing the existence of economic returns to schooling, though the theory is mute on the reasons for that return. But certain aspects of the model strike us as quite wrong: the ideas that a rate of return is in equilibrium with the return on capital and that enrollment responses to rates of return are uniform and symmetrical; the implicit emphasis of the model on abilities and skill acquisition; the emphasis on enrollment changes (supply-side responses) as the only equilibrating mechanism; and above all the dismissal of any effects of class. We propose several possible revisions of human capital models in the following sections. See the discussion of schooling models in David Hogan's essay in this volume and in Randall Collins, *The Credential Society: An Historical Sociology of Education and Stratification* (New York, 1979).

hence, the relationship of skill training in schools to skill use on the job seemed clear enough. For another group of expanding occupations, professional positions, the necessity for schooling came to be argued and accepted as part of the conception of professionalism and expertise, whether additional schooling was functionally necessary or not. Second, and partly as a result of these changes, the economic return to schooling became substantial, probably after 1900 and more certainly by the 1920's, so that staying in school was objectively "worth it." Third, although groups received differential benefits from extended schooling, the possibility of any economic benefits (together with the relative absence of other means of upward mobility) and the development of a widespread belief in schooling as a mechanism of advancement muted criticism of the schools. Political efforts that might have turned against the schools focused instead on gaining greater access to them.

Vocationalism did not work equally well in all parts of the educational system. Programs had varying rates of return. Industrial education programs probably had low- or no-income returns; other vocational programs, principally commercial education, probably did have some returns. Blacks, in comparison to whites, received almost trivial returns from additional schooling, although the small number of black professionals found that schooling could pay off. The sex-segmented labor market meant that returns to schooling were less for women than men, although again, staying in school almost certainly meant a distinct advantage over dropping out of school.[32] For groups like blacks and women, vocationalism served the function that it has continued to serve, that of segregating them into lower-paid and lower-status positions, and then legitimizing this allocation on grounds of merit and ability. For working-class and immigrant youth, in addition to the uncertainty about the return they faced, the ideal of equal opportunity was one in which educational opportunities were provided according to the "evident or probable destinies" of individual students; such forecasts of their future places in the occupational hierarchy were inevitably biased by class and race.[33]

In this sense, then, vocationalism as established early in the twentieth century "worked." It generated a new conception of the role of schooling: as a preparation for occupations, as a mirror of social stratification, and as a certification for occupational access. Schooling on the whole paid off on its economic promises. In areas of inconsistency, such as the obviously low returns to some groups and the tension between meritocratic and egalitarian goals, other mechanisms were available to mute the potential challenges to vocationalism. But vocationalism, in its very success, set up a pattern of behavior, both in schools and in labor markets, that has led to the problems of the 1960's and 1970's. Though at this point we cannot describe precisely how this pattern developed, four problems that have emerged suggest the dilemmas created by vocationalizing the educational system.

First, the promise of economic returns has meant that schooling has been limited as a warehousing device. Warehousing has been possible and legitimate only when the occupational and income payoffs to schooling are rising because of demand patterns outside the control of the schools themselves, as in the early twentieth century and immediately after the Second World War. But when there are no economic returns, or when economic returns are falling, then various difficulties with warehousing arise. One example has been the debate over vocational education since the early 1960's, when the irrelevance of many vocational programs caused a series of reforms, each of them trying to establish the relevance to work of vocational education. Another example has been the falling returns to college education in the 1970's; both those who argued that "overeducation" was the cause and those who tried to raise the economic returns by increasing federal subsidies to higher education agreed that the only justification for extended schooling was economic. In effect, then, schools can be easily used as warehouses only when economic returns are substantial. If returns decline, the schools are charged with irrelevance, and this sets in motion political efforts to reshape the schools.

A second problem, related to the first, is that the vocationalization of the schools has exacerbated the contradictory pressures on the schools that relate to the allocation of social positions over generations. Once schooling became the mechanism of entry into occupations, then gaining access to schools took on a new importance, specifically in the case of those schools and programs known to be "good" (that is, with high economic returns). For lower-class parents, schooling became *the* mechanism of upward mobility; for middle-class parents, it became the institution through which they could insure that their children would maintain or advance their class standing. The vocationalization of schooling became a basis for the politicization of education. But inequalities in political power among groups shaped the outcome of political battles. Middle-class and white parents have typically enjoyed several advantages: political power, familiarity with bureaucratic and professionalized institutions, and the fact that the agenda of the schools has been defined in terms of middle-class occupations, norms, and values. It is not surprising that they have won most of the battles. Nonetheless, minority, immigrant, and working-class parents have been able to draw upon the ideology that sees equalization as a goal of schooling, and by using that ideology politically they have managed to make some slow gains. To all groups, whether middle- or working-class, white or nonwhite, vocationalization has carried the assumption that schools exist for the gain of individuals. The use of the schools for some "public" purposes—as distinct from the "private" purpose of providing economic advantage for one's own children—has thus been made all the more difficult by the vocationalization of education.

Third, the vocationalization of schooling started the process of "leapfrogging" and credentialing.[34] With schooling the mechanism of social and economic advancement, the incentive for each individual was to gain as much schooling as possible (even for those like women and minorities, for whom advanced schooling had limited returns). This process in turn led to increasing rates of high school attendance, and then to increasing rates of college attendance. But the growth in the skill requirements of jobs has not kept pace with the educational attainments of the available work force, except for accidents of changing sectoral composition like the expansion of professional and technical jobs in the postwar period. The consequence is the tendency for jobs requiring relatively low skill to be filled by individuals with higher levels of schooling, a process variously referred to as educational upgrading or, more pejoratively, educational inflation.[35] The decisions of students, individually rational, have led to a situation that is in the aggregate irrational, and where the relation between schooling and work is again problematic. In addition, the process of credentialing makes it more difficult for those without schooling—particularly minorities—to find positions as adults; and it may exacerbate the problem of youth unemployment.[36]

Fourth, vocationalism reinforced the pattern of relying on educational solutions to economic and labor market problems. This was obvious during the 1960's, when human capital theory developed and justified the educational solutions characteristic of that decade: compensatory education and manpower training programs. Even when the source of the problem was thought to lie in changing labor markets—for example, with the threat of technological unemployment in the early 1960's—the solution was still to provide retraining as a way to adjust individuals to new occupations, rather than to investigate possibilities for reshaping the labor market itself. In drawing attention away from the labor market, educational solutions reflect the political unwillingness of the state to intrude into ostensibly private institutions, and at the same time they neutralize political pressure to do so.

Over the long run, vocationalism has generated the problems of credentialing, exacerbated the problems of equalizing opportunity, and heightened conflict within the schools. And at the same time, vocationalism has contributed to the pervasive and recurring charge that schooling is irrelevant. Thus vocationalism is so contradictory in its effects that it cannot resolve the problems it set out to solve. Instead of making school-based training consistent with occupational requirements, it has made the requirements increasingly irrelevant. None of this was inevitable, since alternatives have always been available. One is to emphasize employment programs and training programs (in the schools or in some other institutional setting) geared to the jobs created, rather than continue to have training programs that are uncoordinated with job opportunities and public employment.* Similarly, if youth unemployment is to be considered a serious problem, then

---

*One fairly recent development, however, has been the trend toward giving specific, short training courses in post-secondary community colleges. These courses, often instigated by employers, can be established within a month or two. Students enroll only for the period of time required for the training program itself, and are virtually assured of placement in the firm requesting the training. Though this appears to be a solution to the inflexibility of conventional school-based training programs, it also represents a significant departure from conventional

the expansion of employment programs, as distinct from training programs, seems an obvious prerequisite. For the particular problems of minority youth, there can be no substitute for efforts to reduce labor market discrimination, through Title VII and similar programs; otherwise, education and training programs simply fail to have as much payoff for them as for white students, and therefore fail to give them the intended benefits.* Other efforts might be undertaken to reduce credentialing,[37] and to eliminate training programs that have no payoff in earnings or employment. The elimination of such worthless programs might transform the image of the schools: high schools and colleges could be reserved for "academic" programs, and specific-skill courses could be conducted outside the schools, either under public auspices as in the short courses now a part of community colleges, or in private hands as in proprietary training schools and company-based programs. Such an arrangement would also eliminate one of the mechanisms of tracking within the high schools and community colleges, though of course it would not eliminate the pressure for stratification in the schooling system.

Even though a number of alternatives have been possible, none is likely to be implemented. In the past, evidence of the irrationality of educational solutions has been ignored, particularly in the constant affirmation of vocational education, in the search during the 1960's for solutions in manpower programs, and in the efforts during the 1970's to resurrect manpower approaches in "employment and training programs." The educational solution is too deeply embedded in our institutions; the alternatives are too politically embattled. Alternatives to conventional educational

---

vocational education and one whose justification for receiving public funds is still insecure. The coordination of training programs with existing jobs—those available in the private sector or created in public employment programs—is the heart of Sweden's manpower program. See Kenneth Hauf, Benny Hjern, and David Porter, "Implementation of Manpower Training: Local Administrative Networks in the Federal Republic of Germany and Sweden," Discussion paper, International Institute of Management, Wissenschaftszentrum Berlin (Dec. 1975).

*There is one real exception to our focus on employment rather than training programs. Hispanics in particular lag behind both blacks and Anglos in level of schooling, and this difference appears to account for a good proportion of the Anglo-Hispanic earnings difference. Narrowing the schooling gap is critical to bringing the earnings of Hispanics up to those of other groups, whereas labor market discrimination remains the more powerful barrier for blacks.

solutions have in fact been possible only as adjuncts to programs
for adults. The youth programs of the depression were part of
employment programs for adults; the development of the CETA
and YEDPA youth programs depended on prior demands for
public employment programs for adults suffering from high unemployment; and efforts to combat discrimination, rarely in-
voked for youth, began with efforts to reduce discrimination for
adults. To be sure, the advent of public employment programs,
anti-discrimination efforts, and the Occupational Health and
Safety Administration during the 1960's and 1970's have slowly
changed the conception of what the state might do with respect to
personnel policies and labor markets. But the historical record
still indicates that there can be no real change in programs for
youth until there are corresponding changes in programs for
adults, and that youth are generally the last group to enjoy the
benefits of these efforts. This conclusion suggests how unsatisfactory the resolution of the "youth problem" has been.

Postscript: What We Need to Know

We have offered an interpretation of how the relationship between schooling and work changed after the turn of the century,
and outlined some of the implications of that change for students,
schools, and "youth policy" in general. We are acutely aware of
how tentative our argument is, in respect to both the historical
record and the current relationship between schooling and work.
In speculating about changes, we have emphasized the first three
decades of this century; yet, to the extent that labor market
changes have continued to shape school organization and educational decisions, those changes must be followed into the present. We have also treated the schools as essentially reactive,
although by the 1940's schooling itself was beginning to affect the
labor market, if only by keeping more youth out of the market.
Both our argument and its limitations need to be examined in the
light of extensive research into historical and current sources.

For example, the hypothesis of a major shift in the relationship
between work and schooling in the first decades of this century,
with increasing returns to schooling tied to changes in the labor
market, requires an investigation of the impact of schooling on

the labor market in the nineteenth century, and of whether the returns then were essentially zero for most people, as we suggest. We would expect to find generally rising levels of returns to schooling after 1900. The returns would increase first in areas of the country where more pronounced occupational shifts were occurring, shifts to more retail and clerical positions and to large-scale corporations, and shifts that eliminated young workers. In other areas of the country, such as rural areas and perhaps the underdeveloped South, changing relationships between schooling and work may not be visible. We also need to know why the returns to schooling changed. In particular, our claim that stratified labor markets were important in shaping decisions about schools needs to be tested, and also our claim that deskilling, corporate growth, internal labor markets, and rationalized hiring policies structured these labor markets and established the relationship between schooling and work. The reasons for the use of schooling in the more formal hiring procedures need some investigation, perhaps with the aid of company records or company histories; our hunch is that if we knew more about the use of schooling as a credential early in the century, we would gain significant insight into the current nature of credentialing and some indication of its stability. The relationship between schooling and office and managerial work is another subject on which our data is tantalizing but incomplete: we know that the enrollment in commercial programs boomed, and we have assumed without demonstration that this was economically rational. The final transformation in the early twentieth century that we outlined was a change in the nature of professionalism (more than a change in its magnitude). But for all that has been written about professionalism, we still know less in this area than we need to about actual educational practices and their influence on the schools generally.

A related issue involves the nature of the youth labor market. We have argued that the creation of a secondary labor market did not by itself push young people out; indeed, unskilled jobs in the secondary sector seem well suited to assumptions that youth are unstable and irresponsible. But there is some evidence that by the second decade of the twentieth century employers did not want youth at work in their firms, at least those under eighteen. Why young people suddenly became "unfit" for employment is not clear. Assertions that youth could not be trusted to operate complex machinery or to stay on the job assume that young people's behavior was substantially different from the behavior of those who replaced them. An alternative explanation is that the declining demand for young people may have been designed to protect the labor market against teenage workers. Organized labor, for example, supported vocational education, but stressed its importance in helping those *already* on the job to advance, and demanded it in order to keep high school youth off the labor market. Whatever the explanation, the historical origins of discrimination against youth are important, because the pattern of discrimination has persisted and continues to generate unemployment and dead-end jobs for teenagers.

If the hypothesis of rising returns to schooling after 1900 can be verified, the link between changing returns and attendance patterns will still be unclear. There is no satisfactory explanation for the rising attendance rates in high schools after 1890, though conventional human capital theory would predict rising attendance in response to rising rates of return. Both the levels and patterns of enrollment are of interest. Patterns of enrollment that developed in high schools according to different tracks—academic, industrial, commercial, and agricultural, for example—might reveal which enrollments were motivated by economic advantage and which served purely as tracking mechanisms. The mechanisms that prompted students to change their educational decisions and the ways that schooling made students aware of changing opportunities are critical links in our argument.

Our conception of vocationalism encompasses not only rising returns to schooling, but also the hypothesis that access to occupations over time becomes increasingly dependent on schooling levels. The trend of increasing educational requirements for occupations provides some confirmation of this, but without much sense of how the process occurred or what other routes to occupations were replaced by schooling. It may turn out, for example, that schooling reduced the influence of family and kin. Different areas to examine include the gradual elimination of alternative routes into different occupations, the process of licensing, which for a variety of semiprofessions appears to have escalated educational requirements and limited other mechanisms of access, and the ways that firms responded to the oversupply of educated workers generated by "educational inflation."

Even though the human capital model may help explain rising school attendance during the Progressive era, we find this an incomplete and unbalanced theory. Two implications of the human capital model in particular need to be examined. The first is that attendance falls in response to falling returns, just as it rises when returns are going up. Our hypothesis would be that responses are asymmetric, with falling rates of return having relatively little impact on attendance (until the return falls to zero, perhaps) because of the struggle for any advantage, no matter how small. Second, the human capital model stresses the supply side of the labor market and supply adjustments, as in educational enrollments, to restore the equilibrium rate of return to schooling. Other equilibrating mechanisms exist, and need to be integrated into a more comprehensive theory. One way to restore the equilibrium is to increase the rate of return by lowering the direct costs of attendance, as in recent efforts by middle-class parents to increase federal subsidies to higher education. Another, probably more important, is the response of employers to changing rates of return: if rates fall, then under most conditions the "price" of educated labor is falling relative to uneducated labor, and the normal response to such a price change is to increase the demand for educated labor and to restore (at least partially) the rate of return. However, employers may make this adjustment by using educated labor in occupations previously filled by less educated labor; this would stimulate the process of educational attainments outrunning job requirements, which has been documented for the postwar period. An improved model would encompass rates of return as well as the problems of credentialing and the degradation of jobs that have occurred throughout the postwar period.

Another flaw of the human capital model is that the nature of the relation of schooling to earnings is unexamined. Although there is by now a relatively large literature on credentialing and signaling, it is still far from reaching a decision among the competing hypotheses. There are endless statistical studies examining the economic returns to schooling in the aggregate, and yet there is still almost no data on what kinds of programs pay off—what kinds of vocational programs under what labor market conditions, whether some kinds of skills are most readily taught in schools, whether two-year colleges have the economic returns that many students seem to believe. With the proliferation of training programs in different institutional settings, including high schools, two-year colleges, proprietary schools, various CETA and YEDPA programs, as well as traditional apprenticeship and company-based programs, there is an opportunity to examine the kinds of settings that are appropriate for different occupations and for such goals as equality of access for women and minorities.

Because of the dominance of the human capital model, with its emphasis on the supply side of the labor market, there has been almost no investigation of demand-side effects of schooling on employment and earnings, aside from the common statement that occupational expansion in the postwar period was education-intensive. In particular, the influence of the changing sectoral composition of employment and changing occupational composition within sectors (as distinct from the process of educational inflation for specific occupations) has not been established. Although both of these sorts of change may have increased the return to schooling, they operate in very different ways. Some of the developments in skill training—the role of proprietary schools, for example, and the very recent development of short, specific-skill courses in community colleges—have not been closely examined. Such developments as these imply that some kinds of specific-skill training have been difficult to provide in the schools (and indeed, the public provision of such training might also be undesirable). Finally, although it seems unbelievable, there has been no general theoretical work on the microeconomics of training programs. This could be useful in specifying the different demand conditions under which training programs have an economic impact (in either earnings or employment), and in indicating when educational policies are likely to be worthless.

Finally, there are overarching questions that involve the relationship of the state to schooling and work. We need to ask why public support has so readily been given to the expansion of schooling, rather than to intervention in the labor market. On one level the answer is obvious: by promising to solve social, political, and economic problems through the schools, more fundamental reforms could be avoided. In periods of tension between labor and capital, the promise that education can correct the mismatch between workers and jobs directs attention away from the structural inability of capitalism to provide enough employment, or enough decent jobs, to fulfill expectations about work. Claiming, as educational reformers always have, that education can increase productivity is politically powerful in a society that values productivity so highly.

But it is incomplete to argue that the resort to education has occurred simply because it has successfully avoided "real" problems. After all, schooling has "worked," at least in the sense that it has withdrawn youth from the labor market and provided economic returns to some individuals; and it has become the focus of aspirations to upward mobility, largely (though not entirely) replacing the more family-linked mechanisms of the nineteenth century. At the same time, schooling has not worked well enough to mystify all of the people all of the time. Political battles over access to the schools have intensified, and alternatives to schooling, such as manpower and employment programs, have been instituted. The uncertainty of the educational solution, as the state has grappled with the problems of youth and the preparation of adolescents for adulthood, remains one of the important legacies of the early twentieth century.

Making It in America: Work, Education, and Social Structure

DAVID HOGAN

Introduction

In the course of an intensive investigation of the social life of Muncie, Indiana, in the mid-1920's, Helen and Robert Lynd noted that since the early years of the century there had been a dramatic change in the character of public education. The nature of this change was not difficult to discern. It was all too apparent to the Lynds that a shift had occurred from "the traditional dignified conception of what constitutes education" toward an education that seeks "to train for specific tool and skill activities in factory, office, and home." Two-thirds of the programs in the high school were now of this character; more than any other part of the school curriculum, "these vocational courses consist in learning *how* rather than learning *about*."

The schools, it seemed to the Lynds, had "frankly adopted the canons of office and machine shop: they must change in step with the coming of new physical equipment in machine shops and offices, or become ineffective." Thus

The writing of this essay was supported in part by funds from the National Institute of Education, Grant no. 9-0173. For comments on earlier drafts I wish to thank the participants of the Stanford Conference on Work and Education, in particular Carl Kaestle, David Tyack, and Harvey Kantor. A special debt is owed to Michael Katz for his help in the preparation of the first draft.

actual conditions of work in the city's factories are imported into the schoolshops; boys bring repair work from their homes; they study auto mechanics by working on an old Ford car; they design, draft, and make patterns for lathes and drill presses, the actual casting being done by a Middletown foundry; they have designed and constructed a house, doing all the architectural, carpentry, wiring, metal work, and painting. A plan for providing work in a local machine shop, alternating two weeks of this with two weeks of study throughout the year, is under discussion.

Justifying this "pragmatic commandeering of education," the president of the school board explained: "For a long time all boys were trained to be President. Then for a while we trained them to be professional men. Now we are training boys to get jobs."[1]

For the rest, "the school, like the factory, is a thoroughly regimented world":

Immovable seats in orderly rows fix the sphere of activity for each child. For all, from the timid six-year-old entering for the first time to the most assured high school senior, the general routine is much the same. Bells divide the day into periods. For the six-year-olds the periods are short (fifteen to twenty-five minutes) and varied; in some they leave their seats, play games, and act out make-believe stories, although in "recitation periods" all movement is prohibited. As they grow older the taboo upon physical activity becomes stricter, until by the third or fourth year practically all movement is forbidden except the marching from one set of seats to another between periods, a brief period of prescribed exercise daily, and periods of manual training or home economics once or twice a week.[2]

In this essay I do not intend to explain how these developments came to pass in Muncie, Indiana, or in any other American city for that matter. Nor do I discuss the motives or ideology that impelled or supported the vocationalizing of education. Rather, I examine the evidence concerning structural links between schooling and the economy in the twentieth century, and I evaluate two competing explanations for this realignment of institutional arrangements.

The argument proceeds as follows. First I examine the main varieties of one of the two competing explanations, modernization theory, and assess how well the structural claims of modernization theory stand up to scrutiny. I then examine modernization theory in relation to the status attainment process. Next, I introduce the basic principles of class analysis, the second of the two explanations, and lay out in a highly schematic fashion the principal arguments of a class analysis of the institutional realignment of schooling and the economy. And I conclude with some general observations about the significance of vocationalism in American education.

Modernization Theory: Some Structural Anomalies

The grand, governing principle of modernization theory is that the process of modernization is above all a process of "structural differentiation." The meaning of this is quite straightforward. Briefly, modernization theorists argue that premodern or traditional societies are characterized by low institutional specialization: the boundaries between the family, the state, the economy, and the educational process are weak and nebulous. As modernization occurs, however, institutions specialize; an institutional division of labor develops with respect to the social functions that are performed. Boundaries between institutions become sharper and more defined: between the family and schooling, between the economy and the polity, and so on. It is this process of institutional specialization that is the heart of the notion of structural differentiation.[3]

In modernization theory, the growth and organization of American schooling are approached as an instance, and an important one, of the process of structural differentiation. Because of the breakdown of traditional family-based arrangements for the socialization and training of children, because of the growth of particular technological and normative requirements of modern occupations, and because of the expansion of political participation in modern democratic life, schools come to specialize in the training and socialization of children and to assume responsibility for the training of students for modern occupational and civic roles.

With respect to occupational training, modernization theorists stress two propositions. First, schools are a rational and efficient means of sorting and selecting people so that the talented and motivated attain those positions that are functionally the most important in modern industrial society. Second, schools teach the kind of norms and cognitive skills essential for the preservation of social consensus and for the competent performance of work in modern society. Schooling, Robert Dreeben argues, "involves much more than training competence in job-related skills; it involves as well the shaping of men's states of mind, and gaining their willingness to accept standards of conduct related to holding a job as well as to master its component activities." Of particular importance are the norms of independence, achievement, universalism, and specificity.[4] An important variant of this normative emphasis has been developed by some historians, who have focused on ethnocultural conflict and on the development of "modern" attitudes toward work, schooling, and political life among immigrant groups.[5]

The backbone of modernization theory, however, is the question of technological change and the demand for skilled labor—particularly the claim that industrialization generated a demand for skilled labor and, in turn, for schooling.[6] Douglas C. North argued, apropos of America's industrialization in the nineteenth century, that:

The sustained expansion of manufacturing . . . requires a large investment in human capital. While the operatives in the factory itself may not be required to possess substantial skills, the spread of manufacturing with expansion in the size of the market leads to vertical disintegration and the development of a host of highly trained and skilled ancillary and complementary functions. I am thinking not only of the development of specialized capital-goods industries and wholesale and retail marketing facilities, but equally of the wide variety of professional services which are required.[7]

H. J. Habakkuk was even more emphatic than North about the relationship between industrialization ("mechanization") and skills. Habakkuk contended that machines and skilled labor are complements in production, not alternatives, because skilled workers are required to build the machines. In all probability, he argued, "the manufacture and use of the more capital-intensive technique required more skilled to unskilled labor than the labor intensive."[8]

It is but a short step from here to an explanation of the expansion of schooling. Martin Trow, for example, used a two-step argument. He first noted the great "changes in the occupational structure" reflecting "tremendous changes in the economy and organization of work," a result of large-scale mechanization and bureaucratization. Accordingly, "The growth of the secondary-school system after 1870 was in large part a response to the pull of the economy for a mass of white-collar employees with more than an elementary-school education." But second, he added, "changes in the occupational structures do not provide the whole explanation of the extraordinary growth of secondary and higher education in the United States," for "the changes in the occupational structure have raised the educational aspirations of the large parts of the American population, and the educational system has been responsive to these higher aspirations."[9]

With a closer look at the central assumptions of modernization theory, however, the theory quickly begins to unravel. Two interrelated difficulties stand out. One is that modernization theory relies on a human capital explanation of technology and of increasing skill requirements as the primary cause of the expansion of schooling. The second difficulty, a step further back, is that modernization theory relies on a neoclassical theory of production and the nature of the firm.

The basic argument concerning technology and increasing skill requirements is derived from human capital theory: a growing demand for skilled labor increases the individual returns to investment in education, and, other things being equal (direct and opportunity costs), the demand for education rises. The theory assumes that changes in the mix of goods and services and changes in technology produce an increased demand for skilled or educated labor. This increase in demand leads to a rise in the wage of educated workers, which produces, in turn, an increase in the incentive to invest in schooling and an increase in voluntary enrollment.

To the extent, then, that human capital or market mechanisms operated, we would expect to observe increases in the rate of employment in occupational categories associated with high levels of schooling, and perhaps increases in skill requirements within certain categories or sectors. This expectation rests on the further assumption that production processes provide relatively few opportunities for substitution among workers with different amounts of education (what economists call "low substitution effects"). Given this assumption, observed shifts in employment would indicate underlying shifts in the demand for labor. Likewise, the argument that skill requirements increased as a result of industrialization could be measured by (a) observing whether industrialization did in fact require greater numbers of skilled workers; and (b) observing whether the shift to capital-intensive techniques in fact increased the average level of skill required of industrial workers.

Sadly for modernization theory, the available body of research provides very little support for its claims. Some suggestion of the difficulties facing modernization theory can be gained by noting some of the Lynds' observations of changes in the work life of Muncie between the 1890's and the mid-1920's.

First of all, the Lynds noted that the work of the craftsman was being transformed and his craft disappearing. "Inventions and technology," they wrote, "continue rapidly to supplant muscle and the cunning hand of the master craftsman by batteries of tireless ironmen doing narrowly specialized things over and over and merely 'operated' or 'tended' in their orderly, clangorous, repetitive processes by the human worker."[10] Gradually, "the demands of the ironman for swiftness and endurance rather than training and skill" had led to the "abandonment" of the system of apprentices and master craftsmen. Work had been transformed "from a system in which length of service, craftsmanship, and authority in the shop and social prestige among one's peers tended to go together to one which, in the main, demands little of a worker's personality save rapid, habitual reactions and an ability to submerge himself in the performance of a few routinized, easily learned movements."[11]

Change could be seen everywhere. In a machine shop, 75 percent of the labor force of 800 men "can be taken from farm or high school and trained in a week's time." In a glass plant, 84 percent of the tool-using personnel, excluding foremen, required one month or less of training; in Middletown's leading foundry, "60 percent of all the castings produced are made by a group of newcomers who cast with the help of machines and require only a fortnight or so of training."[12] And with the disappearance of the apprenticeship system, "the line between skilled and unskilled worker has become so blurred as to be in some shops almost nonexistent," with the consequence that avenues of mobility were disappearing. All that was possible was promotion for a foremanship, and that was a relatively rare event. For example, in six Middletown plants employing an average total of 4,240 workers during the first six months of 1923—admittedly a time of economic recession—there were ten vacancies for foremen over the period of 21 months from January 1, 1923, to October 1, 1924. In effect, in a year and three-quarters there was a chance of promotion for only one in 424; but there was some evidence that "the chance of becoming a foreman, small as it is, would appear to be somewhat better than it was a generation ago." And on top of the small chance of becoming a foreman, "increasing technological complexity and the resulting tendency to insert college-trained technical men into a force between foreman and owners appear to hinder a workman's progress beyond a foremanship more than formerly."[13]

Other evidence, of a more general nature, supplements the findings of the Lynds. For one, the expansion of schooling far exceeds the expansion of the occupational structure, which suggests that at best the latter can only explain part of the former.[14] Second, the demand for skilled labor and the proportion of it in the manufacturing labor force has diminished over time. Not only did the Lynds note this phenomenon in *Middletown*, but many others did so as well. Weyl and Sakolski in 1906, in a trade-by-trade analysis, and Paul Douglas in the 1920's, in an industry-by-industry analysis, both observed a decline in skill requirements and in the demand for skilled labor. The Griffens describe such a decline in Poughkeepsie, New York. Alan Dawley found similar trends in the shoe industry in nineteenth-century Lynn, Massachusetts, Brody and Stone in the turn-of-the-century steel industry, and Ozanne in the farm implements industry. Ericksen and Yancey estimated that between 1850 and 1880 the proportion of skilled workers in Philadelphia's manufacturing labor force dropped from 46.9 percent to 36.8 percent, and that between 1910 and 1930 the proportion of skilled workers in hand trades declined from 24.8 percent to 22.8 percent. In Chicago, the percentage of draftsmen, foremen, and other skilled workers dropped from 26.7 percent in 1880 to 17.1 percent in 1930. Harry Braverman estimated that although the number of engineers in the United States had risen dramatically (2,000 percent between 1880 and 1929, for example), "taken together, the technical engineers, chemists, scientists, architects, draftsmen, designers, and technicians represented not more than 3 percent of the total labor force in 1970"; he concluded that all "the technical knowledge required to operate the various industries in the United States" could be found in this group.[15]

Taking a different approach, Folger and Nam estimated that only 15 percent of the increase in education of the American work force in the twentieth century could be attributed to shifts in the occupational structure (that is, as a consequence of an increase in the demand for skilled labor); the rest of the increase, they argue, has occurred within job categories.[16] Moreover, there is some striking evidence, developed and collated by Berg and Collins, that the skill requirements of many jobs in the economy are significantly lower than the educational requirements.[17] There is also persuasive evidence, initially analyzed by James Bright and later reanalyzed by Braverman, that although technological change has created many new jobs, most of them are unskilled monitoring jobs; few require substantial knowledge or technical training. Highly complex equipment does not usually need highly skilled operators, since the skills are built into the machines themselves. As Bright concluded, contrary to his presuppositions, "there was more evidence that automation had reduced the skill requirements of the operating labor force, and occasionally of the entire factory force, including the maintenance organization."[18]

Other evidence suggests that most clerical jobs either have undergone considerable skill dilution or require only low levels of skill, and such jobs account for by far the greatest part of the expansion in the occupational structure of the labor force since 1900. Since 1960, for example, the white-collar sector has expanded by 15 million people, but about four-fifths of this was in sales and clerical jobs.

All in all, the evidence is consistent: the proportion of skilled labor in the labor force has diminished, skill requirements for most jobs are low or diminishing, and educational certificates have little direct relationship to skill requirements. Accordingly, the expansion of schooling cannot be explained structurally by reference to skill requirements and the demand for skilled labor, which is to say that the reliance of modernization theory on the human capital market to link the economy and education is unsupportable.

Modernization Theory: "Expanding Universalism"

According to modernization theory, as a society modernizes, prescription is replaced by achievement as the main determinant of the allocation of income, power, and prestige. People gain wealth, power, and prestige not by virtue of birth, but by virtue of achievement. And the road to achievement starts at the schoolhouse door. In modernizing societies, education increasingly mediates the relationship between family background and economic success. In effect, a modern society is a meritocracy.

This development is held to be desirable for two reasons. First, it is efficient: it makes better use of talent, particularly educated talent. This proposition has been formalized by sociologists into the "functionalist theory of stratification."[19] Second, it is desirable because it is "democratic": the spreading of equality of opportunity by means of education enables people to rise according to their own efforts. In the United States this is called "democratic capitalism"[20] or "expanding universalism." "Objective criteria of evaluation that are universally accepted," Blau and Duncan argue, "increasingly pervade all spheres of life and displace particularistic standards of diverse in-groups, intuitive judgments, and humanistic values not susceptible to empirical verification." They go on:

Education assumes increasing significance for social status in general and for the transmission of social standing from fathers to sons in particular. Superior family origins increase a son's chances of attaining superior occupational status in the United States in large part because they help him to obtain a better education, whereas in less industrialized societies the influence of family origins on status does not seem to be primarily mediated by education.[21]

Although much of this is borne out by history, the record is not as clear-cut as Blau and Duncan suggest. From the mid-nineteenth century onward, education has indeed increasingly mediated the relationship between people's family background and their occupational achievement and income. There is, however, considerable controversy over the strength of the statistical relationships between family background, educational achievement, and occupational success, and over the nature of the linking processes.

Concerning the relationship between family background and educational achievement, the evidence is conflicting. Some researchers have found a substantial impact of family background on educational achievement, others have found none or little. Research findings on the relationship between educational achievement and occupational attainment, particularly for the middle-to-late nineteenth century, are similarly ambiguous.[22] In later periods, however, the association between education and occupational success becomes dramatic; but interpretations of the causal linkage still vary, and scholars differ over the significance of family background. Blau and Duncan argue that "a man's social origins exert a considerable influence on his chances of occupational success," but that his own education and his early job experience "exert a more pronounced influence on his success chances." They conclude that "although most of the influence of social origins on occupational achievement is mediated by education and early experience, social origins have a continuing impact on careers that is independent of the two variables pertaining to career preparation. Education exerts the strongest direct effect on occupational achievements, with . . . the level at which a man starts his career being second."[23]

In various ways, other studies either confirm or conflict with these findings. Although Christopher Jencks went to great pains to demonstrate that education is a relatively modest determinant of adult success, his own figures belie his argument and tend to support Blau and Duncan. Arguing that education left more than half of the variance in occupational attainment unexplained, Jencks downplayed, unjustifiably by most canons of statistical reasoning, the high correlation of .65 between education and occupational status.[24] Moreover, as Raymond Boudon points out, relationships that are objectively indeterminate for the individual may be anything but that with respect to the functioning of the social structure. For example, correlations between education and occupation may be partially influenced by changes in the occupational structure that create a disjunctive between the systems of work and education.[25]

Bowles and Gintis take a different tack. They acknowledge that educational achievement is highly correlated with occupational attainment. For example, an individual in the ninth educational achievement decile has a 34.3 percent chance of attaining a position in the top fifth of income earners, whereas an individual in the bottom decile in education has only a 3.5 percent chance. Nevertheless, they argue, this relationship cannot be explained by cognitive ability, for when IQ is held constant it barely alters the statistical relationship. Thus, among people with identical adult IQ scores, someone from the ninth education decile is still eight times more likely to be in the top income quintile than someone from the bottom decile. Bowles and Gintis therefore conclude that economic success tends to run in the family, "almost completely independently from any inheritance of IQ, whether it be genetic or environmental." Finally, Sewell and Hauser argue, following Blau and Duncan, that higher education is an important determinant of occupational success; that a father's occupational status still directly affects a son's occupational status; and that, contrary to Bowles and Gintis, cognitive ability matters a great deal.[26]

Despite controversy of this sort, there is little disagreement that education is the prime institutional factor in the relationship between the family and occupational success. The role of education in the status attainment process represents an important and even pivotal aspect of modernization. Yet one issue, the relationship between educational achievement and income, poses a severe challenge to the part of modernization theory that posits an increasingly "universalistic" process of status attainment.

In twentieth-century America the gap between the least educated and the most educated, in years of schooling, has progressively diminished; and yet, contrary to what modernization theory predicts, a concomitant reduction in the income gap between the richest and the poorest has not materialized.[27] Lester Thurow, for example, points out that in 1950 the bottom fifth of the white male population had 8.6 percent of the total number of years of education, and the top fifth had 31.1 percent. By 1970, the bottom fifth had risen to 10.7 percent and the top fifth had fallen to 29.3 percent. But despite this movement toward equality of educational achievement, the distribution of income among white males in fact became even more unequal. Between 1949 and 1969 the share of total income going to the lowest fifth fell from 3.2 percent to 2.6 percent, and the share going to the highest fifth rose from 44.8 percent to 46.3 percent.[28]

Moreover, as Mincer and Chiswick point out, a significant increase in school achievement would only reduce income inequality by a negligible amount, even if other offsetting factors were removed. The income gap between blacks and whites reveals the same discrepancy. Between 1952 and 1968 the mean education of black male workers rose from 67 percent to 87 percent of that of white male workers (a 29 percent increase), yet median wage and salary incomes rose only from 58 percent to 66 percent, an increase of only 13 percent. Moreover, most of this increase in income could be attributed to black emigration from the South, where the relative income of blacks was lower.[29]

The standard, or neoclassical, explanation of income discrimination is the one developed initially by Gary Becker.[30] Assuming that black and white workers, or male and female workers, did not differ in their access to human capital or in their marginal productivity at work, Becker would argue that black-white and male-female differences in income can be explained by exogenous "tastes for discrimination" on the part of employers. Employers failing to hire blacks and women, with their lower wage rates, would place themselves at a competitive disadvantage in respect to other employers. The most obvious difficulty with this explanation, of course, is its bogus problematic. Employers have indeed employed blacks and women; they have done so, however, not in labor markets characterized by wage competition, but in highly segmented and stratified labor markets—whose roots go back into the nineteenth century—characterized by job competition. Furthermore, this explanation assumes a theory of production in which purely technical, input-output cost considerations predominate, an assumption that cannot be substantiated. Finally, it assumes a simple human capital mechanism linking education to the economy.

In other words, the theory of human capital misconstrues the nature of the linking mechanisms between education and the labor market. An adequate account of the relationship between education and income requires an explanation of the structural links between education and the network of labor markets; a description of when and why these links developed and how they were sustained; and an account of the genesis of labor market segmentation and the relationship of this segmentation to the organization of production. To answer these questions, however, requires a theoretical framework different from modernization theory and its academic progeny, the functionalist theory of stratification and neoclassical human capital theory.

The Theory of Class Structuration

Essentially, class analysis is an analytical tool, or rather a set of tools, for explaining how societies of a particular kind develop and function over time. A market in labor is a structure of social relations: the class relations between labor (no matter how well or poorly paid) and capital (no matter how benevolent or malevolent, and whether owner-controlled or managerially administered). The Lynds described the disappearance of economic self-sufficiency or independence; nearly all of those "who earned Middletown's living" worked for wages in order to buy "the material necessities of life."[31] It is the development of a structure of social relations and institutional arrangements around labor markets that is the analytic focus of class theory.

The growing importance of class relations in American history can be measured by the growing importance of the market in labor. At the time of the signing of the Declaration of Independence, 80 percent in the non-slave U.S. labor force were self-employed entrepreneurs (by far the most were farmers), and about 20 percent were wage and salaried employees. One hundred years later only 36.9 percent were self-employed entrepreneurs; wage and salaried employees had increased to 62 percent; and 1.1 percent were salaried managers and officials. By 1974, 83 percent were wage and salaried employees; 8.2 percent self-employed entrepreneurs; and 8.8 percent salaried managers and officials.[32] Where once the majority of non-slave Americans were economically independent, by the time of the Grant administration a clear majority were selling their labor in the market. Where once the majority lived as self-sufficient or commercial farmers, or worked in "ten-footers" making shoes or in bakeries, saddleries, or blacksmith or wagon-making shops as independent commodity producers, by the late nineteenth century most belonged to the wage-labor force of industrial capitalism and lived in urban areas.* This process of "proletarianization"—the progressive expansion of markets in labor—is the distinguishing feature of capitalist societies. The principal object of class analysis is to explain how and why the capitalist mode of production developed and overwhelmed alternative modes of production.

Of course, the structure of a society is far more complex than its productive relations, no matter how important they are. In capitalist societies, although the existence of labor markets at the point of production is definitive, class relations are not limited to the social relations of production. Societies also have political and ideological relations; but in capitalist societies these are progressively "structured" into a class form consistent with the basic relations of productive activity. Together these class relations constitute the "class structure" of capitalist societies.[33] These structures are not structures of inequality or of groups, but of class *relations*. At different times these structures will vary in composition, strength, and cohesion; class analysis seeks to explain why and how.

In addition, interlaced through the structure of class relations are webs of institutional arrangements, some obvious, others not:

*Even as late as 1873, three-quarters of the American population lived in rural areas and half worked in agriculture; but by the 1890's rural families constituted less than two-thirds of the population and the agricultural work force was down to 42 percent. By 1900 agriculture accounted for 30.9 percent of the labor force; by 1910, 17.4 percent; by 1972, only 3.8 percent. At the same time, whereas in 1790 only 5.1 percent of the population lived in towns of over 2,500 and in 1830 only 8.8 percent, by 1860 19.8 percent lived in such towns; by 1910 the figure had reached 45.7 percent, and by 1920 it was well past the halfway mark. By 1970 almost three times as many people lived in urban areas as in rural. U.S. Bureau of the Census, *Historical Statistics of the United States, Colonial Times to 1970* (Washington, D.C., 1976), pt. 1, pp. 11–21; Blake McKelvey, *American Urbanization: A Comparative History* (Glenview, Ill., 1973), pp. 24, 37, 104; Michael Reich, "The Evolution of the U.S. Labor Force," in Richard E. Edwards, Michael Reich, and Thomas Weisskopf, eds., *The Capitalist System* (Englewood Cliffs, N.J.; 1972), p. 182.

the private ownership of the means of production and the product of the labor process; the technical organization of production and its relationship to the opportunity structure and to mechanisms of mobility; the spatial distribution of these opportunity structures; the differentiation of labor markets by race, sex, ethnicity, region, and education; the social organization of family life and the relations between the sexes and the generations; the stratification system and its relationship to the opportunity structure; and the degree of articulation between social institutions, such as schooling, and the economy. Together, the structure of class relations and their surrounding institutional arrangements constitute what Nicos Poulantzas terms "the social division of labor as a whole."[34]

The social division of labor did not, obviously, spring up overnight, not even in a society that fancies itself to be the offspring of an immaculate conception between Calvin (or Locke, or some eighteenth-century Scottish moral philosopher) and the Virgin Forest. Rather, it was the product of almost 200 years of American history. It was to deal with such a history that class analysis was designed. With class analysis it is possible to study the way a society like America, increasingly characterized by markets in labor, is transformed from an overwhelming rural agricultural society into a mature industrial capitalist society.

The principal analytical tool provided by class analysis to explain such developments is the concept of class structuration, or what Anthony Giddens calls structuration around the "class principle." Giddens views this as the most appropriate way to conceptualize how a society becomes progressively characterized by class structures.[35] In America, after the advent of labor markets early in the nineteenth century, the "class principle" became the prevailing mode of structuration. By the end of the century, a distinctive capitalist structure of social relations and institutional arrangements was well established. Alternative modes of structuration, associated with different modes of production and ideologies, had for the most part been pushed into the dustbin of history. Something of the nature of class structuration can be illustrated by a few developments in American life in the past 150 years.

As noted earlier, a market in labor did not suddenly appear. It took almost a hundred years for the labor market to reach a point where the overwhelming majority of workers were wage earners. Indeed, even in the post-Second World War era new groups of workers, such as blacks and women, have been incorporated into the wage labor system.[36] Purely capitalist labor markets, in which workers were stripped of all ownership of the means of production and entered the labor market with nothing but their labor to sell, developed slowly, and usually only after great resistance and conflict. (Homestead, 1892, is a conspicuous example of this process in the steel industry.) The creation of a distinctively capitalist labor process wholly designed and controlled by capital—or what Marx called the shift from formal to real subordination—was also long and drawn-out, varying within and between industries and often engendering considerable conflict. The opportunity structure of America in the 1920's was very different from that of fifty years before: in particular, education had come to constitute the principle mechanism of social mobility. Finally, and of particular relevance to the present essay, new institutional networks gradually evolved between the economy, education, and the family, changing the institutional relations of American society.[37]

The transformation of political and ideological structures was more complex, in part because of the peculiar juxtaposition of the political and industrial revolutions in America, which is of considerable importance in understanding the process of class reformation in America. From the early years of the nineteenth century, political and ideological relations were under continual pressure and were a source of social conflict. Successive waves of immigrant groups, who arrived in America with little in common except grit and poverty, were eventually forged into an ethnically differentiated working class with common and parallel cultural forms and institutions. The issues relating to class formation are not just empirical and theoretical, but conceptual and even epistemological. It is these issues that are at the center of the recent controversy between E. P. Thompson and the Althusserians.[38] This controversy need not detain us here, although it should be emphasized that it cannot be avoided in any concrete analysis of the process of structuration.

In the remainder of this essay I will discuss three of the topics that a class analysis of education highlights: the structural links

between education and the economy; the organization of schooling; and the political and ideological mechanisms that link education to the economy.

The Structuration of Schooling and the Economy

What links the economy to education, what mechanisms create
and sustain these links, and what is the relationship between
education, skills, and productivity? The answers to the first and
third questions are closely related, and turn out in the end to
hinge upon the relationships between the labor process and labor
market structures. The answer to the second depends on the
answers to the first and third.

One may approach the relationship between education, skills,
and productivity from three perspectives. It might be argued that
they are not linked, or that they are linked but only indirectly, or
that they are directly linked. Randall Collins's conflict theory of
education stratification and Ivar Berg's theory of credentialism
are leading expressions of the first view: educational credentials
represent simply the impact of demographic demand and supply
factors, rather than work-related skill requirements. For Lester
Thurow, the linkage is indirect; educational credentials are important not for any skills they signal, but because they screen
workers for the kinds of personality or character traits assumed to
be associated with various levels of productivity.[39]

Bowles and Gintis, on the other hand, on the basis of research
by themselves, Edwards, and others, argue that educational qualifications do not reflect cognitive or technical skills that employers seeks, but personality or affective traits compatible with
the social relations of production. Thus education is linked to
productivity, but not to skill requirements technically conceived.
Productivity is a question not of the technical relations of production, but of the social relations of production. The relationship
between productivity and education varies, however, with the
nature of the labor market. Education has little relationship to
productivity in male secondary labor markets; some relationship
in female secondary labor markets; and only "fairly little" relationship to primary blue-collar productivity. In independent primary labor markets, however, educational credentials often have

a very close relationship to both skill requirements and job productivity.[40]

We are now in a position to describe in some detail the nature of the links between education and the economy. Schools are linked not to the economy in general, but to the labor process and labor markets. And the structure of labor markets is dependent on the organization of the labor process, in what Edwards calls "structures of control." It is these structures of control that determine the nature of the demand for labor and the nature of the links between schooling and the economy.

The cornerstone of the argument is the relationship between the structure of the labor market, the structure of control, and behavior requirements. Edwards first distinguishes between four major structures of control, and the corresponding worker attributes that a firm expects and rewards. In "simple" control, characteristic of entrepreneurial firms in which the owner exercises direct personal control over the labor force, no particular set of personality attributes is required, apart from a general deference to the employer's power. In "hierarchical" control, characteristic of firms too big for simple control, the principle of control is nevertheless similar: each boss, whether a foreman, supervisor, or manager, recreates in his shop the situation of the capitalist with entrepreneurial power. Each boss has full rights to fire and hire, evaluate and promote or demote, discipline, reward, and so forth. In effect, the negative sanctions are the more important; workers need to obey the boss and be sufficiently deferential. But the required behavior varies greatly according to the particular foreman and the conditions of employment.

Simple and hierarchical control structures are particularly characteristic of secondary labor markets, which include small manufacturing jobs, service and retail jobs, and temporary and typing-pool office work. In "technical" control, characteristic of firms in subordinate primary labor markets (automobile and steel plants, assembly-line production work, and machine-paced clerical work), machinery and the flow of work are designed so that the worker must follow the dictates of the machines and the industrial engineers. In technical control the system forces workers to respond to machine pacing, but beyond that it leaves workers relatively free from other demands on their behavior, besides punctuality, regularity, deference to supervisors, and the ability to work consistently at high speed in boring, monotonous jobs. In the fourth structure of control, however, "bureaucratic" control, characteristic of firms in the independent primary labor market, personal attributes are of considerable importance. Edwards delineates three principal areas of compliance or behavior within such firms: rules orientation; predictability and dependability; and internalization of the firm's goals and values.[41]

Edwards next attempts to link the segmentation of the labor markets to the segmentation of the labor process, arguing that the two are historically linked: each labor market structure corresponds to a particular form of labor control. Labor markets, in other words, "are segmented because they express a historical segmentation of the labor process; specifically, a distinct system of control inside the firm underlies each of the three market segments."[42] The fundamental basis of the segmentation of labor markets is to be found in the labor process, and not in the labor market itself.

The third and final step of Edwards's argument is to link two sets of issues: on the one hand, the nature of the job skills, behavioral requirements, experience, and other technical characteristics of the labor force, and on the other, schooling. He does so in a fashion very different from human capital approaches:

These characteristics are usually thought to create different types of labor (and so they do), and therefore to be the basis themselves of different treatment in the labor market. The relevance of these technical attributes, even their preeminence in certain cases, cannot be denied. However, the analysis presented here suggests that it is the system of control that creates the context within which experiences, training, schooling, skills, and other attributes assume their importance.[43]

It is now possible to see why experience and schooling do not explain secondary workers' income but do explain primary workers' income: secondary work is organized so as to minimize the need for experience and schooling, whereas primary work is organized so as to utilize these factors.[44] In effect, it is not wage competition but the nature of work that determines income.

All of this is more than plausible; yet Edwards's account is not without its difficulties. These, however, are less conceptual and theoretical than empirical. For example, he simply asserts, rather than demonstrates, the existence of tight structural links between the labor process and the labor market, the labor market and schooling. The task facing class analysis, then, is to demonstrate the existence of such structural linkage.

The general research program suggested by a class analysis of the linkage between schooling and economy is thus, in principle, quite straightforward. It consists of three analyses: (1) the structure of labor markets and the development of distinctive control structures within the labor process; (2) the organizational features of schooling that seemingly have structural links to the economy; and (3) the political and ideological mechanisms that link schooling to the economy.

In general, it is clear that the structural links between schooling and the economy have varied considerably over time. That schools play important functional economic roles in twentieth-century American capitalism, and that they are linked not to the economy in general but to labor markets and labor processes in particular, in no way implies that this was the case in the nineteenth century. Indeed, for much of the nineteenth century, schooling did not play an important role in allocating students to the labor force. (Nor was schooling so important for attaining status as in the twentieth century.) The chief role of schooling was to teach children the dominant bourgeois political and ideological practices of nineteenth-century America. It was only during the Progressive era that schooling was given, or took up (there is some dispute), the economic responsibility of training, certifying, and differentiating the labor force.[45]

The establishment of structural links between the economy and schooling during the Progressive era was not a simple affair. Moreover, we can assume that as the structure of control of the labor process and the nature of the labor market changed, so too the process of recruitment into the labor force changed. These considerations force attention to three features of the historical development of these relationships that class theory brings out. One is the development of capitalist labor markets (in which workers had nothing to sell but their labor power) that have subsequently become stratified by race, sex, ethnicity, geography, and education. A second is the transformation of the labor process, largely because of mechanization, from one with a great deal of craft control to one designed and controlled mainly by capital and very little by labor. The third consists of changes in the training and recruitment of the labor force: vocational education and vocational guidance, business and trade schools, employment agencies, union hiring halls, internal labor markets, and so on.

The analysis in each of these areas will need to be sensitive to variations by region, by industry, and even within particular industries. The aim of such analyses would be to describe and, if possible, to measure the development of simple, hierarchical, technical, and bureaucratic forms of control; the development of corresponding segmented labor markets; and the creation of internal labor markets, which Doeringer and Piore assert are characteristic of most large firms.[46]

Educational credentials are crucial mechanisms in internal labor markets, perhaps more significant in internal labor markets than in secondary or subordinate primary labor markets, though not more than in independent primary markets. In this connection, it is necessary to analyze the development of professional labor markets. It seems that educational credentials grew increasingly significant as professionals attempted to create and guard a separate labor market for their services. Magali Larson's account of how practitioners of medicine and law were able, since the nineteenth century, to create in effect a primary labor market for their services is exemplary. She treats professionalization as a process in which producers of special services sought to set up a controlled market for their expertise and "to translate one order of scarce resource—special knowledge and skills—into another—social and economic rewards." These goals were achieved by creating a monopoly of expertise in the market and a monopoly of status in the stratification system. These monopolies were based on a principle of legitimacy derived from socially recognized expertise; that is, on a system of education and credentialing. As the main function of professions shifted from the economic one of linking expertise and the market to the ideological one of justifying inequality of status, it became crucial to restrict education, the source of social legitimacy.[47]

In short, the theoretical core of the analysis of the structural relations between work and schooling is the analysis of the labor process and its transformation over the past 150 years or so. Not only did the demand for skilled labor change significantly, but also the character of the skills themselves. The continual reconstitution of the labor process upon new technical and social foundations generated a demand for new kinds of skills and new kinds of schooling. The skills were increasingly less technical than social and affective; they relied less on cognitive skills and judgments than on attitudes and behavior appropriate to the organization of the labor process. These social skills, and their internal differentiation, were increasingly necessary, since the specialized and mechanized labor processes placed a premium on social and affective traits. Productivity, and not just social control or protection of the prerogatives of capital, demanded a properly socialized and disciplined labor force.

Other lines of research also support the validity of this class analysis. One line concerns the structural relationships between education and inequality. Boudon, for example, analyzes the relationship between income, occupational structures, and education, and finds the key issue to be whether the expansion of school attendance and the decrease in educational inequality brings about a decrease in the inequality of social mobility. For Boudon the expansion of education is generally consistent with a highly stable mobility structure. This is because the growth in the number of high-status positions has not been commensurate with the growth in the supply of educationally qualified individuals, so that the occupational chances of persons at lower levels of education decrease as the demand for them is outstripped by the supply of educationally qualified persons. Those with the most education retain their traditional advantage, but for groups at intermediate levels of schooling, occupational opportunities decline. Potential gains in status, by means of increased schooling, are lost because of declining occupational opportunities. Consequently, the pattern of social mobility remains unchanged by increases in educational achievement.[48]

Although there is ample evidence that the problem occupying Boudon is real, there are difficulties in his explanation.[49] But rather than summarily dismissing this approach, we might consider other lines of argument. One such line is suggested by Ralph Collins. Whereas Boudon argues that there is no reason to expect an increase in social mobility or equality even if there is greater equality of education, Collins argues that greater educational achievement by less-educated groups will not increase social mobility if the more educated groups are able to maintain a relative advantage over the less educated.[50]

Collins, whose approach is based on a Weberian theory of status competition, proposes that competition and conflict between status groups generate an increased demand for schooling that has little or nothing to do with skill requirements in the economy. People seek education because they desire status and believe that education is the way to attain it. Low- and middle-status groups will thus seek to raise their relative position in the competition for status. And since educational qualifications both symbolize high status and are important in achieving it, these low- and middle-status groups attempt to gain higher educational credentials. But of course to the extent that such groups are able to increase their educational qualifications—for example, from five to seven years—high-status groups will seek to preserve their relatively privileged position by raising their own qualifications. In response, low-status groups will again attempt to close the gap, and so on in a continuous spiral.

The principal consequence of this spiral, according to Collins, has been to increase the supply of educated labor. This in turn has allowed employers continually to upgrade the educational requirements of jobs that to all intents and purposes have not changed in their objective skill requirements; thus the credentials gap noted by Berg.[51] Cognitive skills are produced in excess of the demand for them; an imbalance appears between the demands of the economy and the supply of educated labor. Because of this, the expansion of educational achievement does not necessarily decrease inequality of opportunity. High-status positions are still out of the reach of most low-status groups, despite levels of education that earlier would have entitled them to such positions. On such grounds one could explain the loss of faith in education suggested by the titles of two recent books, *The Case Against College* and *The Over-educated America*. By Collins's account, confidence in education as a means of social mobility has decreased with the inflation of educational credentials and with the growing belief by employers that job-specific training, rather than educational credentials, is the better way to acquire high-performance workers.*

To some extent, Collins's position can be supported by what Thurow calls a "job opportunity" model of the relationship between education, work, and inequality. For Thurow, the American economy is characterized less by wage competition (as theorists of human capital assume) than by "job competition." Instead of people looking for jobs, there are jobs looking for "suitable people." In a labor market based on job competition, an individual's income is determined by (1) his relative position in the labor queue and (2) the distribution of job opportunities in the economy. Although education can affect the shape of the labor queue, this does not mean that it changes the distribution of income, since this is a function, not only of the labor queue, but also of the distribution of job opportunities.[52]

This is a provocative argument, with important implications for understanding the function of education in the economy. Thurow summarizes the implications in this way: "In a labor market based on job competition, the function of education is not to confer skill and therefore increased productivity and higher wages on the worker; it is rather to certify his 'trainability' and to

---

*As a model to explain the relationship between education and income or mobility, Collins's model has much to recommend it. As an explanation of the expansion of schooling, however, it has difficulties. First of all, it does not explain the politics of educational expansion; that is, it does not explain the politics of compulsory education, neighborhood schooling, differentiated education, vocational education, testing, and the stratification of higher education. Recent research suggests that elites imposed many of these features on the educational system in an effort to ensure the incorporation of students into the various ideological practices of capitalist society and to develop institutions that would effectively channel students into a differentiated and stratified labor market. Second, Collins's theory of status competition seriously misconstrues the motives of working-class parents—and many middle-class parents—in sending their children to school, and it fails to account for such motives or explain their significance in different class cultures. For the most part these deficiencies are due to Collins's undifferentiated notion of market. Working-class and middle-class educational behavior was less a search for status than a rational response to a wage-labor society—education was widely believed to be first and foremost the key to economic survival. People send their children to school in order to enhance the market value, whatever its fluctuations, of their children's labor power. Educational behavior, then, cannot be understood independently of the structure of class relations, particularly in the wage-labor system. Finally, Collins's theory of status competition fails to consider the organizational features of schooling.

confer upon him a certain status by virtue of this certification. Jobs and higher income are then distributed on the basis of this certified status."[53]

In other words, the labor market is not primarily a mechanism for matching the demands for and supplies of different job skills (acquired in school, for example), but one for matching trainable individuals with training ladders: "Since most skills are acquired on the job, it is the demand for skills which creates the supply of job skills." Employers attempt to pick and train workers so as to generate the desired productivity with the least investment in training costs. For new workers and for entry-level jobs, it is the "background characteristics" of the workers—their age, sex, race, ethnicity, educational attainment, previous skills, and so forth—that form the basis of selection. The "national labor queue" thus depends on the distribution of these background characteristics and on employers' ranking of different background characteristics for the "screening" of individuals. Alterations in the distribution of education can influence the shape of the labor queue, but not necessarily the distribution of income, since this is also shaped, perhaps decisively, by the distribution of job opportunities.

At this point in the argument, however, both Thurow and Collins run into difficulty. In Collins's case, his theory of status competition simply does not provide any explanation for the distribution of job opportunities in the economy, and it fails to give an adequate account of the shape of the labor queue. Thurow has similar problems. A number of economists have observed that job opportunities are not homogeneous across the labor market, and indeed that different kinds of job opportunities cluster together in different, stratified labor markets: secondary, subordinate primary, and independent primary.[54]

Moreover, the returns to education within each labor market are strikingly different. Robert Buchele found, for example, that for workers in secondary labor markets (where jobs have low skills, low pay, no security, high turnover, and little chance of advancement), there was some slight benefit for each year of schooling achieved, but that they received no additional returns for any further schooling commenced after starting work. Paul Osterman calculated that the effect of education in increasing earnings was four to six times greater for workers in primary labor markets (those characterized by job security, relatively stable employment, higher wages, and extensive linkage between a worker's successive jobs) than in secondary markets. Similar results were obtained by David Gordon and by Carnoy and Rumberger. In subordinate primary labor markets (the traditional working-class jobs in unionized, mass-production industries) each year of schooling gives the average worker more than a 6 percent raise, whereas in the secondary market it is only about 1.5 percent. College education—at least for the first three years—also paid off in higher returns; but the highest returns were for secondary schooling. Finally, in independent primary markets (professional or quasi-professional work), each year of schooling increases the average worker's pay by 10 percent. Buchele estimated that each year of schooling after college generated an extra $2,000 a year in income for supervisory workers. Large returns were common at other levels of education as well, particularly college.[55]

There is convincing evidence, then, that labor markets are stratified according to the character of the job opportunities available, and that rates of return to education vary dramatically between labor markets. The fact that educational equalization has not been matched by income equalization might thus be explained in terms of the disproportionate concentration of educational improvement among workers in secondary labor markets.[56] And indeed it might be argued that no amount of educational upgrading in these markets could improve income distribution, since it is not the amount of education that determines the income, but the character of the job and the labor market.

The effects of labor market stratification on income distribution are compounded by labor market segmentation, the horizontal division of labor markets by race, sex, age, and ethnicity. These divisions in the labor force segment the national labor queue into different groups, with blacks, Hispanics, and women clustered into secondary labor markets in a pattern of ethnic stratification established in the nineteenth century. Returns to education for blacks, for example, are significantly lower than those for whites, even within the same market.[57]

This evidence concerning education and income provides further support for the class structuration analysis described earlier, and it indicates some additional lines of research that should be included in a comprehensive structural study of schooling and the economy. We now need to turn to the second and third parts of this analysis, concerning the organizational features of schooling that are linked to the economy and the political and ideological mechanisms that link schooling and the economy.

The Organization of Schooling

Two kinds of explanations dominate current research on the organizational characteristics of schooling that link schools to the economy. One emphasizes the socialization of children; and the other emphasizes various "allocation" processes within schooling.

The first approach specifies some organizational feature of the school that is said to be responsible for socializing children into the normative requirements of the world of work. Thus, in the late 1960's and early 1970's, a number of historians, following on Robert Merton's analysis of the bureaucratic personality, argued that the formal bureaucratic structures of education were responsible for the socialization of children. These structures represent the rationalization of the educational process, the centralization of control and supervision, the differentiation of functions, and the standardization of appointments and promotions.[58] In the most comprehensive of the studies in this area, David Tyack described the normative goals of the "administrative progressives" for schoolchildren: punctuality, regularity, attention, silence, obedience, and precision. He also attempted to specify the particular bureaucratic features of schooling that he believed were responsible for inculcating these norms: class grading, uniform courses of study, standardized written examinations, competition for grades, intense activity, and strict rules of behavior.[59]

Other scholars have pursued similar approaches to the organizational links between schooling and the economy. Robert Dreeben, for example, drawing on the work of Parsons, Inkeles, and Stinchcombe, attempted to link the ecological features of the school with normative requirements of modern occupational life—universalism, specificity, achievement, and independence.[60]

Dreeben stressed that the age-graded, relatively autonomous classrooms of a particular size, composition, differentiation, scheduling, and reward structure provide students with the social experiences necessary for learning occupational norms. Schools teach students to work for the sake of grades rather than because of their personal emotional relationship with the teacher. They teach that performance and competence—what you do rather than what you are—are the basis of rewards and status. Because classrooms are large collectivities, children experience impersonality. Yearly promotions, staff specialization, and the large size of schools systematically provide students with lessons in forming and breaking transitory relationships. This helps form the ability to distinguish between positions and persons. Schools reward merit and achievement with extrinsic rewards, grades, and promotions. And school experiences teach children to distinguish between superordination and subordination, that is, between authority and obedience. As Dreeben suggests, "Schooling, insofar as it entails repeated and systematic variation of persons (teachers, pupils), situations (school grades, class size), and areas of conduct, provides a setting in which different types of subordination with their corresponding principles of legitimacy can be experienced."[61]

This is a powerful and useful model of the organization of schooling, and one whose arguments find strong support in the writings of other observers. Nevertheless, it has difficulties, and requires some modification and extension. One approach that attempts to overcome some of these difficulties has been outlined by Bowles and Gintis. Like Dreeben, they argue that the principal structural connection between school and work is in the organization of schooling. But they also insist that schools systematically vary in what they call the social relations of education, and also in the normative orientation toward work that is generated. Bowles and Gintis claim that the major aspects of educational organization replicate the relationships of dominance and subordinancy that exist in the economic sphere. Specifically, "the social relations of education—the relationships between administrators and teachers, teachers and students, students and students, and students and their work—replicate the hierarchical division of labor." Students, as a consequence of the social relations of

education, are socialized into the appropriate personality characteristics, habits, and modes of self-presentation required by modern bureaucratic and hierarchically organized enterprises. Most
schools, Bowles and Gintis argue, teach the kind of qualities and
personality traits essential for performing low- and middle-level
jobs: obedience, punctuality, respect, orderly work habits, the
ability to follow instruction. Schooling that differs from this pattern in its social relations is for the most part engaged in "soft
socialization": the production of workers for upper-level jobs
whose main requirement is the "internationalization of norms."
Bowles and Gintis thus argue that systematic differences exist in
the social relations of education, and that these differences play
an important role in the intergenerational reproduction of inequality.[62]

So far so good. But Bowles and Gintis go on to claim, rashly,
that this correspondence mechanism is the only important link
between work and schooling. They stress that it is the *form* of the
social relations of education that is crucial to the socialization of
future workers.

The heart of the process is to be found not in the *content* of the educational encounter—or the process of the information transfer—but in
the form: the social relations of the educational encounter. These corres-
pond closely to the social relations of dominance, subordination, and
motivation in the economic sphere. Through the educational encounter,
individuals are induced to accept the degree of powerlessness with which
they will be faced as mature workers.[63]

This is somewhat exaggerated. Though Bowles and Gintis present evidence of a statistical correspondence between the personal attributes required for success in work and in school, the
evidence is thin, at best only suggestive, and certainly not conclusive. Furthermore, they neglect linking mechanisms other than
the correspondence between the social relations of production
and education. Other educational processes also need to be considered. Basil Bernstein has developed a provocative theory, for
instance, that the form of the relations between curriculum,
pedagogy, and evaluation embody important ideological mes-
sages, educational "codes," that are structurally linked to production codes. Bernstein also argues that a historical shift from

"collection" to "integrated" educational codes has occurred because of changes in the division of labor that have affected skill requirements in modern industry.[64] A number of researchers have pointed to what Pierre Bourdieu called the "cultural capital" of schooling—its normative order of symbols, rituals, knowledge, meanings, values, practices, and relationships—as a crucial mechanism of the cultural reproduction of class relations.[65]

Bowles and Gintis seem to have something similar in mind when they discuss "types of personal demeanor, modes of self-presentation, self-image, and social class identification." But they limit their argument to the link between "the structure of social relations of education" and "job adequacy."[66] The issue is much more complex than this; and it is simply too reductive to view the cultural capital of the school or the social relations of education as directly determining what Paul Willis calls "the subjective and cultural formation of particular kinds of labor power."[67] As Willis's own study demonstrates, many working-class students contest the official normative order of the school and attempt to create their own counter school culture. Schools may well articulate and legitimize particular values and behavior; but it by no means follows that these are internalized as specific personalities.

That students create their own school cultures is no great surprise—Hollingshead, Coleman, Stinchcombe, and many others have shown this. What is new and provocative about Willis's work is that he shows schooling to be less a process of imposing meanings than a cultural contest, a process of negotiation between different orders of meaning, rooted in the clash between the cultural capital of the school and the process of (counter) cultural formation among working-class children. It is not so much that working-class children are socialized into the norms and behavior compatible with the social relations of production; rather, out of an effort to resist official labels and meanings and to create a counterculture of fraternity and self-worth, they create a culture that feeds them right into working-class jobs—a process of "self-induction" that is as tragic as it is poignant. Schools, then, are less institutions of socialization than arenas of cultural conflict, negotiation, and class reproduction. As well as any study yet published, Willis's book exposes the layers of cultural and symbolic contests within schools, and lays bare how economic and social pressures are transformed and lived out in schools, not simply mirrored or reproduced. It is in this sense and this sense only that we can say that schools are *hegemonic* institutions, and that the process of class reproduction is both an economic and a cultural phenomenon.[68]

For sociologists and ethnographers analyzing the structural linkage between schooling and work, these approaches, each of which stresses the socialization of students as the crucial link, present no methodological difficulties. This is not so for historians, who have no way to demonstrate that children in past years were in fact socialized into the patterns of thought and behavior intended by educators, or, assuming that such socialization did take place, what particular organizational features of schooling were responsible. This methodological difficulty does not amount to a theoretical difficulty for socialization approaches to the relationship between work and schooling, but it does force attention to alternative (although not necessarily incompatible) approaches.

One such approach is called "allocation theory" by sociologists. Allocation theorists claim that adult success is assigned to individuals on the basis of the type and duration of schooling received, whatever they may have learned in school. Schooling is viewed as a set of instructional rules that classify and allocate individuals for positions in society. Thus schooling *symbolically* redefines graduates as possessing particular qualities and skills as a result of attendance at school or college, and this occurs independently of whether there have been any *actual* changes in competence, skill, or values.[69]

From this perspective, the importance of school organization is that it legitimates the claim of students to having had particular kinds of education. The major source of organizational diversity and change in schools is the symbolic conceptions or definitions of graduates that schools wish to project to their clients, such as employers. The linkage between schooling and work is to be found in the legitimation of particular student characteristics, rather than in any actual internalization of specific behavior or attitudes. The organization of schooling is thus approached less as a structure of socialization processes than as a mechanism of stratification, a set of sorting and selecting processes that classify students and allocate or distribute them among different curriculum tracks and occupations. As Jencks suggests, "Schools serve primarily as selection and certification agencies, whose job is to measure and label people, and only secondarily as socialization agencies, whose job is to change people."[70]

Both the socialization and the allocation models of the organizational processes linking schooling to the economy contain much of value. The question is not either-or; both are required, for each explains different, but interconnected, facets of the relationship. Allocation models stress the connection between labor markets and the stratification and labeling processes within the school. Socialization models stress, in various ways, the connection between the school itself and the labor process. Of course, the relative importance of the two mechanisms will often vary at different times and in different labor markets. But this is a matter of empirical investigation, not of a priori theorizing.

The Mechanisms Linking Schooling and the Economy

It is one thing to delineate the structural linkage between schooling and work, and entirely another to determine the mechanism that creates and sustains the links. For neoclassical economists, and those sociologists and others influenced by them, economic and educational change are mediated by the mechanisms of the human capital market. In the neoclassical model, educational change, whether organizational innovation or increased school attendance, is viewed as a market-based response to changes in the demand for skilled labor that flow from technological change and occupational specialization.

The first difficulty faced by this theory can easily be anticipated: its assumptions about the demand side of the process, as we have seen, are simply erroneous. But this difficulty in itself is not sufficient to destroy the argument that market processes govern economic and social change. A much greater difficulty for market-based explanations is the supply-side process. By and large, people do not send their children to school simply out of a conviction that education is economically beneficial, although certainly this is an important consideration.

Even more seriously, organizational innovation in schools is not just a market response to economic change. In a very fundamental sense, educational changes are also the product of cultural, ideological, and political conflicts in the society. The major reforms of the Progressive era—for example, compulsory education, differentiated education, centralized educational administration, and child-centered pedagogy—were not simply "economic" responses to "economic" changes (and certainly not to the economic changes stipulated by modernization theory). They were also political responses to events that were in part political in nature. Schools, moreover, like other large organizations, encompass "competitive," "incompatible," or "contradictory" processes and structures. There is tension between the principles for recruiting teachers, students, and administrators; between vocational goals and citizenship training; between the need to motivate and the need to discipline; and between the competing authority of teachers, administrators, interest groups, and parents.[71] Organizational development is more a political process and less the outcome of some bureaucratic imperative.[72]

It is for these reasons that schooling ought not to be approached as an economic institution operating in a competitive market. Schools function, it seems, to some extent independently of the market system. They are not an economic institution in the same sense as, say, a firm, a bank, or a labor market. The main reason for this is that the structural and institutional links between the economy and schooling contain political and ideological mechanisms not under business control or some other direct economic influence. Schooling does not respond to economic changes in any simple fashion, and certainly not automatically, as modernization theory predicts.

Thus the notions of "functional fit" and "invisible hand" are inappropriate for describing the relationship between schooling and the economy. "The independent internal dynamics of the two systems (work and schooling)," Bowles and Gintis point out, "present the ever-present possibility of a significant mismatch arising between the economy and education."[73] Consequently, they argue, important "contradictions" or noncorrespondences between the economy and schooling frequently develop.

To disqualify functionalist logic as a historical explanation, however, is not to deny that important functional relations exist between work and schooling. Though a particular configuration of workplaces and organizational innovations may be "functional" for capitalism, the configuration is nevertheless contingent on various political and ideological processes. It is all too easy, as Ira Katznelson suggests, "to confuse the difference between the claim that capitalism and schooling have a functional relationship with the claim that schooling was the required institution to perform a given function for the reproduction of the system."[74] There are few better reasons why the relationship between the economy and schooling should be studied historically.

If the human capital market does not govern the relationship between economic and social change, what kinds of political or ideological processes do? Interest group pluralism? Class determinism? Class conflict? Ideological hegemony? Professionalism? The general theoretical literature on the form of political processes in America is extensive and unsettled. This larger debate is reflected in writings on educational politics.[75]

For a variety of reasons, which I have outlined elsewhere, most current analyses of educational change are unsatisfactory.[76] The most promising approach is a model proposed by Bowles and Gintis. On a day-to-day basis, they argue, educational politics reflects a pluralist politics of interest-group conflicts and ethnocultural antagonisms, but within an economic and political framework shaped by the effects of capital accumulation. Occasionally, when the schools appear inadequate to employers or reformers or when social disorder threatens, the political process changes. A politics of pluralist accommodation is then replaced by a politics of structural change, as reformers or educational elites try to realign the school with the needs of the economy or to resolve pressing social and political conflicts.

The demand for vocational education during the Progressive era, for example, was a political and ideological response, primarily of efficiency-minded educators and business groups, to the transformation of the labor process and the development of segmented labor markets. The outcome was a triumph for the advocates of vocational and differentiated education. It was thus a political triumph for those advocating a close calibration of public schooling with the labor process and the labor market, or in the terms of class analysis, advocating the structuration of American education around the "class principle."[77]

Such a model of educational politics is simple and elegant. With some modification, notably the inclusion of ideological processes as a form of class conflict rather than as a reflection of economic interest, it would be a cogent and accurate explanation of educational politics in America. There is no omnipotent invisible hand of the human capital kind, nor a functional fit that Parsonians imagine, nor a class determinism that social-control historians worry about. There are only concrete political struggles, sometimes assuming a class character and sometimes not, between groups of people with different goals and interests reacting to different circumstances.

These political processes that link schooling to the economy are of course also linked to the larger political processes of American history. It is impossible to analyze educational politics adequately without locating them in the historical context of industrial capitalism. Two examples illustrate this problem. One was the tension that the development of industrial capitalism created between the promise of republican independence and the reality of wage employment and economic dependency. This tension was exacerbated by the profound impact of industrialization on American opportunity structures; the old equation of hard work and economic independence was upset. The result was a redefinition of economic success, from the old republican idea of yeoman and entrepreneurial independence to an ideology of status mobility. Not only did the meaning of success change, but also the means, from the virtues of frugality and industry to the personality traits of sociability, charm, and will power. The visions of Franklin, Jefferson, and Paine gave way to the dicta of Horatio Alger and Russell Conwell, and these in turn to the pat formulas of Norman Vincent Peale and Dale Carnegie.[78]

A second example is a variety of tensions at the heart of liberal social theory: tension between possessive individualism and the legacy of an eighteenth-century intellectual tradition based on compassion, sentiment, and sympathy; between self-interest and republican virtue; between individual achievement and social equality; between utility and morality.[79] Some of the products of these tensions are crucial to an adequate understanding of the public philosophy of American education: the transmutation of avarice from a vice into a virtue; the redefinition of equality as equality of opportunity; the reduction of equality of opportunity into equality of educational opportunity; the metamorphosis of democracy into meritocracy; and the birth of "contest" mobility and "expanding universalism."*

Conclusion

In this essay I have argued that the role of education in America has been shaped by the forces of industrial capitalism as part of a broad transformation of American society. This transformation has involved the creation of a market in labor; radical changes in work, opportunity structures, and mobility paths; the restless and ceaseless movement of people; the stratification of labor markets; new ideological formations; and new patterns of institutional alignments. As a consequence, new structural links have been forged between schooling and work. At the same time, schooling has increasingly mediated the relationship between family background and occupational attainment.

It is important to emphasize that the connections between schooling, the labor process, and the labor market developed only over many decades, and to the accompaniment of considerable political conflict. For many years after the first appearance of capitalism as a coherent cultural configuration, schooling was not linked in any structural sense to the labor process or the labor market. For much of the nineteenth century, schooling grew because of the particular ideological commitments of Americans, and it served largely political and ideological functions. It was not until the late nineteenth century and the Progressive era that

---

*Yet despite the fact that meritocratic ideology has been the single most important source of the legitimation of inequality in America, no systematic study has so far appeared on meritocratic ideology or on the rise of education as the principal institutional means of legitimating social authority and inequality. For studies of related issues, see Samuel Haber, *Efficiency and Uplift: Scientific Management in the Progressive Era, 1890–1920* (Chicago, 1964); Thomas L. Haskell, *The Emergence of Professional Social Science: The American Social Science Association and the Nineteenth-Century Crisis of Authority* (Urbana, Ill., 1976); Burton J. Bledstein, *The Culture of Professionalism: The Middle Class and the Development of Higher Education* (New York, 1976); and Loren Baritz, *The Servants of Power* (Middletown, Conn., 1961).

schooling was linked structurally to the economy. The key to this linkage was the continued transformation of the labor process (the shift to real subordination), the development of stratified labor markets, and the vocationalizing of education; these have been the focus of this paper.

Of course, the structuration of education and capitalism includes far more than the creation of structural links between work and schooling. It also includes the "modernization" of inequality and incompetence; the articulation of ideologies of legitimation; the growing significance of "cultural capital" and processes of cultural reproduction; and the growing importance of such institutions as vocational guidance, employment agencies, private trade, technical, and business schools, colleges, and professional schools in the transition from school to work. I have not attempted to analyze these issues, or to discuss how education and the mechanisms that link schooling to the family and to work came to play a major role in status attainment. These are all aspects of the structuration of schooling that a comprehensive account of the impact of capitalism on American education could hardly neglect.

Finally, I have not attempted to document the recurrent tensions in American history between the political purposes of schooling, inherited from the Revolution and the common-school reform movement, and the unremitting pressure of the market conception of schooling. This conception has led to the demand of business groups for a certain training and differentiation of workers; to the effort by parents of all classes, creeds, and races to use education as a means of improving their children's chances in the labor market; and to the recent career-education movement, which has sought to inculcate the work ethic in children and to provide them with entry-level skills.

These are all rational responses to the market economy. But as some educators recognized during the Progressive era, these developments also threatened the primary political purpose of schooling: the development of republican citizens. The Progressive period was in fact the second time the great ideological conflict of American education was fought out between these two principles of social and educational organization. There were compromises, to be sure, the chief of which was the abandonment of the effort to establish dual systems of secondary education and the acceptance of the comprehensive high school. This compromise has of course been avoided in higher education, where a highly stratified system has appeared, helped in no small measure by the Carnegie Commission on Higher Education.

By 1920 vocationalism had triumphed. If the triumph of the market in politics, as in the economy, left nothing but the pursuit of self-interest; if in culture it left nothing but narcissism and the psychedelic bazaar; if in human relations nothing but the cash nexus, in education it has increasingly left nothing but vocationalism. It is this forging of new institutional alignments between the economy and schooling that a class analysis of American education can make intelligible.

The Historical Development of

Black Vocational Education

JAMES D. ANDERSON

Introduction

The original intent of this essay was to explore past research on
black vocational education and guidance, to examine the relation
of education to work, and to develop an agenda for future research. Preliminary research, however, revealed that there are
few secondary sources to appraise. There are, to be sure, some
writings on the Hampton-Tuskegee program of industrial education; most are concerned with the educational ideas of Samuel
Armstrong and Booker T. Washington and the critique of this
form of industrial education by W. E. B. DuBois. But even in this
area, the focus of nearly all the published writings on black
vocational education, it is rare to find a systematic analysis of
institutional practices that affords a view of the actual vocational
education experiences of black students. On black vocational
education in general, Clyde Hall's *Black Vocational, Technical,
and Industrial Arts Education* (1973) is the only published monograph that attempts to chronicle the entire subject. But it is not
really a history of black vocational education. Rather, it gathers
bits and pieces of information on the founding dates, the first
leaders, and the sources of financial support for hundreds of black
secondary schools, normal schools, land-grant institutions, and
colleges that offered any technical or industrial training. It is, in

fact, a directory. Some unpublished dissertations offer good historical insights, but they are uniformly specialized, and do not offer a comprehensive view of black vocational education over time.

Accordingly, this essay sketches the development of black vocational education from the mid-nineteenth century to the present. Vocational education is here defined broadly, to include training for specific trades, instruction in work behavior and work attitudes, and vocational guidance programs. First, I look at the early and disappointing efforts, from 1830 to 1860, to establish black trade and technical schools. Second, I discuss the ideas and practices of the post-Civil War industrial normal schools that dominated the field of black vocationalism from the late 1860's to the turn of the century. Third, I turn to the "1890 Black Land-Grant Institutions," tracing their policies and practices to 1930. Fourth, I trace the rise of black vocational guidance during the Great Depression, the analysis going up to the Second World War era. Fifth, I conclude with a discussion of recent trends in education and unemployment among black youth, and with some suggestions for future research.

Early Efforts for Black Trade and Industrial Education, 1830–60

The historian Benjamin Brawley, in a short pamphlet, showed that black leaders and white antislavery leaders were interested in establishing black trade and industrial schools as early as the eighteenth century.[1] This interest increased significantly with the emergence of militant abolitionism and the Negro Convention Movement in the 1830's. In 1829 the black leader Samuel Cornish, then editor of *The Rights of All* in New York, suggested that Northern Afro-American communities support "one general college embracing all the mechanic arts, with a thorough classical education." There was some discussion of Cornish's proposal, but it was not until white abolitionists proposed an actual location for the college and guaranteed initial funding that the endeavor was seriously undertaken. In June 1831 black male activists from the major Northern urban centers assembled in Philadelphia for the First Annual Convention of the Free People of Color. At this convention, Simeon S. Jocelyn, William Lloyd Garrison, Arthur Tappan, Benjamin Lundy, Thomas Shipley, and Charles Pierce came before the delegates to propose the establishment of a Negro "Manual Labor College" in New Haven, Connecticut. Black leaders supported this proposal so that black youth, "in connection with a scientific education," could acquire a "useful mechanical and agricultural profession." After Tappan committed $1,000 to the project, estimated to cost $20,000, plans were made for blacks and whites to raise the balance jointly. Cornish was selected to coordinate the black fund-raising efforts.

Early on, all seemed auspicious that the black Manual Labor College would receive general support from Northern white communities and prove itself a success within a short time. However, New Haven whites, foreshadowing future opposition to black trade and industrial education, "were as one in their protest" against the plan, and forced the initial project to be abandoned. In 1833, still attempting to realize the goal of a black mechanical and agricultural school, black and white abolitionists sought to transfer their resources to an academy in Canaan, Connecticut. But in Canaan, the white townspeople demolished the building that was erected to start a black manual labor college; again, the plan was squelched almost before it began. This hostility in both New Haven and Canaan surprised the black and white proponents of the college. But the project was considered "to be of too great importance to be abandoned without further efforts being made to effect it," especially since Cornish had already collected nearly $3,000.

Whatever the reason for the opposition, the supporters of the college seemed convinced that such a plan could be realized, and the idea persisted through the 1840's and 1850's. At the national black convention of 1847, a committee on education reported in favor of "a collegiate institution, on the manual labor plan," and a committee of 25 was appointed to carry out the idea. This plan was also abandoned. Still, at the 1853 Annual Convention of the Free People of Color, which met in Rochester, New York, there was a renewed interest in a mechanical and agricultural college. The efforts were led by some of the best-known black leaders of the era, such as Frederick Douglass, James W. C. Pennington, James McCune Smith, Alexander Crummell, Martin R. Delany, and William C. Nell. These leaders and their white colleagues, however, were never able to overcome Northern white resistance, and the idea of a black manual labor college was eventually discarded altogether.[2]

Although no black manual labor college was established in the pre-Civil War era, the early campaign for black trade and industrial training underscored problems that have characterized black vocational education throughout the nineteenth century and into the twentieth. The campaign was shaped in peculiar ways by a pervasive racism in the apprenticeship system. Frederick Douglass discussed the issue in 1853:

Prejudice against the free colored people in the United States has shown itself nowhere so invincible as among mechanics. The farmer and the professional man cherish no feeling so bitter as that cherished by these. The latter would starve us out of the country entirely. At this moment I can more easily get my son into a lawyer's office to study law than I can into a blacksmith's shop to blow the bellows and to wield the sledgehammer. Denied the means of learning useful trades, we are pressed into the narrowest limits to obtain a livelihood.

Such labor-market discrimination placed the black school in the impossible position of attempting to elevate blacks to skilled jobs in the workplace by offering them vocational opportunities that were denied them in the white-controlled apprenticeship system.

To be sure, blacks did not see the vocational school as a panacea for labor-market discrimination. Douglass, for instance, was well aware of the school's inability to remodel the social order. Reflecting on the employment problems of well-educated black youth, he asked: "Can the daughters find schools to teach or the sons find books to keep? Do abolitionists give them employment in their stores or counting-houses?" In fact, educated blacks usually could not find employment in fields for which they were trained. The situation was the same, if not worse, for those pursuing the skilled trades. Yet Douglass, insisting that blacks had to "learn trades or starve," supported the manual labor college plan as an alternative to the racist apprenticeship system in the skilled trades. He and other black leaders were not relying on vocational education as a solution to labor-market discrimination. Primarily, they sought to prevent the educational system from operating under the philosophy that blacks had a special place in the economy and, more importantly, that it was the purpose of education to keep them in that special place. On the contrary, they urged the schools to act on the assumption that it was better for black youth to be trained for skilled work and not get it than for them to have the opportunity arise suddenly and not be prepared. Further, a well-trained black working class would more forcefully direct attention to labor-market discrimination, whereas a poorly trained one would reinforce strongly the myths of black inefficiency.[3]

A manual labor college or trade school, therefore, would not so much solve labor-market problems as make them apparent. Ample vocational education opportunities, it was believed, would make unequal apprenticeship opportunities appear even more unjust and irrational. These views, of course, overestimated the ability of schools to depart from trends in the dominant social and economic institutions. The schools merely transmitted the racism that existed in the political system and the economy. Thus the sort of racism in the apprenticeship system was also reflected in vocational training opportunities. There has not been a single trade or technical school of even modest quality established for blacks, in the nineteenth century or later, that has had the promise of training a cadre of skilled black workers. Several mid-nineteenth-century black institutions were identified as manual labor schools, but none of them offered viable trade and technical training programs. Vocational training at the Peterboro Manual Labor School in New York and Emlen Institute in Ohio was mainly unskilled toil that enabled students to support themselves while attending school. The Philadelphia Institute for Colored Youth was given a donation in 1837 for the establishment of a department of mechanic arts and agriculture. But the Quaker board of trustees did not act on the idea until 1889, when a new industrial building was erected to offer four-year courses in bricklaying, carpentry, printing, tailoring, and shoemaking. The institute remained predominantly a literary school, and only a few students were instructed in the industrial department, which lasted from 1889 to 1902.[4]

There was little chance that mid-nineteenth-century black educators could manipulate schools so as to counter the racist apprenticeship system. Still, they saw some merit in their own fight to achieve black occupational advancement through education. Ideologically, the campaign to drive a wedge between vocational opportunities in schools and those in the workplace, however unrealistic, seemed worthwhile. Schools, by denying black youth good vocational training opportunities, might rationalize and make acceptable the intolerable contradictions generated by the racism of the workplace. If schools channeled black youth into "their place," labor-market racism could be disguised as an educational problem, and this would draw attention away from the basic source of black inequality in the labor market. Black educators and leaders, therefore, attempted to forfend against such a development by forcing the schools to provide mechanical and technical training that could not be obtained by apprenticeship. This they failed to accomplish. Black educators and leaders began to comprehend the improbability of separating schooling from the dominant values and trends in the nation's economic mainstream. Racism did not stop at the schoolhouse door, but pervaded every aspect of the educational system; and opportunity in vocational education was no more liberal than in apprenticeship.

The Industrial Normal School

Immediately after the Civil War, when the campaign for black public education was launched on a grand scale, a new variety of industrial education was emphasized in privately supported normal schools. Between the founding of Hampton Institute in 1868 and the death of Booker T. Washington in 1915, Northern businessmen-philanthropists and Southern white school reformers came to recognize "Negro industrial training" as the appropriate form of education to assist in bringing racial order, political stability, and material prosperity to the South. In their opinion, the model most suitable for the socialization of the newly emancipated black people, and hence for the amelioration of Southern racial and political conflict, was being developed by Samuel Chapman Armstrong at Hampton Normal and Agricultural Institute in Hampton, Virginia.

The historiography is most confused on the social purposes of the normal-school model of industrial education. Some, like Clyde Hall, contend that Armstrong and his staff "wanted to see the skilled artisan traditions continued that existed among blacks during slavery." Others, like Allen W. Jones and Donnie D. Bellamy, see the chief aim of the Hampton-Tuskegee model as that of helping black farmers turn their labor into assets for themselves. Still others, like August Meier, emphasize on the one hand the moral aspects of normal-school industrial education and on the other hand its value in preparing black youth for "lives as small individualistic entrepreneurs."[5]

The traditional emphasis on Hampton as an agricultural and mechanical school has obscured the fact that it was founded and maintained primarily to train black teachers for the American South. Hampton did not even offer trade certificates until 1895, and then only to a tiny minority of its students. In 1900, for instance, only 45 of Hampton's 656 students were enrolled in the Trade Department. From the school's inception until well into the twentieth century, it was devoted almost exclusively to teacher training. Indeed, the intention to become a teacher was a condition for admission at Hampton in the early years. Not surprisingly, between 1872 and 1890, 604 of Hampton's 723 graduates became teachers. The pattern was basically the same for other black normal schools, which abounded in the post-Civil War South. Tuskegee Institute and smaller industrial normal schools, such as Snow Hill (Alabama) Normal and Industrial Institute, Fort Valley (Georgia) High and Industrial School, and the Utica (Mississippi) Normal and Industrial Institute, were based on the Hampton model of industrial education.[6]

According to this model, black industrial teachers would exemplify and transmit the Puritan work ethic to the Afro-American working class. Hence a sharp line divided the manual labor college idea of the 1830's from the post-Civil War industrial training curriculum. The manual labor college plan proposed to train workers for specific trades and technical occupations that blacks could not readily enter as unskilled laborers. The industrial normal school program was aimed primarily at instilling the "proper" work attitudes, especially among the masses of unskilled black workers. Indeed, the normal school advocates expected the majority of black workers to remain in the South as unskilled domestic and agricultural laborers. From this point of view, there was one major problem: ex-slaves had the "wrong"

attitude toward work. Blacks, the industrial normal school proponents argued, had inherited from slavery a proclivity for extended leisure that prevented their seeing steady, routinized work
as a moral duty. The white slavocracy, so the story went, had for
generations scorned work as beneath its dignity, and Afro-
Americans, when they became free, adopted a similar prejudice in
their struggle for recognition and self-respect. This attitude
blinded many black workers to the dignity and possibilities for
self-improvement in the simple, manual tasks in which the majority of them were engaged.

This was the more ingenious and polite version of the lazy-
shiftless-Negro tale. At other times, however, industrial normal
school advocates were not so polite. In 1891 Armstrong maintained that of the eight million or more blacks, "a large third, say
three millions . . . are a 'low down' shiftless class . . . lazy . . .
living from hand to mouth . . . grossly immoral." The majority of
the others, he believed, had not internalized the right attitudes
toward work. Hence, "The Negroes who are to form the working
classes of the South must be taught not only to do their work well,
but to know what their work means."[7]

But first it was necessary to condition the ideas, personality,
and attitudes of the teachers who were expected to model and
transmit the Hampton-Tuskegee values among the Afro-American
working class. For Armstrong, Hampton students would be properly drilled in the "habits of living and labor . . . in order that
graduates may be qualified to teach others these important lessons of life." He considered hard labor the first principle of
civilized life, and he drilled Hampton students in manual labor
routines so that the teacher-graduates could inculcate industri-
ousness in Southern black schoolchildren. "If you are the right
sort of man, you will engage in any sort of labor, and dignify it,"
declared Armstrong. Indeed, "A man had better work for nothing
and find himself than to spend his time in idling and loafing."
Therefore Armstrong encouraged blacks to "Plow, hoe, ditch,
grub; do anything rather than nothing." Routine and repetitive
manual labor activities were developed at Hampton and other
industrial normal schools in order to condition teacher-graduates
to serve as missionaries of the Puritan work ethic in Southern
black communities.[8]

Hampton's industrial education system comprised three inter-related areas: the academic program, the manual labor system, and a strict social discipline code. The academic program, aside from preparing students to teach common school, was designed to inculcate prospective teachers with the proper attitudes toward work. It was believed, however, that such attitudes could only be learned in actual work processes. Hence the manual labor system was developed, in order to mold character through steady, hard labor. The daily discipline routine served to control the entire 24 hours of each day; "only thus can old ideas and ways be pushed out and new ones take their place," said Armstrong. The heart of Hampton's industrial education program was established in 1879 when Armstrong created the Night School. It opened with 36 students, who were required to labor ten hours a day, six days a week, eleven months a year, for two years. They attended academic classes for two hours in the evening. Two years of work and night school were equivalent to one year of the normal-school course. In the last two years of normal-school work the students attended classes four days and worked two days each week. The Night School came to represent the industrial normal-school idea. By 1893, 305 of Hampton's 541 black students were enrolled in the Night School. Tuskegee Institute, founded by Hampton graduate Booker T. Washington in 1881, replicated the night school concept, and other black industrial normal schools patterned themselves on the Hampton-Tuskegee model.[9]

Hampton's student-teachers were chiefly farm laborers, domestic servants, and mill hands. "Much of the labor that goes into our industries," reported Armstrong, "is neither skilled labor nor apprentice labor, but is made up of the great body of unskilled laborers who come here to work a year or two at whatever work the school may be able to give them." Male students worked in the sawmill, on the farm, in the kitchens as dishwashers and pantry boys, in the dining rooms as waiters, and in the cottages and smaller buildings as houseboys. Female students received even less diverse "training," and were encouraged to do little except "plain sewing, plain washing and ironing, scrubbing, mending, etc." In the words of the Hampton faculty, normal-school students learned "how to work steadily and regularly, to attend promptly at certain hours to certain duties," and they "gained new ideas of the value of manual labor." Instruction in work attitudes was the main purpose of the Hampton normal-school industrial education, not the training of students for specific occupations in skilled trades. As Armstrong put it, "We do not mean to say that much is not learned by every faithful student in these departments; he or she will be a better cook, laundress, or farmer, and surely much-needed lessons in promptness and thoroughness are inculcated, but still the object in view is not to teach a trade but to get the work done." [10]

After 1895 a small minority of Hampton students did receive trade certificates in such practical work as carpentry, woodworking, bricklaying, harness making, blacksmithing, and wheel-wrighting. This small number of artisan-graduates was not viewed as any attempt to change significantly the status of black workers in the labor market. Indeed, the vocational courses at Hampton were consistent with the occupations that claimed the largest number of black male artisans: milling, carpentry, masonry, blacksmithing. More important, however, the Hampton program was aimed ultimately at teaching the proper work attitudes to the large number of unskilled agricultural and domestic workers. At the turn of the century, 53.7 percent of black workers were agricultural laborers and 33 percent were in domestic and personal service. Industrial normal-school advocates were not only content with the overall position of black wage earners; they considered it necessary for the development of the Southern economy. The aim of training servants, for instance, was widely advertised. Industrial normal-school student-teachers were taught "proper" work attitudes by having to do unskilled work so that they would have no problems in teaching the "dignity of labor" ethic to children of farm laborers and servants. In contrast to the manual labor college idea of the 1830's, the post-Civil War industrial normal school had the underlying philosophy that black youth should limit their career choices to those occupations in which large numbers of blacks were then engaged, and to eschew those in which only a few or no blacks were found. [11]

Not surprisingly, the industrial normal-school model spread rapidly across the South between 1880 and 1900. In addition to such well-known normal schools as Tuskegee, Penn Normal, Snow Hill, and Utica, scores of kindred schools were modeled on the Hampton program. Schofield Normal and Industrial School and Voorhees Industrial School in South Carolina; St.

Paul Normal and Industrial School, Manassas Industrial School, and Christianburg Industrial Institute in Virginia; High Point Normal and Industrial School in North Carolina; and Okalona Industrial College in Mississippi were among the many small industrial normal schools emphasizing teacher training through manual labor. This was the form of industrial education that most Southern black students experienced. The Hampton program was adopted as the normal-school model, and a watered-down version became the standard curriculum in elementary and secondary schools, especially in rural areas. In the early twentieth century the majority of Southern rural black students attended elementary and secondary schools based on the Hampton-Tuskegee manual labor idea.[12]

The Black Land-Grant Institutions, 1890–1930

In 1862 the United States Congress passed the first Morrill Act, which provided for the establishment of a land-grant institution in each state to educate citizens in the fields of agriculture, mechanic arts, home economics, and "scientific and classical studies." In the South, however, blacks were generally not permitted to attend the institutions first established under the Morrill Act of 1862; although the federal law provided for separate but equal facilities, only Mississippi and Kentucky established institutions for blacks under the first Morrill Act, and only Alcorn University was designated "land-grant." To overcome this problem, a second Morrill Act was passed in 1890, specifically to support land-grant institutions "for the education of colored students in agricultural and mechanic arts."[13] Thus the black land-grant institutions are today referred to as "the 1890 Land-Grant Institutions."*

Although these institutions were set up to train black students in mechanical and agricultural vocations, the Southern states, when they actually responded to the federal guidelines, designed

---

*The black land-grant institutions are: Alcorn State University, South Carolina State College, University of Arkansas-Pine Bluff, Alabama Agricultural and Mechanical University, Prairie View Agricultural and Mechanical University, Southern University, Virginia State College, Kentucky State University, University of Maryland-Eastern Shore, Florida Agricultural and Mechanical University, Delaware State College, North Carolina Agricultural and Technical University, Fort Valley State College, Langston University, and Tennessee State University.

programs that corresponded closely to the industrial education model of Hampton and Tuskegee. Tennessee State University, for example, initially set as its goal the preparation of students "to fill positions as foremen, first-class workmen, and teachers of their craft." This stated goal was altered in 1914, when the mechanical department proclaimed its intention to upgrade the skills of those already employed in trades and to make skilled workmen of those who had "no knowledge of the trade processes." The trade offerings at Tennessee State paralleled those introduced at Hampton in 1868, replicated at Tuskegee in 1880, and adopted at other black normal schools and land-grant institutions in the late nineteenth and early twentieth centuries. As with Hampton and Tuskegee, there were special certificates for students who chose to pursue intensively and to complete particular trade courses. Certificates in such trades as carpentry, bricklaying, and tailoring could be gained after three successive years' study. These courses at Tennessee State, however, were sparsely attended. In the 1921–22 school year, during the period in which the largest number of students received certificates for advanced trade work, six students were awarded certificates. There were 583 students in regular attendance that year.[14]

Samuel Henry Shannon's case study of Tennessee State helps us to understand the meager attractiveness of the trade program as an avenue to future employment. Labor-market racism dampened or destroyed most students' enthusiasm for the trades. Nashville's local plumbers' union would only allow blacks to work occasionally, as helpers and nothing more. In the electrical field the opportunities were not much better. Blacks were not allowed to work for white electrical contractors; and if blacks chose to work independently, they had difficulty finding an electrical company that would sell them equipment. One black electrician recalled being arrested by the local police for practicing his trade: "The police itself would catch us with the tools working and arrest you for vagrancy." Access to unions was also difficult in the so-called trowel trades; but since bricklaying and plastering skills had been passed down for generations within the black community, white contractors felt they could ill afford not to have their services. One black bricklayer, a member of Nashville's Bricklayers Union Local 4, estimated that white members outnumbered blacks "about six to one" in the union, but there were "more Negroes in the field than was the white." Hence blacks, even when outnumbering whites in a particular trade, faced enormous difficulties in gaining union membership and finding profitable employment. This reality served to discourage many black students from pursuing the few trades that were offered in land-grant institutions.[15]

A few students, however, did complete the trade courses at Tennessee State, and their experiences reveal another problem: the serious gap between vocational training courses and the world of work. Practicing black artisans did not take the school's vocational training seriously, either as a "practical" place to learn or as a source of future workers "in the field." First, as W. E. B. DuBois discovered, the vast majority of black tradesmen, including the best and most successful, learned their crafts outside of schools: 41 percent in apprenticeship programs and 37 percent by "pick-up" on the job. Only 21 percent attended trade school. Second, the trade graduates were regarded by successful artisans as highfalutin theoreticians who could not perform on the job. One experienced bricklayer stated that no more than "one or two" former Tennessee State students qualified to practice their trade. He described the problem of a school-trained employee, with his "little certificate":

I had to let this fellow go because he didn't know how to lay brick right. He only knew how to stand there and argue and give equations and what not, which didn't even make sense to me, much less to the fellows that worked for me. So they weren't ready. Maybe one out of twenty . . . all it takes is to spread the mortar and lay the brick. The foreman and the superintendent got the damn theory.

This gap between vocational training and the world of work helped limit the number of Tennessee State graduates who succeeded as skilled artisans. Between 1912 and 1922, of the 518 graduates who listed their occupations in the July 1923 catalogue, only fifteen were employed as tradesmen. This was the general trend among land-grant school graduates; only a few became artisans.[16]

The agriculture department had similar problems. There were three principal agricultural vocations for which the land-grant schools sought to prepare students: agriculture teaching, farm demonstration work, and individual farming. Students above the seventh-grade level were generally required to take agriculture. But evidence gathered from student transcripts and catalogues reveals that there was only token adherence to the requirement. Of the total course work taken by Tennessee State students between 1914 and 1922, no more than an estimated 5 percent was in agricultural studies. The vocational listings of graduates reflect the low priority that agriculture, as a field, held for students. There were actually no graduates at all between 1912 and 1922 who gave farming as their occupation.

Some external realities accounted for this situation. It was nearly impossible for blacks to obtain land, and the alternatives of tenant farming and sharecropping were unattractive. And for those students interested in a career in "scientific" farming, land-grant institutions were poorly equipped, with neither the financial resources nor the extension and research facilities necessary for training students adequately. Tennessee State's request to the state legislature for an agricultural building to house laboratory work and technical instruction, for a campus-based agricultural experiment station, and for agricultural extension workers went unrecognized. It was not until 1956 that a separate agricultural building was finally constructed. Indeed, a hundred years elapsed between the founding of the first black land-grant college, in 1866, and the first grant of funds for agricultural research to a black land-grant college by the United States Department of Agriculture, in 1967. In sum, the vocational agriculture curriculum had little impact on students in the areas of farm demonstration, extension work, individual farming, and agricultural research.[17]

It was under these circumstances, in both trades and agriculture, that land-grant institutions followed the Hampton-Tuskegee pattern of normal-school industrial education. Unable to train students adequately or to place them in skilled agricultural or trade occupations, the land-grant institutions directed their efforts at preparing prospective agricultural and mechanical teachers for the South's black public school system. As one former Tennessee State instructor explained: "It later got around to the point where you were not taught to go around and do the job itself. You were taught to teach." Since the agricultural and trade programs gave only an inadequate preparation for practical work in the field, teacher-graduates could do little more than attempt to inculcate the value of hard labor through simple hand work. They had virtually no experience with modern plants and the equipment of modern industry; DuBois properly called them "tinkers and repairers." They were best prepared to meet the common problems of repairing schoolhouses, instructing their students in the use of tools, and teaching simple agriculture, cooking, sewing, and various elementary lessons in unskilled hand labor. The majority of land-grant graduates, therefore, became teachers in the Southern black public schools. Few actually sought to apply their manual skill directly in farming and trade vocations.[18]

In vital respects, it was the educational practices in the industrial normal schools and the land-grant institutions, not the Washington-DuBois debates, that gave vocational and industrial education a negative image in the black community. The black land-grant institutions differed sharply from the white ones. Black land-grant institutions placed a heavy emphasis on manual labor or hard toil, practices that had been generally discarded in white institutions by 1890. The most crucial differences, however, were in the curriculum. The black institutions, until after the First World War, served mainly as normal schools, whose teacher-graduates would instruct in the black public schools of the South. Manual training, focusing on such work as carpentry and bricklaying, was incorporated into the black land-grant curriculum to teach trades to a few students. At white land-grant institutions most students were not in teacher-training; and by 1890, fields like carpentry and bricklaying were already being abandoned in favor of scientific agriculture, engineering, and the broadening of the curriculum to include medicine, law, and business. The white colleges were becoming full-fledged, highly respectable scientific and technical universities. The black land-grant colleges, on the other hand, were looked down on by black students in private colleges as two-year high schools for the training of agricultural and industrial teachers.

The black land-grant colleges did not shed this image until after the Second World War. One Tennessee State instructor recalled that his institution was "not quite regarded as being respectable" by black college students. Another instructor remembered that the land-grant students "were designated as farmers or as hayseeders." The lack of a college curriculum did not help matters at all. In the early twentieth century, only one black land-grant school was offering a curriculum beyond the two-year normal course. In 1909 Florida Agricultural and Mechanical awarded the first baccalaureate degree ever by a black land-grant institution. Yet no trend was established. In 1914 the Florida school remained the sole black land-grant institution offering a four-year, degree-granting curriculum. It had twelve baccalaureate students, out of 5,997 students enrolled in black land-grant schools during the 1914–15 academic year. And in 1932, when these schools enrolled a total of 5,698 students, 4,059 were preparing for some kind of teaching. Thus the black experience with "vocational education" in the land-grant and industrial normal-school setting came to mean either teacher training at a precollegiate level or a routine manual labor that, for one reason or another, did not lead to gainful employment in skilled occupations.[19]

The early goals of black trade and industrial education, formulated by leaders like Douglass and Cornish in the mid-nineteenth century, remained important as long as skilled occupations were considered of first importance. Elevating the black laborer and ultimately establishing a prestigious artisan and skilled-labor class were themes continually heard from the 1830's through the 1920's. Yet when the industrial normal schools and land-grant institutions were firmly entrenched, they discarded the black uplift ideology by their deeds if not by their words; and the advent of "Negro industrial education" for traditional "Negro jobs" meant the end of the brighter side of black vocational education. Black youth came to view academic and professional education as the only paths leading out of unskilled agricultural and domestic labor.

From the mid-nineteenth to the early twentieth century, blacks hoped to establish high-quality mechanical and technical schools that could prepare black youth for skilled and semiskilled positions in the rapidly expanding industrial economy. Their hopes were never realized. Neither federal government, state government, nor private philanthropy would foot the bill for well-developed black mechanical and technical schools. Black industrial schools found themselves limited to two options: they could train teachers for the segregated black elementary and secondary schools, or they could prepare blacks to be good agricultural and domestic laborers and thus reproduce the mostly unskilled, dead-end occupational structure that locked blacks in poverty. Why did black industrial education develop along these lines, especially since many schoolmen, philanthropists, and politicians regarded vocational and industrial education as peculiarly fitted for the laboring classes? Basically, it was because the black working class was treated differently from native and foreign-born white workers, and the educational opportunities of blacks corresponded closely with their opportunities in the labor market.

The industrial revolution virtually bypassed the black working class, because the racism of employers and unions tended to keep blacks from skilled and semiskilled industrial occupations. As early as 1899, W. E. B. DuBois, in his seminal work *The Philadelphia Negro*, drew attention to the concentration of blacks in menial, low-wage jobs. He found race discrimination to be the principal reason for this. Some, however, suggested other, nonracist reasons for the poor economic showing of blacks at the turn of the century. Such factors as rural background, level of education, residential segregation, male-absent households, length of residence in the city, and population size were considered fundamental sources of black inequality. Recent studies of black employment during the industrial revolution underscore DuBois's earlier findings. Elizabeth Pleck, studying blacks in Boston between 1865 and 1900, found that nonracist factors were relatively insignificant barriers to black economic opportunity. "It seems clear," she concluded, "that the one overriding disadvantage blacks faced was the deeply rooted racial prejudice of their fellow Bostonians." An inferior education, for instance, typified Irish peasants and southern Italians as much as blacks; still, a European immigrant who had just arrived in Boston had a far better chance of securing a well-paying job than a black whose ancestors had been in the North for generations. For the most part, blacks were crowded into menial jobs because of the racist policies and practices of city government, department stores, trade unions, and manufacturers.[20]

David Katzman and Kenneth Kusmer found similar patterns in their studies of Detroit and Cleveland. The meteoric rise of manufacturing in Detroit required an extraordinary supply of labor, but the jobs were held almost exclusively for native and foreign-born whites; black workers were kept outside of Detroit's white-organized factories. In 1890 there were no blacks in Detroit's brass and ship industries, and only 21 blacks were found among the 5,839 male employees in the tobacco, stove, iron, machine, and shoe industries. In 1910 only 25 blacks were recorded among 10,000 mostly foreign-born, semiskilled operatives and laborers who worked in Detroit's automotive factories. Similarly, Cleveland blacks participated very little in the upsurge of industrial activity there. In 1890 only three blacks were employed in the city's rapidly expanding steel industry, and virtually none worked as semiskilled operatives in factories. What jobs blacks were able to obtain in industry were almost all in the unskilled labor category; only a handful attained skilled or even semiskilled positions in factories before the Great Migration. In Cleveland, as elsewhere, the industrial firms producing steel, oil, rubber, machinery, and refrigerated meat demanded an ever-increasing supply of laborers. Blacks, however, were shunted aside in the competition, becoming an isolated and marginal segment of the industrial labor force.[21]

The same racism shaped black educational opportunities, and largely explains why black vocational and industrial education bore little or no relationship to the occupations created by the industrial revolution. As has been shown by David Tyack, whether schoolmen believed in or merely acquiesced in labor-market racism, they tended to prepare blacks for unskilled, dead-end occupations that actually required little or no schooling. As the ranks of black laborers became filled with disappointed men, the chronic despair spread to the educational system. According to Tyack, in 1915 a New York social investigator reported that the restriction of industrial opportunities was "sapping the ambition of the colored boys and girls, and that they were not making the effort put out by their parents and grandparents to secure an education." Ironically, during the depression years black education would be blamed for the lack of black occupational advance, and many schoolmen would accept the blame.[22]

The Depression and the Rise of Black Vocational Guidance, 1930–48

From the national economic depression of the 1930's through the wartime resurgence of Northern industry in the early 1940's, more emphasis was placed on black vocational training than during any other period in Afro-American history. The *Journal of Negro Education*, from its origin in 1932 to 1979, devoted only one of its yearbooks and special issues to the question of black vocational education, and that was the special issue in January 1935 entitled "The Vocational Guidance of Negroes." It is important to note that the *Journal*'s yearbooks and special issues were aimed at a comprehensive and thorough coverage of the most urgent problems in black education and related areas. Between 1930 and 1942, the area of black vocational guidance, which was largely concerned with the adjustment of black youth to the urban workplace, commanded the attention of the most noted black intellectuals. Such researchers as E. Franklin Frazier, Charles S. Johnson, Allison Davis, Ira De A. Reid, Alain Locke, Rayford Logan, Charles H. Thompson, Doxey Wilkerson, Benjamin E. Mays, Ralph W. Bullock, Robert C. Weaver, Ambrose Caliver, and W. E. B. DuBois addressed the problems of guidance, vocational education, and the occupational preferences of young blacks. Similarly, white intellectuals such as John Dollard, W. Lloyd Warner, Robert Sutherland, T. J. Woofter, and George Zook were preoccupied with vocational training and its relation to the "crisis of Negro youth in the twentieth-century city."[23]

The widespread concern over black vocational guidance, between 1930 and 1948, was generated mainly by the rapid increase in the black youth population in the twentieth-century city and the impact of the economic depression on that population. The increase in young urban blacks was of course part and parcel of the Great Migration that took place between 1910 and 1930. The expansion of Northern industry, in response to the First World War, and the sharp decline in the flow of immigrants from Europe opened up job opportunities for blacks in Northern cities. The repressive labor system in the agricultural South, the devastation of cotton farming by the boll weevil, the mechanization of agriculture, and related factors caused rural blacks to seek new opportunities in Southern cities also. This movement to the city was highly selective of young adults, who were less bound to the rural South and more anxious to respond to new opportunities.

The impact of the Great Migration was tremendous. In the 30 years between 1900 and 1930, the urban black population increased by more than three million. When the migration subsided in 1930, 56.3 percent of the black population was still rural; but this contrasted with 66 percent in 1920 and 72.7 percent in 1910. To an urban black population of only 790,000 in the North in 1910, approximately 1.3 million were added by 1930; and the urban black population in the South increased from 1,850,000 in 1910 to 2,961,000 in 1930. The main migration trend was from rural areas and small urban centers to Northern cities of 100,000 or more inhabitants. In 1930 there were 233,903 blacks in Chicago, 430 percent more than in 1910; 327,706 were in New York City, 257 percent more than in 1910; and 219,599 were in Philadelphia, 160 percent more than in 1910. In the seventeen Southern cities with populations of more than 100,000 in 1930, blacks constituted 25.2 percent of the aggregate. Blacks represented more than 38 percent of the population in Birmingham and Memphis; more than 33 percent in Atlanta, Jacksonville, and Norfolk; and more than 27 percent in Washington, New Orleans, Richmond, Nashville, and Chattanooga.[24]

Consequently, the population of young blacks in American cities increased enormously between 1910 and 1930. Of the 5,193,913 urban blacks in 1930, 447,155 were from 15 to 19 years of age, and 560,215 were from 20 to 24. Black youth from 15 to 24 years old numbered more than 59,000 in New York City, more than 38,000 in Chicago and Philadelphia, more than 25,000 in New Orleans, Washington, and Baltimore, and more than 20,000 in Birmingham and Detroit. The rapid growth of the urban black youth population, culminating as it did on the eve of the Great Depression, created a very real social crisis in cities across the nation. The Great Migration brought them to the urban centers seeking new job opportunities, but before they could adjust to city life the depression had placed disproportionately large numbers of them on the unemployment and relief rolls. The position of the Northern urban black was particularly desperate, and remained so throughout the 1930's. In 1939, 12.8 percent of the whites and 45.3 percent of the blacks in Cincinnati were unemployed. In March 1940 the percentage of whites out of work in Philadelphia, Chicago, Detroit, and New York varied from 12 to 18 percent; for blacks the range was from 30 to 39 percent. These were the figures for all black workers; the rates of unemployment were even higher for black youth. In 1935, for instance, two-thirds of New York City's blacks between the ages of 16 and 24 were either unemployed or out of school and seeking work.[25]

Black liberal intellectuals and educationists were in agreement that schools and colleges contributed to the creation and perpetuation of this large-scale youth unemployment. To be sure, they all agreed that the high unemployment was due mainly or in part to a "sick economy." Yet they were equally convinced that black youth shouldered more than their share of the economic depression because black vocational guidance and education had been approached without plan or purpose. Reports reaching observers of the educational scene in the 1930's indicated clearly that a large proportion of black adolescents were in desperate need of vocational guidance. Two such reports were conducted by Ralph W. Bullock and Benjamin E. Mays in 1930. Bullock made a study of occupational choices of 1,833 black high school boys in North Carolina, Tennessee, Georgia, Virginia, Missouri, and the District of Columbia. Mays, then student secretary of the National Council of the YMCA, studied the occupational choices of 1,714 black students in 22 black colleges. Both studies sought to find out what occupations black youth were expecting to enter; the reasons they were inclined toward these occupations; the kind of vocational guidance black youth received from the schools and colleges; and the extent to which black students chose to follow the occupations of their fathers.[26]

Both researchers were alarmed at the high percentage of black students planning to attend college or do graduate work, and who had already decided on medicine, teaching, law, or another of the professions as a career. Bullock's questionnaires revealed that upon graduation from high school, 1,601 of the 1,833 boys, or 87.6 percent of them, were planning to enter college. Significantly, the percentage of boys expecting to go to college increased from the ninth grade through the twelfth: 83.7 percent of the ninth graders, 86.9 percent of the tenth graders, 90.2 percent of the eleventh graders, and 91.4 percent of the twelfth graders. Mays discovered that 90 percent of the 1,714 college students he interviewed planned to continue their study by doing graduate work or enrolling in professional school. Both groups expressed occupational preferences that differed sharply from their fathers' occupations.

In Bullock's high school sample, 1,415 boys reported their father's occupation; 88 percent of the fathers were engaged in occupations of the unskilled, semiskilled, domestic-and-personal-service sort, and 12 percent were in professions and highly skilled occupations. Only 5 percent of the boys who gave their fathers' occupations were planning to enter the same occupation as their father. More of the college students were inclined to follow their fathers' occupations, but these were primarily in the professions or in occupations in which the parents had already established a successful business. Still, out of 1,366 college students who gave their fathers' occupations, only 163, or 12 percent, preferred to follow that occupation.[27]

Both Bullock and Mays were dissatisfied with their findings and with what they indicated about vocational training in black high schools and colleges. They were particularly concerned that the vocational aspirations of black high school students were leading to the development of two distinct black classes, "the common labor mass and domestic servants at the bottom, and the professional class at the top." In Bullock's high school sample, 52 percent of the students were planning to enter eleven occupations of the professional type: medicine, teaching, law, pharmacy, engineering, architecture, dentistry, science, art, painting, and music. Mays found that 85 percent of the black college sample grouped themselves in roughly the same professions, leaving only 15 percent distributed among 49 other occupations. Very few of the high school or college students chose the skilled, mechanical, artisan, technical, commercial, and business occupations that, according to Bullock, constituted "the real economic backbone of any group, race, or nation." Similarly, Mays complained that little was being done "to build up a great middle class of skilled and technically trained [black] people."[28]

The narrow range of black student career choices was taken as solid evidence that they received little vocational guidance and were allowed to choose their occupations indiscriminately. This was viewed as not only bad for the black community, but harmful to individual students as well. The authors argued that many of the students would drop out before entering or finishing college, and in order to live they would have to work like the vast majority of black workers, at unskilled personal service and domestic occupations. "But why this turmoil and disappointment?" asked Mays. Much of it could be avoided, he reasoned, by providing black youth with "the help of men trained in the technique of vocational adjustment, to help them find their way in the vocational world."

Both Mays and Bullock maintained that black high school and college students were concentrated in a narrow range of occupational choices because of the tendency to seek opportunities where trails had already been blazed (where blacks had already made good), and because the occupations chosen by most of them were arbitrarily selected. In an effort to find out why those particular occupations were selected, a careful examination was made of the reasons the students gave for their choices and of the vocational guidance literature they had read. Bullock found that only 6.6 percent of the high school students listed any material that could be classified as occupational or vocational guidance literature. Similarly, Mays concluded that the college students were "stumbling along rather blindly and haphazardly toward their careers." Students chose their occupations on the basis of "interests and likes," "desire to be of service to society," "remuneration," "special fitness for the job," "satisfaction," and "the influence of parents and friends." When these statements were analyzed with the aid of interviews, the researchers found them to be "weak and meaningless"; the occupational choices "were based on meager and unreliable information."[29]

Such studies sparked a widespread emphasis on black vocational guidance in the 1930's. Writers were careful to distinguish vocational guidance from "vocational education." Vocational guidance was defined as "the giving of information, advice, and the direction of experience with regard to choosing an occupation, preparing for it, entering it, and progressing in it." On the other hand, vocational education was viewed as "the training of pupils for some particular occupation or vocation." There were three familiar dimensions of vocational guidance: (1) inspirational, (2) informational, and (3) diagnostic. The second and third were the most important. The function of vocational guidance was to gather and disseminate occupational information, to provide counseling based on occupational information and a careful study of the individual, and to do placement and follow-up work.

It was proposed that vocational guidance programs begin no later than the junior high school and continue through high school, college and professional school, and even through a person's occupational life. Such programs would give students a knowledge of the workaday world, inform them of the requirements for entering various occupations, and make them aware of the occupational demands on their time and of the financial rewards for different kinds of work.

The vocational guidance movement caught fire in the early 1930's. By 1932 the need for federal involvement was seen as particularly necessary in the field of black education. Citing the deplorable vocational opportunities in black schools across America, critics lashed out at the Hoover administration for not addressing the relationship between urban schools and the economic health of black communities. In 1933, however, Franklin D. Roosevelt's administration brought into national prominence a number of Progressive reformers whose educational views favored the organization of vocational guidance programs. Clark Foreman, President Roosevelt's trusted advisor on racial affairs, George Zook, the choice for commissioner of the U.S. Office of Education, and Secretary of the Interior Harold L. Ickes, who was placed over the Office of Education, called for the reorganization of black education with particular attention to vocational education and guidance.[30]

In May 1934 Ickes called a National Conference on Fundamental Problems in the Education of Negroes; the general chairman was Zook. Dr. Ambrose Caliver, the black serving as federal specialist on the education of Negroes, was in charge of the immediate direction of the conference, which was set up to consider the special and peculiar problems of black education arising from the economic and social conditions of the 1930's. The reports to the conference were given by fourteen committees over a period of several months. The committee on vocations, chaired by T. Arnold Hill, industrial secretary of the National Urban League, reported:

The difficulties encountered by Negroes in employment make vocational guidance more of a necessity for them than for white students. Even if guidance were not accepted as an essential function of education, it would be necessary for those entrusted with the education of Negro youth to employ the principle of guidance if the large number of Negro students now completing schools and dropping out before graduation are to find employment. . . .

The report concluded that neither black teachers nor black students were sufficiently aware of the requirements of business and industry and the changes then occurring among workers to prepare graduates for success and advancement in the labor market. The committee on vocations called for new approaches, new courses of study, and new techniques in vocational education and guidance.[31]

The following year, the *Journal of Negro Education* emphasized the same themes: "The fact that many Negroes have found and still find it exceedingly difficult to enter many occupations solely because they are Negroes necessitates a guidance machinery that will not only meet *normal* vocational needs but will also successfully overcome the additional barriers of race." Black writers in this special issue rejected the "old" philosophy of black vocational guidance, which, as we have seen, advised black youth to pursue occupations where many blacks were already found and to eschew those with few blacks. This policy, the writers argued, tended to confine black youth to the lowest forms of labor; it accepted the assumption that blacks had a special "place" in the national economy and that it was the function of education to keep them in that place.

Instead, the editors and writers proposed a blueprint for change. First, black vocational guidance would recognize the historical fact that even though blacks found many occupations extremely difficult to enter in significant numbers, there were black individuals successfully engaged in most occupations. Instead of accommodating to existing patterns, the black vocational guidance advocates called for a concerted and systematic investigation of how individuals overcame racial barriers. The insights of successful workers could then be used so as to widen the occupational horizon of blacks in general. Second, black writers rejected the idea that black youth should be guided mainly into occupations servicing the black community, such as those of social worker, nurse, teacher, lawyer, and doctor. This idea was based on the belief that black professional and social service workers could do their work more effectively for the black community because they understood and were more sympathetic to black clients. Hence jobs servicing black clients were recommended as special, almost exclusive opportunities for black youth. Though recognizing some elements of truth in this position, black writers rejected the idea because it placed vocational choices on a racial instead of an individual basis, and it entrenched further the racial categorization of employment opportunities. Black vocational guidance advocates took the nonracist path, "that the occupational future of the Negro is inextricably bound up with that of all other workers in the country without consideration of race, and that only a policy of vocational guidance which recognizes this fact can be of any real value to Negroes."[32]

In this view of vocational guidance, black education had a new role that was unalterably linked to what was happening to black youth in the industrial economy. Existing curricula and vocational guidance programs were now seen as double-edged swords, capable of including or excluding blacks from the nation's economic mainstream. The new outlook also allowed critics to castigate both black educators and white school counselors for leaving black students in "apparent confusion as to the actual possibilities of work and the methods of training." Sensing a tremendous gap between blacks and whites in vocational training opportunities, guidance services, apprenticeship education, and many other fields of specialized training, black critics lashed out especially at the ghetto schools of the North.

They blamed the ghetto schools for contributing to both the creation and the perpetuation of the vocational opportunity gap. "Such schools," said the black sociologist Ira De A. Reid, "regularly commit atrocities in the name of occupational guidance for Negroes." As outlined by the 1935 conference on Vocational Guidance and Education for Negroes, these atrocities normally took two forms: guiding black youth into jobs that were fast becoming obsolete, and preparing them for occupations that served to entrench them further among the unskilled. Many of the critics fixed the blame on ignorant white counselors who often acted without knowledge of the vocations black youth desired to enter or had already entered successfully. "The chances are two to one," Reid contended, "that the Negro students themselves know far more about these opportunities than the person or persons counseling them." A substantial number of critics, however, charged that the ghetto schools were guilty of deliberately denying black youth access to supportive guidance services and high-quality vocational training courses.[33]

To support these charges of willful neglect, black critics pointed to a variety of techniques used by Northern school systems to repress black ambition. In a Boston school, for instance, a separate school assembly for black students was ordered for the purpose of showing them the virtues of manual training and predominantly black schools. In New York City the Board of Education attempted to restrict course offerings in the Harlem vocational schools to areas "where Negroes can expect jobs." Under this plan electrical training would no longer be offered to blacks as long as electrical contractors refused to employ them and as long as trade unions excluded them from most apprenticeships in the skilled trades. At Wadleigh High School in Harlem, black girls were told by the principal not to register for commercial courses, on the grounds that they would not have the opportunity after graduation to use such knowledge. Similar charges surfaced in the aftermath of the Harlem Riot of March 1935, when Mayor LaGuardia appointed an interracial commission of influential New Yorkers to investigate the root causes of the disturbances. Before the subcommittee on education, Harlem residents accused Charles Pickett, principal of the New York Industrial High School, of deliberately misguiding black students on vocational possibilities. Pickett's school, they maintained, was the dumping ground of Harlem's educational system.[34]

Similar attacks on vocational guidance in ghetto schools occurred elsewhere. In the fall of 1935, Chicago's black South Side Citizens School Committee exposed conditions at Washburn Trade School. Like trade schools in other sections of the city, the South Side school offered apprenticeship and technical courses but made admission to them particularly difficult for blacks. The school's black students were invariably guided by the advice of vocational counselors to enter the "lower" vocational track, and were refused the use of certain school equipment on the grounds that blacks rarely became members of trade unions in the areas using those machines and tools. Unused machinery was often stored away in the school's basement, rusting and deteriorating, at the same time that black students were denied a chance to learn. Similarly, on the West Coast black critics condemned the rulings of local school boards barring blacks from taking vocational courses unless they could provide letters from employers promising them jobs after graduation.[35]

Black-controlled programs fell under different criticisms. Nevertheless, critics charged that black schools had been singularly remiss in their development of vocational guidance programs. "So far as I know," wrote Bullock, "there is not a single Negro college in America that has a department or school offering major courses in vocational and educational guidance." In his study of more than 200 public schools and colleges, he found no appreciable emphasis on helping students to decide what occupations they would enter after finishing school. Black public schools and colleges could not continue to neglect this phase of education, Bullock maintained, "and lay claim to meeting the educational needs of students." Mays reached the same conclusion: "Vocational Guidance has been almost wholly neglected in our high schools and colleges." Hill, of the Urban League, criticized black educators who considered vocational guidance from the standpoint of how it might be "slipped into a school program without disturbing the time-honored educational pattern." For Hill, "educational aims should be consonant with social demands," and the lessons of five years of unprecedented unemployment, 1930–35, proved the need for a restructuring of the black educational system. Above all, "students must be prepared for the occupational readjustment which will be forced upon them by constantly changing economic conditions."[36]

It was an interesting analysis of black economic conditions during the Great Depression that allowed vocational guidance advocates to blame the schools for the status of black laborers. Focusing not on the causes of the general rate of unemployment, but almost exclusively on the specific causes of the disproportionately high rate of black unemployment, critics easily attributed the catastrophic position of black workers to the lack of vocational guidance. Vocational guidance advocates maintained that black workers experienced disproportionately high unemployment because they were concentrated in a few occupations that were especially hard hit by the depression, such as the building trades. Hence black laborers would not have suffered as much if schools had guided them toward greater occupational diversification. The vocational guidance advocates did not mean to suggest that black workers would not suffer from some discriminatory unemployment in another period of economic decline. Rather, they argued that occupational diversification would make the black workers' position in the developing economy less marginal than it had been in the period of prosperity after the First World War, and would lessen the possibility that blacks would have a similar rate of unemployment in another major depression.

Vocational guidance advocates also blamed the schools for not preparing black workers for unexpected occupational changes or "technological unemployment." It was assumed that blacks were disproportionately unemployed because they did not have the appropriate education and the farsightedness to adapt to scientific and technological revolutions in the economy. In this context, vocational guidance had a particular appeal that was missing from "vocational education" or trade and technical training. For instance, almost half the black male skilled workers were pushed out of their usual occupations between 1930 and 1936. A third of those displaced went into unskilled jobs and 17 percent were without work. Clearly, these workers were not unemployed because they lacked technical training. The basic problem, contended vocational guidance advocates, was an education that did not prepare people to meet the requirements of working and living in a modern industrial economy. Thus youth needed more education about making intelligent occupational choices and a satisfactory adjustment to an ever-changing scientific and technological economy. Interestingly, in the 1930's this education was defined as more sociological than technological. "The type of vocational instruction most necessary for the vast majority of high-school students is not technical, but social," insisted Hill. Social education or vocational guidance would involve teaching black youth about labor problems, occupational diversity, production and consumption, efficiency, employment discrimination, and related social issues.[37]

Increasing black vocational opportunities with well-developed school guidance programs was more easily said than done. Indeed, black vocational education and guidance practices in the

1930's generated much disillusionment. This was well illustrated in 1936 when Caliver, the federal specialist, conducted a nationwide survey of vocational education and guidance opportunities for blacks. The survey, employing five hundred black relief workers, collected data on 27,366 black high school and college students in 150 urban and rural communities in 34 states. The theme of the survey's final report was that vocational opportunities for blacks had changed little from the mid-1920's to the mid-1930's. The land-grant colleges still prepared their vocational education students to teach home economics and vocational agriculture. Few of the black high school and college students were enrolled in trade and industrial courses. Students enrolled in such courses were generally concentrated in bricklaying, carpentry and woodwork, masonry, shoemaking and shoe repairing, and tailoring.

Caliver's report documented the number of blacks and whites enrolled in the federally aided vocational courses in secondary schools in eighteen states. White students were registered in 24 different occupations in the all-day schools, 36 in the evening schools, and 33 in the part-time and trade extension curricula. Black students were registered in 12 different occupations in the all-day schools, 14 in the evening schools, and 8 in the part-time and trade extension courses. There were no blacks enrolled in such trades as boat building, boiler work, fire fighting, general mechanics, greenhouse work, internal-combustion engines, ironwork, marble carving, natural gas, petroleum, power plant operations, practical engineering, pulp and papermaking, refrigeration and air conditioning, shipbuilding, sign painting, steelmaking, surveying, textiles, and upholstering; and there was only one black among the 878 students in welding. Moreover, there were very few blacks enrolled in blueprint reading (11 out of 1,434); commercial art (38 out of 1,028); electricity (160 out of 2,843); machine shop (118 out of 2,695); metal trades (9 out of 1,070); printing (28 out of 1,805); and radio mechanics (33 out of 1,283). Black students, concentrated in vocations such as bricklaying and tailoring, were far from achieving the kind of occupational diversity advocated by vocational guidance enthusiasts. In fact, black students had virtually the same vocational opportunities as before the vocational guidance movement.[38]

Information reaching Caliver's Washington office from schools across the nation proved uniformly dismal with respect to the vocational future of black youth. An official of the Pittsburgh Urban League reported that many black high school students dismissed the survey's vocational questionnaire as a joke. "One lad," she reported, "said he hoped to secure the position of janitor at his own funeral." In Oakland, California, the public school system flagrantly discriminated against black youth in the assignment of students for vocational training courses. Teachers and guidance counselors were found to be ignorant of black employment possibilities, and many seemed content to set low limits for black students. Racism in trade unions and businesses made these limits a reality.[39]

The sad state of education and vocational opportunity for black youth was also documented in social science research sponsored by the American Youth Commission of the American Council on Education. In 1939 the Commission, acknowledging the desperate state of black youth, funded seven studies to "determine what kind of person a Negro youth is or is in the process of becoming as a result of the limitations which are placed upon his or her participation in the life of America." Between 1940 and 1942, these studies were published by the American Council on Education. Reid prepared a preliminary volume reviewing published and unpublished studies of black youth in America. Drawing heavily on government publications and doctoral dissertations, Reid produced *In a Minor Key: Negro Youth in Story and Fact*. Two noted black social scientists conducted original research projects on black youth in the lower South. One, Charles S. Johnson, wrote a classic on rural youth, *Growing Up in the Black Belt*. The other, Allison Davis, teamed with the white psychologist John Dollard to produce an equally significant volume, *Children of Bondage*, which analyzed the psychological effects of caste and class discrimination on black youth in urban areas of Louisiana and Mississippi. W. Lloyd Warner, in *Color and Human Nature*, collaborated with two other researchers to explore the personalities of ghettoized youth in black Chicago. E. Franklin Frazier studied black youth in Washington, D.C., and Louisville, cities between the Deep South and the Northern ghettoes, and chose to call his book *Negro Youth at the Crossways*. J. Howell Atwood and others, in *Thus Be Their Destiny*, wrote a collection of short essays on black youth in small Northern communities. In *Color, Class, and Personality*, Robert Sutherland summarized the findings of the entire project and presented recommendations for a program of educational and social planning.[40]

These studies were uniformly pessimistic in disclosing the mounting frustration of black youth in America. Schooling as it existed was not part of the solution, it was part of the problem. "Present conditions in and around the rural schools are far from conducive to the proper personality development of these [rural] youth," wrote Johnson. "A traditional, lifeless curriculum; the harsh, unintelligent disciplinary punishment; and the emphasis upon rote learning must share the blame with poverty for excessive retardation, and for the unrest and dissatisfaction of Negro youth." Davis and Dollard concluded that "the great majority of lower-class Negro children in Southern cities are retarded in graded schools," and they laid much of the blame on middle-class teachers and students. The Negro lower-class child was not allowed to make the proper responses in school because he was "stigmatized by teachers and their favored students on grounds of the 'ignorance' of his parents, the dialect which he speaks, the appearance of his clothes, and, very likely, the darkness of his skin." Frazier uncovered similar problems among black youth in the border-state cities. "Because of their social status and dark complexion, lower-class youth are subject to discrimination on the part of teachers as well as on the part of other pupils." The discrimination was brutal enough to cause the dark lower-class children to develop "feelings of inferiority and resentment."[41]

Class distinctions within the race, however, were considered merely part of the larger problem, which was "the ceiling of economic and social ascent." As Sutherland put it, "the main basis of frustration is economic—the denial of the same chance as others to get an education and a reasonably secure and satisfying job." Many black youth expressed misgivings about the value of education, since so many avenues of employment were closed to them. The lack of employment opportunities, Frazier maintained, convinced many lower-class youth "that illegal and antisocial means of making a living must be resorted to and are justified."

Clearly, the poor quality of schooling documented by the social scientists stood in marked contrast to the vocational goals of black youth. Johnson, for instance, discovered that of 851 rural boys, 38.1 percent wished to enter professional careers, 17.2 percent skilled trades, 9.3 percent "clerical" work, and 10.9 percent unskilled nonfarm labor; only 8.9 percent were inclined to do farm work. The occupational choices of the girls were even more heavily concentrated in the professions. Of 1,399 rural girls, 65.3 percent wanted professional careers, 11.5 percent clerical or retail work, 9.1 percent skilled work, and 6.5 percent personal and domestic service; only 1.2 percent wanted farm work. The girls were not only more pronounced in their preference for professional careers, but more positive in their rejection of farming. And they were not merely rejecting a "man's occupation"; they were similarly opposed to being a farmer's wife. Vocational opportunities in black schools were hardly relevant to the occupational preferences of black youth. Indeed, Johnson concluded: "The gap between occupational expectation and reality is at present so great as to suggest that the expectation itself borders on fantasy." The researchers concluded that little could be done to help black youth without broad political and economic reforms.[42]

By the late 1930's both liberal and radical black critics were moving away from the public schools as the way to solve the vocational training and unemployment problems of black youth, but for different reasons. The radicals rejected the two basic assumptions that undergirded the liberals' vocational guidance policy: (1) that black unemployment problems were solvable without fundamentally restructuring the economy; and (2) that a reorganization of the school curricula was essential for bringing black youth into the economic mainstream. They considered both assumptions unwarranted, especially the second. Unless labor-market racism was eliminated, John P. Davis declared, the New Deal could offer "nothing new for the Negro except maintenance of his inferior status by government fiat." The black columnist George Schuyler denounced "those charlatans who pretend to see a time when this vast army of young Negroes will be employed privately"; most "will have to work for the state, earning just enough to keep them alive and out of mischief." Ralph Bunche, taking a more radical position, argued that schooling was "compelled to reflect the *status quo*" and could do little about the economic condition of black youth:

We are living in an economy of capitalism, and our educational system consistently harmonizes with the dominant capitalistic pattern. Our schools are extremely sensitive to the functions of capitalism. . . . When capitalism is hard-pressed with criticisms of its shortcomings, the schools are expected to provide its advocates, and if they demur, for reasons of educational ideas, capitalism tightens the economic screws until the schools surrender.

Schools would not be permitted to "remodel the social order"; they could not, therefore, solve the problems "of the masses of working-class Negroes." There was only one sensible path for the schools to take, to provide black youth with a "good, sound training in the fundamentals of education." Frazier took a similar stance: "If the vast economic forces which control the destinies of Negro industrial workers and farmers cannot be influenced by the educational process, an intelligent recognition of this fact is better than chimerical schemes for advancement which are bound to result in disillusionment." These critics did not push for any serious reorganization of the school curricula.[43]

Black liberals, failing to open up vocational training opportunities for black youth in the public schools, attacked the problems of education and unemployment with New Deal relief programs. They pushed for and nearly gained equal representation for black youth in the National Youth Administration, the Emergency Education Program, and the Civilian Conservation Corps. These programs were established ostensibly to increase the employability of each enrollee by providing counsel, guidance, vocational instruction, and work experience. The number of blacks receiving aid from the National Youth Administration rose from 5,000 a month in 1933 to 28,500 in 1937, and nearly 180,000 black students were supported by the agency to continue in high school. Black monthly enrollment at Emergency Education Program classes mushroomed from 50,000 in 1935 to over 500,000 in 1939. Thousands of black youth were enrolled in the Civilian Conservation Corps, which was established in 1933 to take armies of unemployed young men and give them healthful work and beneficial experiences in conservation camps. Many of the vocational training courses in these relief programs, such as cooking, table-waiting, laundering, tailoring, and shoe repairing, were reminiscent of the land-grant and industrial normal-school programs. But black liberals like Mary McLeod Bethune, Reid,

Weaver, Hill, and Caliver gave the federal programs high marks because they offered black youth their first real chance to be clerks, stenographers, supervisors, typists, bookkeepers, store managers, and the like. The promise of nondiscriminatory employment training opportunities in federal programs kept dissatisfaction at a minimum.[44]

Vocational training opportunities in federal education programs, followed by increased employment in the wartime defense-related industries, did much to cast black vocational education and guidance programs into oblivion. A million black workers entered civilian jobs between 1940 and 1944. In 1943, when a drop in the number of white applicants for defense training created an acute shortage of skilled labor, many black workers were hired. By 1944 the number of black workers in skilled jobs had doubled. These workers entered both new industries and plants where before the war few blacks, if any, had been employed. The wartime emergency created overnight more industrial and occupational diversification for blacks than had occurred in the preceding 75 years. Although the vocational guidance programs had been designed especially to achieve such diversification among black workers, the programs had virtually no impact on blacks' position in the labor market. Clearly, the war could place blacks in skilled jobs faster and in greater numbers than the schools. The resurgent wartime economy significantly decreased the unemployment rate for black youth. In 1948, for instance, the teenage male unemployment rate was 7.6 percent for nonwhites and 8.3 percent for whites. The fact, however, that blacks had to wait for a wartime economy to recoup the occupational losses sustained during the depression was an indication that the problems might recur under peacetime conditions.[45]

Education and Youth Unemployment, 1950–79

Throughout the 1930's and into the 1940's, advocates of black vocational education and guidance had called for a reorganization of the school curriculum in order that schooling might do more to prepare black youth for employment. The more they studied the relationship between education and work, however, the more they realized that there was little relation between the type of curriculum pursued and the occupations of secondary school graduates and nongraduates. Reid's 1938 survey of 213,983 white-collar and skilled black workers revealed that less than one-fourth had taken some form of business or trade training. One-third of the workers had received their fundamental training on the job, and a high school diploma appeared to be the most important factor in gaining access to white-collar or skilled occupations. In 1939 Weaver, with data obtained from 78,330 black male skilled workers, concluded "that vocational education for skills has been least effective among Negroes where it has been most loudly championed." In 1940 Caliver, studying the relation of education to the occupational status of 20,260 black high school graduates, found that high school graduates, irrespective of curriculum, received better occupational opportunities than nongraduates. The 64.8 percent of graduates and nongraduates who had no vocational training, as well as the 11 percent who admitted that their vocational training did not help them in securing work, dealt crippling blows to the vocational guidance campaign. The absorption of many black youth into the wartime labor market, then, came as a welcome relief for those who had run out of educational proposals to solve the problem of black youth unemployment.[46]

Against this background, the question of academic versus vocational education for black youth, which had been much debated from 1930 to 1940, became far less important in the postwar period. Black educators and civil rights leaders turned their attention to the issues of school desegregation and equality of opportunity in academic secondary schools and colleges. The irony of this position was that it placed black educational goals squarely in line with the much-criticized educational and vocational preferences of black youth during the 1930's. Occupational choice surveys in the 1930's, 1940's, and 1950's revealed that the majority of black high school students aspired to jobs that required mainly academic training in and beyond high school. The majority of black youth aspired to professional or semiprofessional occupations. Approximately 19 percent chose occupations in the clerical and sales fields. The desire to be in the skilled trades declined steadily from 1930 to 1960. In 1930 Bullock found that 20 percent of black high school boys aspired to skilled trades; in 1940 sur-

veys showed 15 to 19 percent with this aspiration; Paul Lawrence's 1950 survey of 460 California black students indicated 9
percent; and B. A. Turner's 1964 study indicated only 3.2 percent. Black youth, convinced that racism by unions and management blocked their entry into apprenticeship programs, concentrated almost exclusively on traditional academic preparation.
Thus, when the 1950's witnessed a strong emphasis on the
"search for talent," black youth were ready to respond. The new
federal policy of aid to education, designed to increase college
enrollments, fitted well with the long-term academic interests of
black youth.[47]

The post-Brown social climate, the "search for talent," and the
attendant educational opportunities had an enormous effect on
black academic performance. The median number of years of
school completed by blacks increased from 5.8 in 1940 to 12.3 in
1976. Thus in 1976 there was no significant difference in this
respect between blacks and whites, for whom the median was
12.6 years. As Dorothy K. Newman points out, the upsurge in
black educational achievement was extraordinary because so
much of the "catching up" took place in a few short years. In
1960, 42 percent of blacks 20 to 24 years old had completed high
school, compared to 66 percent for whites of the same age. In
1974, the figure for blacks had risen to 72 percent, compared to 85
percent for whites. Current reports show that young blacks continue to improve their high school completion rate. The U.S.
Commission on Civil Rights documented that in 1976 over 74
percent of blacks 20 to 24 years old had completed high school.[48]

The percentage change in college enrollment, though its significance may be exaggerated, was still startling. In the years
between 1966 and 1976, the number of black students enrolled in
college increased from 282,000 to 1,062,000, or by more than 275
percent. In that period the percentage of blacks soared from 4.6
percent to 10.7 percent of all collegians. To be sure, there are still
noticeable differences between black and white college enrollments. First, of the total black and white high school enrollment
in 1977, blacks were approximately 18 percent. Yet the black
percentage in college was only 12.5 percent. Second, the distribution of students among two-year colleges, four-year colleges, and
universities is statistically significant along racial lines. For the

black collegians, in 1975–76, 34 percent were enrolled in two-year colleges, 44 percent in four-year colleges, and 16 percent in universities. For whites, only 23 percent were enrolled in two-year colleges, 44 percent in four-year colleges, and 33 percent in universities. Such distributions undoubtedly produce differential access to professional and employment opportunities. Third, there is a noticeable difference between blacks and whites in the proportion completing college. As of 1976, among 25- to 29-year-olds, for every 100 white males, 34 were college educated, whereas only about 11 out of 100 minority males or minority females were college educated. "In other words," reports the U.S. Commission on Civil Rights, "most minority and female groups remain only about 30 percent as likely as majority males to have a college education." Thus significant inequalities persist.[49]

There have, however, been tremendous gains since the Brown decision. During these years blacks have virtually doubled their median years of school completed, doubled the proportion who are high school graduates, almost tripled their rate of college attainment, and increased sharply their enrollment percentages in high school and college. Clearly, the academic achievement level of the black population has not reached parity with whites. But when one takes a look at black educational attainment since 1950, the gains are highly visible. And these gains are even more remarkable when we reflect on the fact that they were achieved by a relatively low-income minority group, in mostly segregated schools, and under considerable repression by the dominant society.

If these educational gains are · solid—and since educational attainment (the number of years of schooling completed) is supposedly a prime determinant of access to occupations—it is important to look at the impact of post-1950 schooling on black participation in the labor force. If we look at the relationship between educational attainment and participation in the labor force, we find that many whites with good and respectable jobs have neither had nor needed much formal education. Dorothy K. Newman, in *Protest, Politics, and Prosperity*, documents that in 1950 white high school dropouts made up half the experienced civilian labor force. That year, white workers who had not finished high school constituted 65 to 70 percent of all the skilled and semiskilled workers in industry (in crafts or production jobs); 50 percent of the police; 40 percent or more of all sales workers; and 30 percent of all clerical workers.

In 1960 this picture had not changed significantly. Whites without high school diplomas still made up 46 percent of the labor force. Although by that time 42 percent of the blacks 20 to 24 years old had completed four years of high school or more, virtually none had access to these occupations. In 1960 whites constituted 95 percent of the clerical workers (bank tellers, 99 percent; secretaries, 98 percent; telephone operators, 97 percent), 97 percent of the salespeople, 95 percent of the crafts workers (compositors and typesetters, 98 percent; electricians, 99 percent; airplane mechanics, 96 percent; tool and die makers, 100 percent), 96 percent of the bus drivers, and 98 percent of the police. In short, white high school dropouts had much greater access to such occupations than black high school graduates. The statistics for 1970 show the persistence of this pattern: one-third of the total labor force still consisted of white workers who had not finished high school, and black high-school graduates still found it extremely difficult to get jobs as salespeople, clerical workers, police, and craftsmen.[50]

Black youth still find it almost impossible to gain access to the skilled trades. What Frederick Douglass said in 1853, that it was easier for his son to enter law than mechanics, rings true today. Between 1950 and the present, there have been very few black apprentices in the United States. The U.S. Census Bureau reported that blacks constituted 1.9 percent of apprentices in the labor force in 1950 and 2.5 percent in 1960. According to census figures, there were 2,190 black apprentices in 1950 and 2,191 in 1960. Significantly, the only apprenticeship classifications in which blacks even approximated their proportions of the total work force in 1960 (10.6 percent) were the building trades. Within the building trades, however, black workers were concentrated primarily in the laborers' jobs and in the trowel trades (cement masons, plasterers, and bricklayers) and carpentry. In 1965 a survey by the President's Committee on Equal Employment Opportunity of 989 construction industry contractors, 281 employer associations, and 731 unions uncovered the gross underrepresentation of blacks in apprenticeship programs. The survey showed that in 30 Southern cities, of 3,696 apprentices selected for the five building trades (plumbers, electricians, sheet metal workers, ironworkers, carpenters), only 26 were black; and 20 of these were in the carpenter's union, the one that has traditionally been the most accessible to blacks. In non-Southern cities, of the 5,908 apprentices in the five building trades, 133 were black, 70 of whom were carpenters.[51]

Since 1950, in good times or bad, the black youth unemployment rate has remained substantially higher than the white, and usually twice as high. Joblessness among black teenagers from sixteen to nineteen, for instance, soared from 16.5 percent in 1954 to 36.3 percent in 1978, compared to 12.1 and 13.9 percent for white teenagers. Moreover, according to the National Urban League, the 1978 figures are low. Using a hidden unemployment index, adjusted for temporary and part-time employment as well as for potential workers discouraged from seeking jobs, the Urban League estimated that more than 60 percent of the black teenagers were without full-time jobs in 1978. In Vernon Jordan's opinion, "Black America today verges on the brink of a disaster."[52]

Why is it that blacks' remarkable increase in educational attainment has not significantly increased their chances of finding and holding a job or of getting better jobs and making more money? As any student of black history would suspect, there is no dearth of rationales to explain this phenomenon. One, however, has emerged as most popular in rationalizing the persistent high unemployment rate among black workers despite such changes as economic growth, migration, and advances in schooling. Black joblessness is attributed to the worst of three kinds of unemployment. One kind is cyclical, caused by layoffs and the inability of the economy to produce new jobs during economic downturns. Another is the so-called frictional unemployment, which encompasses those workers who are between jobs, entering the labor market, or temporarily laid off. The third kind, called structural unemployment, is advanced to explain the persistently high unemployment rates among black Americans. Structural unemployment encompasses the pockets of seemingly intractable joblessness that exist in varying degrees whether the economic cycle is in boom or bust. Unlike cyclical and frictional unemployment, structural unemployment is not directly related to the economic cycle, but to the skills, training, or background of the workers. In the case of black workers, the structural unemployment concept holds that it is not so much their race that causes them to be unemployed as their lack of the skills, training, or background to find and hold a job. This is in effect a return to the political-educational rationalizations of the depression years, which blamed black youth unemployment on either poor education or miseducation, and drew attention away from underlying causes such as the basic inequality in the labor market.

In vital respects, the myth that blamed black unemployment on poor educational training has been exploded. If the lack of education, and not labor market racism, was the primary factor, then employment rates for black and white youths with similar education would be comparable. Instead, white high school dropouts have had lower unemployment rates than black high school graduates, and indeed lower rates than black youth with some college education. Thus, as the National Urban League said recently, "the myth that a lack of skills has kept black teenagers out of the labor force is not an adequate explanation." This position differs sharply from the one taken by Hill of the Urban League in the 1930's. Hill was strongly influenced by the social climate that blamed black youth unemployment on a lack of education and promised rewards for educational achievement. The upsurge in black education between the mid-1960's and early 1970's has sharpened to an intolerable degree the contradiction between blacks' educational attainment and their job opportunities.[53] For many civil rights leaders, professional educators, and researchers, the present crisis will open the way to new questions about the whole relation of education to black youth unemployment, especially in the twentieth-century city.

Conclusion

In March 1978, ten months after being founded, the National Association for the Advancement of Black Americans in Vocational Education held its first annual convention in Dallas, Texas. The meeting drew over 200 black vocational educators, besides politicians like Congresswoman Shirley Chisholm and government officials like Ernest Green, an assistant secretary of labor. The participants agreed that the most critical issue facing black Americans, particularly the young, is the high rate of unemployment. Two factors, inadequate training and discriminatory hiring practices, were singled out as major causes of the disproportionately high unemployment among black youth. The association dedicated itself to "work directly" to overcome the problem of inadequate training and to "work indirectly" to overcome the problems of job isolation and employment discrimination. Such action, such concerns, and even such views of the causes of black youth unemployment are not new. They remind us of Frederick Douglass's concerns in the mid-nineteenth century and of W. E. B. DuBois's arguments early in this century; and they are strikingly similar to movements and issues during the Great Depression. DuBois, in 1912, said: "Race prejudice, more than any other single factor, retards the Negroes' development in the economic world." And he bitterly criticized the industrial schools for "teaching mere hand work" and for failing to train black students for "modern industry."[54]

New directions in black vocational education, therefore, should raise new questions, or at least answer old ones in such a complete manner that they will not recur in the same forms over the next one hundred years. For instance, precisely how much of the black youth unemployment rate can we actually attribute to "inadequate training," and what constitutes the appropriate amount and quality of education for gaining access to stable, well-paying jobs. The United States Employment Service has looked at jobs in terms of the worker traits required for successful performance. Its job-analysis manual, *Dictionary of Occupational Titles*, first published in 1944 and updated in 1956 and 1965, provides specifications for several thousand occupations. The Bureau of Labor Statistics published less-detailed information over the same period of time in its *Occupational Outlook Handbook*. These reference works agree that the overwhelming majority of American workers have had as much formal schooling as their jobs demand, or more. This has been as true for black workers as for white. As Dorothy Newman put it, "Both the *Dictionary* and the *Handbook* still make the important point that most jobs in the labor force can be learned on the job, in a short time, and without a high-school diploma—jobs the white labor force has long managed to hold without a diploma. . . ." It is with this reality clearly in mind that we must explore the relationship between education and black participation in the labor force.[55]

We should also ask similar questions about employment discrimination as a determinant of the extent to which young blacks participate in the labor market. Sociologists such as William J. Wilson and Nathan Glazer claim that labor market racism is abating rapidly. "In the economic sphere," contends Wilson, "class has become more important than race in determining black access to privilege and power." However, economists like Stanley H. Masters and Irwin Garfinkel are convinced that labor market discrimination is still important as an explanation for black unemployment and black-white income differentials. Though acknowledging a more liberal climate since 1965, Masters concluded that "there does not appear to have been any significant decrease in labor market discrimination in the century following the Civil War." Garfinkel documented that labor market discrimination "accounts for from 43 percent to 60 percent of the total earnings gap between black and white males. . . . If labor market discrimination were eliminated, the earnings of black men would increase by 25 percent to 35 percent." Clearly, we need to know more precisely what to attribute to labor market discrimination and what to attribute to inadequate training before we can decide where to concentrate our resources in order to solve the problems of black youth unemployment and underemployment.[56]

Finally, general policy recommendations are likely to be better if they arise from an understanding of the educational, social, and economic problems of black youth over time. A history of black youth in the twentieth-century city, covering such areas as population characteristics, social groups, family, schooling, vocational aspirations, marriage, work, unemployment, crime, and imprisonment is badly needed.

"Marry, Stitch, Die, or Do Worse":

Educating Women for Work

GERALDINE JONÇICH CLIFFORD

Introduction

In the nineteenth century, when the campaign for women's education finally bore dramatic results, the author and lecturer Caroline Dall argued that to deprive women of education was to keep them from respected and decently rewarded employment. Society's command to the uneducated women, Dall said, was "Marry, stitch, die, or do worse."[1] Dall, forced into teaching at age nineteen by her father's business reverses and later trapped in a difficult marriage, was one of many Americans struggling to resolve personally the many-sided "Woman Question."

Across the continent, near Fidalgo, Washington Territory, another Caroline had a family talk prompted by her father's "blues about me"; afterward she confided to her diary, "I have never longed to be a man—I am glad that I am a woman—but sometimes my womanhood is almost a burden." Carrie White, two generations younger than Dall and also a sometime teacher, was confused by her parents' seemingly contradictory behavior. Following one clash with her father, she wrote:

He then said, "you ought to be willing to do something to make a living." I replied that I was and thought I did do something towards it. But the idea of father making such a speech. Is he growing tired of me and thinks it would be a relief to have me off his hands? I wonder if I had better try it! But when I had a small position offered me in Whitman College they did not want me to accept it. Well if the time does ever come when they think me a burden it will be very very bitter for me and I shall almost regret that I did not continue teaching and so make a calling for myself where I could be independent.[2]

Each of these two Carolines had received schooling, probably somewhat more than the average male of her generation, social class, and region. For these women, as for progressively more American women in the nineteenth and twentieth centuries, the educational question became less that of access to schooling than "the rather damaging one of what they are going to do with their learning once they get it."[3] Decisions about work, like decisions about education, were rooted in family life and in shifting personal and social expectations about the family. By the turn of the century, it was widely reported that many well-educated, middle-class wives yearned for "careers," unlike young shop girls and factory hands, who still planned to get married and stop working.[4] Of course, not all women agonized about work or risked family dissension. Economic pressure denied choice to some, and cultural imperatives caused others never to consider alternatives. Nonetheless, economic and social change and cross-cultural contacts were raising new possibilities. So was education. While society debated and educators made their nervous, inconclusive adjustments to the fact that women were increasingly employed outside the home, individuals and families reached their decisions about schooling and work. And increasingly, the actions of women with respect to schooling had occupational ramifications.

In 1800 the women's share of the labor force was a mere 4.6 percent; in 1850 only one worker in ten was a woman. But in 1900 females age fourteen and older made up 18.3 percent of the labor force, and in 1920, 20.4 percent. The rate continued to grow despite the depression years of the 1930's and the layoffs of women workers after the Second World War. The 1950 census showed women to be 27.9 percent of the work force. Recent increases have been dramatic: to 37.1 percent in 1960; 42.8 percent in 1970; and 46 percent in 1978.[5]

Three other changes in women's employment are noteworthy. One was the shift from manufacturing and domestic labor to white-collar work; between 1900 and 1940 the percentage of women in nonmanual occupations grew from 28 to 45 percent. The second was the lengthening of the average woman worker's expected employment life: from the frequently cited figure of seven years in 1890 to 25 years in 1960.[6] The third was the development of a strong association between the amount of formal schooling a woman had and the kind of job she had; in 1973, for example, female high school graduates were two and one-half times more likely to hold clerical and sales jobs than nongraduates, and half as likely to work in the service and operative sectors.[7]

Little is known of the ways in which women were prepared and encouraged to join the labor force. When and how did the roles of home and school change in shaping women's consciousness of work and of the choices among available occupations? Moreover, public schools, when they began to give vocational guidance and training, interacted with social class, ethnicity, and region. How did gender fit into the equation?

In this study I address these issues by analyzing the interacting roles of the family, work, and education for work. Decisions and actions concerning education and work are rarely free from family influences, deliberate and subliminal. This was especially true in the nineteenth century because there was less compulsion to attend school, among other reasons. I also argue that such decisions were most securely rooted in the family in the case of girls, since their future role as family members was central to their life planning.

As is made clear in other essays in this volume, the new social history of education has borrowed social-structural models, using them to order data and to explain what happened over time to educational institutions workplaces, and their inhabitants. By design, econometricians, political economists, sociologists, and demographers often give little attention to individual experience and personal meanings. History, however, is a humanity as well as a social science. The meanings people attach to their experiences; their sense of what drives or limits their actions; the victories and defeats of their lives; what builds them up and what tears or wears them down; the struggle within as well as the struggle without—these are also the data of history. Therefore, this paper incorporates many first-person accounts from individual American women like Carrie White. Would that space permitted many more women to speak here!

Educating the Sexes for Work

The history of women and work in the United States may be divided into two parts: the pre-vocational education era, and the vocational education era. In the first period, essentially from the late eighteenth century through the nineteenth, schooling was not thought to be directly related to vocational preparation or vocational guidance. For either sex, job skills were to be learned at the work site. The home and family were typically important, and indeed critical, in that occupational learning. For males, formal and informal apprenticeship and practical experience eased the transition from predominantly agrarian labor to commercial and industrial labor. For females, there were fewer alternatives to home instruction. But as household life slowly changed and as outside opportunities for work and training came into view, many mothers and aunts became less adequate as role models and imparters of economic skills. By the early twentieth century, it was claimed that many middle-class housewives were inadequately equipped even to teach domestic skills to their hired girls.[8]

In an age when schools and jobs were not "matched," the length of school attendance did not predict occupational entry or persistence. Persons with similar or identical educational backgrounds might work in widely divergent occupations; conversely, persons with a given occupation might have quite different educational credentials. The majority of Americans schooled in the nineteenth century attended nonurban common schools. By midcentury, those who attended the longest were probably girls and those boys looking primarily to occupy spare time; boys with clear occupational goals had left the common schools to gain work experience or, less frequently, to attend more advanced schools.[9] Oliver Johnson, recalling his Indiana boyhood of the 1840's, wrote, "Boys and girls could go to school just as long as they wanted to, or as long as they paid for their term. . . . I think a lot of us kept going to school more for a pastime and to get away from the monotony of home life than we did for book learning."[10] Neither schooling nor work was as rigidly age-graded as it would become, and youth moved quite freely in and out of school and back and forth between school, work, and their families.

Below the college level, the amount of schooling boys and girls received became quite similar as the nineteenth century matured. Most of that schooling, moreover, was not gender specific— despite some efforts to have it so.[11] When Bradford Academy opened as a coeducational school in that Massachusetts town in 1803, the tuition was twenty cents a week. If boys wished to study the mathematical principles of navigation and surveying, a thirty-cent charge was added; girls could have painting, drawing, and embroidery for just five cents more. Both sexes, however, got a curriculum that stressed grammar, penmanship, parsing, and elementary science. The Kanawha County, West Virginia, school records for 1840 list the boys' curriculum as reading, writing, and arithmetic, and the girls' as reading and spelling; whether practice conformed to this is not known, but neither sex got a very generous curriculum. When Colburn's *Intellectual Arithmetic* (1821) was introduced, some female students reported being told, "If you expect to become widows and have to carry pork to market, it may be well enough to study mental arithmetic."[12] Nevertheless, Colburn's text became a staple for generations of students of either sex.

The children's reader *Good Behavior* (1881) specified that girls get precedence coming and going at recesses. Such decorum, imperfectly achieved at best, was probably better observed than were the recommendations for the provision of separate entrances, physical dividers, and segregated departments. At Bradford, the boys' and girls' departments were often combined, simply because it was hard to keep teachers, and the number of boys lagged dangerously. Notwithstanding a literature that urged physical separation, teacher and student diaries suggest that practice departed widely from precept;[13] separation was impracticable, and many Americans were just not that fussy about details.

The clearest case of discrimination against women involved colleges, most of which did not admit women before 1865. In that year, however, only 1 percent of all American students were collegians. So loose was the relationship of education to work that access to the traditional learned professions could be gained by varying combinations of self-study, apprenticeship, and non-collegiate schooling. In 1876, however, the National Education Association created an Industrial Section, acknowledging a growing interest in adapting schools to students' vocational futures.[14] Many youngsters age fourteen or older were then neither in school nor prepared by schooling for the work they found or hoped to find. Numerous studies reported their dislike for school and their failure to see its worth. Some educators, therefore, advocated job training in the new junior high schools, in trade schools, or in vocational high schools. Even females, certain educators stressed, should at least receive manual training, the development of eye and hand, as the broadest foundation of an industrial education that was being described as the birthright of every American child.[15] Although in 1920, for example, more students were found in general education than in vocational classes, vocationalism nonetheless triumphed, historians have argued, with the acceptance of the principle that schools have a primary obligation to prepare youth for jobs, with the appearance of vocational guidance, and with some differentiation of curricula according to the probable occupational destiny of the pupil.[16]

In the vocational education era, schooling became a sufficiently universal and extended experience that the amount of schooling broadly, if crudely, came to define occupational placement. In many ways, however, the distinctive spheres of men and women workers were preserved. As will be seen, gender represents a crucial link between the pre-vocational and vocational periods.

The School of Life: The Pre-Vocational Education Era

In the nineteenth century almost all women worked—in the home, in the factory, in the schoolhouse. Employments such as these showed two characteristics: they were accessible to women of differing educational qualifications, and more importantly, they demonstrated society's capacity to use gender stereotypes to meet new demands for labor.

The Younger Worker at Home. The home worker, whether in her own or another's household, inherited an ages-old pattern of domestic employment. Labor shortages in the United States may have enhanced women's value—and widened somewhat their range of duties beyond the house, gardens, poultry yard, and pasture—but gender continued to define the expected work roles.[17] On the Indiana frontier, Peggy Johnson, a young mother of three, wrote, "If ever there was true happiness on earth it is in our own family. . . . Here everyone appears to be anxious to do what is right . . . each one Cheerfully performs the duty of his station. . . . I stay at home and . . . feel a great pleasure in the performance of what I consider my duty."[18]

Although many jobs were sexually defined, there was some sharing, especially among women, children, servants, and other dependents. As children grew, they assumed more of the domestic work, under maternal supervision. Large farm families dispensed with hired help as the sons gradually took over; this, at least, reduced the number of persons for whom the girls and women cooked, sewed, and laundered.[19] Daughters, by their wedding day, had learned virtually all they needed to know to run a household. If they did not marry or returned to their childhood homes as marital casualties or widows, the care of aging parents or family unfortunates was honorable employment. In the Luellen family in Pennsylvania, Aunt Polly was like the biblical Martha: "the devoted slave" of her parents, a crippled brother, and an imbecile sister.[20] Even so, an astute girl like Florence Peck might reflect on the fact that when her grandmother died, her Aunt Lucy found her "*life* work taken away."[21] Circumstances permitting, then, a "modern" girl might try to spend her life differently.

Women contributed variously to the family economy in the nineteenth century. Many households produced articles and services both for home consumption and for cash or barter. On a Kansas farm, John Ise's mother did laundry for bachelors and widowers, along with her butter and egg business and her daily chores.[22] More indicative of economic change, however, was the placement in New England farmhouses of the wholesale businesses of sewing shoes, spinning yarn, and weaving cloth. By 1800, women were sewing the uppers of shoes and boots, and by the 1830's, 60 percent of the total output of Lynn, Massachusetts, came from scattered domestic manufacturing.[23]

Textiles were historically women's work. Indentures had commonly specified that girls "be instructed in the art of a spin-

ster, seamster, and housekeeping"—the words of Phoebe Carpenter's 1803 agreement with Enoch Cate concerning her daughter Sarah.[24] In the 1830's Benjamin Barnard's four daughters, but
never his three sons, might all be spinning "flax and tow in the
spring and wool in summer."[25] As tow spinning grew less important and other household duties lighter, Nancy Barnard was permitted to leave her Vermont home to attend the academy in
Westminster, Massachusetts, where she had relatives to board
her in exchange for housework. For Jane Conine of Wyoming
County, New York, it was domestic strife—a stepmother whom
she loathed—that drove her, around 1850, to live with various
families as a seamstress.[26] She soon ended up, like Nancy Barnard, in another extension of the "woman's sphere," presiding
over a school, before taking final refuge running an Indiana
household as John Hawkins's wife.

Kathryn Sklar argues convincingly that the expansion of the
household manufacturing system in late eighteenth- and early
nineteenth-century New England enabled many girls both to
reimburse their parents for the small costs of district schooling
and to purchase for themselves additional education in female
seminaries and coeducational academies. These schools proliferated to meet the new demands. By getting more schooling, young
women became more employable as teachers in common schools
and academies.[27] The additional element in this equation was the
reduced demand for young women's labor at home. Especially in
the Northeast, women were slowly losing some of their productive and reproductive functions. Except in new areas of settlement, household manufacture was increasingly restricted to
household use; first in urban middle-class families, and then
widely, the "manufacturing mother" was becoming the housewife. Meanwhile, more men were leaving the household to work,
go to sea, or take up land in the West.

Until the 1890's the surplus of permanently single women grew
progressively larger, and the average age of first marriage rose.
Among the marrying, birth rates dropped. On the average,
women in 1800 had 7.04 children; in 1850 the figure was 5.42; by
1900 it was 3.56.[28] Lower infant and child mortality meant that
proportionately more children survived, but since women were
pregnant or nursing during a smaller part of their lives, they

required less household assistance from their daughters. More schooling became available, too, and this further diminished the child-care demands on daughters. New educational and work careers grew to fill the void.

The Factory Girl. When seventeen-year-old Sally Rice left her family in Vermont in 1838 to "work out" in the Holmeses' farmhouse near Union Village, New York, she was following an ancient tradition. Domestic service historically offered girls housing, family protection, and employment that used home-learned skills. Of her new situation Sally wrote,

They are very anxious that I should live with them as long as I work out anywhere. . . . I have got so that by next summer if I could stay I could begin to lay up something. I am most 19 years old. I must of course have something of my own before many more years have passed over my head. And where is that something coming from if I go home and earn nothing? What can we get off that rocky farm?[29]

There were also new alternatives to domestic labor for farmers' daughters. When the Boston Manufacturing Company opened its large mill in Waltham in 1814, it found farm girls eager to earn dowry money, to add to family income, or perhaps to help a brother into college.[30] By the 1830's and 1840's, the famed Lowell mills employed thousands of young women and children, with girls outnumbering boys five to one. In 1845 Sally Rice explained to her father her decision to work in Connecticut's Masonville mill: "Well knowing that you were dolefully prejudiced against a cotton factory, and being no less prejudiced myself, I thought it best to wait and see how I prospered." While visiting her young suitor's sisters, she was asked to learn to weave, but "I did not fall in with the idea at all because I well knew that I should not like it as well as housework and knowing that you would not approve of my working in the mill. But when I considered that I had got myself to take care of, I knew I ought to do [it;] that way I can make the most and save the most."[31]

The Lowell mills' dormitories, rules of conduct, and regulated living reflected social expectations about home-like protections. Long hours of hard work, sobriety, and church attendance "in a measure reflected the social standard and practices of their homes."[32] Sally Rice, like others, found a church and entered a routine of twelve- to fourteen-hour days tending three pounding looms. Machinery had so reduced the level of necessary skills that she learned the work in one week. Being readily learned, mill employment was easily abandoned.[33] Like others, Sally intended a brief career:

I like it quite as well as I expected but not as well as housework. To be sure it is a noisy place and we are confined more than I like to be. I do not wear out my clothes and shoes as I do when I do housework. If I can make 2 dollars per week besides my board and save my clothes and shoes I think it will be better than to do housework for nine shillings. I mean for a year or two. I should not want to spend my days in a mill.*

Sally Rice had only a common-school education. Yet she and most other Yankee mill operatives had more formal schooling than the Irish girls who succeeded them in Lowell or Cohoes, New York, or the Italian women workers of Buffalo and Providence, or the North Carolina girls when the textile mills went South late in the century. That link between factory employment and educational aspiration, reported in Lucy Larcom's widely read reminiscences, was more than myth. One woman recalled her experiences in Lowell around 1837, where she alternated mill work and school from age fourteen: "I was ambitious to do something for myself in the way of earning money to pay my expenses at an Academy; and being too young to teach school in the country, not strong enough to do housework or learn a trade, I went into the card-room of the Fremont Corporation."[34] A Clinton, Massachusetts, factory worker who nightly studied Weld's *Grammar* explained in 1851 why she meant to enter Oberlin College:

I have earned enough to school me awhile, & have not I a right to do so, or must I go home, like a dutiful girl, place the money in father's hand & then there goes all my hard earnings, within prison walls, my sleepless nights & gloomy days, & all for what. . . . But if I go to Oberlin I take comfort & forget all these long wearisome mill days & perhaps I prepare

*Sally Rice to Hazelton Rice, Feb. 23, 1845, in Nell W. Kull, "I Can Never Be Happy There in Among So Many Mountains—The Letters of Sally Rice," *Vermont History*, 38 (1970): 54. The unhealthy swamp surrounding the mill drove Sally away in a few months. In 1847, after another short stay in farm work, she married James Alger and settled in Worcester, Massachusetts.

myself for usefulness in this life. . . . If I am necessarily detained at home I shall think all is for the best. I merely wish to go because I think it the best way of spending the money I have worked so hard to earn.[35]

Among prosperous families, of course, factory employment was regarded as evidence of misfortune rather than opportunity. After a visit to Greenfield, Massachusetts, in 1837, Mary Todd reassured her friends that the rumors about the Farnums were ill founded: "Their Father did not fail as was reported, neither are the girls working in a factory."[36] Before the Civil War, factory work paid better than teaching, given the seasonal and short-term nature of the common schools. Nonetheless, manufacturing jobs were to become less important to women: in 1850 women made up 24 percent of all manufacturing employees, by 1900, only 19 percent. The daughters of New England Protestant farm families increasingly abandoned the mills to immigrant job seekers, and the factory came to represent in many more minds the workplace of the unlucky or the unambitious. An orphaned Mary Bartlett, when she left her cousin's house in 1870 to live with her guardian George Nye, related that "Mrs. Nye said if she couldn't get a school she would have to work in the factory."[37] For Mary, however, and for others eager or needing to make their own way, if local schools did not require teachers there was always "the West," a place of unmet educational needs and single men. A case in point was Urania Richards of Gill, Massachusetts, who left the Lowell mills around 1840 to teach school in Ohio. Reporting her marriage in 1847, the Lowell *Voice of Industry* advised: "Sisters of New England, 'Go ye and do likewise.' "[38]

The Schoolmistress. It was sometimes argued that to send eastern women to educate and Christianize the West was futile and wasteful, that such organizations as the Ladies' Society for the Promotion of Education at the West would quickly lose their recruits to the "School for Life." In 1858, for example, the Board of National Popular Education reported that it had sent 481 teachers to the West, and 75 of them had married. Nevertheless, it was considered a "source of no-little satisfaction, that we have been instrumental in furnishing seventy-five good wives to as many gentlemen of the West." Indeed, in 1846 the *New York Evangelist* argued that:

In regard to forsaking the teachers office for domestic alliances, which is predicted as a serious embarrassment, no evil or disappointment is anticipated; *for it is believed, that in all cases, the school room is the truest avenue to domestic happiness.* Every such departure can be made good by new recruits, who will find their best friends and firmest supporters in their predecessors, settled around them as the wives and mothers of the most influential members of society.[39]

Many in the nineteenth century believed that preparation for teaching and experience in the classroom were good for a woman's ultimate career as a wife and mother; undoubtedly, this belief still influences the career decisions of young women. Such a view stimulated a high turnover rate in the female teaching force, and the resulting large group of former teachers in the citizenry probably acted to promote a strong public sentiment in favor of public education.

The turnover among female teachers was truly extraordinary, as was the large share that teaching had of the outside work experience of women in a century when most women worked only at home. Data for Massachusetts before the Civil War, when women numerically dominated the schools, show that in any given year teaching did not constitute more than 2 percent of the employment of all white women aged 15 to 60, the vast majority of whom were employed in their own or related households. Of all white women of the state, however, one in five had taught *at some time* in her life, and probably one in four of the native-born women had been teachers.[40]

In 1839, specifically to prepare teachers, Massachusetts opened the first public normal school in America. By 1860 there were four in the state, two for women and two coeducational. Frances Merritt was a "normalite" at the all-female Framingham Normal School in 1854 and 1855. In her diary she recorded her reflections after an instructor raised the issue of the "woman's mission":

There is so much truth in what Mr. Stearns said to-day of woman's mission. His view seems to be just the right one. Better exercise the influence God has given her over the heart, mind and will of all mankind in the most lovely and becoming manner, than to speak about women's rights, or to step out of her Heaven-ordained sphere.

I am glad these rights have been talked of, nevertheless, for I think that many true women, after seeing a few experiments tried, will rejoice more heartily in the lot to which God has appointed them, and to be more awake to its high and holy requirements.[41]

Although the number of public normal schools in the nation grew from thirteen in 1860 to 135 in 1890, they educated only a small proportion of all teachers. Most teachers acquired else-where whatever passed for occupational skills—and whatever understanding they had of the relationship between their occupation and their sex. Many of the students in the proliferating normal schools had already been teachers, their enrollment signifying a desire to advance in the profession rather than an initial preparation for teaching. In the 1874 class of the Illinois State Normal School, for example, all of the fifteen male students had taught; five had been principals of graded schools, and one a county superintendent. The experience of the eighteen women totaled 20.8 teaching years.[42]

A small but important segment of teachers first entered teaching from female seminaries and coeducational academies that promised disciplined study enabling a woman "to regulate her own mind, and to be useful to others."[43] Many such institutions educated teachers only incidentally. In the process, however, of appealing to the more serious-minded girls by teaching them algebra and geology, they were also equipping them to be teachers, even in the higher grades.[44] Other seminaries, like Mount Holyoke, had been founded to prepare good Christians to be good teachers; in its first half-century, 80 percent or more of its students became teachers, without benefit of pedagogy courses or practice in model schools. Along with supplying teachers for new seminaries in the South and West, Mount Holyoke sent women abroad, to the foreign mission field; to the South to teach reading and Bible study on Sundays to factory-employed children and later as "teachers of the contraband"; and to Oklahoma to teach Indian children.[45] These women taught in schools that saw different destinies for men and women: boys were taught farming, livestock raising, and manual arts; girls received "constant instruction in needle, household, and all kinds of work that properly fall to the share of woman in civilized domestic economy."[46] Organized on the manual labor principle, mission schools also required different work of the two sexes, as had Oberlin College and the scores of other manual labor schools popular in the 1830's and 1840's. Thus school experiences reinforced the lessons learned at home in childhood about the respective spheres and appropriate conduct of each sex.

Although teaching in mission schools in distant climes glamorized teaching, most women teachers in the nineteenth century remained, at least through their initial experience, within the family orbit. Whatever education in teaching they possessed they gained in the undifferentiated local common schools. This was supplemented by occasional county or state teachers' meetings ("institutes"), where most had their first opportunity to form a new identity and ties that transcended those of the family and the neighborhood. With experience, teachers could gain additional independence by taking a school progressively farther from their family and from familiar surroundings. But many novices and short-term teachers stayed put; a study of the living conditions of the women teachers of Michigan in 1860 found 66 percent living with their families of origin.[47]

Throughout the century, family influences continued to ease the entry into teaching, as recent historians have similarly found in the recruiting of factory workers. Diaries and letters show that women were often drawn into teaching by the example of relatives, and that family initiative and influence were responsible for filling many teaching posts.[48] Cassie Wiggins reported that she became a teacher in large part because of her mother's disappointment at not having been allowed to attend an academy in Pennsylvania during her youth in the 1850's, and also because her Aunt Mag, a teacher, had been a boarder in her Iowa home in the 1870's.[49] The national landscape was peppered with families, like the Kennedys of Kentucky and Indiana, the Applegates of Oregon, and the Funkhousers of Maryland, in which teaching seemed as natural as breathing.[50] Relatives filled in for teachers who were sick or had other business, as when Rebecca Bright finished her sister Abbie's term at the Danville, Pennsylvania, school so that Abbie could visit in the West.[51] Jabez Brown, a resident of Wisconsin who combined farming and teaching through the 1850's and 1860's, inducted his sons, daughters, nieces, nephews, and neighbors' children into teaching; he talked to officials about hiring them, broadcast the news of school vacancies, and ensured that these youngsters passed the teachers' examinations and collected their wages.[52] When Lydia Murdoch attended the Bellefield School in Pittsburgh in the 1880's, "at different times there were three of one family teaching in that school, relatives of the boss, Chris Magee."[53]

Becoming a teacher was made easier by the personalized nature of nineteenth-century teaching, even in city neighborhoods and the colleges. It was also helped by the spread of public and private schooling, outward from New England and Ohio, into rural and urban areas, and upward well into the years of adolescence. This growth created students, teaching jobs, and teachers. Thus, whereas the daughters of rural England became domestic servants away from home, their American counterparts more often became teachers. Of course, the wages were poor and sometimes uncertain: Eunice Will's contract with the Sutherland Springs, Texas, School Board specified employment for "three months, or until the public fund appropriated to the community school is exhausted."[54] Many a teacher reported the failure of parents to pay the rate bill agreed on. Women teachers almost always earned less and experienced other discrimination. In graded common schools, the female teacher was the "assistant teacher" and her male colleague the "master" or "principal." Male high school teachers were addressed as "Professor" and their female counterparts as "Miss." One is reminded of the 1805 catalogue of Bradford Academy, which reported having "twenty-nine Students and forty-six Females" enrolled that year.

Poor wages and the possibility of other occupations discouraged male careers in teaching. Except in the South and in some primarily rural states, males were unavailable or unwilling to compete except for high school positions and, later, for the administrative posts that men came to dominate. If America was to have universal schooling, perhaps it would have to conclude that teaching was, as Horace Mann contended, "truly feminine" employment.*

---

*As the Roman Catholic Church in America expanded its parochial schools, the proportion of women religious in jobs other than teaching declined. In Boston in 1880, 40 percent of the nuns were in teaching, hospital work, or social work with orphans, the poor, the handicapped, and the elderly; by 1940 that figure had shrunk to 12 percent. See Mary J. Oates, "Organized Volunteerism: The Catholic Sisters in Massachusetts, 1870–1940," *American Quarterly*, 30 (1978): 654–55.

In the Indiana of 1828, "there was no such thing as a woman teacher," remembered Oliver Johnson. "It wasn't a woman's job, any more than milking a cow was a man's job."[55] By the time of Johnson's death in 1907, two of every three public school teachers in the United States were women; twelve cities in seven states reported hiring only women; and women made up 967 of the 1,070 teachers in San Francisco and two-thirds of the high school teachers in Los Angeles. In the nation's urban high schools in 1907, where girls were 57 percent of the students, women were 53 percent of the teachers. What aspirations and expectations were raised or confirmed by these experiences? Of what significance was it that in the smaller but much talked-of sector of manual and industrial training, women were less in evidence—only 36 percent of the students and 34 percent of the teachers?[56]

From Latin to Life: The Vocational Education Era

One of the earliest governmental actions on behalf of sex-segregated vocational education might be that described in an 1832 treaty between the United States and the Winnebago Indians. The federal government agreed to establish a school near Fort Crawford or Prairie du Chien

for the education, including clothing, board, and lodging, of such Winnebago children as may be voluntarily sent to it: . . . said children to be taught reading, writing, and arithmetic, gardening, agriculture, carding, spinning, weaving, and sewing, according to their ages and sexes, and such other branches of useful knowledge as the President of the United States may prescribe.[57]

But vocational education was slow to take root. Around 1913, Amanda Stoltzfus, former principal of the first Texas public school where manual training, home economics, and elementary agriculture were offered, traveled through the state as a rural school lecturer for the Extension Department of the University of Texas. She reported on a lecture she gave—on "The Good School"—in a schoolhouse with windows blown out by a recent storm:

It was most interesting to find a class of forty or fifty high school boys from a small town taught by a frail little woman. The girls were fewer in number, but all these and with others from a lower grade were crowded into one recitation room. . . . I described the modern school with its vitalized course of study related to the life of the people, to the life the boys and girls were expected to lead. I described the work of domestic economy, of manual training and agriculture, and told that today high schools no longer demanded of the young farmer a four year course in Latin. The smile that passed over the fine faces of these pupils told the story that they were all attempting the classical course. There was no science work in the school.[58]

Even in rural east Texas, some of these girls were destined to work outside the home, and even outside the area. As early as 1890, nearly half of all American women worked during the years between school and marriage.* Some educators were arguing, therefore, that schools must develop a differentiated curriculum so as to meet the sexes' different vocational roles. As a Canadian supervisor of manual training and household arts wrote in 1918, equity demanded such a curriculum, but implementation remained problematic:

Until very recently school systems were organized and courses drawn up on the assumption that the needs of the boy and the needs of the girl were identical and could be met by a study of the same subjects, but the subjects were chosen, and their content and extent determined almost entirely with reference to the supposed needs of the boy. This assumption dominated the entire system from the kindergarten to the University. It is now admitted that differentiation is necessary, but this differentiation in materials, means, and methods has not yet been satisfactorily worked out.[59]

Large city systems like those of Boston and New York developed a few separate high schools for boys or girls, organized around specific occupations. The Cleveland Technical High School proposed a complete separation, since it aimed "to prepare youth of both sexes for a definite vocation and for efficient industrial citizenship." As Superintendent Elson explained in 1909, separation exists "not for reasons of sex, but because of the

*In 1890, during those eight to ten years before marriage, 2.5 million of the 6 million single women over age fifteen worked for pay, and also another quarter-million under age fifteen. These figures do not include the uncounted women working in home industrial production. Robert Smuts, *Women and Work in America* (New York, 1971), pp. 23–24.

widely different kind of work"; a technical school should relate academic work closely to the shopwork, "so that the chemistry which the girls have, being chiefly applied chemistry, is different from that taken by the boys."[60]

Vocational educators were limited by academic conservatism, by the small size of most high schools, and probably by the premise that most females took jobs only briefly and reluctantly. Hence academic subjects ordinarily remained coeducational, poorly articulated with vocational education, and little affected by rhetoric about "becoming practical." Where available, "Business English" and "Commercial Math" were found to resemble closely the general courses.[61] Even where vocational courses were more highly developed, the matching of graduates to their intended vocations was imperfect at best. A 1915 study of Boston's Mechanic Arts High School (founded in 1892) showed its graduates and those of the English High School similarly distributed in employment.[62] Although most Mechanic Arts students wanted to go directly into manual trades, the Boston School Committee's purpose for the school was preparation for "advantageous entrance into industry on the business and directive side." And the "controlling aim" of the faculty was to give the 15 percent interested in higher education a general education and to prepare them for engineering colleges. Much has been made recently of sex segregation in vocational schools and classes, but the fact that Mechanic Arts was a high school for boys did not deprive girls of all opportunity to enter the Massachusetts Institute of Technology. MIT admissions data for 1911 reported students entering from Girls High, English High, and Boston's coeducational neighborhood high schools; and the Girls High entrants had the best success rate in MIT class standing.

Boston had sufficient population and the economic diversity to warrant school and course differentiation, whatever its results, but most communities nationwide did not. In the first decade of this century, more than 36 percent of high school pupils attended schools with three or fewer teachers; schools with one to three teachers were five times as numerous as those with five to ten teachers, and ten times those with ten or more teachers.[63] Small schools required a degree of versatility that did not augur well for specialized teaching of a high order. In response to an article challenging educators to enrich the curriculum of the six-teacher, six-year high school, a Nebraska schoolman proposed in 1933 a plan whereby only three teachers could offer all the basic academic subjects, hygiene, and fine arts, plus three vocational courses in grades seven and eight: practical arts for boys, homemaking for girls, and business and agriculture.[64] Some four decades later, a female graduate of a small (265 students) midwestern high school complained: "I wanted to take world history, but the principal said there wasn't enough kids for it so I had to take shorthand. And I wanted to take sociology and economics, but there wasn't enough kids for them either so I had to take home ec."[65]

The meaning of differentiation by gender cannot be measured, then, solely by reference to the provision, as happened in the United States, of courses largely limited to one sex. A cross-national study published in 1933 underscored the influence of coeducation. In Germany's system of single-sex schools, for example, except for needlework there was little along the lines of America's home economics. Yet in the *academic* classes taught to girls, the investigator observed: "Sex differences are stressed in the selection and handling of the educational materials with a view to developing and guiding the attitudes and interests which it is believed are peculiar to the female sex. . . . Girls' education in America [conversely] is almost inseparate from boys' education, since coeducation prevails."[66]

Different societies also approached vocational guidance differently. In Europe vocational guidance was developed in employment bureaus and labor exchanges, for the elementary school leaver who would work or attend a full-time or part-time vocational school.[67] The offering of occupational information in schools was unique to America, where, although vocational and educational guidance were confused, the likelihood was greater that girls would receive some early orientation to the work world. But many questioned the adequacy of such counseling. For example, it was charged that women teachers could not give proper vocational guidance, and that parochial school faculties were even less equipped by trade and industrial experience.[68]

Nonetheless, teachers did respond to their students' desire for job information. St. Louis teachers surveyed occupations and publicized the results, urging girls to prepare for jobs.[69] Groups of New York City eighth-graders attended the Manhattan Trade School for Girls for a two-week orientation to occupational possibilities, and took various commercial and industrial performance tests.[70] A committee of teachers working with the Bureau of Vocational Guidance of the Buffalo Chamber of Commerce urged other teachers to caution girls who wanted to escape from school: "Those who find it hard to get along in school with the assistance of their teachers will find it much harder to get along in business or in the industrial field, where no one is especially concerned as to whether they succeed or fail."[71] Despite these and other efforts, however, the American Youth Commission reported in 1938 that among those who had received vocational guidance, girls were somewhat less likely than boys to have found it satisfactory, and the largest group of former students who had not received guidance was that of homemakers.[72]

Vocational courses for girls represented an accommodation by schoolmen to a variety of realities: the continued commitment to women's prime (that is, domestic) vocation; the desire to "do something" for the girls while the boys went off to their "real" vocational courses; the practical scheduling problems of balancing boys' offerings and girls' offerings so as to preserve the basic coeducational mix in the rest of the curriculum; the hope of prolonging school attendance by adding nonacademic subjects; and the goal of Americanizing the daughters of the immigrants. Adjustment to the fact of women's employment may well have been the least pressing demand. Nonetheless, a women's position *among workers* was coming to be broadly defined by the amount, if not the kind, of formal schooling she possessed. The girl who left school for work after the eighth grade typically entered different work than the girl with high school experience. And the professions were increasingly being restricted to those with college education.

The Eighth-Grade Graduate. For many girls who left school around age fourteen, domestic service was their first job. For decades this was the largest source of employment for women of all ages, and it retained importance for those of lesser education, newcomers to America, and racial and ethnic minorities. When

Mary and Emma Minesinger, whose mother was a Shoshone Indian, completed their sporadic Montana schooling, each was hired as a housemaid in Missoula.[73] In 1920 three-fourths of employed black women worked as farm laborers, servants, and domestic laundresses.[74] As domestic employment slowly shifted its workplace to hotels, office buildings, and institutions, however, its share of all working women declined, from 60.7 percent in 1870 to 18.2 percent in 1920.

In England, "service" had historically been a major employment for both men and women. In 1924 an English housemaid recalled how her failures in job-hunting left her no occupational alternative:

I can only vaguely imagine what my mother must have felt. All that time, and all those books, and all my education—I know she was inarticulate—but I can see now the hurt in her eyes, that after all that, her daughter, her eldest, gawky, clever, talented daughter was going "into service," as she herself had done at the age of twelve—without education.[75]

Europe experienced a servant shortage as a result of education, competition from other work, and emigration, which had once supplied many American households with servants. In America, however, women simply would not stay in service. A study of New York's West Side around 1912 found 70 percent of wage-earning mothers in domestic service, but only 5 percent of their daughters; democratic America had acquired a "servant problem."[76] Characteristically, some tried to solve it with education, proposing that home economics courses and "schools of domestic science" add to their functions the task of training girls to be efficient, loyal, and satisfied domestic servants. Such an investment in education was justified, it was argued, in view of the findings of Lucy Salmon and others that the average domestic employee could save as much as a city schoolteacher or more. But the distaste for domestic service was strong. Even when a school proclaimed itself a trade school for homemakers, as the public School of Domestic Science and Domestic Art in Rochester, New York, did in 1909, the students feared that they were being trained for domestic service. The Rochester school had to be reorganized with an emphasis on dressmaking and millinery.*

Many girls preferred factory work to domestic service. But as a group of Boston teachers put it, there were few other alternatives for the girl who has to leave school at an early age with an incomplete education and lack of knowledge of English grammar, spelling, and arithmetic.[77] Nor indeed was factory work everywhere available. Much of the difference in female labor-force participation between the large cities (where 31.9 percent of women residents were employed in 1920) and the less urban districts (18.8 percent) is explainable by the amount of industry present. In one-industry towns even high school graduates, who usually shunned the factories, had few alternatives. A study of southern cotton mills concluded that the odds of a graduate's entering mill work were 9 to 1 for boys and 99 to 1 for girls. No wonder most mill town youngsters in the 1920's were leaving school for the mill at age fourteen.[78]

Boys and girls, like their fathers and mothers, worked at different kinds of jobs, often in different industries. In Paterson, New Jersey, for example, men were mainly found in the ironworks and women in textile factories. Although women were skilled cigar makers in Slavic countries, in Pittsburgh's cigar factories these same women were relegated to the lowest jobs.[79] Unskilled boys and girls had the most menial and poorly paid jobs, with minimal opportunity to learn much of economic value. But boys had the more varied work and tended to be less confined; whereas girls were runners in the factory, boys could be runners about the city.† Even in small towns, girls had less freedom. When Cassie Wiggins tried to emulate her brother in door-to-door selling, she was effectively stopped by a woman who gave her a tongue-lashing for her "unladylike conduct in going about as a peddler."[80]

---

*The school was not helped by the practice of transferring to it other schools' "undesirable and dull pupils"; see Albert H. Leake, *The Vocational Education of Girls and Women* (New York, 1918), p. 178.

†Katherine Anthony, *Mothers Who Must Earn* (New York, 1914), p. 42. When St. Louis surveyed its evening school enrollment in 1875, the girls attending were nearly all employed as servants, laundresses, milliners, sales clerks, nurses, or seamstresses and dressmakers. The boys were employed in about sixty different occupations. See Selwyn K. Troen, *The Public and the Schools: Shaping the St. Louis System, 1838–1920* (Columbia, Mo., 1975), p. 133.

The women workers who attended the Bryn Mawr Affiliated Summer Schools for Workers in the 1930's, when interviewed, did not mention vocational education. Theirs were mainly stories of leaving school early, often voluntarily, of blasted dreams and dead-end jobs.[81] What potential for learning was there in a shoe factory, where 150 to 200 separate operations stood between the worker and the finished product? Educators like Willystine Goodsell lamented "the bleak road which leads from one deadening occupation to another" and considered ways to put zest and meaning, as well as job skills, into the curriculum of part-time schooling for the young factory girls.

Yet society still refused to confront the reality that women worked. It was widely believed that the expectation of marriage caused girls "to look upon their employment as a temporary makeshift and therefore [they] are not anxious to learn their trade properly." Since many girls left school because they disliked it, educators and others thought girls were less able to be reached through night schools or continuation schools. Even among the more intelligent girls, it was reported, there was little interest in "occupational success in itself." The principal of New York City's East Side Continuation School advocated the requiring of each female continuation school student under age sixteen to take a course in homemaking. Such beliefs undoubtedly retarded the development of continuation and trade schools for girls; in 1910, of the 193 trade schools in operation, only 26 taught girls.[82]

Night schools offered girls and women other opportunities, however. Females often outnumbered males in night school vocational classes. In St. Louis evening classes, the percentage of females grew from 11.9 to 41.5 percent from 1910 to 1920.[83] Moreover, these students were often highly motivated. A society matron who worked beside Perry, New York, mill hands reported on such workers, children of immigrant families. "A great many of the girls and boys," she observed, "took correspondence courses in stenography, drawing, bookkeeping, illustrating, etc., etc. The purely mechanical work of the mill does not satisfy them. They are restless and ambitious."[84]

A Jewish immigrant from Poland spoke for herself about her expectations of work and education:

When mother died I thought I would try to learn a trade and then I could go to school at night and learn to speak the English well. So I went to work in Allen Street [Manhattan] in what they call a sweatshop, making skirts by machine. . . .

I am going back to night school again this winter. Plenty of my friends go there. Some of the women of my class are more than forty years of age. Like me, they did not have a chance to learn anything in the old country. It is good to have an education; it makes you feel higher. Ignorant people are all low. People say now that I am clever and fine in conversation. . . .

Some of the women blame me very much because I spend so much money on clothes. . . . Those who blame me are the old-country people who have old-fashioned notions, but the people who have been here a long time know better. . . .[85]

Those who left school characteristically went to work to add to family income, often working in the same factory as other family members. Sometimes their wages were paid to their father, following a European tradition. The employment of children in the Cohoes mill in the 1880's permitted their mothers to remain at home; and such practices continued in the twentieth century. Daughters in the French-Canadian community of Manchester, New Hampshire, contributed nearly all their earnings to the family, and their mothers and younger siblings gradually withdrew from factory work as a consequence. In Scranton, Pennsylvania, in the 1920's, child labor provided 35 percent of Polish family income; records were often falsified so that underage children could work.

Notably among Italians, sons might go to work so that their sisters as well as their mothers could stay at home.[86] Among Buffalo's Italians, sons and daughters left school in about the same proportions. Around 1910, of those aged fifteen to nineteen, 79 percent of the sons and 82 percent of the daughters were not in school. Sons went to work, and daughters helped out at home.[87] The Italians of New York City, because of high fertility, needed their children's contribution to family income. In the words of one historian, "With so many children . . . consumers had to be turned into wage earners as soon as possible, [and] long term education became even less feasible."[88] Female grade school leavers commonly headed not for work but to help at home; this was not unique to recent immigrants. A study in the 1910's of early school leavers in Bloomington, Indiana, found most boys employed as common laborers or looking for work. Over 43 percent of the girls, however, worked only at home.[89]

Less employment opportunity for girls was a factor. Another was the presence of work at home that did not tax the skills of young girls. In addition to the ordinary household duties, girls could contribute indirectly to family income by assisting with the lodgers and boarders who were important in many households.[90] Moreover, an uncounted number of girls and women, especially in immigrant neighborhoods, took in laundry, made lace, jewelry, artificial flowers, and cigars, or did finish work for the garment industry. It was reported that many within a thirty-mile radius of Troy, New York, worked at home for its collar and cuff industry.[91] Daughters who assisted in piecework at home protected their mothers from the discrimination in the labor market that might come from the handicaps of language and foreign ways.

This sort of work at home also contributed to frequent absence from school, especially by those children under age fourteen not legally permitted to work. With time this problem lessened. There was much less domestic manufacturing among New York City's immigrant Jewish population, for instance, after 1900, when the garment and cigar making unions became stronger and prosperity increased. School attendance became more regular and prolonged, and Jewish girls began to appear in the city's high schools in startling numbers.[92] Among Italians of a later generation, New Deal efforts to regulate domestic manufacture helped to promote school attendance. The girl or boy with some high school education, equipped to compete for society's "clean" jobs, became more common.

The High School Girl. On January 24, 1898, at Claude Bowers's graduation from Indianapolis High School, the platform held five boys and nine girls, a ratio typical of the nation's high schools. Class honors went to three, all girls. "Like most honor people, they are more than ordinarily commonplace—mere drudges," Bowers noted sourly in his diary.[93] Male high school graduates being rather the exception among young men of the day, rather exceptional careers might be predicted for this group. They did not disappoint, producing a rabbi, a physician, a businessman, and a diplomat. (The occupation of the fifth is unknown.) The girls, for their part, took notable advantage of the expanding opportunities for women to pursue higher education, to prepare to inhabit "that strange new world that is arising alike upon the man and the woman, where nothing is as it was, and all things are assuming new shapes and relations."[94] Two of the female graduates attended Vassar College, one the new University of Chicago, another Butler University, and another Indianapolis Normal School. Two of the nine, both of them married women and daughters of clergymen, had unusual careers: one was a journalist-poet and the other a dealer in fine arts. From the rest of this group of Indianapolis women, there emerged only those few careers that came to typify women high school and college graduates: three housewives, two teachers, and two secretaries.

Between the First World War and the onset of the Great Depression, the percentage of mid-adolescents (ages fourteen to seventeen) in high schools rose from 62 to 73 percent. Among the nation's seventeen-year-olds, under one in five graduated from high school in 1920; the figure was nearly one in three in 1930 and one in two in 1940. The career success of those like Claude Bowers's male classmates might furnish a reason for boys to stay in school. But what of the girls, who continued to predominate in high school enrollments, although by a decreasing margin? Why did they persist in high school, when, if they did not end up in full-time housework, they tended to be concentrated in a very few "women's fields"? In these they functioned as "social housekeepers and assistant professionals," in the roles of librarian, nurse, social worker, teacher, and office worker.[95]

The explanation is not that social expectations changed with respect to the relationship between work and marriage in the woman's life cycle. In 1940 eleventh-grade girls in nine Brooklyn high schools were asked their choice of work for the near future and for later.[96] Their most popular immediate choices were secretarial work, women's wear jobs (such as dressmaking and millinery), and teaching. Of their plans for ten years later, the largest group said "housewife"—this despite everyday evidence of male unemployment during the depression and a slow rise in the employment rate of married women.* In 1900 young, single women had the highest female employment rates; in 1940 the pattern remained remarkably similar, except that the very youngest girls were kept out of the labor market by prolonged school attendance during the high school years.

When Joseph Van Denburg studied New York City high school students around 1910, he contrasted their drudgery and continued dependence with the more attractive and free lives led by their employed friends. "In every way," he concluded, "the work of the high school pupil seems hard, uninviting, and entirely out of keeping with what appear to be the realities of life. The contrast between the abstractions of algebra and the life of the neighborhood is too great to be bridged, save by an arch of faith which few indeed can construct."[97]

Yet the realities of life do help to explain why parents sent their sometimes unwilling daughters through high school. Adolescent girls after the turn of the century had fewer household duties than in the nineteenth century, when Boston school officials directed that schoolgirls be given no out-of-school lessons.† In 1914 it was noted that "probably one-third of the kitchen work has gone, or for households that patronize bakeries, perhaps one half," and that the majority of American families used bakeries and store-bought clothing.[98] Because families were smaller and more small children were in school, many girls could confine their domestic assistance to after-school hours. Historians also think that because families were smaller, parents made a greater psychic and economic "investment" in their children, including more schooling.[99]

---

*Despite legal and cultural barriers to working by married women, the depression's economic effects and the presence of so much education in the female population increased the rate of gainful employment of the married: from 11.7 percent of the female labor force in 1930 to 15.2 percent in 1940. See Mary P. Ryan, *Womanhood in America; From Colonial Times to the Present* (New York, 1975), p. 315. By 1974 married women accounted for nearly 58 percent of all women workers. In U.S. Department of Labor, *Handbook of Women Workers* (Washington, D.C., 1975), p. 3; Valerie Kincaid Oppenheimer, *The Female Labor Force in the United States: Demographic and Economic Factors Governing Its Growth and Changing Composition* (Berkeley, Calif., 1970).

†The Boston regulations of 1857–61 stated that boys' assignments during out-of-school hours should be no longer "than can be acquired in an hour's study by boys of good capacity." Marion Talbot, *The Education of Women* (Chicago, 1910), p. 71.

Although many high school girls expressed themselves as undecided about future occupation, often because they hoped or expected to marry, their behavior indicated that they or their parents sensed other realities of life. One was the diminished demand for unskilled labor; the women's share of factory employment was declining and machines were doing what beginners used to do. Another was the knowledge that occupational skills and experience were a form of insurance against life's uncertainties, and that there was ample evidence a woman might have to support herself and others. Although premature widowhood was growing less common, there were prolonged economic depressions during the 1890's and 1930's, involvement in five foreign wars, and rising divorce rates.[100] Many parents felt an increasing obligation to see that their daughters had some training for employment.

A high school education gave that, for girls more than for boys, given the differing labor markets for the sexes. The academic or general course equipped girls to be teachers, office workers, and sales clerks, with little or no additional or expensive study required. Girls learned how to speak, behave, and dress properly, to meet strangers, and to take directions, without the necessity for vocational courses or commercial tracks. If high schools offered no classes in typing, shorthand, or bookkeeping, brief courses in night schools, secretarial schools, and business colleges were available in many communities. In Chicago in 1910, 32 percent of all high school students elected a commercial subject, and forty business schools enrolled 19,000 students. Indeed, a common reason given for leaving high school before graduation was to go to business college. In Cleveland, the public schools' enrollment in commercial courses was one-tenth that found in similar courses in the private and parochial schools.[101]

Commenting on the irony of history, Chesterton is supposed to have observed of the women's rights movement that 20 million young women rose to their feet with the cry that "We will not be dictated to!"—and promptly became stenographers. Twentieth-century high school girls profited, nonetheless, from the fact that office jobs were in the process of becoming "women's work."

This was a profound reversal. When Mary Grant asked to help

her father in his rural Ohio bank during the Civil War, she found him unwilling, "even though so many men have enlisted here that it is difficult to obtain hands in all employments."[102] The Civil War opened a few government jobs to women in Washington, but in 1870 men were still 97.5 percent of the American clerical labor force. Clerkships had been apprenticeships to business careers, and in 1906 men still outnumbered women as students and faculty in commercial and business schools. Especially before the First World War, discussions of public school commercial courses typically mentioned their appropriateness for both boys and girls, unlike the industrial arts and domestic sciences courses. Gradually, however, clerical work became women's work.

With the growing need for clerks in businesses and corporations, the woman "typewriter" began to appear in many late nineteenth-century stores and offices. So much did women come to be associated with the office machine that two teachers at the Technical High School in Newton, Massachusetts, wrote in 1913:

Every woman and girl in this twentieth century should congratulate herself on the numerous means open to her for self-support and, if need be, for helping to fill the family exchequer,—means which are not only remunerative . . . but which are pleasant, respectable, and capable of widening the outlook of the worker. The inventor of the typewriter ought to be an honorary member of every women's club in the land, for, to how many women has it furnished the means of independence?[103]

Store and office employment grew at a faster rate than the female labor force, and by 1920 the census listed stenographers and typists in third place and saleswomen and clerks in fourth place among all white, native-born women in the work force. The percentage of women among federal civil service employees grew more slowly, from 16 percent in 1923 to 23 percent in 1950; most federal female white-collar workers were clerical employees, however. The telephone companies hired the first women telephone operators in 1878; there were 200,000 in 1925. Exchanges preferred girls with high school experience and would not hire girls below age seventeen; a study of Boston's telephone operators in 1912 found 87 percent had been to high school.[104]

As the pattern of occupations for women changed, so too did

their schooling. New York City's Washington Irving High School, sometimes disparaged as "Washing and Ironing School," was a model comprehensive high school, preparing its 6,000 female students for college or to be bookbinders, library assistants, dressmakers, and buyers, among other things. But the most popular offering among these girls, largely from poor immigrant families, was the commercial course. By 1930, in New York City, clerical jobs comprised 30 percent of the female labor force. Working-class women found the hours and pay better, the work more secure, the workplace cleaner.[105] Jewish girls, besides, had the additional resource of the city's many small Jewish businesses, which needed a clerk, bookkeeper, or general office girl. In smaller communities, of course, there were fewer clerical or other jobs that called for the training offered by the general education of the high school.* Black women, even in large northern cities, were rarely found in clerical work; only 1 percent of their nonagricultural employment in 1920 was in clerical and sales jobs.

Black women were, however, found in teaching, the other large employer of the high school educated. Teaching ranked seventh in the share of all black women workers in 1920; that figure represented 30,000 out of 1.5 million black women workers. In the late nineteenth century, many southern school boards yielded to pressure to hire black teachers for black schools.[106] The enrollment of black girls in the St. Louis schools went up after the reversal in 1877 of a policy against hiring black teachers in the city's black schools.[107] A New York City survey published in 1911 reported that "the colored girl with intellectual ability, particularly if she comes of an old New York family, is apt to turn to teaching."[108]

At a time when relatively few immigrant males advanced from the working to the middle class through schooling, their sisters could be upwardly mobile through teaching. First- and second-generation Norwegian immigrant women were teaching in Iowa in the 1860's and probably earlier.[109] Girls dominated the Catholic

---

*In 1920 one quarter of all women age sixteen and over were in the labor force. The figure for cities of more than 100,000 was 32 percent; that for smaller cities (under 25,000) and rural areas, 19 percent. Joseph A. Hill, *Women in Gainful Occupations, 1870 to 1920*, Census Monographs no. 9 (Washington, D.C., 1929), p. 9.

high school classes of Boston, and many Irish girls became teachers in the city's public schools. In 1900 Lotus Coffman found that "old stock" Americans made up 63.5 percent of all women teachers; but native-born daughters of foreign parentage were 27 percent, a disproportionately large part of the nation's teachers.[110] By 1920, the census reported, teaching ranked fifth among the occupations of women with foreign or mixed parentage, employing 7.5 percent (over 153,000) of all such women.

One such teacher was Henrietta Szold, daughter of a Baltimore rabbi. After graduating from Western Female High School in 1887, she promptly returned to the school (at age 17) as a teacher; later she became the principal. Subsequently she taught in a private school before turning to Zionist causes.[111] Although an exceptional woman in many respects, Szold was not alone in finding few obstacles standing between a high school education and a teaching post. When Ruth Hill graduated from the Beloit (Kansas) High School in 1896, most of her small class hunted teaching vacancies after a few weeks of summer "normal" to prepare for the teacher's examinations.[112] Indiana, in 1907, was the first state to require that all licensed teachers be high school graduates. Normal courses appeared in certain high schools, like the Girls High Schools in Boston and San Francisco. Chicago's very first public high school established a normal department, which restricted entry to girls and gave them preference when teachers were hired for the city schools.[113] Normal schools attached to the public school system, as in St. Louis, also eased entry into teaching.* When Garlin Hill wrote to her sister, a former teacher, of her plan to enroll at the State Agricultural College at Corvallis, Oregon—many "ag' schools" turned out more teachers and preachers than farmers—she was candid: "I do not care to go there, but perhaps I had better make a teacher of myself. What else can I make of myself? It costs lots of money to make anything else of one's self."[114]

Some state normal schools were hardly more than substitutes

---

*The concept of "eased entry," developed by Lortie, includes the provision of accessible, low-cost institutions of a non-elitist character, which can be viewed as a partial compensation for those entering the rather poorly paying or lower-status semiprofessions. See Dan C. Lortie, *Schoolteacher: A Sociological Study* (Chicago, 1975).

for high schools. Pennsylvania had the largest number of normal schools. A study early in this century found that 44 percent of the students in them had no work above the common schools; only 12 percent had completed a full, four-year high school course. The recruiting agent sent out by these schools, according to one critic, "discovered that his strongest appeal to the parents is to show them that a son or daughter can save a year's time in obtaining a permanent teacher's certificate by attending."[115]

The New York City high schools, more demanding than the Pennsylvania normal schools, also led smoothly into teaching. Van Denburg found that nearly twice as many high school girls chose teaching as all other occupations combined, and that the persistence of girls in high school was high. The reasons were clear:

For teaching, the way is open through free training schools to actual positions attractively paid. No initiative is required, but merely the compliance with certain scholastic standards. . . . Until a girl marries she finds in teaching a gentle position with apparently short hours and long vacations. Moreover, most girls are very fond of their teachers, and the impulse to emulate them is very strong indeed.[116]

I began this section on the high school girl by asking why girls would remain in schools when the range of their probable occupations was narrow. We now see, from the perspective of the family, some suggestions of an answer. The general high school curriculum led many young women directly into clean, respectable white-collar jobs. If necessary, specialized secretarial and pedagogy courses were available. For many parents of the students Van Denburg studied, education was part of "a grand struggle upward." Their sons, even if born in poverty, might become merchants and lawyers; their daughters would become stenographers, sales clerks, and teachers, able to support themselves and their aging parents and to assist younger siblings.

For the student, of course, schooling is more than an academic or vocational enterprise; it is a profoundly social experience as well. A child, once asked why he went to school, responded, "Because that's where my friends are!" Student diaries demonstrate how preoccupied youngsters have been with friendships and rivalries, with the development and testing of social skills, and with the gaining of an identity in a group other than the family. Compared with this agenda, the curriculum runs a distant second. Girls who attended the ungraded common school of the nineteenth century and the high school of the early twentieth probably did not have the intense preoccupation with sociability that James Coleman found in the 1950's and reported in his *Adolescent Society*.[117] Nonetheless, during the preceding decades many an adolescent girl without occupational goals may well have gone to school because "that's where her friends were."

And it may also be argued that schooling increases the hunger for participation in society. Highly educated women, besides, are less likely than the average to live among their families of origin, and therefore they have to seek society elsewhere. The young, single women of the nineteenth century who came into cities, apparently in greater numbers than men, were probably seeking not only work but also companionship. Many women felt an intolerable isolation on the farm or in the home, shut away from what Parsons called the "sociability of the workroom" and from the stimulation that men received when they left the house to go to town.[118] Work, too, can be a place where one's friends are.

The College Woman. Caroline Dall's manifesto was "I ask for woman, then, free, untrammeled access to all fields of labor." Many saw the eventual realization of that goal in the opening of colleges and universities to women. From 1900 to 1910 alone, the number of nurses increased by 700 percent and that of women college faculty by 600 percent; optimism seemed warranted. "The day is past when half of the people in the world are occupied in one vocation and the other half in an interesting variety of occupations," asserted a California home economist; "the modern women may choose from the variety."[119] Nevertheless, as concerns women and their work, college has in crucial ways been a mere continuation of high school.

For the middle-class housewife, college courses in child development, fine arts, comparative political theory, and body mechanics constituted an ad hoc homemaking curriculum. A college-educated housewife was better equipped to discover John B. Watson, to form parent-cooperative nursery schools, to join the

League of Women Voters, and to appreciate the perfect soubise. Such an education was at least less self-conscious than the un-standardized domestic science of the high school, mired as it was in the rhetoric of the woman's "true profession."

At the same time, teaching remained the principal outside employment for educated women. "I do not think a lady is educated till she has had some experiences in teaching children," Mary Lyon had told the Mount Holyoke students in the 1840's.[120] The counterparts of the women who had, in the nineteenth century, qualified for teaching by going to a common school or academy like Mount Holyoke, began, toward the end of the century, to set off for places like Ann Arbor and Madison, Vassar and Sophie Newcomb. As women moved into colleges—they received a third of all bachelors degrees by 1916 and were 47 percent of all under-graduates by 1920—the job requirements of teaching followed them. Secondary-level normal schools were upgraded into teachers colleges. Some private and most public universities quickly established education departments for the training of prospective elementary school teachers (females), often leaving, however, the training of high school teachers (males and females) to other departments. For women, teaching dominated the Department of Labor's category "professional and technical occupations." In 1973, 43 percent of all women in this category were teachers, and at no time between 1870 and 1970 did teaching fall below fifth among the ten leading occupations of *all* women workers.[121]

A census in 1918 of nearly 12,000 women graduates of nine eastern colleges who had ever been employed revealed that 83.5 percent had been teachers. As Willystine Goodsell explained, "Teaching is, of course, the path of least resistance for those women who desire to utilize as promptly as possible the information that they have acquired in college as a means of gaining a livelihood."[122] Among the 1912 graduates of five women's colleges, Mabel Robinson found 54 percent in the teaching profession. Robinson observed acidly:

It is scarcely likely that over half the graduates of five women's colleges have peculiar aptitude for the teaching profession any more than half of the registered alumnae at the intercollegiate bureau have peculiar aptitude for secretarial work, or that half the graduates of any five men's colleges have either aptitude or desire for any one vocation.[123]

College-educated teachers tended to act like their common-schooled predecessors, retiring from the classrooms, temporarily or permanently, to domesticity. And the college-educated teachers were even less likely than earlier women to capture administrative positions in public education.

Office workers also came out of the colleges; secretarial work was second only to teaching in Robinson's sample. The relative ease of entry was an inducement, as was, recalled Alice Parsons, "the delusion still cherished in girls' colleges" that to learn some office skills was to escape the traditional fields. Looking backward from 1926, she wrote:

Those of us who were in college in those days heard prodigious rumors about this great new possibility opened up to women. Girls who didn't want to teach were no longer faced with the alternative of going home and twiddling our thumbs. They might, if they studied typing and stenography and were very clever and efficient, become the Confidential Secretaries of men who were doing frightfully interesting things. . . . No one would have suggested this as a means of launching a boy on any other career than that of typist or stenographer. . . . It has little to do with being a good doctor, forester, dietician, or sculptor.[124]

There were, to be sure, some new careers for college women. By the 1920's some nursing education had moved out of hospital schools and into baccalaureate programs. Nurses came to be the second largest group of women professionals. By 1910, three-quarters of library workers were women. Courses in library science developed in a variety of colleges, including state teachers colleges and their successor institutions. The arguments that women were ideal library workers bore an unmistakable resemblance to that applied earlier to teaching.[125]

The turn-of-the-century women's colleges have been characterized as celebrating what Barbara Harris calls "a peculiar blend of intellectual achievement, social service, and genteel feminism." This was put to use in social work, which expressed a persistent belief in the nurturant, self-sacrificing qualities of women. Jane Addams spoke of the settlement-house work in terms of the "great mother breasts of our common humanity, with its labor and suffering and its homely comforts."[126] By 1920, college-trained women caseworkers and social researchers had come to dominate at least the lower rungs of this new profession. The new and growing bureaucracies of "social housekeeping" provided jobs for college-educated social workers and high school–educated clerks.

Women who themselves stepped outside the usual woman's roles, like Catharine Beecher, Sarah Josepha Hale, Jane Addams, and Ellen Richards, helped create a few large fields of work for the woman with advanced education, yet did not challenge gender stereotypes or redefine the woman's spheres. Woman's natural instruction of children in the family proved her superiority as a teacher. Her traditional almsgiving function demonstrated the humanitarian selflessness needed at charitable and relief agencies. The nursing profession was born of woman's "love of ministering to those in need," her observant nature, her "gentle touch."[127]

It was becoming important, however, that training for women's professions also be scientific, efficient, and expert. A scientifically oriented home economics, which had scant success in the high schools as preparation for employment, became established in universities, especially in the land-grant institutions. Graduates did indeed find varied careers, as extension agents, dieticians, research scientists, product developers and testers, institutional managers, and professors in universities that otherwise employed very few women on the faculty.

An advantage claimed for the field of home economics as an occupation for college women was that "the name itself prevents any possibility of considering the field unsuitable for women and usually eliminates any competition with men."[128] It also encouraged university officials to make of home economics and other fields clearly for women the equivalent of a distinct "ladies college" within a university. Cornell founded a department of home economics in 1900, and restricted admission to women; law and engineering were reserved for men, and female enrollment in other professional schools was limited. Cornell professorships for women were confined to home economics until 1947, when a woman was named assistant professor in the college that educated the most women, Arts and Sciences. Women interested in economics or chemistry were directed into home economics and food chemistry.*

The segregation that many women experienced in their studies rested in part on institutional devices: quotas, restrictions on scholarships, the unavailability of hospital internships for women medical graduates. Individual women also made choices that reduced their options. As a high school student in 1901, Florence Peck made a decision about education that helped to shape later decisions. As she explained in her diary:

Tried chemistry. And flunked. It is the horridist of hateful things to flunk. I will, I shall "drop" it. . . . I wont need it for the U[niversity] of R[ochester] and that is where I shall go on account of the "lonesome dollars" in the E. C. Peck family.[129]

Florence Peck subsequently prepared herself to teach kindergarten.

Other women were making similar decisions against careers in science. When St. Louis added several new courses in its high schools between 1900 and 1920, the percentage of girls electing the "Scientific Course" declined from 38 (over half the boys' figure) to 2.9 (one-seventh the boys' figure); the percentage of girls in the "General Course" grew from 35 in 1910 to 62 in 1920. Surveys of high school physics and chemistry classes in the late twenties found boys outnumbering girls three to two, but with girls slightly more numerous in biology and botany.[130]

That girls did not fail in school as often as boys was undoubtedly encouraging. On the other hand, the opportunity to skip a grade, which girls were generally denied, might have produced a greater desire for achievement, and this might have sent more girls into demanding fields. As Charles Keyes explained:

The larger number of boys among the ground-gainers is in part due to a hesitancy on the part of teachers and parents to let the girls undertake the extra work necessary to gain a grade, in part to the more ready accep-

*Cornell University went so far as to form separate alumni associations and to build a student union, in 1925, with a side door for women. Serious discrimination began, however, with an 1884 policy requiring all women students to live in campus dormitories; by limiting the number of "female beds" the university was able to restrict the admission of women students. See Charlotte Williams Conable, *Women at Cornell: The Myth of Equal Education* (Ithaca, N.Y., 1977).

tance of the conventional schedule by girls, and for girls by their parents. On the other hand, the larger number of boys looking ahead to business careers or to college and professional life were stimulated to save time.[131]

Only a few days before graduating from Girls High in San Francisco, two of Harriet Levy's girl friends announced their decision to go to the university and sought her company. She recalled:

I had never considered a university education, as girls whom I knew had not gone to college. The proposal coming suddenly associated itself with no image. I knew nothing of qualifications for admission, or of entrance examinations. I had not even seen the University of California, nor been to Berkeley. . . . I told Father. . . . He would ask the advice of Nathan Sachs, the wholesale dry-goods merchant. Mr. Sachs told Father that education was fine for a boy, but would spoil the chances of a girl. Men did not like smart wives. . . . We decided to take the chance.[132]

For both sexes the decision about a field of study, or even the decision to continue in school, could be capricious, perhaps due to the choices and experiences of friends, to accidental encounters, or to flights of fancy. Such decisions were easier for women to make, in the sense that few fields of study and vocational preparation appeared feasible, despite the unquestionably true assertion that some women were to be found in virtually all occupations. There were sharp differences between the sexes in the college studies they pursued. Besides education, nursing, home economics, and librarianship—fields where women took at least two-thirds of the degrees—women were the majority in English, journalism, and fine and applied arts. Men, meanwhile, earned 90 percent or more of the degrees in engineering, business, agriculture, law, medicine, pharmacy, and the physical sciences. The tendency of women to go to teachers colleges and liberal arts colleges and men to go to technical colleges and universities was another reflection of the separate men's and women's labor markets.

Every census from 1900 to the present shows most female workers in occupations where most of their fellow workers (frequently 70–80 percent) are women. Although the two world wars, like the Civil War, opened more varied work to women, the gains were often transitory; or the newly opened fields, such as teaching and nursing, relentlessly became women's work. Moreover, during the Second World War professional workers did not benefit as much as craft and industrial workers. Nor were the employment gains of wartime periods necessarily permanent. After the Armistice of 1918, Elizabeth Adams had cautioned: "It is no time for easy optimism nor for relaxed effort. There is considerable reaction from the professional hospitalities extended during the war; and women who worked shoulder to shoulder with men are discovering that the masculine shoulder may be coldly turned."[133] Over 2 million workers were laid off following the end of the next war.

Women were less than 3 percent of the 2.3 million veterans who attended college on the G.I. Bill.[134] The federal policy of education benefits to veterans intensified a quarter-century decline of women as a percentage of college students; in 1950, at 31 percent, they reached a low not seen since 1880. Those women who did attend college and enter the labor market concentrated, more than before, in preparing to teach those children whose birth testified to the renewed strength of the domestic imperative. Middle-class women began marrying earlier and having children at the same rate as the poor. This further reduced the proportion of women receiving higher education, at a time when going to college was a national mania among young men and their families.

Conclusions

If the story of women's work is made more richly textured and complex by looking at different women's experiences, it has also been made more starkly simple. Individual-level data, together with studies of work in America, women in the work force, women's education, and vocational education, lead to the first conclusion of this study: for women, it is the mere fact of their gender that has, more than any other thing, determined their places in the work world. More than social class, parental occupation, region lived in, or ethnic background, their sex has largely specified the kinds of occupations women may enter, the patterns of their entering and leaving the work force during the life cycle, their duration in the labor force, their earnings, their vulnerability to unemployment, and their opportunities for advancement relative to male workers.

At the outset I proposed that a woman's decisions with respect to work and schooling had to be compatible with the ideology giving primacy to a woman's role within the family, whether as a daughter, wife, or maiden aunt. The life-history data and the secondary sources we have seen shape a second conclusion: that this compatibility could be manifested in four general ways. All four ways were evident during the two centuries surveyed in this study, coexisting in time even as one overtook another in importance.

First, women could add to the family economy directly by working for and within the family circle. For women like Peggy Johnson and Mrs. Ise—as for most women in the colonial and early republican periods—there was almost no option but the family corporation: the family farm or business. Only for a small number of women is this important work today, except among recent immigrants.

Second, women could go outside the home and family to a job that was somehow perceived as congruent with family roles. Early factory work in the textile mills, teaching, and nursing are clear examples of employment that the workers themselves, like Frances Merritt, viewed as traditional female work. It was suited to God-given or biologically determined feminine qualities; it was important to family welfare; and it was good preparation for marriage. Such work, although performed away from home, often retained symbolic features of the home, such as the parietal rules governing the non-work behavior of mill girls and the quasi-domestic conditions of the small "nursing home" hospital, the library, and the settlement house. In this context, an additional attraction of teaching as a "full-time" employment was the compatibility of the calendar and the hours of work with domestic responsibilities, this at a time when single teachers still had duties in their own families and married women began to teach in significant numbers. Also, high turnover permitted reentry into the occupation after one's own children were grown, which created the familiar bimodal age distribution in teaching characteristic of the mid-twentieth century.

Third, women in a wide range of occupations could work until marriage or pregnancy brought an early and permanent retirement from the labor force, as for Abbie Bright and millions of other workers. Employment, thus, did not interfere with woman's "true profession." Maybe it even supported domesticity, since the working girl could earn for a dowry and her savings could contribute to family formation. Such money could have been critical when prolonged schooling made it more difficult for a young man to become established enough to marry and retire his wife by his middle to late twenties. Moreover, it was argued, employment increased a woman's chances for marriage by widening her contacts with eligible men.

Fourth, working before marriage, or even after marriage and childbearing, could be justified by its material contribution to family welfare. For instance, single women, by working, had long permitted younger siblings to stay in school, brothers to receive otherwise unobtainable advanced schooling, and mothers to work only at home. Perhaps more widespread in the middle class was the fact that the working daughter's economic independence lightened both the financial and psychic burdens carried by aging parents. The prolonged dependency of children caused by extended schooling or late marriage, the absence of pension and social security systems, the increased reliance on consumer goods, and even the workings of the mortgage system weighed heavily on a solid middle-class family like the Whites of Fidalgo. Providing adequate education and encouraging work experience for female children were hedges against such contingencies. And of course the education industry itself generated part of the problem: in one way or another parents had to pay more for more and better education of their children.

Despite all these real, family-bound reasons, social commentators never became fully reconciled to women in the labor force. Women's motives were often trivialized, their economic contributions slighted. It is a commonplace to read that single women take jobs only to fill in the time between school graduation and marriage, to meet prospective mates, or to save for a trousseau. Moralists have scorned the young woman who works for "pin money, luxuries, and good times," and social disapproval of the married working woman has been still more intense.[135] Of course, the startling increase in the labor force participation of married women, including those in the 25–34 range, and a pattern of unprecedented persistence among older women workers—shown in the accompanying figure—need some justification. The most

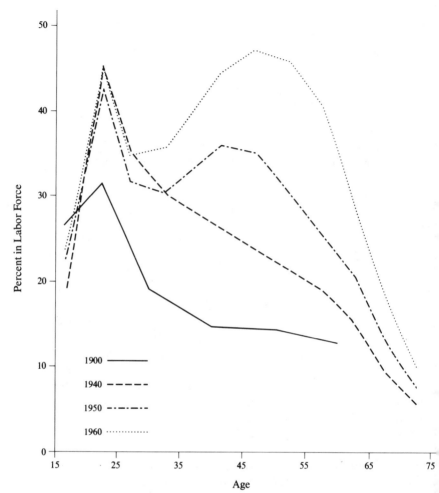

Female Labor Force Participation by Age, 1900, 1940, 1950, 1960.
(Source: Valerie Kincaid Oppenheimer, *The Female Labor Force in the United States* (Berkeley, Calif., 1970), p. 9.)

common explanation is the moderately acceptable one that married women are employed solely out of economic necessity: to supplement a husband's inadequate earnings or because they are divorced or separated. This makes their working palatable by linking it to family goals, as with the employment of children in the nineteenth century.[136] Except by feminists, it is seldom proposed that many women might seek employment out of the same motives as men.

The life-history materials we have seen show that women worked for many different reasons; this is my third conclusion. Some of the reasons for working were: because they wanted to, like Nancy Barnard; to get away from home, like Jane Conine; to cut or loosen the ties with the family and the neighborhood; to attain economic independence as a precondition for emotional freedom; out of loneliness; to avoid the feeling of being a burden, like Sally Rice; to seek adventure, like Urania Richards; because their friends had done so; to meet new people; to do God's work; to benefit society; to pursue further education, like the unknown Lucy Ann and Ruth Hill; to see if they could do it. And regardless of educators who seemed oblivious to the stronger hold that employment was gaining among women, schooling did figure in the process. Education *has* contributed to work incentives, both by contributing to ego development and by raising the level of "wants" that can be met only by increased earnings. As the French say, *"L'appétit vient en mangeant"*—"The appetite grows with eating." Such a function for education should not be underestimated.

Various kinds of data show how anomalous and complex the role of education has been. Schooling proved unable to satisfy either the aspirations of radical feminists for equal access to all work or the desires of conservative men and women for a greater commitment to homemaking as woman's "true vocation." Yet it is quite probable that the social character of schooling, as well as the pride of accomplishment female students experienced, encouraged subsequent decisions to enter the labor force. The decisions to work were evidently not encumbered by the fact that women workers continued to be concentrated in low-paying or low-status "women's" occupations.

Sexism is too unidirectional and crude a concept for understanding how men and women experience differently the rewards and punishments meted out by the family, education, and work. Discriminatory treatment there has been. In schools, males are singled out far more frequently for discipline, for identification as "retarded" or "emotionally disturbed," and for placement in "ungraded classes" and custodial institutions.* To a point, females have been more successful and better rewarded by schools. That point was and is still reached where education is clearly articulated with work in *non-female fields*. There, women students have often faced rebuff or hostility—from teachers and administrators, male students, dispensers of scholarships and internships, potential employers, union officials, male workers, government, and even their families.

Like women themselves, well-meaning educators have found it hard to cope with changes in women's labor force participation, given the fact that the reigning ideal has remained that of the contented, full-time homemaker. In the earlier period, discussions of female education seldom mentioned occupational objectives, except the preparation of teachers, who were seen more clearly as moral stewards than as working women. "I would confidently assert, as biological fact, the males are the race; the females are merely the sex told off to recruit and reproduce it," wrote Grant Allen. "All that is distinctively human is men—the field, the ship, the mine, the workshop; all that is truly woman is merely reproductive—the home, the nursery, the schoolroom."[137] Not surprisingly, both advocates and opponents of female education focused on issues of morality, health, and fertility—not on work.

Even when vocational education became accepted as an explicit function of schooling, girls were seldom mentioned. For one

*Commenting on the fact that studies showed more males than females in institutions for the feeble-minded, Leta S. Hollingworth correctly observed that institutional statistics "may be merely an index of the degree to which it is easier for one sex to survive outside of institutions than it is for the other." Noting that, among the institutionalized, males were the less severely retarded, she linked this to society's expectation that women would need less institutional care because many would marry rather than follow competitive careers: "Men . . . form a highly competitive class, working in rivalry with each other for a wage. The boy who cannot compete becomes an object of concern" and is, more frequently, directed to an institution. "Social and economic pressure bears very unequally upon the sexes in the matter of commitment to institutions for the feeble-minded," *The Psychology of Subnormal Children* (New York, 1922), p. 12.

thing, vocational curricula were intended to keep boys longer as students, whereas girls were already overrepresented in school. Home economics proliferated without much challenge, because it posed no threat to old assumptions. As a federal publication stated in 1918, home economics "finds its place in the school curricula because it furnishes vocational education in that occupation in which 93 percent of all American women ultimately engage and because it gives prevocational training to the industries in which the majority of all women wage earners enter, . . . pursuits evolved from employment formerly carried on within the home."[138]

Below the university level, job training and "content related to vocations" was little seen, despite considerable evidence that girls too were concerned about remunerative employment and occupational preparation. Except for occasional study units on budgeting, grooming, and time management for working girls, home economics courses emphasized household management, domestic cooking and sewing, family relationships, home nursing, and child care.[139]

Commercial courses might be accounted the most far-reaching response of schools to the fact of women's employment. As early as 1920 in the eastern states, half or more of the girls entering high school elected some business subjects in preparation for office work, which became the largest source of employment for female high school graduates. Still, in the first year of the depression, Office of Education statistics showed under one girl in five enrolled in a commercial course. And three decades later the enrollment in high school shorthand was only 7 percent, though general-education and college objectives had boosted enrollment in typing classes to over half of all ninth graders.[140] Business, then, was relying most on the prevocational general curriculum—and on the enduring cultural expectations that socialized women for the "women's" jobs, which now included clerical and sales work.

To explain the gender-segmented work force or the "collapse" of career orientation among college-educated women by the 1920's,[141] it would be tempting but shortsighted to put too much stock in curricular differentiation by gender. The sometimes-obligatory course in home economics, whose "controlling purpose" was to prepare girls "for useful employment as house daughters and homemakers,"[142] no more shaped female participation in the labor force than the sometimes-obligatory course in industrial arts or drafting shaped male careers. Illiberal and ungenerous as it was, the refusal to admit girls to many shop or vocational agriculture classes was only symptomatic of society's attitudes and the economy's needs. It was not itself a *cause* of the exclusion of women from male occupations.

Sex-specific instruction developed only to a very modest degree in the elementary and secondary schools. The enrollment in new women's professional curricula in the universities—for teaching, social work, librarianship, nursing, and home economics—was dwarfed by the number of women who elected non-professional majors in English, psychology, the arts, and modern languages—studies that themselves led far more women into housewifery, the public or private school classroom, and the business office. It was, then, the academic curriculum that equipped women with the minimal job skills and socialization to work that they needed to enter the labor force.

By being unspecialized and inexpensive, the academic curriculum was "practical," given the near-universal expectation that women wanted and would have short careers as paid workers. Because such education was cheap, it did not pay off handsomely, as economists reckon these things. Male-female wage differentials persisted, female advancement was restricted, and women remained more vulnerable to unemployment. But it is incorrect to say that schooling had little or no vocational payoff for women. A new labor economics must consider the rewards of work to women according to criteria rather different from those traditionally applied to men. Erich Fromm has stated that "Women are equal because they are not different anymore."[143] Although it was very agreeable of him to say so, this is not yet true—and may never be so, as long as we humans remain in some sense the prisoners of our different histories.

Work, Youth, and Schooling: Mapping Critical Research Areas

DANIEL T. RODGERS AND DAVID B. TYACK

One of the major premises of the essays in this volume is that the relationships between work, youth, and schooling were decisively transformed in the early years of the twentieth century.[1] Few historians of youth or education would disagree with that premise. That the early twentieth century forms something of a watershed in the history of work, youth, and schooling has long been recognized. The landmarks of the transformation are well known: the growth of schooling rates at the expense of child labor, the transformation of secondary schools into mass institutions, the mounting concern with the problems of youth and dead-end jobs, the elaboration of a vocational education curriculum and a structure of vocational schools and classes, and, still more generally, the rise of the theory and practice of educational vocationalism itself.

What makes the essays in this volume revisionist studies lies in the kinds of explanations they seek for these relatively familiar problems. Taken together, they first broaden the scope of vocational schooling to encompass the history of the vocationalizing of American education and the creation of modern work-school links. And second, they trace the roots of these changes back into the social history of the times—into the realms of ideology and interest-group politics, into the transformation of the workplace and career lines, into the consolidation of the corporate economy, and into the enduring inequalities of race, sex, and class.

Most explanations of the rise of vocationalism in American education fall, roughly speaking, into three broad camps. Accounts by advocates of vocational education typically argue that "traditional" schooling (which they often denigrate as "academic" or "culturist") was ill adapted to the talents and interests of working-class youth, who were entering high schools in increasing numbers, and also to the needs of a specialized, urban-industrial society. What drove change—and created vocational schooling—was a coalition of Progressive reformers in education, enlightened business and labor groups, and responsive politicians who passed legislation like the Smith-Hughes Act. The result was a transformed high school, in which fewer students dropped out from boredom or frustration. Pupils gained skills that made them more productive and well-paid workers, and the schools meshed with the economy as socially efficient institutions.

Explanations of vocational schooling by a second group—functionalist sociologists and neoclassical economists—do not lay such stress on the reformers, but they nevertheless arrive at similarly optimistic conclusions about the vocationalizing of education. These scholars argue that the transformation of the industrial economy produced major shifts in social structure and heightened skill requirements in occupations. Thus businessmen and political leaders made a calculated set of decisions to invest in education so as to prepare people to discharge these new functions. During the Progressive era this took the form of efforts to expand enrollments and to introduce specialized training courses into the high schools. Neoclassical economists, arguing from human capital theory, add that families and individuals, sensing the shift in opportunities, chose to invest in extended education and school-based skill courses, in the hope that a short-term loss of income would result in long-term economic gain. Though set against a backdrop of large-scale economic and social changes, this explanation stresses individual decisions as the unit of analysis and rational estimates of fiscal return as the driving force in educational change.

The third explanation, a neo-Marxist one, relies not on a political economy of autonomous, calculating individuals but rather on a model in which class conflict drives change. The analysis starts with the entry of workers into new social relationships of production under consolidated corporate capitalism; it reveals the unrest and conflict these relationships generated, and shows how businessmen turned to education as a means of socializing and disciplining employees to their new roles. The new, differentiated system of schooling sorted and trained employees for their niches in the economy with increased precision, and at the same time obscured actual inequalities with a mystifying rationale that the schools were providing opportunities equal to every person's talents.

If the "house history" version of vocational education now seems unduly sanguine and self-serving, as several of the authors in this volume suggest, both the neoclassical and neo-Marxist interpretations seem to us somewhat incomplete and a priori, lacking in the cultural complexity that lends "verisimilitude to an otherwise bald and unconvincing narrative." People bring to decisions about schooling and work not only a rational calculus of advantage, but also a rich mixture of cultural values; and those values, in turn, take shape within social relationships and opportunities structured by class, race, sex, and age. If the neoclassical analysis oversimplifies social history, the neo-Marxist concern with the emerging dominance of the large-scale corporation carries its own dangers of distortion. The actual relationship between capitalism and education in the United States, we suggest, has been more variegated than simply that produced by the new social relationships of production in the most advanced sectors of the economy.

The essays of this volume are ventures into this more complex social history of the relationship between work and education. Being exploratory, often deliberately so, many of them leave as many unresolved questions as they do answers. In this concluding essay we will try to bring many of those questions together, to pose others, to advance a few hypotheses, and to suggest some of the ways in which the artificial distinctions between the history of schools, family, business, labor, and ideology might be further broken down—to map, in short, some of the topics and research terrain that seem most in need of exploration. Let us suggest the most critical areas on that map in shorthand fashion:

First, what were the relationships between work and schooling during the nineteenth century, before the expansion of secondary education and the emergence of an explicit vocational curriculum? What vocational functions did the schools perform in their "prevocational" era, and for whom? What relationship did the "prevocationalized" schools have to the surrounding nineteenth-century economy?

Second, what explains the rise and triumph of a new, much more explicit vocationalism in American education after the turn of the century? Why did pressures arise for a wholesale reconstruction of the older connections between work and schooling? The question is familiar, but that familiarity should not be allowed to disguise how much yet remains to be known about the interaction of economics, ideology, and power in that vocational transformation.

Third, what transformations in the work-school relationship did employers make on their own, independent of the vocationalized schools? What, in particular, is the history of the ascendancy of school-based credentials in hiring? When and where did credentialism originate, how did it affect the employment of young workers, and what impact did it ultimately have on the schools themselves?

Fourth, once the vocational transformation was well established—once the structure of credentials, academic tracks, and institutional and curricular reforms, all zealously designed to further the efficiency of the social machine, was set in place—how did the resulting structure work in practice? How did young people find their way into work, and what functions in that process did the vocationalized secondary schools actually perform? What, in short, is the history of the relationships between youth, work, and schooling after the time with which most historical accounts conclude, the pivotal period when the Smith-Hughes Act was passed?

Fifth, how are we to explain the most enduring, though now implausible, legacy of the vocational transformation—the belief that the schools were the most effective lever with which to correct the problems and injustices Americans perceived in their economy? Whence, in particular, came the assumption that investment in expanded education was ipso facto an investment in expanded employment and equal opportunities? Put more broadly, what role did the vocationalization of the schools play in cementing the American people's habit of seeking pedagogical remedies to the "problems" that beset them—whether dead-end youth jobs or carnage on the highways?

To answer such questions requires close-grained study of how youth learned about and obtained jobs; inquiry about how these routes into work differed by region, sex, race, ethnicity, and class; assessment of the importance of networks of family, friends, and neighbors in comparison with school-based training and placement; and intensive investigation of particular communities to pinpoint the linkages between schools, ideologies, and local labor markets. Changes in ideology and institutional structures take on different meanings when seen as part of the lives of particular people in particular times and places. In the rest of this essay we attempt to sketch, in a tentative fashion, what the answers to these questions might entail.

Work and School Before Twentieth-Century Vocationalism

"The idle Fool/is whipt at school." So a child made acquaintance with the peculiar shape of the letter F in the reading schools of seventeenth-century New England. There was obviously more to that juxtaposition than simply a turn of phrase. Even the alphabet bore down on a child heavily loaded with meaning. So did long division in eighteenth-century Concord. "If you buy a Pasture Sufficient to Summer 15 oxen and 20 young creatures and give 700£ for it, how Long will it be before you make the money you gave, if you have 3£ per head for summering the creatures?"[2] Education—even education of the most stripped-down, reading-writing-and-reckoning sort—never takes place free of a massive tangle of cultural norms and expectations. Down the gullet with the alphabet have gone complicated ideas of damnation and democracy, of boundless success and sexist stereotypes. The assumptions of capitalism slipped in early with the multiplication tables. Perhaps most pervasive of all was work, for from the beginning of formal schooling in America work was never far away from the core of the curriculum.

That the schools had always been, in a fundamental sense, vocational schools would have been hard to gather from most of the rhetoric of vocational education's partisans in their triumphant decade of the 1910's. The Prossers, the Deweys, and the cast of the influentials assembled in the National Society for the Promotion of Industrial Education all thought of themselves as ventilating the cloistered schoolrooms with an unfamiliar gust of reality. By intruding courses in everyday work into the schools, they hoped to wrench public education out of its ostensible isolation from the workplace and into a new acknowledgment of the everyday economic world. When the vocational education movement found its first historians, they generally sustained that assumption of a dramatic revolt against "academic" formalism. The movement's central achievement, in this reading, was a specifically designated vocational education curriculum; the year of triumph was that of the Smith-Hughes Act, 1917; and the drill presses and cooking stoves that dominated the new classrooms contrasted with the familiar rows of bolted desks as symbols of the schools' new mission to prepare youth for practical tasks.

But in fact the schools had always prepared people for work, in many ways and on many levels. For some students, to begin with, the schools had been places of explicit skill training, long before the vocational transformation. Nowhere was this more true, ironically enough, than in those same late nineteenth-century high schools that the vocationalists derived for their impractical devotion to an outmoded curriculum. For students from the right sorts of background and bound for the right occupations, the prevocationalized schools were eminently practical places. One of the oldest and straightest of career lines, that toward college, seminary, and the ministry, ran directly through the secondary school, as did the paths to most other professions. So did the much broader and shorter path from the normal class of an urban high school to a position as schoolmistress. In many late-nineteenth-century cities the largest single contingent of secondary school students was made up of young women enrolled in normal classes, working to master the specific curriculum of their district in a way that would vault them directly into elementary school teaching.

The relationship between the schools and business careers was never so clear-cut; but youths who gambled on clerkships as the entry point could gain a good deal of specific vocational training from the schools, at least in such skills as penmanship and ciphering. By the end of the century and in still greater numbers, young, urban, native-born women could capitalize on the same instruction to work their way through the schools into the expanding secretarial and commercial positions opened to women.

To how many other jobs did the nineteenth-century schools offer a pathway? What other direct economic value did their instruction impart? Clearly, neither the bookish curriculum nor the preponderance of female students in the nineteenth-century secondary schools ought to be taken—as the vocationalists were prone to read the evidence—as proof of the inutility of the unreformed high schools. Such features of the schools might be better read as signs, worth much more careful exploration than the problem has received, of who stood most to gain from the kinds of vocational training the nineteenth-century schools did in fact offer.

For most students, nonetheless, the vocational lessons of nineteenth-century schools took the form not of specific skills, but of general habits, norms, and relationships—all in some measure calculated to link the classrooms with the economic world outside. The maxims of punctuality, regularity, industry, and silence, so insistently drummed into pupils in the nineteenth century, were saturated with the theme of preparation for work. So was the equally insistent training in competition, from the sustained competition of the Lancasterian schools, to the spelling bee, to the class rankings in colleges. The heroics-filled declamatory exercises of the late nineteenth-century high schools were an explicit rehearsal for work. And for a very different class of children, destined not for entrepreneurial adventures but for a wage earner's obligations, so were the straight, rigidly disciplined rows of schoolchildren that could be seen in virtually any end-of-the-century urban grade school.

The relationship between this pervasive indoctrination in economically useful habits and the surrounding nineteenth-century economy has to some extent been obscured by the focus of recent writing on the connections between schools and large-scale industry. Factories, and the social relationships of factory production, are only part of the story. Capitalism not only entailed a new—and often exploitative—relationship between employers and workers in large factories. It also meant an unbound and mobile labor system; the protection of private property; a complex system of national and even international markets; socialization to habits of thrift, sobriety, and order, which were as useful to the small entrepreneur as to the employee; and an ideology that justified competition and inequality by portraying success as the result of qualities of individual character. If the large-scale factory haunted the imagination of nineteenth-century Americans, it remains true that only a relatively small proportion of workers toiled in such places. The nineteenth-century capitalist economy was on the whole one of small enterprises: of the family farms that still constituted the most common single mode of production; of small industrial concerns where older work techniques and shop cultures persisted; and of small commercial establishments.

By the same token, the mainstream of public education in the United States in the nineteenth century was the one-room rural school and the graded school of the town or small city, institutions that corresponded somewhat with productive relationships in the family farm or the small shop or business. A large proportion of youth who were trained in such schools moved to cities as urbanization accelerated. Thus much of the contribution that schooling made to the development of the economy took place not in the urban school bureaucracies that resembled the massive organizations of corporate capitalism, but in schools that reflected an earlier stage of economic development.

It was in this context—farther from the shadow of the factories than many recent accounts suggest—that most nineteenth-century children were socialized by the schools into the habits and disciplines of work. There children were taught, as we have said, norms of behavior that may have helped some of them adapt to the patterns of wage employment typical of the new large-scale workplaces. But the more important and, as yet, not fully explored lessons of the schools may have consisted of the attitudes and habits appropriate to the expanding small-scale entrepreneurial capitalism in which the schools were in fact embedded— lessons for the Nebraska farmer who produced wheat for a world market, for the Indiana druggist's son who wanted to become a doctor, or for the California peddler who wanted to strike it rich selling a new gadget.

The "prevocationalized" schools were thus linked to work both as skill-training institutions for the few and as socializing institutions for the many. Perhaps the most crucial relationship with the economy, however, was ideological. On the whole, the public schools, like churches and other agencies of cultural transmission, conveyed a class-rooted set of values that made the triumph of capitalism and the republican form of government seem virtually synonymous, self-evidently correct, and providential. Particularly through such conservative textbooks as those analyzed by Ruth Elson, nineteenth-century schoolchildren learned to think of their political system as inextricable from an open market and to see themselves as potential capitalists, not bound by feudal or mercantile restrictions, but each able to try the main chance.[3] They learned what may have been the most important vocational lesson of the nineteenth-century schools: that economic success was the result of individual character and effort, that cooperation between employer and employee was the norm, and that there was no alternative to the political economy identified as providentially American.

It is not our intention to exaggerate the vocational aspects of public schooling in the nineteenth century. Then as now the schools served a multitude of functions. They were public institutions of a scale then unique in the United States, and they were imbued with millennial aspirations. The habits and values they tried to inculcate in the young were designed as much to produce good and orderly citizens as ambitious and perseverant workers—to the extent that these characteristics were thought to be separable at all.[4] Public schools performed many private tasks as well, not the least of which may have been to occupy the time of a good many daughters of middle-class families prior to marriage. Where and with what impact the vocational lessons of the schools entered into this much larger baggage of things taught and learned offers a crucial arena for historical research. But the vocational transformation of the twentieth century cannot be grasped for what it really was without recognizing that the use of the public schools for a wide variety of vocational purposes has a history that stretches back to well before the arrival of the gospel of efficiency.

The Revolution in the Curriculum

What then was new about the vocational transformation in the early twentieth century? The key changes were: the extension of schooling to much larger numbers of children, particularly to those who in previous generations would have left the schools for work at a younger age; the expansion of vocational education out of its narrow, white-collar confines into domains formerly left to on-the-job training, and the extension of skill training to new sorts of students, particularly urban working-class boys; the construction of a separate vocational education curriculum that was advocated by a broad coalition of business, labor, and reform groups, financed by new public sources, and controlled by a new and self-conscious force of vocational education teachers; and the inauguration of a set of new practices designed to guide and sort students into jobs and educational tracks calibrated far more precisely and deliberately than ever before.

What was *revolutionary* about the vocational transformation, however, is not to be found in these specific measures so much as in the assumption that held them together: that the public schools and entry-level jobs should be meshed into an interlocking structure, through which young people could be propelled from childhood through schooling to work, all with an unprecedented efficiency and concentration of effort. Very few educators before the turn of the century, for all their concern with vocations, had thought it their mission to use the schools to train a whole nation for its work or to smooth out the trajectory of young people's careers, and much less to solve the host of problems at the workplace and in the nation at large for which vocational education would be touted as a solution. What was most audacious about the revolution was its breadth. Vocationalism was a call to refashion the schools into a comprehensive set of bridges to work; its promise was of a social instrument capable of mitigating problems as far afield as the dead-end job of a young box maker and the competitive weakness of America in international trade.

Why did it come about? Why did the older forms of vocational preparation and the older methods of finding work seem in need of such drastic repair? And why this choice of remedy?

The "house history" of vocational education stresses the problem of keeping older children, particularly boys, in schools past the age of fourteen or fifteen. At the turn of the century young people were leaving school in droves, even for the dullest and least remunerative jobs. In the minds of many educators of the time, this assumed the dimensions of a crisis. Since the perceived problem was the lifelessness and artificiality of the secondary school curriculum, the educators' answer was to inject a large dose of reality into the schools, seizing for the purpose the sort of skill training that would hold the interest of the so-called hand-minded student.

We find this school-centered story of problem resolution to be persuasive in some ways, although we concede the justice of Larry Cuban's arguments about the element of self-interest in the movement. There was, indeed, a serious problem of repeaters piling up in the elementary grades—what contemporaries called "retardation" or "laggards"—and a dramatic attrition of students in secondary education. Educators may have been accurate in believing that high schools were much better adapted to those heading for white-collar occupations than those likely to do blue-collar work. The disproportion in secondary education of girls over boys, as students and graduates, was a particular concern of vocational educators; there can be no doubt that the retention of urban, working-class boys was central in the thinking of a very large number of advocates of vocational schooling, at both the local and the national level.*

Believing that white-collar training was well established—per-haps even overdeveloped—the drafters of the Smith-Hughes Act focused on industrial training, continuation schools, and domestic science rather than the commercial, secretarial, and teacher-education programs that enrolled many girls. Thus, much of the revolution in curriculum was designed to correct what many of them saw as a "feminized" high school and to attract more working-class boys. In part the reforms did exactly that, yet preserved older ideas of the "woman's sphere" by subsidizing the training of women as homemakers.

The vocational curriculum may have served the schools inter-nally in a second way as well, by alleviating problems of student discontent and discipline. For many young people, the new shops and kitchens were surely more pleasant places to spend part of the day than the academic classrooms. There young people could move around, converse more freely, and produce a hot meal or

---

*We are indebted to Katherine Poss, a graduate student at Stanford, for calling our attention to this dimension of vocational education; she is writing her dissertation on this topic.

some metalwork, more tangible achievements than the conventional classroom encouraged. There too, particularly after compulsory school laws took hold, school administrators could unload many of their morale and discipline problems, by giving students a respite from regular classroom routines. Such intrinsic rewards of vocational classes as a more pleasant school day have not, however, been stressed by writers on vocational schooling, perhaps because hedonism was suspect to the perfervid advocates of social efficiency, who much preferred education for the ulterior and practical motive of fitting students for "life."

The struggle to hold young people longer in school, however, was central to the curricular revolution. And nothing seemed more clearly to demonstrate the success of that investment in a more interesting curriculum than the contemporaneous rise in school enrollments. But interpreting that evidence is full of challenges. To begin with the supply side of the labor market, the enactment of stricter child labor laws and the creation of effective compulsory schooling laws and enforcement systems, with their legions of "child accounting" officials and truant officers, muddy the waters. And on the demand side, as Norton Grubb and Marvin Lazerson suggest, there is evidence that employers began to discriminate sharply and voluntarily against young workers. In part this was done by mechanizing the young people's tasks out of existence by such inventions as the cash register and the pneumatic tube, which eliminated the need for cash boys and girls; the telephone, which destroyed the jobs of many messengers; and new machines, as in the glass industry, that displaced boys as assistant workers. And in part it was done simply by choosing to hire older, and presumably less transient, employees.[5]

Which of these pressures most effectively shaped students' decisions to stay in or to leave school? Vocational educators themselves in the Progressive era tended to blame the high attrition rate on the boring or irrelevant curriculum rather than on economic necessity. It was not that families needed the earnings of their teenage children; rather, youth were just not interested in what the school had to offer. Parents might be greedy for the wages of their children, but that problem could be solved by compulsory schooling laws.

Much of the recent work in family and labor history, however, makes it clear that economic necessity did indeed play a critical role in decisions to leave school. As a rule, urban working-class families at the turn of the century found it impossible to make do on the wages of the male head of the household alone. They did so only by employing the earning power of other family members, children and teenagers in particular; by pooling their earnings into a single, parentally administered family wage; and by struggling hard against the centrifugal tendencies toward autonomy of family members. What kind of job a child was sent into, how much of a young worker's pay was conscripted for the family's necessities, and above all which children were to stay in school and how long they should remain there—all of these were family, that is to say parental, decisions, and to a considerable extent economic ones.[6]

Not all kinds of families decided on those matters alike, as the marked variation in schooling patterns among different ethnic groups shows. A simple zeal for learning often pulled against the force of economic calculation, in a thread that runs from the workingmen's agitation for public schooling in the early nineteenth century through the immense, tragically doomed aspirations of black schoolchildren that James Anderson describes. No family could effectively keep a thoroughly uninterested, alienated child in school—or at home either, for that matter. How, in the end, did all these forces balance out? How, in reality, were decisions to leave school made, and how are they made now? To a great extent we do not know, even for recent years, despite some useful sociological studies. The more educational history reaches out toward the materials of labor history and economic history, however, the less it seems that boredom in itself is a sufficient answer.

Once the trail of economic calculation is taken up, the limits of the "house history" of the curricular transformation become apparent; for the crucial national debate over vocational education turned not nearly so much on problems within the schools as on an acute economic and social crisis in the nation at large. It is with this broader context that both the neoclassical and neo-Marxist interpretations begin. In particular, both interpretations recognize that the curricular transformation occurred at what seems to have been a critical moment in the development of

American industry. The rise of the massive corporation, the rapid invention of new forms of bureaucratic organization, and the aggressive drive toward new labor economies (most strikingly symbolized by scientific management) all point to a momentous transition: from the relatively small-scale, haphazard, and competitive entrepreneurial economy of the late nineteenth century to the modern, highly rationalized industrial structures that were superimposed on that older economy in the early twentieth century.[7] The drive for vocational education in the schools appeared almost precisely at this transition point in American industrial life, and it cannot have been unconnected with it.

But those connections are far from clear-cut; and both the neoclassical and neo-Marxist arguments, for all their insights, ultimately run up against recalcitrant evidence. The neoclassical argument that vocational education represented a conscious investment in human capital in the form of more highly trained employees is hard to reconcile with accumulating evidence that the aggressive rationalization of industry did not increase the general level of skills required. In fact, much work was effectively deskilled as jobs were simplified by the subdivision and mechanization of tasks.[8] There was—and is—little evidence that vocational training of the sort most commonly provided in secondary schools does in fact raise lifetime earnings. Were parents and children deceived into investing, hopefully but unwisely, in a training that was for many ultimately superfluous?

And on the demand side, it is not clear just what it was that business advocates of vocational training hoped to gain by their noisy, ambitious campaign to insert training for jobs into the schools. Is it possible that business promoters of vocational education did not see how effectively their deskilling operations were resolving the supposed skill crisis they talked about with such alarm? To believe that is to cast doubt on the image of employers as aggressively rational planners shaping society to their interests; was it true that the left hand did not know what the right hand was doing? Or did the need for skills differ radically in different labor markets? We shall return to that question later.

But perhaps skills were not really what employers were most concerned about. Samuel Bowles and Herbert Gintis argue that capitalists were most concerned about preparing workers to accept the new social relationships of production and mitigating conflict at the workplace.[9] But it is hard to find convincing evidence that vocational education classes were more effective in such socialization than the traditional, highly disciplined classrooms of the nineteenth century were in reproducing the hierarchical relations and traits of character the industrialists desired. If regimentation, acceptance of bureaucratic rules, and resignation to a high degree of social inequality were what was needed, it is difficult to think of a more effective training machine than the unreformed urban schools Joseph Rice observed just before the turn of the century.[10]

We know next to nothing about the internal workings of the early vocational education classrooms, but to the extent that vocational classes served the internal needs of the schools by reducing classroom discipline and softening hierarchical relations, they may actually have prepared students less well for the increasingly intense discipline of the workplace. Moreover, if the industrialists had something to gain from passing a portion of their socializing costs on to the public, they did so at the cost of direct control over that process—a bargain that by the 1920's, with the emergence of a distinctive high school subculture, had begun to show some important disadvantages. Nor is it clear that industrialists (unlike, for example, the employers of the commercial course graduates) took much immediate advantage of the sorting functions of the vocationalized schools, or that they preferred the schools' judgments to those of their own rapidly expanding personnel bureaus.

None of this argument refutes the possibility that the vocational education movement drew crucial support from industrial capitalists hoping to create a new sort of work force. But it seems impossible to strike a useful connection between the general deskilling of industry and the determined skilling of pupils without a significant detour through politics, perceptions, and ideology, even when helped along by such encompassing phrases as human capital, social reproduction, and industrial crisis. Most of the essays in this volume begin at this impasse. They are skeptical of any simple arc from problem to reform to resolution, and equally skeptical of simple economic functionalism. They also suggest some of the inquiries that might offer ways out.

To begin with, we need to know considerably more than we do about the sources of support for vocational education, particularly at the state and local level. Support came from virtually everywhere, or so the vote on the Smith-Hughes Act would lead us to believe. But the Smith-Hughes coalition was potentially a fragile one, shot through as it was with tension between labor's dream of prying open the doors to advancement and management's vision of the schools as an efficient training and sorting mechanism. How long did that alliance hold together? To what extent was it duplicated at the state and local levels, where, as Larry Cuban suggests, things often looked very different? Who pushed first and hardest within local school districts for vocational education courses: employers, labor spokesmen, state education officials, local school personnel, or parents? Scholars have provided some preliminary answers to such questions— especially to those about the ideological controversies—but much of the early political history of vocationalism remains obscure.[11]

Harder to answer is the question of how children and parents voted on vocational education in practical ways. Who enrolled in the new vocational education courses? From what backgrounds did they come? Which kinds of vocational courses did they seek out in greatest numbers? How much of that demand was voluntary, and how much of it coerced? This last is a particularly difficult matter to resolve, given the pressures of compulsory schooling laws, employer hiring practices, and internal tracking in the schools (whether by outright sorting or by indirect combinations of academic failure and counseling). Despite the popularity of "social control" arguments in the recent historical writings on vocational guidance and tracking, we find ourselves puzzled about the answers for those questions. We suspect that families did indeed make choices, but choices within a framework congruent with the interests of the new corporate capitalists. Careful study of local enrollment patterns, newspapers, and other sources should yield a good many clues. And the question at stake is a crucial one: did the schools turn to and sustain vocational education because of the press of eager students; or did the schools—

because of external and internal pressures—establish vocational education courses and then proceed, by sorting or otherwise, to fill the new classrooms up?

There is also a great deal we need to know too about industry and about the shifting patterns of skill requirements in the twentieth century. The general trend has clearly been toward a convergence on semiskilled jobs. Employers used the economies of mechanization to lop off vast numbers of the least skilled of their workers—the brute haulers and shovers of materials, like F. W. Taylor's famous coal shovelers and pig iron carriers, who played such a vital role in the nineteenth-century economy. At the same time, employers launched an even more aggressive attack on those skilled jobs where their dependence on the workers was most complete. The result was a wholesale destruction of the industrial occupations on which much of the strength of the nineteenth-century labor aristocracy had rested.

It is equally clear, however, that these trends were very unevenly spread through the economy, and that to a great extent they remain so. The sweatshops and the giant U.S. Steel flourished at the same time, just as high-technology electronics and fast-food franchises have boomed together since. Even within U.S. Steel early in this century two quite distinct labor systems existed side by side: an army of highly transient unskilled workers, and a much smaller and considerably more privileged corps of craftsmen whose skills remained indispensable. Recognizing the economy for the diverse and highly segmented structure that it is may help explain the seeming paradox of a drive for skill enlargement in a deskilling society. Particular industries did in fact face acute skill and labor crises at the turn of the century. But before we can try to resolve on these lines the impasse into which the skill question has led us, historians will have to be much more specific about the identity of businessmen who pushed for vocational education; about the relation of those businessmen to unions and to contests over the control of jobs; about the structure of work processes in the industries and enterprises they represented; and about the specific labor markets from which they drew.[12]

Finally, we need to know far more about ideology. No one can read very far into turn-of-the-century social analysis before stumbling over the explosion of concern with social efficiency. The dream of organizing the discreet, loosely rattling pieces of society into a single, functionally integrated machine was not the only social vision abroad in early twentieth-century America. It contended with a set of older appeals to the dignity of work, to civic virtue, and to the dream of upward mobility, all of which fused in the rhetoric of vocational education's proponents. But the vision of society made over as a smoothly working unit was stronger and more enduring than the rest. Corporation apologists, scientific managers, and vocational educators—both the intensely practical and many of their Deweyite opponents—all shared that vision in one form or another, and it lured them compellingly toward such mechanisms of social linkage as vocational education courses. Many historians describe the dream of social efficiency as a major structural break in the pattern of American thought, akin, for example, to the rifts between mercantile and laissez-faire assumptions or between hierarchical and democratic political theory.[13] If that is true, and if ideologies do have important consequences in action, then not much else would seem to matter. The ideology of efficiency would seem to have made a vocational education curriculum a virtually inescapable social invention.

Despite over a decade of historical appeals to the turn-of-the-century "search for order," however, we still have much to learn about this set of social assumptions. Aside from amorphous references to the contemporaneous rise of the industrial corporation, we know very little about where the ideology of social efficiency came from. Nor do we know why it triumphed so completely and easily, why it succeeded in appealing simultaneously to such disparate groups as socialists and scientific managers, and why it has had such persistence. Finally, in the realm of education, we do not know whether the full-blown ideology came first, or whether ideology and piecemeal social experiments, like vocational education itself, rose together in a more complex and reciprocal relationship. The "search for order" has become the historian's deus ex machina; but rather than explaining events, it shifts the agenda of questions.

Above all, it is clear that we need to know much more about society: about pressure groups, family wage calculations, skill structures, economic segmentation, and ideas. Only then can we know what we would like about even the internal history of vocational education.

The Demand Side: Employers and Credentialism

The new bridgework between classrooms and jobs was not all constructed from the side of the schools. In the twentieth century employers began to change their hiring practices in ways that may have had a significant impact on the opportunities open to young workers, and ultimately on the schools themselves. But here educational and labor historians have barely begun to catch up with educational sociologists, and the questions vastly outnumber the answers. When and in what parts of the economy did employers begin to discriminate against young workers? When and where did the assumption that young workers were unstable and immature begin to override the fact that seems to have mattered much more in the nineteenth century, that young workers were much cheaper workers?

To bring the question still closer to the schools: when and where did the certification of some minimum of education become common as a factor in hiring decisions? The ascendancy of educational credentials as formal job requirements seems to have been a fairly recent phenomenon, with the turning point perhaps not earlier than the Second World War.[14] But high school and college diplomas certainly had a symbolic value well before that, and a good number of questions remain. What, for example, was demanded of a clerk in the late nineteenth century or early twentieth: a good hand, an apparent ability at arithmetic, a neat appearance, an expression of reliability, and what, if anything, else? In what context did anyone begin to ask not only of clerks but of prospective factory employees whether they had been to school? What, in short, was the historical context of the rise of modern credentialism?

If historians can find appropriate payroll and personnel department records, they will surely have sufficient theories of credentialism to test. Some observers of contemporary education say that school credentials are useful guarantees of specific skills. Others stress that school certificates signify that people have been socialized into the norms and expectations employers find useful (for example, in business administration). Finally, critics of the whole structure argue that employers use credentials simply to slice off part of the queue of applicants.

Knowing more precisely in what context the use of educational credentials became widespread might help advance that debate considerably. Did the use of educational achievement records or school diplomas begin in occupations requiring particular skills? And did vocational training certificates lead the way, or more general symbols of school achievement? Or, on the contrary, did credentialing first assume importance in occupations relatively low in skill requirements but badly overstocked with applicants? Or did credentialing begin, as Grubb and Lazerson suggest, in large, bureaucratically managed corporations, in a zeal to rationalize—even to overrationalize—the whole of the production process? Once the shift began, how did it proceed? Were the familiar concomitants of hiring—kinship, neighborhood ties, ethnic bonds, a good word to the supervisor, a strong back, an eager expression—completely pushed aside by diplomas, and if so, how rapidly? Finally, what did the transition mean for the structure of opportunity? The last question, the most important of all, is full of imponderables. But the others ought to be fairly easily answerable.

The merging of hiring and educational criteria altered industry and opportunities; to what extent did it also alter the schools? What impact, for example, did changes in hiring practices have on school enrollments or on the distribution of students through the schools' curricular tracks? To what extent did employers influence curricular decisions not by directly intervening in educational debates, but by establishing hiring norms that the schools then scrambled to meet? How were the credentials themselves—the traditional system of grades and diplomas—altered as they ceased to serve essentially as internal ranking mechanisms and grew in external economic significance? Once the vocational revolution is seen, as these essays insist it should be, as a series of interlocking social decisions extending far beyond the schools, questions of this sort become inescapable. As the schools increasingly learned to stamp students with credentials, in what ways did credentialing stamp the schools themselves?

The Blueprint and the Reality

The bridgework that employers built toward school certificates and the bridgework that schools built toward jobs never exactly met. The result was not the neatly joined piece of social machinery so many early twentieth-century educators and employers had in mind, but a creaky, jerry-built structure, full of gaps and contradictions. As many of these essays contend, the economic payoff of investment in vocational education has not been nearly so clear as the proponents of vocational education assumed it would be. Nor has the rationalizing of hiring procedures created the meritocracy its advocates touted. Nevertheless, the ungainly construction these essays describe remains a structure, and a markedly enduring one. What remains to be asked—much more closely than historians have asked to this point—is how that structure actually worked, what impact it had on society, and how in particular it shaped the lives of the young people who moved and were moved through it. Once historians begin to look past the formative years of vocationalism, into the 1920's and beyond, the challenges are immense.

At first glance, the contrast between the new and the old seems stark. In the nineteenth century, as recent work in social history has made increasingly clear, the family was an overwhelmingly important institution. Among the institutions connecting youth and work it had no real rival. For a young person, getting a job, acquiring skills, and advancing at work were all in great measure determined by family connections. The tightest of families, to be sure, could not stem the terrific countervailing instability of late nineteenth-century economic life, in which a boss's whim in disciplining and firing was virtually unchecked, cyclical unemployment was endemic, and job security was fragile, particularly among the youngest and oldest workers. But in comparison with the informally exercised power of the family and the coercive instability of the economy, such formal social institutions as the schools counted for relatively little in most people's lives.

Then into this structure was suddenly intruded a vast network of expanded and reconstructed schools, guidance counselors, vocational tracks, and personnel departments. Few areas of American life have been formalized and bureaucratized so swiftly, or offer a better arena in which to judge the consequences of the twentieth century's compulsive search for social efficiency. But what real differences did that transformation make in the traditional relationships between youth and work? Or, as Joseph Kett cautions, did it perhaps not alter many of those older relationships at all?

Most of the work on vocational education has focused on its formative period and its most recent history, jumping from Smith-Hughes to the "career education" of the 1960's and thereby skipping the implementation phases of the 1920's and the crises of the Great Depression and the Second World War. For these periods we need to ask the sorts of questions we have already raised. How did young people find their way into vocational courses? What was taught there, as skills and as ideology? How did the new layers of vocational training—high schools, community colleges, separate private technical schools, vocational tracks within colleges—relate to one another? How did young people proceed into jobs and from one job to another? To what degree was there a separate youth labor market, and how was it in turn riven by barriers of sex and race?

These are such obvious questions that it is startling how little historians actually know about these matters. One reason is the compartmentalization of history into labor history, family history, educational history, and so on. Labor history, for all its new scope and excitement, has not shifted its attention far from its bedrock concern with working-class militancy and ideology. Family history has not intersected much with educational history. The vast new historical industry of mobility studies has revealed far more about the statistical contours of occupational and social mobility than about its underlying processes. Geraldine Clifford's piecing together of the work and schooling histories of young women suggests the kind of painstaking digging in the sources that remains to be done for virtually every group in the twentieth-century population.

Furthermore, the full study of vocationalism in education needs to look well beyond the vocational courses themselves. The vocationalization of the schools affected all students, not just those in the explicitly designated vocational tracks. Intelligence testing and the curricular segregation of the schools, for example, had as much impact on those who came out on the top of the heap as on those on the bottom or in the middle. So did the massive assumption, by no means confined to the vocational curriculum, that the function of education was career preparation, to be judged in great part by its economic payoff. In these and other ways, what sorts of social relationships did the vocationalized schools teach? The issue is full of obvious cross-currents, particularly at the secondary school level; IQ testing, athletics, civics discussions, and high school fraternities do not necessarily run in the same direction. But the question of the socializing impact of the schools clearly needs to be advanced into the period after 1920 by researchers with a sense of what came before. In what ways did the sorts of human materials the schools tried to produce change as a result of the vocational transformation, if they changed at all? There are big answers in the educational literature to these questions, but not, as yet, many effective, close-grained comparisons.

Finally, what sorts of ideological relations did the schools assume with the increasingly bureaucratic, corporation-dominated economy? How long did school texts and teachers continue to preach the maxims of nineteenth-century, small-scale, entrepreneurial capitalism: thrift, enterprise, perseverance, and the prospect of acres of diamonds in one's backyard? When and in what fashion did these give way to the celebration of cooperation, the glad hand, and institutional loyalty—if so they did? What is the history of high school (or college) economics and social studies textbooks akin to what Frances FitzGerald has drawn for history teaching?[15] Clearly, the nation's economic mission had been substantially transformed by the 1920's; what role did the schools play in shaping the ways Americans comprehended their strange, new, but still apparently providential destiny?

All this post-1920 terrain is criss-crossed by broad and serviceable trails, blazed by students of contemporary education.[16] But one of the essential questions remains an explicitly historical one. The vocational reformers had envisioned both transformed schools and a transformed society. Once the dust of construction had settled, what relation was there between their ambitious blueprints and reality?

Educational Answers to Economic Problems

The professional vocational educators assembled in the AVA looked at that relationship and pronounced it a satisfactory one. They had seized upon classrooms and curricula in the firm conviction that they could thereby move the economy itself; and so, they contended, they had. Looking at subsequent crises of unemployment, declining productivity, inequality, or sagging industrial morale, the vocationalists and their allies in government have continued to suggest that the most efficacious answers lie in better training in the public schools.

What is more surprising, as many of the essays in this volume suggest, is that this faith has commanded so much assent in the nation at large. The social crisis that terrified many Americans after the turn of the century seemed massive. As participants in the debate described it, it was a compound of dead-end jobs and juvenile delinquency, smoldering industrial unrest and German economic competition, business trustification and, most unnerving of all, a perceived breakdown in cultural homogeneity. That school courses in shop skills and nutritious cooking should have carried so much reassurance in the face of such momentous challenges is not a little puzzling. But even as astute a scholar as Paul Douglas thought that part-time continuation schools could undo the havoc wrought by the destruction of industrial apprenticeships, in much the same way that John Dewey thought the right sort of education would revolutionize work by revolutionizing what young workers expected of it.[17] In retrospect, the disproportion between means and ends seems immense, and the confidence naive. Why did Americans expect so much of the schools? Why have they so often chosen to transform deeply rooted economic and social relationships into a pedagogical matter?

On one level, the answer is fairly obvious. Politically powerful groups have turned to the schools because they often seemed the only serviceable tool at hand. From the nation's beginning, a great deal of American political energies have been spent in drawing a distinct and careful line between the realm of things public and of things private. The line between these two domains has moved around a good deal, and in perceived emergencies, like those of the 1930's and the world wars, it has moved rather far and grown unusually indistinct. The legacy has been a series of experiments in more direct public intervention into the problems of youth and jobs, from skill-training programs independent of the public schools (like the Job Corps) to outright job creation (as under the CCC). But such incursions have generated major resistance and, on the whole, been quickly aborted. The schools, on the other hand, endowed with expansive public purposes, lie clearly within the realm of things public. Americans like Douglas and Dewey have eagerly turned to the schools in times of crisis in part because there are not many unmistakably public institutions in the American polity—once one goes beyond schools, armies, police, and libraries—and in part because pedagogical solutions generate so much less economically entrenched resistance than more direct measures.

But the deeper question is why the appeal to education, and to vocational education in particular, has endured despite so much evidence of the inability of education to work a significant change on the structures of jobs and opportunities facing young workers. How did the vocationalists manage to convince so much of the public not simply that the schools should be tried, but that the bridge from school to jobs really worked as the blueprints had promised?

That answer will not be simple. Nonetheless, part of it, we suspect, will lie in a deeper recognition of the symbolic function education serves in American political life. Americans have long been prone to turn specific anxieties into a sense of social breakdown too pervasive to admit specific definition, and hence all the more open to essentially symbolic solutions. Just as deep is the habit of finding those solutions in the reconstruction of the lives of some conveniently located part of the dependent population— whether they be the asylum-housed mentally ill in the nineteenth century, or poor relief recipients, or schoolchildren.

The schools, however, have occupied a central place in this drama of American politics. From sex education to school prayers to work, school policy has been the stage on which Americans have fought out the destiny of their nation in a set of symbolic but intensely serious battles. As David Cohen and Bella Rosenberg have observed, the ritualistic rhetoric and theatrical poses that have occurred on this stage cannot be dismissed simply as mystification—though mystification there often was. In an important sense, Americans have created a dramatic arena called public education, in which they reconcile their millennial social visions with the realities that stand in the way.[18]

The social history of the vocational transformation in education is still far from complete. Social historians and educational historians still have a great deal to learn from each other about the role of the schools in bridging the chasm between youth and work. The final task for historians of vocationalism in education, however, may be to see through the old arguments over policy to the public gestures and dramatic rhetoric that have often held the shaky structure of social assumptions and educational institutions together.

NOTES

NOTES

Kantor and Tyack: Introduction

1. Quoted in W. Carson Ryan, *Vocational Guidance and the Public Schools,* U.S. Bureau of Education Bulletin, no. 24, 1918 (Washington, D.C., 1919), p. 28.

2. For general surveys of the rise of vocational education, see Lawrence A. Cremin, *The Transformation of the School: Progressivism in American Education, 1876–1957* (New York, 1964), ch. 2; Edward A. Krug, *The Shaping of the American High School, 1880–1920* (New York, 1964), ch. 10; Arthur G. Wirth, *Education in the Technological Society: The Vocational-Liberal Studies Controversy in the Early Twentieth Century* (Scranton, Pa., 1972); Marvin Lazerson and W. Norton Grubb, *American Education and Vocationalism: Documents in Vocational Education, 1870–1970* (New York, 1974); Berenice M. Fisher, *Industrial Education: American Ideals and Institutions* (Madison, Wis., 1967); and Melvin Barlow, *History of Industrial Education in the United States* (Peoria, Ill., 1967).

3. For a review of studies evaluating vocational programs, see Beatrice G. Reubens, "Vocational Training for *All* in High School?" in James O'Toole, ed., *Work and the Quality of Life: Resource Papers for "Work in America"* (Cambridge, Mass., 1974), pp. 299–338; and Larry Cuban, in this volume.

4. W. Norton Grubb and Marvin Lazerson, "Rally 'Round the Workplace: Continuities and Fallacies in Career Education," *Harvard Educational Review,* 45 (1975): 451–74; Martin Carnoy and Henry M. Levin, *The Limits of Educational Reform* (New York, 1976); and Levin, "A Decade of Policy Developments in Improving Education and Training for Low-Income Populations," in Robert Haveman, ed., *A Decade of Federal Anti-Poverty Programs: Achievements, Failures, and Lessons* (New York, 1977), pp. 123–88. In this volume see the papers by Cuban, Kett, Hogan, and Grubb and Lazerson.

5. See for example Ellwood Cubberley, *Public Education in the*

United States: A Study and Interpretation of American Educational History, rev. ed. (Boston, 1934); Leonard Koos, The American Secondary School (Boston, 1927); and Charles Prosser and Thomas Quigley, Vocational Education in a Democracy (Chicago, 1949). For an appraisal of Cubberley's influence on educational historiography in the United States, see Lawrence A. Cremin, The Wonderful World of Ellwood Patterson Cubberley: An Essay on the Historiography of American Education (New York, 1965).

6. This body of scholarship includes: Michael B. Katz, The Irony of Early School Reform: Educational Innovation in Mid-Nineteenth Century Massachusetts (Cambridge, Mass., 1968); Katz, Class, Bureaucracy, and Schools: The Illusion of Educational Change in America (New York, 1971); Clarence J. Karier, Paul C. Violas, and Joel H. Spring, Roots of Crisis: American Education in the Twentieth Century (Chicago, 1973); Spring, Education and the Rise of the Corporate State (Boston, 1972); Violas, The Training of the Urban Working Class: A History of Twentieth-Century American Education (Chicago, 1978); and Walter Feinberg and Henry Rosemont, Jr., eds., Work, Technology, and Education: Dissenting Essays in the Intellectual Foundations of American Education (Urbana, Ill., 1976).

7. Samuel Bowles and Herbert Gintis, Schooling in Capitalist America: Educational Reform and the Contradictions of Economic Life (New York, 1976).

8. James S. Coleman et al., Youth: Transition to Adulthood (Chicago, 1974). For a discussion of the current romance with work, see Eleanor Farrar McGowan and David K. Cohen, "'Career Education'—Reforming School Through Work," The Public Interest, 46 (1977): 28–47.

9. Helen Marot, Creative Impulse in Industry: A Proposition for Educators (New York, 1918).

10. On the history of professionalism in the United States, see Burton J. Bledstein, The Culture of Professionalism: The Middle Class and the Development of Higher Education in America (New York, 1976); Mary O. Furner, Advocacy and Objectivity: A Crisis in the Professionalization of Social Science, 1865–1905 (Lexington, Ky., 1975); Thomas L. Haskell, The Emergence of Professional Social Science: The American Social Science Association and the Nineteenth-Century Crisis of Authority (Urbana, Ill., 1977); and Magali S. Larson, The Rise of Professionalism: A Sociological Analysis (Berkeley, Calif., 1977).

11. See for example David Hogan, "Education and the Making of the Chicago Working Class, 1880–1930," History of Education Quarterly, 18 (1978): 227–70; Miriam Cohen, "Italian-American Women in New York City, 1900–1950: Work and School," in Milton Cantor and Bruce Laurie, eds., Class, Sex, and the Woman Worker (Westport, Conn., 1977), pp.

120–43; Michael B. Katz and Ian E. Davey, "Youth and Early Industrialization in a Canadian City," in John Demos and Sarane S. Boocock, eds., *Turning Points: Historical and Sociological Essays on the Family* (Chicago, 1978), pp. 81–119; Clyde and Sally Griffen, *Natives and Newcomers: The Ordering of Opportunity in Mid-Nineteenth-Century Poughkeepsie* (Cambridge, Mass., 1978); and Selwyn K. Troen, *The Public and the Schools: Shaping the St. Louis System, 1838–1920* (Columbia, Mo., 1975), ch. 6.

12. Lester Thurow, "Education and Economic Equality," *The Public Interest*, 28 (1972): 66–81. Also, see Dorothy K. Newman et al., *Protest, Politics, and Prosperity: Black Americans and White Institutions, 1940–75* (New York, 1978).

13. For further reviews of recent studies of women and work, see Susan J. Keinberg, "The Systematic Study of Urban Women," in Cantor and Laurie, *Woman Worker*, pp. 20–42, and Alice Kessler-Harris, "Women's Wage Work as Myth and History," *Labor History*, 19 (1978): 287–307.

14. William H. Chafe, *Woman and Equality: Changing Patterns in American Culture* (New York, 1977), p. 31.

15. *Ibid.*

16. On the problems of work, youth, and school in the 1970's and 1980's and proposals for reform, see Sidney P. Marland, Jr., *Career Education: A Proposal for Reform* (New York, 1974); National Commission for Manpower Policy, *From School to Work: Improving the Transition* (Washington, D.C., 1976); Special Task Force to the Secretary of Health, Education, and Welfare, *Work in America* (Cambridge, Mass., 1973); Frank Viviano, "The New Lost Generation," *Working Papers for a New Society*, 7 (1980): 42–47; Coleman et al., *Youth*; and Grubb and Lazerson in this volume.

Kantor: The Economic and Political Context

1. Committee on High Schools and Training Schools, Board of Education, New York City, 1914, "Vocational Guidance," in Meyer Bloomfield, ed., *Readings in Vocational Guidance* (Boston, 1915), p. 307.

2. David B. Tyack, *The One Best System* (Cambridge, Mass., 1974), pts. 1 and 2; Joseph F. Kett, *Rites of Passage: Adolescence in America, 1790 to the Present* (New York, 1977), chs. 1–4; Lewis Solmon, "Estimates of the Costs of Schooling in 1880 and 1890," in *Explorations in Economic History*, Supplement, vol. 7, no. 4, p. 575; Lee Soltow and Edward Stevens, "Economic Aspects of School Participation in Mid-Nineteenth-Century United States," *Journal of Interdisciplinary History*, 8 (1977): 221–43; Carl Kaestle and Maris Vinovskis, *Education*

and Social Change in Nineteenth-Century Massachusetts: Quantitative Studies (National Institute of Education, Research Report for Project no. 3-0825, 1976).

3. Quoted in David B. Tyack, "Bureaucracy and the Common School: The Example of Portland, Oregon, 1851–1913," *American Quarterly,* 19 (1967): 489. On nineteenth-century attitudes concerning education and success, see Irvin G. Wyllie, *The Self-Made Man in America* (New York, 1954); Thomas C. Cochran, *Business in American Life: A History* (New York, 1972), ch. 6; Ruth Miller Elson, *Guardians of Tradition: American Schoolbooks of the Nineteenth Century* (Lincoln, Neb., 1964), ch. 8; and Selwyn K. Troen, *The Public and the Schools: Shaping the St. Louis System, 1838–1920* (Columbia, Mo., 1975), ch. 6.

4. For general surveys of the rise of vocational education, see Lawrence A. Cremin, *The Transformation of the School: Progressivism in American Education, 1876–1957* (New York, 1964), ch. 2; Edward A. Krug, *The Shaping of the American High School, 1880–1920* (New York, 1964), ch. 10; Melvin Barlow, *History of Industrial Education in the United States* (Peoria, Ill., 1967); Charles Bennett, *A History of Manual and Industrial Education, 1870–1917* (Peoria, Ill., 1937); Berenice M. Fisher, *Industrial Education: American Ideals and Institutions* (Madison, Wis., 1967); Sol Cohen, "The Industrial Education Movement, 1906–1917," *American Quarterly*, 20 (1968): 95–110; C. H. Edson, "The Reform of Vocational Education: The Relationship Between Jobs and Schooling," *Urban Education*, 7 (1978): 451–62; Selwyn K. Troen, "The Discovery of the Adolescent by American Educational Reformers, 1900–1920: An Economic Perspective," in Lawrence Stone, ed., *Schooling and Society: Studies in the History of Education* (Baltimore, 1976), pp. 239–51; Arthur G. Wirth, *Education in the Technological Society: The Vocational-Liberal Studies Controversy in the Early Twentieth Century* (Scranton, Pa., 1972); and Marvin Lazerson and W. Norton Grubb, *American Education and Vocationalism: Documents in Vocational Education, 1870–1970* (New York, 1974).

5. Robert H. Wiebe, *The Search for Order, 1877–1920* (New York, 1967); Samuel P. Hays, *The Response to Industrialism, 1885–1914* (Chicago, 1957).

6. U.S. Bureau of the Census, *Historical Statistics of the United States, Colonial Times to 1970* (Washington, D.C., 1975), 2: 666.

7. Alfred D. Chandler, Jr., *Strategy and Structure: Chapters in the History of American Industrial Enterprise* (Cambridge, Mass., 1962); Chandler, *The Visible Hand: The Managerial Revolution in American Business* (Cambridge, Mass., 1977).

8. Chandler, *Visible Hand*; David F. Noble, *America By Design: Science, Technology, and the Rise of Corporate Capitalism* (New York,

1977); C. Wright Mills, *White Collar* (London, 1951); Cochran, *Business*, chs. 14–16.

9. Daniel Nelson, *Managers and Workers: Origins of the New Factory System in the United States, 1880–1920* (Madison, Wis., 1975), pp. 6–9.

10. Daniel T. Rodgers, *The Work Ethic in Industrial America, 1850–1920* (Chicago, 1978), p. 24.

11. Frederick Winslow Taylor, *The Principles of Scientific Management* (New York, 1911), p. 36. It is difficult to determine how many firms introduced scientific management, particularly since manufacturers often adopted principles of Taylor's system despite opposing many of its specific components. Taylor's system, for example, also involved incentive wage schemes and plans for functional foremanship that many employers opposed. Still, the proliferation of cost-accounting techniques, production control systems, and centralized purchasing suggests that many manufacturers adopted the idea of scientific management, if not the specifics of Taylor's system itself. See Harry Braverman, *Labor and Monopoly Capital: The Degradation of Work in the Twentieth Century* (New York, 1974); Samuel Haber, *Efficiency and Uplift: Scientific Management in the Progressive Era, 1890–1920* (Chicago, 1964); Nelson, *Managers and Workers*, esp. ch. 4; Noble, *America by Design*; Chandler, *Visible Hand*; David Montgomery, "Immigrant Workers and Managerial Reform," in Richard Ehrlich, ed., *Immigrants in Industrial America* (Charlottesville, Va., 1977), pp. 97–110; and Richard C. Edwards, *Contested Terrain: The Transformation of the Workplace in America* (New York, 1979), pp. 77–104.

12. Walter E. Weyl and A. M. Sakolski, *Conditions of Entrance to the Principal Trades*, Bureau of Labor Bulletin no. 67 (Washington, D.C., 1906), p. 692.

13. *Ibid.*, pp. 692–93.

14. Paul H. Douglas, *American Apprenticeship and Industrial Education* (New York, 1921), ch. 5; Weyl and Sakolski, *Conditions*, pp. 691–780; Braverman, *Labor*; Alan Dawley, *Class and Community: The Industrial Revolution in Lynn* (Cambridge, Mass., 1976), chs. 2–3; and David Hogan, "Capitalism and Schooling: A History of the Political Economy of Education in Chicago, 1880–1930." Ph.D. diss. (Univ. of Illinois, 1978), ch. 2.

15. Robert S. Lynd and Helen M. Lynd, *Middletown: A Study in Modern American Culture* (New York, 1929), pp. 40–42.

16. Quoted in Braverman, *Labor*, p. 147.

17. Lynds, *Middletown*, p. 43. Much recent scholarship has debated whether the organization of work reflects the desire of employers to control labor or the drive for efficiency under the competitive spur of the

market. Historically, however, these two forces are difficult to differentiate. As David Gordon has noted, manufacturers who discovered the most successful combinations of efficiency and control probably gained a comparative advantage over their competitors, since they could both reduce costs and control their workers. See Gordon, "Capitalist Efficiency and Socialist Efficiency," *Monthly Review*, 28 (1976): 19–39; Katherine Stone, "The Origins of Job Structures in the Steel Industry," *Review of Radical Political Economics*, 1974, pp. 113–73; Braverman, *Labor*, ch. 9; and Hogan in this volume.

Similarly, scholars have debated the impact of technological development on the organization of work. Generally, it is suggested that mechanization led inevitably to large-scale production, the systematizing of tasks, and the rationalizing of work. David Noble and others have challenged this "neutral" conception of technology, suggesting that the forms technology took, though certainly limited by the laws of physics, were also the technologies most appropriate to the social relations of a capitalist economy. For alternative views, see Noble, *America by Design*; Dawley, *Class and Community*, chs. 2–3; and Stephen Marglin, "What Do Bosses Do?," *Review of Radical Political Economics*, 1974, pp. 60–112. For a recent example of the impact of social relations on technology, see Noble, "Social Choice in Machine Design: The Case of Automatically Controlled Machine Tools, and a Challenge for Labor," *Politics and Society*, 8 (1978): 313–48.

18. David Brody, *Steelworkers in America: The Nonunion Era* (New York, 1960), p. 32. Also see Stone, "Job Structures," p. 133.

19. Douglas, *American Apprenticeship*, ch. 5; Weyl and Sakolski, *Conditions*; Braverman, *Labor*; Hogan, "Capitalism," pp. 77–94; and Clyde and Sally Griffen, *Natives and Newcomers: The Ordering of Opportunity in Mid-Nineteenth Century Poughkeepsie* (Cambridge, Mass., 1978).

20. Lynds, *Middletown*, p. 43.

21. Weyl and Sakolski, *Conditions*, p. 692.

22. Douglas, *American Apprenticeship*, p. 116.

23. *Ibid.*, pp. 118–19.

24. Stone, "Job Structures," p. 133.

25. See Hogan, "Capitalism," pp. 80–85.

26. Edwards, *Contested Terrain*; Chandler, *Visible Hand*; Noble, *America By Design*; and Mills, *White Collar*.

27. Braverman, *Labor*, p. 299. See also Margery Davies, "Woman's Place Is at the Typewriter: The Feminization of the Clerical Labor Force," in Richard Edwards, Michael Reich, and David Gordon, eds., *Labor Market Segmentation* (Lexington, Mass., 1975), pp. 279–96.

28. Rodgers, *Work Ethic*; James B. Gilbert, *Work Without Salvation: America's Intellectuals and Industrial Alienation, 1880–1910* (Baltimore, 1978).

29. See Herbert G. Gutman, *Work, Culture, and Society in Industrializing America* (New York, 1976), ch. 1; Dawley, *Class and Community*, chs. 2, 5; Paul Faler, "Cultural Aspects of the Industrial Revolution: Lynn, Massachusetts, Shoemakers and Industrial Morality, 1826–1860," *Labor History*, 15 (1974): 367–94; Bruce Laurie, "'Nothing on Compulsion': Life Styles of Philadelphia Artisans, 1820–1850," *ibid.*, pp. 336–66; Daniel T. Rodgers, "Tradition, Modernity, and the American Industrial Worker: Reflections and Critique," *Journal of Interdisciplinary History*, 7 (1977): 655–81; and E. P. Thompson, "Time, Work-Discipline, and Industrial Capitalism," *Past and Present*, 38 (1967): 56–97.

30. For early twentieth-century studies of labor turnover, see Sumner H. Slichter, *The Turnover of Factory Labor* (New York, 1919); Paul Douglas, "The Problem of Labor Turnover," *American Economic Review*, 8 (1918): 306–16; and Don D. Lescohier, *The Labor Market* (New York, 1919). For recent summaries of these and other studies, see Rodgers, *Work Ethic*, pp. 163–65, and Nelson, *Managers and Workers*, pp. 85–86.

31. David Montgomery, "Workers' Control of Machine Production in the Nineteenth Century," *Labor History*, 17 (1976): 485–509.

32. *Ibid.*; David Montgomery, "The 'New Unionism' and the Transformation of Workers' Consciousness in America, 1909–22," *Journal of Social History*, 7 (1974): 508–29; James R. Green, "Comments on the Montgomery Paper," *ibid.*, pp. 530–35; and Montgomery, "Immigrant Workers."

33. James Weinstein, *Ambiguous Legacy: The Left in American Politics* (New York, 1975), p. 7.

34. Nelson, *Managers and Workers*, p. 102. Also, see Rodgers, *Work Ethic*, ch. 2; Noble, *America By Design*, ch. 10; and Bruno Ramirez, *When Workers Fight: The Politics of Industrial Relations in the Progressive Era, 1898–1916* (Westport, Conn., 1978), ch. 8.

35. Montgomery, "Immigrant Workers," p. 104.

36. Nelson, *Managers and Workers*, p. 103.

37. Loren Baritz, *The Servants of Power: A History of the Use of Social Science in American Industry* (Middletown, Conn., 1960).

38. Montgomery, "Immigrant Workers," p. 109. See also Nelson, *Managers and Workers*, ch. 8; and Noble, *America by Design*, ch. 10.

39. Rodgers, *Work Ethic*, p. 59.

40. Gilbert, *Work Without Salvation*, pp. 110–11.

41. Wirth, *Education*, ch. 2.

42. Quoted in *ibid.*, p. 118. On the NAM and vocational education, see also Lazerson and Grubb, *American Education*, pp. 18–19.

43. Quoted in Wirth, *Education*, p. 58. On the attitudes of organized labor toward vocational education, see also Philip R. V. Curoe, *Educational Attitudes and Policies of Organized Labor in the United States* (New York, 1926), ch. 6; and for valuable studies on organized labor and vocational education in Chicago, see George Counts, *School and Society in Chicago* (New York, 1928), ch. 9, and Hogan, "Capitalism," ch. 10.

44. Quoted in Grubb and Lazerson, *American Education*, p. 21.

45. Wirth, *Education*, ch. 3, and Hogan, "Capitalism," ch. 10.

46. Quoted in Wirth, *Education*, pp. 113–14.

47. Quoted in *ibid.*, p. 137.

48. Quoted in *ibid.*, p. 102.

49. For a review of early twentieth-century studies of young workers, see Douglas, *American Apprenticeship*, ch. 4; and W. Carson Ryan, *Vocational Guidance and the Public Schools*, U.S. Bureau of Education Bulletin no. 24, 1918 (Washington, D.C., 1910), pp. 38–59.

50. Helen M. Todd, "Why Children Work: The Children's Answer," *McClure's Magazine*, 40 (1913): 68–79.

51. Edith Waterfall, *The Day Continuation School in England: Its Function and Future* (London, 1923), pp. 154–55.

52. Quoted in Ryan, *Vocational Guidance*, p. 47.

53. Douglas, *American Apprenticeship*, p. 97.

54. *Ibid.*, p. 85.

55. *Report of the Commission on Industrial and Technical Education*, Commonwealth of Massachusetts, Senate no. 349 (April 1906): 87.

56. On school attendance and employment for working youth, see the studies in Bloomfield, *Readings*.

57. On professionalism, see Burton J. Bledstein, *The Culture of Professionalism: The Middle Class and the Development of Higher Education in America* (New York, 1976); and for the influence of professionalism on vocational educators, see Kett, *Rites,* ch. 6, and Kett in this volume.

58. Lazerson and Grubb, *American Education*, pp. 33–40.

59. For accounts of the conflict over the Cooley bill, see Hogan, "Capitalism," ch. 10, and Lazerson and Grubb, *American Education*, pp. 33–37.

60. Quoted in *ibid.*, p. 36.

61. Quoted in *ibid.*, p. 37. For Dewey's position, also see Wirth, *Education*, pp. 210–15.

62. Quoted in Lazerson and Grubb, *Vocationalism*, p. 37.

63. *Report of the Commission on National Aid to Vocational Educa-*

tion, House of Representatives, 63d Congress, 2d sess., doc. no. 1004 (Washington, D.C., 1914), p. 33.

64. Federal Board of Vocational Education, *Sixteenth Annual Report to Congress* (Washington, 1932), p. 61.

65. William H. Dooley, *The Education of the Ne'er-Do-Well* (Boston, 1916); and E. M. McDonough, "Organization and Administration of a Continuation School," *Industrial Arts Magazine*, 10 (1921): 203–25.

66. Edward Mayman, "The Evolution of the Continuation School in New York City," *The School Review*, 41 (1933): 196.

67. Douglas, *American Apprenticeship*, p. 268.

68. *Ibid.*, pp. 267–68.

69. *Ibid.*, pp. 123, 268.

70. Ryan, *Vocational Guidance*, p. 17; Bloomfield, *Readings*, p. vi.

71. On the history of vocational guidance, see John M. Brewer, *The History of Vocational Guidance: Origins and Early Development* (New York, 1942); W. Richard Stephens, *Social Reform and the Dawn of Guidance* (Terre Haute, Ind., 1968); and Wirth, *Education*, ch. 5.

72. Bloomfield, *Readings*, p. v.

73. Charles William Eliot, "The Value during Education of the Life-Career Motive," in Bloomfield, *Readings*, p. 4.

74. Edward L. Thorndike, "The University and Vocational Guidance," *ibid.*, p. 100.

75. Frank E. Spaulding, "Problems of Vocational Guidance," *ibid.*, p. 74.

76. Helen T. Woolley, "Charting Childhood in Cincinnati," *ibid.*, p. 231.

77. Alice P. Barrows, "The Dangers and Possibilities of Vocational Guidance," *Child Labor Bulletin*, 1 (1912): 46–48.

78. Woolley, "Cincinnati," p. 231.

79. On women and work in the early twentieth century, see Edith Abbott, *Women in Industry: A Study in American Economic History* (New York, 1910); *Report on the Condition of Women and Child Wage Earners in the U.S.*, 61st Congress, 2d sess., Senate Document No. 645 (Washington, D.C., 1910, 1911, 1920); Robert W. Smuts, *Women and Work in America* (New York, 1959); Leslie Woodcock Tentler, *Wage-Earning Women: Industrial Work and Family Life in the United States, 1900–1930* (New York, 1979); Alice Kessler-Harris, "Women's Wage Work as Myth and History," *Labor History*, 19 (1978): 287–307; Davies, "Woman's Place"; and Geraldine Clifford in this volume.

80. Cree T. Work, "High School Training for Girls," *Sierra Educational News*, 7 (1911): 20. On vocational schooling for young women, see Clifford in this volume; Albert Leake, *Vocational Education of Girls*

and Women (New York, 1918); Willystine Goodsell, *The Education of Women: Its Social Background and Its Problems* (New York, 1924), especially the review of education for working girls, ch. 7; and Thomas Woody, *A History of Women's Education in the United States*, vol. 2 (New York, 1974; orig. ed. 1929), chs. 1–2.

81. Quoted in Goodsell, *Education*, p. 211.

82. *Ibid.*, p. 213.

83. Henry Perkinson, *The Imperfect Panacea: American Faith in Education, 1865–1965* (New York, 1968).

84. Lynds, *Middletown*, p. 194.

Cuban: Federal Vocational Education Legislation

1. Edward A. Krug, *The Shaping of the American High School*, vol. 2 (New York, 1972), pp. 310–11.

2. Franklin Keller, *The Double-Purpose High School* (New York, 1933), p. 181.

3. Report of the Panel of Consultants on Vocational Education, *Education for a Changing World of Work* (Washington, D.C., 1964), p. 2.

4. John D. Russell et al., *Vocational Education* (Washington, D.C., 1938); Panel of Consultants, *Education*; General Report of the Advisory Council on Vocational Education, *Vocational Education: The Bridge Between Man and His Work* (Washington, D.C., 1968); Comptroller General's Report to the Congress, *What is the Role of Federal Assistance for Vocational Education?* (Washington, D.C., 1974).

5. Melvin Barlow, *Burkett: Latest Word from Washington* (Washington, D.C., 1977), p. 30.

6. Marvin Lazerson and W. Norton Grubb, eds., *American Education and Vocationalism: Documents in Vocational Education, 1870–1970* (New York, 1974), raises this point explicitly.

7. Lawrence A. Cremin, *The Transformation of the School: Progressivism in American Education, 1876–1957* (New York, 1964), p. 56; Melvin Barlow, *History of Industrial Education in the United States* (Peoria, Ill., 1967), pp. 51–66; Grant Venn, *Man, Education, and Work* (Washington, D.C., 1964), pp. 56–57; Sol Cohen, "The Industrial Education Movement, 1906–1917," *American Quarterly*, 20 (1968): 110; C. H. Edson, "The Reform of Vocational Education," *Urban Education*, 12 (1978): 452; Vincent P. Lannie, "The Development of Vocational Education in America: An Historical Overview," in Carl Shaefer and Jacob Kaufman, eds., *Vocational Education: Social and Behavioral Perspectives* (Lexington, Mass., 1971), p. 17; Berenice M. Fisher, *Industrial Education: American Ideals and Institutions* (Madison, Wis., 1967), p. 135.

8. Arthur G. Wirth, *Education in the Technological Society: The Vocational-Liberal Studies Controversy in the Early Twentieth Century* (Scranton, Pa., 1972), pp. 80–82, 162; Melvin Barlow, *The Unconquerable Senator Page* (Washington, D.C., 1976); W. Richard Stephens, *Social Reform and the Origins of Vocational Guidance* (Washington, D.C., 1970), pp. 53–67; Charles Bennett, *A History of Manual and Industrial Education, 1870–1917* (Peoria, Ill., 1937), pp. 507, 535–50.

9. House Committee on Education and Labor and Senate Committee on Labor and Public Welfare, *A Compilation of Federal and State Education Laws* (Washington, D.C., 1975), p. 522.

10. Russell, *Vocational Education,* p. 46.

11. Among Prosser's writings are Charles Prosser and Charles Allen, *Vocational Education in a Democracy* (New York, 1925) and Layton Hawkins, Charles Prosser, and J. C. Wright, *Development of Vocational Education* (Chicago, 1951).

12. Barlow, *Unconquerable*, p. 48; Lannie, Fisher, Barlow, and many authors of vocational education textbooks have drawn extensively on Prosser's writings. In the 1964 Panel of Consultants report, the only historical reference to the Smith-Hughes Act cites one of Prosser's works.

13. Prosser and Allen, *Vocational Education*, pp. 441–57.

14. Russell, *Vocational Education*, pp. 44, 46.

15. *Ibid.*, pp. 129, 130, 228, 229.

16. *Ibid.*, pp. 113–14.

17. Barlow, Venn, Grubb and Lazerson, Wirth, and Fisher have already been cited. See also Michael Imber, "Compulsory Continuation Schools for Young Workers: An Early Attempt to Combine Schooling and Work" (Stanford University, Boys Town Center for the Study of Youth Development, n.d.).

18. Melvin Barlow, "Bicentennial Issue," *American Vocational Journal*, 51 (1976): 64, 75; Barlow and M. D. Mobley, "Impact of Federal Legislation and Policies Upon Vocational Education," in Barlow, ed., *Vocational Education* (Chicago, 1965), pp. 191, 193–96.

19. Venn, *Man, Education, and Work*, pp. 63–66.

20. Wirth, *Technological Society*, p. 219.

21. Lazerson and Grubb, *American Education*, pp. 20, 31–32; Imber, "Compulsory," p. 8.

22. Marvin Lazerson and W. Norton Grubb, "Rally 'Round the Workplace: Continuities and Fallacies in Career Education," *Harvard Educational Review*, 45 (1975): 459, 462.

23. Lannie, *Development*, p. 17; Venn, *Man, Education, and Work*, pp. 47, 57; Barlow, *Burkett*, p. 57; and Lazerson and Grubb, *American*

Education, disagree with the view that the 1963 law was a departure in either policy or practice.

24. Panel of Consultants, *Education* (pp. 11–17), documents the statements on high unemployment and rapid technological development. See also Venn, pp. 6–15, 119–23; Grubb and Lazerson, *American Education*, pp. 44–45; Advisory Council, *Vocational Education*, p. 3; Barlow, "Bicentennial Issue," p. 77; and Douglas Kliever, *Vocational Education Act of 1963: A Case Study in Legislation* (Washington, D.C., 1965), p. 14.

25. Panel of Consultants, *Education*, p. 109.

26. *Ibid.*, pp. 224–36.

27. Kliever, *Vocational Education Act*, pp. 13–63; Barlow, *History*, pp. 430–52.

28. *Ibid.*, p. 440.

29. Garth Mangum, *Reorienting Vocational Education* (Ann Arbor, Mich., 1968), pp. 10, 12–13.

30. David Rogers, "Vocational and Career Education: A Critique and Some New Directions," *Teachers College Record*, 74 (1973): 490–91.

31. Harry Summerfield, *Power and Process: The Formulation and Limits of Federal Educational Policy* (Berkeley, Calif., 1974), pp. 140–68; Todd Endo and John Wirt, "Federal Program Analysis," Rand, July 1, 1974, pp. V–1–36; Mary Ellis, *A Report to the Nation on Vocational Education* (Flagstaff, Ariz., 1975), p. 9.

32. Advisory Council, *Bridge*, pp. 197–204; Ellis, *Report*, pp. 9–10.

33. Barlow, *Burkett*, pp. 57–66; Summerfield, *Power and Process*, pp. 140–68; Endo and Wirt, "Analysis," pp. V–1–36; Mangum, *Reorienting*, p. 75. This pattern of a national study and its recommendations being incorporated into legislation holds for the 1914 National Commission, the 1963 Panel of Consultants report and the 1968 Advisory Council study. The 1938 Russell Report is an exception.

34. U.S. Office of Education, *The Vocational Amendments of 1968* (Washington, D.C., 1969), Foreword, p. iii.

35. GAO Report, p. iv.

36. Ellis, *Report*, pp. 21–45, 46.

37. National Institute of Education, "A Plan for the Study of Vocational Education," Dec. 30, 1977, pp. 1–36.

38. Few annotated bibliographies of writings on vocational education are available. A recent one is in Grubb and Lazerson, *American Education*, pp. 51–56, which, however, does not deal with the scanty literature on federal legislation.

Basically, most writers on the topic of vocational education legislation have embraced a set of core beliefs, usually unstated, on the value of vocational education. They believe that vocationalism in the schools is in the national interest and that it will improve the life chances of the majority of students, those who choose not to continue their formal schooling. These core beliefs rest on the premise that the existing economic system is worthwhile but in need of better linkage with formal schooling. Prosser, Bennett, Barlow, Venn, Russell and others generally shared these beliefs, though differing among themselves over strategies.

Prosser and Barlow, for example, were passionate promoters of vocational education and participants in legislative battles. What they wrote mirrored their faith. Venn, Evans, Keller, and others—also vocational educators—were pragmatic supporters of vocational education, seeing some legislative and bureaucratic strategies as better than others. Their prose lacked the evangelical ring of true believers. They analyzed and criticized, collecting and using evidence dispassionately and recommending and making improvements.

Wirth, Fisher, Krug, Cohen, Cremin, and Grubb and Lazerson are historians who have written about vocational education and touched upon federal legislation. Wirth, Fisher, Cohen, Krug, and Cremin deal mostly with the ideological debates at the turn of the century and later. Their analyses of the arguments put forth by partisans and critics of vocationalism provide a useful mapping of the intellectual (but not the operational) terrain. Except for Cohen, there seems to be general agreement between these historians and the judgments of Russell and Venn on the significance of federal legislation. Also, with some exceptions, there does not appear to be any serious questioning of the core beliefs described above. Wirth and Krug do raise questions about the wisdom of the reformers' views and the doubtful legacy they bequeathed to mid-twentieth-century educators. Cohen raises far more grave questions about the reformers' intentions and their basic assumptions about the purposes of schooling. Most writers, however, did not raise these issues.

Grubb and Lazerson move beyond Cohen. They reject Prosser's and similarly situated advocates' assumptions. Their premise is that the economic system produces massive inequalities in resources and opportunities. Schools, they argue, can do little to ease or remove those inequalities; if anything, schools strengthen these inequalities by duplicating them in each generation of students. Their conclusion that vocational education has failed repeatedly despite reformers' intentions has also led them to see vocational education as a politically safe reform that will leave the basic workings of the economic system untouched. See their essay in this volume.

Even though Lazerson has identified himself as a revisionist and Grubb's work places him in that category as well, their long essays on career education and the introduction to their book of selections on vocational education soften some of the pronouncements made by radical historians on the motives of reformers, the functions of schooling, and the domination of minorities and the poor by economic elites. Nonetheless, they see continuities in vocational education that tie current efforts to install career education with early twentieth-century reformers' efforts in getting vocationalism accepted. Lazerson and Grubb pay little notice, however, to the development of vocational legislation after 1920.

39. "Fifty Years of Progress in Professional Organizations," *American Vocational Journal*, 31 (1956): 91–97.

40. Barlow, *Unconquerable*, p. 26; Stephens, *Social Reform*, p. 132.

41. *Ibid.*; Barlow, *History*, p. 132; Summerfield, *Power*, p. 141.

42. Barlow, *Burkett*, p. 162; Barlow, "Bicentennial Issue," pp. 87–88.

43. Barlow, *Burkett*, pp. 25–43; Summerfield, *Power*, pp. 130–68; Russell, *Vocational Education*, pp. 20–23.

44. Venn, *Man, Education, and Work*, p. 60; Russell, *Vocational Education*, p. 22.

45. Krug, *Shaping*, pp. 310–11.

46. Barlow, *Burkett*, pp. 57–66.

47. Stephen K. Bailey, *Education Interest Groups in the Nation's Capital* (Washington, D.C., 1976), p. 28.

48. Barlow, *Burkett*, p. 10.

49. One veteran lobbyist stated, "But for the American Vocational Association and its predecessors, there would be no such financial aid today"; M. D. Mobley, "History of Federal Funds for Vocational Education," *American Vocational Journal*, 31 (1956): 98. Norton Grubb also explores the issue of the resiliency and persistence of vocational education in the face of critical evaluations. He dismisses the AVA and the "vocational education establishment" as a "cynical explanation" for the Phoenix-like reappearance of vocational education. See his "The Phoenix of Vocational Education: Implications for Evaluation," in National Institute of Education, *Planning Papers for the Vocational Education Study* (Washington, D.C., 1979), p. 195.

50. Lazerson and Grubb, *American Education*, p. 32; Cohen, "Industrial Education," pp. 101, 104, 110; see Gallup Poll cited in *Reform of Secondary Education* (New York, 1973), Appendixes A and B.

51. Grubb, "Phoenix," pp. 196–99, 200–202; Barlow, *Unconquerable*, pp. 61, 91, 112, 113; Grubb and Lazerson, *American Education*, pp. 17–28.

52. David K. Cohen and Bella H. Rosenberg, "Functions and Fan-

tasies: Understanding Schools in Capitalist America," *History of Education Quarterly*, 17 (1977): 123–24.

53. *Ibid.*

54. Grubb, "Phoenix," p. 210.

55. Endo and Wirt, "Analysis," p. V–32. The growing literature on the implementation of federal programs includes: Richard F. Elmore, "Organizational Models of Social Program Implementation," *Public Policy*, 26 (1978): 185–228; Walter Williams and Richard Elmore, eds., *Social Program Implementation* (New York, 1976); Robert Herriot and Neal Gross, eds., *The Dynamics of Planned Educational Change* (Berkeley, Calif., 1979); Jeffrey Pressman and Aaron Wildavsky, *Implementation* (Berkeley, Calif., 1973); Jerome Murphy, "Title I of ESEA: The Politics of Implementing Federal Education Reform," *Harvard Educational Review*, 41 (1971): 35–63.

56. Williams and Elmore, *Social Program Implementation*, p. 202.

57. Don Gentry, "Federal and State Governance of Vocational Education," in *Planning Papers*, pp. 40, 42; Mike Kirst, "Research Issues for Vocational Education: Compliance and Enforcement of Federal Laws," *ibid.*, pp. 56, 66.

58. Research on this point, the looseness and independent behavior within a school system, continues to grow. See Karl Weick, "Educational Organizations as Loosely Coupled Systems," *Administrative Science Quarterly*, 21 (1976): 1–18; Paul Berman and Milbrey McLaughlin, *Federal Programs Supporting Educational Change*, vol. 3, *The Process of Change*, and vol. 4, *Findings in Review* (Santa Monica, Calif., 1975); and Richard Weatherly and Michael Lipsky, "Street-Level Bureaucrats and Institutional Innovation: Implementing Special Education Reform," *Harvard Educational Review*, 47 (1977): 171–97.

59. The literature on the issue is substantial. See John Goodlad, *Looking Behind the Classroom Door* (Worthington, Ohio, 1974); Louis Smith and Pat Keith, *Anatomy of Educational Innovation* (New York, 1971); Neal Gross, Joseph Giacquinta, and Marilyn Bernstein, *Implementing Organizational Innovations* (New York, 1971); Richard Carlson, *Adoption of Educational Innovations* (Eugene, Ore., 1965); Charles Silberman, *Crisis in the Classroom* (New York, 1971); Larry Cuban, "Determinants of Curriculum Change and Stability," in Gary Sykes and Jon Schafferzick, eds., *Value Conflicts and Curriculum Issues* (Berkeley, Calif., 1979); and Berman and McLaughlin, *Federal Programs*.

60. Eleanor Farrar, John DeSanctis, and David Cohen, "Views From Below: Implementation Research in Education" (Cambridge, Mass., 1978), pp. 7–9; see also Pressman and Wildavsky, *Implementation*; and Jerome Murphy, "Title V of ESEA: The Impact of Discretionary Funds

in State Education Bureaucracies," in Williams and Elmore, eds., *Social Program Implementation*.

61. Prosser and Allen, *Vocational Education*, pp. 442–50; Hawkins et al., *Development*, pp. 135–77, 199–212.

62. *Ibid.*, pp. 167–68; V. R. Cardozier, "Vocational Education and Federal Control," *American School Board Journal* (April 1965): 30–32.

63. Russell, *Vocational Education*, p. 36.

64. *Ibid.*, p. 40.

65. U.S. Department of the Interior, Office of Education, *The Program of Studies Bulletin, 1932*, no. 17 (Washington, D.C., 1933), p. 128; Federal Security Agency, Office of Education, *Home Economics in Public High Schools, 1938–1939* (Washington, D.C., 1941), p. 8.

66. *Program of Studies, 1932*, p. 159.

67. Thomas Norton, *Education for Work* (New York, 1938), p. 49; *Home Economics*, p. 3.

68. Carl Withers [pseud. James West], *Plainville, U.S.A.* (New York, 1945), p. 79.

69. Keller, *Double-Purpose High School*, p. 106.

70. Hawkins et al., *Development*, p. 106.

71. *Ibid.*, p. 262.

72. Norton, *Education*, p. 108.

73. Gladys Branegan, *Home Economics Teacher-Training Under the Smith-Hughes Act, 1917 to 1927* (New York, 1929), pp. 42–43; Council of State Governments, *The Forty-Eight State School Systems* (Chicago, 1949), p. 188.

74. Russell, *Vocational Education*, p. 72.

75. Hawkins et al., *Development of Vocational Education*, p. 198. We know very little about the daily activities of supervisors. An article that contains descriptive data on pre-World War I vocational education supervisors performing their tasks in segregated black schools is what needs to be done for state supervisors under Smith-Hughes funding. See James D. Anderson, "Northern Foundations and the Shaping of Southern Black Rural Education, 1902–1935," *History of Education Quarterly*, 18 (1978): 371–96.

76. Hawkins et al., *Development*, p. 160; Panel of Consultants, *Education*, p. 166.

77. Russell, *Vocational Education*, p. 34.

78. Mangum, Rogers, Ellis, and the Advisory Council and GAO reports have been cited already; Michael Kirst and Joel Berke, *Federal Aid to Education* (Lexington, Mass., 1972).

79. Advisory Council, *Vocational Education*, pp. 123, 157.

80. Kirst and Berke, *Federal Aid*, p. 359.

81. GAO report, p. 11.

82. Rogers, "Vocational and Career Education," pp. 477, 490.

83. Leonard Lecht, *Evaluating Vocational Education: Policies and Plans for the 1970's* (New York, 1974), p. 58.

84. Imber and Farrar et al. point out the top-heavy goal load that vocational education legislation carries with it. Summerfield focuses on OE-AVA ties in his study; Kirst, "Research Issues for Vocational Education," concludes that vocational educators are the major obstacle to local and state compliance with the federal mandate; the GAO report points to stubborn state officials and understaffed OE bureaucrats.

85. The Farrar et al. study of Experienced-Eased Career Education is one example of how the rephrased question can be approached. The complicated texture of local responses to programs, once sketched out and filled in, will help answer the question.

Kett: The Adolescence of Vocational Education

1. Arthur G. Wirth, *Education in the Technological Society: The Vocational-Liberal Studies Controversy in the Early Twentieth Century* (Scranton, Pa., 1972), chs. 2–4. *Congressional Record*, 64th Cong., 2d sess., 1914, 54, pt. 1: 714–24, 749–54, pt. 2; 1080–81.

2. Beatrice G. Reubens, "Vocational Education for All in High School?" in James O'Toole, ed., *Work and the Quality of Life in America: Resource Papers for Work in America* (Cambridge, Mass., 1974), p. 313; Carroll W. DeSelle, "A Follow-Up Study of the Graduates of San Jose Technical High School," M.S. thesis (Oregon State College, 1940), p. 9.

3. Selden C. Menefee, *Vocational Training and Employment of Youth* (Washington, D.C., 1942); Charles Brecher, *Upgrading Blue Collar and Service Workers*, Foreward by Eli Ginzberg (Baltimore, 1972), pp. 23–25, 36–38, 54, 72–78. See also John T. Grasso, "The Contributions of Vocational Education, Training and Work Experience in the Early Career Achievements of Young Men," Ph.D. diss. (Ohio State University, 1975); Harry M. Levin, "A Decade of Policy Developments in Improving Education and Training for Low-Income Populations," in Robert H. Haveman, ed., *A Decade of Federal Antipoverty Programs: Achievements, Failures, and Lessons* (New York, 1977), pp. 171–74.

4. As early as 1920 an educator, Percy E. Davidson, referred to "such unexampled returns on the capital invested" in education; see his "Equality of Educational Opportunity: The Views of the Economists," *School and Society*, 12 (Dec. 4, 1920): 540.

5. David M. Gordon, *Theories of Poverty and Unemployment* (To-

ronto, 1972); Bennett Harrison, "Public Employment and the Theory of the Dual Economy," in Harold L. Sheppard, Bennett Harrison, and William J. Spring, eds., *The Political Economy of Public Service Employment* (Lexington, Mass., 1972), p. 44; Sidney P. Marland, Jr., *Career Education: A Proposal for Reform* (New York, 1974); T. H. Fitzgerald, "Career Education: An Error Whose Time Has Come," *School Review*, 82 (Nov. 1973): 91–105.

6. William Haber et al., *Manpower in the United States: Problems and Policies* (New York, 1954), p. viii.

7. Marvin Lazerson and W. Norton Grubb, "Rally 'Round the Workplace: Continuities and Fallacies in Career Education," *Harvard Educational Review*, 45 (1975): 451–74. It is difficult to see in Marland's ideas a single novel component except the synthetic nature of his proposals.

8. On the relationship between the report of the Commission on National Aid to Vocational Legislation and congressional debates, see Nicholas Ricciardi and Ira W. Kirby, eds., *Readings in Vocational Guidance: Trade and Industrial Aspect* (New York, 1932), chs. 2, 3. On the politics of the Smith-Hughes Act, see Dewey W. Grantham, Jr., *Hoke Smith and the Politics of the New South* (Baton Rouge, La., 1958), pp. 264–67.

9. Wirth, *Education*, chs. 7–9.

10. *Fourteenth Annual Report of the Federal Board for Vocational Education, 1930* (Washington, D.C., 1930), p. 13.

11. For an example of this effort to build a consensus, see the "Report of the Commission on National Aid to Vocational Education," *House Docs.*, 63rd Cong., 2nd sess., 1913–14, no. 1004, 2 vols. in 1 (Washington, D.C., 1914), 1: 18–34.

12. See for example *ibid.*, pp. 18–22; *Fourteenth Report, 1930*, p. 13; *Report of the [Massachusetts] Commission on Industrial and Technical Education, . . . April, 1906* (Boston, 1906), pp. 30–98; Douglas, *American Apprenticeship and Industrial Education*, 100–106; J. Adams Puffer, *Vocational Guidance* (Chicago, 1913), p. 35; John I. Sowers, *The Boy and His Vocation* (Peoria, Ill., 1927), p. 99.

13. Dewey's ideas about vocational education were complex, and were suffused by the connotations which the word "work" had for him. By work Dewey meant not merely a job, but productive labor that helped one reach one's human potential. For a full discussion of Dewey's ideas, see Arthur G. Wirth, "Issues Affecting Education and Work in the Eighties: Efficiency versus Industrial Democracy, A Historical Perspective," *Teachers College Record*, 79 (Sept. 1977): 55–67. As Wirth notes (p. 62), Dewey's aspiration was "to redesign industrial and educational institutions so they would be supportive of democratic values." See also

Charles A. Prosser and Charles R. Allen, *Vocational Education in a Democracy* (New York, 1925), p. 240; and David Snedden, *Vocational Education* (New York, 1920), p. 25.

14. John V. Brennan, "The Schools and Vocational Guidance," in Meyer Bloomfield, ed., *Readings in Vocational Guidance* (Cambridge, Mass., 1924), p. 79; H. D. Kitson, "Suggestions Toward a Tenable Theory of Vocational Guidance," *ibid.*, pp. 103–8; William Rosengarten, *Choosing Your Life Work*, 2nd ed. (New York, 1924), p. vii.

15. Their thinking about dead-end jobs owed a good deal to the *Report of the [Massachusetts] Commission on Industrial and Technical Education*. On contemporary fears of tramping and drifting, see Alice W. Solenberger, *One Thousand Homeless Men: A Study of Original Records* (New York, 1914); Josiah F. Willard, *Tramping with Tramps: Studies and Sketches of Vagabond Life*, pref. by Andrew D. White (1899, repr. ed. College Park, Md., 1969).

16. Prosser and Allen wrote: "In the professional field the advance from unorganized or pick up training to organized instruction has already reached a considerable stage of development." *Vocational Education in a Democracy*, p. 25.

17. Meyer Bloomfield, "Finding One's Place in Life," in Edwin Markham, ed., *Foundation Stones of Success*, 10 vols. (Chicago, 1917), 7: 56.

18. Prosser and Allen, *Vocational Education*, pp. 28–29.

19. For an example of the oversimplified juxtapositions of past and present that pervaded the movement, see *ibid.*, pp. 29–31. A related view was that, with the decline of the family as a working unit, families no longer provided vocational models for youth. See Puffer, *Vocational Guidance,* p. 18.

20. See for example Albert Barnes, "The Choice of a Profession," in *Miscellaneous Essays and Reviews*, 2 vols. (Boston, 1855), 1: 211–12.

21. Daniel T. Rodgers, *The Work Ethic in Industrial America, 1850–1920* (Chicago, 1974), pp. 7–14.

22. Richard C. Maclaurin, "Vocational Guidance," in Bloomfield, *Readings*, p. 18.

23. Erville B. Woods, "The Social Waste of Unguided Personal Ability," *ibid.*, p. 31.

24. Quoted in Charles A. Bennett, *A History of Manual and Industrial Education Up to 1870* (Peoria, Ill., 1926), p. 369; see also *ibid.*, chs. 6, 9, 10; William Maclure, *Opinions on Various Subjects, Dedicated to the Industrious Producers*, 3 vols. (New Harmony, Ind., 1831–38), 1: 56–58. My point is not that promoters of industrial education before 1850 had all been radicals; some, like Philipp von Fellenberg, had conservative

philosophies. Both in Britain and America, moreover, the mechanics' institutes, which grew out of a broad philosophy of useful education, were suffused by paternalism. But the radical potential was at times actualized.

25. Lapp and Mote, *Learning to Earn: A Plea and a Plan for Vocational Education* (Indianapolis, 1915), pp. 74–75. For an example of the claims of vocational reformers to a radical heritage see C. R. Mann, *The American Spirit in Education*, U.S. Bureau of Education Bulletin no. 30 (Washington, D.C., 1919), pp. 7–27, 62.

26. Arthur Pound, *The Iron Man in Industry* (New York, 1922), p. 200; Douglas, *American Apprenticeship and Industrial Education*, p. 124.

27. On the foreign-born dominance of the American working class, see U.S. Dept. of the Interior, Census Office, *Report on the Population of the United States at the Eleventh Census: 1890*, pt. 2 (Washington, D.C., 1897), p. cxlv. The fear was pervasive that white-collar occupations were overstocked and that the schools were turning out too many would-be clerks and not enough honest workmen. See for example *Fourth Annual Report of the [Massachusetts] Bureau of Statistics of Labor* (Boston, 1873), pp. 393–94; *Annual Report of the Board of Education of the State of Connecticut, . . . 1870* (New Haven, 1870), pp. 40–44. On manual training as the staging ground for many vocational educators see David Snedden, "The Vocational-Education Movement: A Critical Inventory of Policies," in Edwin A. Lee, ed., *Objectives and Problems in Vocational Education*, 2nd ed. (New York, 1938), p. 360. For claims that vocational education would attract native-born youth to the manual trades see *Report of the [Massachusetts] Commission on Industrial and Technical Education*, p. 46, and *Congressional Record*, 64th Cong., 2d sess., 1914, 54, part 2, 1081.

28. *Report of the Commission on National Aid to Vocational Education*, 1: 28; Prosser and Allen, *Vocational Education*, p. 85.

29. Stuart Chase, "200,000 Students and 4,000,000 Alumni," *Fortune*, 7 (June 1933): 67; *The I.C.S. System of Instruction by Mail and the Results Achieved* (Scranton, Pa., 1905), Preface.

30. *Twenty-Fifth Annual Report of the [U.S.] Commissioner of Labor, 1910: Industrial Education* (Washington, D.C., 1911), p. 145 and *passim*.

31. Prosser and Allen, *Vocational Education*, p. 83.

32. Frederick W. Taylor, "Taylor's Testimony Before the Special House Committee, in Taylor, *Scientific Management: Comprising Shop Management; The Principles of Scientific Management; Testimony Before the Special House Committee* (New York, 1947), p. 41.

33. William H. Beveridge, *Unemployment: A Problem of Industry* (London, 1910).

34. Mary Van Kleeck, *A Seasonal Industry: A Study of the Millinery Trade in New York* (New York, 1917), *Artificial Flower Makers* (New York, 1913), and *Women in the Bookbinding Trade,* (New York, 1913). Louise C. Odencrantz, *Italian Women in Industry: A Study of Conditions in New York City* (1919, reprint. ed. New York, 1977); Sumner Slichter, *The Turnover of Factory Labor*, intr. by John R. Commons, New York, 1919); Don D. Lescohier, *The Labor Market* (New York, 1919); Herman Feldman, *The Regularization of Employment: A Study in the Prevention of Unemployment* (New York, 1925).

35. Lescohier, *Labor Market*, pp. 265–67, 18.

36. Slichter, *Turnover*, p. 6.

37. Frederick A. Mills, *Contemporary Theories of Unemployment and Unemployment Relief* (New York, 1917), p. 138.

38. Quoted in *ibid.*, p. 84.

39. *Ibid.*, p. 139.

40. Lescohier, *Labor Market*, p. 165.

41. *Ibid.*, p. 108.

42. *Ibid.*, p. 133; Feldman, *Regularization*, p. 422.

43. *Report of the [Massachusetts] Commission on Industrial and Technical Education*; Maurice B. Hexter, *Juvenile Employment and Labor Mobility in the Business Cycle* (Boston, 1927), pp. 13–14.

44. Snedden expressed these ideas in many places. See his *Vocational Education,* pp. 21–22 and his *American High Schools and Vocational Schools in 1960* (New York, 1931), pp. 108–14.

45. August B. Hollingshead, *Elmtown's Youth: The Impact of Social Class on Adolescents* (New York, 1949), pp. 363–74; Percy E. Davidson and H. Dewey Anderson, *Occupational Mobility in an American Community* (Stanford, Calif., 1937), pp. 103–113.

46. Snedden, "Vocational-Education Movement," p. 385.

47. Bloomfield, "Finding One's Place," pp. 42–43.

48. Lloyd G. Reynolds and Joseph Shister, *Job Horizons* (New York, 1949), p. 80.

49. *Ibid.*, pp. 62–63, 85–88. Hollingshead's *Elmtown's Youth* foreshadowed aspects of the critique of this theory put forward by Reynolds and Shister, for Hollingshead showed how social class conditioned occupational expectations as well as outcomes. A later study substantially supporting Reynolds and Shister is Charles A. Meyers and George P. Schultz, *The Dynamics of a Labor Market* (New York, 1951), pp. 73–74. In recent years a number of historians have explored the relationship between ethnicity and occupation. See for example Josef J. Barton, *Peasants and Strangers: Italians, Rumanians, and Slovaks in an American City, 1890–1950* (Cambridge, Mass., 1975); Virginia Yans-McLaugh-

lin, *Family and Community: Italian Immigrants in Buffalo, 1880–1930* (Ithaca, N.Y., 1973); and Thomas Kessner, *The Golden Door: Italian and Jewish Immigrant Mobility in New York City, 1880–1915* (New York, 1977). (New York, 1977).

50. Odencrantz, *Italian Women*, pp. 272–75, 280–84.

51. Frank W. Taussig, *Principles of Economics*, rev. ed. (New York, 1915), 2: 130.

52. J. E. Cairnes, *Some Leading Principles of Political Economy, Newly Expounded* (New York, 1874), p. 68.

53. Douglas, *American Apprenticeship*, pp. 266–67.

54. *Ibid.*, p. 266.

55. Thomas N. Carver, *Essays in Social Justice* (Cambridge, Mass., 1915), p. 364.

56. Taussig, *Economics*, 2: 237–38.

57. *Ibid.*, p. 138.

58. *Ibid.*, p. 139.

59. Taussig mentioned the argument, but it was not among those used by the Commission on National Aid to Vocational Education.

60. See Grubb and Lazerson, conference paper.

61. Joseph F. Kett, *Rites of Passage: Adolescence in America, 1790–Present* (New York, 1977), ch. 8.

62. *Fourteenth Annual Report of the Federal Board for Vocational Education*, p. 10.

63. *Ibid.*, p. 14.

64. An example of this tendency to deflect criticism by calling for better vocational programs can be found in Albert Westefeld, *Getting Started: Urban Youth in the Labor Market* (New York, 1943, 1971), p. 146. In response to Menefee's negative assessment of vocational education (which had the distinction of being the first serious study of the effects of vocational education), Westefeld concluded that "the most thorough and specific sorts of training appear to be the most effective." He based this on Menefee's data, yet nothing Menefee said really supported this conclusion.

65. *Vocational Education Act of 1963: Hearings Before the General Subcommittee on Education of the Committee on Education and Labor, House of Representatives, Eighty-Eighth Congress, First Session, Title V–A of H.R. 3000 and H.R. 4955* (Washington, D.C., 1963); *Vocational Education Amendments of 1968: Hearings Before the General Subcommittee on Education of the Committee on Education and Labor, House of Representatives, Ninetieth Congress, Second Session, on H.R. 16460* (Washington, D.C., 1968).

Grubb and Lazerson: Education and the Labor Market

1. For a more thorough review of current issues, see W. Norton Grubb, "Schooling and Work: The Changing Context of Education," in Charles Benson and Michael Kirst, eds., *Education, Finance, Governance, and Organization: Future Research Directions* (Washington, D.C., 1980).

2. We have argued some of the historical continuities in several places; see Marvin Lazerson and W. Norton Grubb, *American Education and Vocationalism: A Documentary History, 1870–1970* (New York, 1974); W. Norton Grubb and Marvin Lazerson, "Rally 'Round the Workplace: Continuities and Fallacies in Career Education," *Harvard Educational Review*, 45 (1975): 451–74; and W. Norton Grubb, "The Phoenix of Vocationalism: Hope Deferred is Hope Denied," *New Directions in Schooling and Work,* 1 (1978): 71–90. On the 1930's and 1940's, see Robert S. Lynd and Helen M. Lynd, *Middletown in Transition* (New York, 1937), esp. pp. 47–50, and Howard Bell, *Matching Youth and Jobs: A Study of Occupational Adjustment* (Washington, D.C., 1940).

3. Congressional Budget Office, *Policy Options for the Teenage Unemployment Problem*, Background Paper no. 13, Sept. 21, 1976, updated with data from the Bureau of Labor Statistics. For the effect on adulthood of unemployment in youth, see Paul Osterman, *Getting Started: The Youth Labor Market* (Cambridge, Mass., 1980); and R. B. Freeman and D. A. Wise, *Youth Unemployment: Summary Report*, National Bureau of Economic Research (Cambridge, Mass., 1979).

4. On the G.I. Bill, see Keith Olson, "The G.I. Bill and Higher Education: Success and Surprise," *American Quarterly*, 25 (1973): 596–610. For two-year colleges, see Jerome Karabel, "Community Colleges and Social Stratification," *Harvard Educational Review*, 42 (1972): 521–62; and Burton Clark, "The 'Cooling-Out' Function in Higher Education," *American Journal of Sociology*, 45 (1960): 569–76. On the absorption by colleges and universities of the unprecedented numbers of young people in their late teens during the late 1960's, see Norman Ryder, "The Demography of Youth," in President's Science Advisory Committee, *Youth: Transition to Adulthood* (Chicago, 1974).

5. The reasons for the deterioration include the large size of the age cohort, which came from the end of the baby boom, and increased participation rates. For some notions about increases in participation rates, see Congressional Budget Office, *Policy Options*, pp. 17–19.

6. For some evidence on variation in information, see "Knowledge of the World of Work," *Career Thresholds*, vol. 1, ch. 5, U.S. Department of Labor Manpower Research Monograph no. 16 (Washington, D.C.,

1970). On unemployment rates for blacks and Hispanics, see *Employment and Training Report of the President, 1978*, Table A-20; and *Workers of Spanish Origin: A Chartbook*, Bureau of Labor Statistics, Bulletin no. 1970, 1978, Table C-14. For evidence that racial differences in the rates reflect discrimination, and cannot be explained by the educational and demographic differences between white and black youth, see Osterman, *Getting Started*.

7. For evidence on the preference of employers to hire older workers, see Paul Barton, "Youth Unemployment and Career Entry," in Seymour Wolfbein, ed., *Labor Market Information for Youth* (Philadelphia, 1975); *Youth Unemployment and Minimum Wages*, Bureau of Labor Statistics Bulletin 1655, 1970; and Daniel Diamond and Hrach Bedrosian, *Hiring Standards and Job Performance*, U.S. Department of Labor Manpower Research Monograph no. 18, 1970.

8. For evidence that child labor laws do seem to affect employment patterns for those under eighteen, see Daniel Mitchell and John Clapp, "The Effects of Child Labor Laws on Youth Employment," in *Conference Report on Youth Unemployment*. However, employers tend not to be able to indicate what child labor laws are violated in specific cases, and so the authors interpret their actions as a way of avoiding the risk of violating child labor laws rather than the constraints of the laws themselves. For the conflicting evidence on the minimum wage, see CBO, *op. cit.*, pp. 33–39; and Osterman, *Getting Started*.

9. See the discussion of work-based programs in Michael Timpane, Susan Abramowitz, Sue Berryman Bobrow, and Anthony Pascal, *Youth Policy in Transition* (Rand Report R-2006-HEW, June 1976); and the discussion of career education in Grubb and Lazerson, "Rally 'Round the Workplace."

10. Bradley Schiller, "Program Outcomes," in *CETA: An Analysis of the Issues*, National Commission for Manpower Policy, Special Report no. 23 (May, 1978).

11. Charles Killingsworth and Mark Killingsworth, "Direct Effects of Employment and Training Programs on Employment and Unemployment: New Estimates and Implications for Employment Policy," in *Conference Report on Youth Unemployment*.

12. Randall Collins, *The Credential Society: An Historical Sociology of Education and Stratification* (New York, 1979), p. 4. Data on individual cities reveal the same phenomenon of increasing school attendance; in Providence, R.I., for example, high school attendance went from 10.6 percent of the age group in 1880 to 53.6 percent in 1925. Joel Perlmann, "Education and Social Structure in Providence, R.I., 1880–1920," unpublished. The data on Providence are especially significant because

unlike most such data they take into account population growth. See also David Hogan, "Capitalism and Schooling: A History of the Political Economy of Education in Chicago, 1880–1930," Ph.D. diss. (University of Illinois, Urbana, 1978), pp. 352–54.

13. *Ibid.*, pp. 352–430; Perlmann, "Education"; Michael Olneck and Marvin Lazerson, "The School Achievement of Immigrant Children, 1900–1930," *History of Education Quarterly*, 14 (1974): 453–82.

14. For the traditional human capital model, see Martin Trow, "The Second Transformation of American Secondary Education," *Comparative Sociology*, 2 (1961): 144–66. For the alternative, see Samuel Bowles and Herbert Gintis, *Schooling in Capitalist America* (New York, 1976). On skill levels in general, see Harry Braverman, *Labor and Monopoly Capital: The Degradation of Work in the Twentieth Century* (New York, 1974).

15. Joseph Speakman, "Unwillingly to School: Child Labor and Its Reform in Pennsylvania in the Progressive Era," Ph.D. diss. (Temple University, 1976); Daniel Nelson, *Managers and Workers: Origins of the New Factory System in the United States, 1880–1920* (Madison, Wis., 1975), ch. 7.

16. See for example Jane Addams, *The Spirit of Youth and the City Streets* (Urbana, Ill., 1972 ed; first pub. in 1909); Anthony Platt, *The Child Savers: The Invention of Delinquency* (Chicago, 1969).

17. Joseph Kett, *Rites of Passage: Adolescence in America, 1790 to the Present* (New York, 1977).

18. Our description of the nineteenth century draws on Kett, *Rites*; Michael Katz, *The People of Hamilton, Canada West: Family and Class in a Mid-Nineteenth Century City* (Cambridge, Mass., 1976); Clyde and Sally Griffen, *Natives and Newcomers: The Ordering of Opportunity in Mid-Nineteenth Century Poughkeepsie* (Cambridge, Mass., 1978); Carl Kaestle and Maris Vinovskis, *Education and Social Change in Nineteenth Century Massachusetts* (New York, 1980); David Montgomery, "Workers' Control of Machine Production in the Nineteenth Century," *Labor History*, 17 (1976): 485–509; John Modell, Frank F. Furstenberg, Jr., and Theodore Hershberg, "Social Change and Transitions to Adulthood in Historical Perspective," *Journal of Family History*, (1976): 7–32; and Michael Katz and Ian Davey, "Youth and Industrialization in a Canadian City," in John Demos and Sarane S. Boocock, eds., *Turning Points: Historical and Sociological Essays on the Family* (Chicago, 1978).

19. Griffens, *Natives and Newcomers*, chs. 7–9. See also the kind of mobility described in Herbert Gutman, "The Reality of Rags-to-Riches 'Myth': The Case of the Paterson, New Jersey, Locomotive, Iron, and

Machinery Manufacturers, 1830–1880," in Gutman, *Work, Culture, and Society in Industrializing America* (New York, 1976). See also the discussion in Hogan, "Capitalism and Schooling," ch. 2.

20. Robert Averitt, *The Dual Economy* (New York, 1968).

21. On internal labor markets, see Peter Doeringer and Michael Piore, *Internal Labor Markets and Manpower Analysis* (Lexington, Mass., 1971).

22. Nelson, *Managers and Workers,* ch. 8.

23. On some of the potential reasons for using the amount of schooling completed as a hiring credential, see V. Lane Rawlins and Lloyd Ulman, "The Utilization of College-Trained Manpower in the United States," in Margaret Gorden, ed., *Higher Education and the Labor Market* (New York, 1974).

24. Selwyn Troen, "The Discovery of the Adolescent by American Educational Reformers, 1900–1920: An Economic Perspective," in Lawrence Stone, ed., *Schooling and Society: Studies in the History of Education* (Baltimore, 1976).

25. Osterman, *Getting Started.* David Montgomery suggests that older workers may have wanted to keep youth out of the labor market since young people were "notorious for their proclivity to 'rate busting'" under piecework schedules; see Montgomery, "Immigrant Workers and Managerial Reform," in Richard L. Ehrlich, ed., *Immigrants in Industrial America, 1850–1920* (Charlottesville, Va., 1977).

26. The costs added to production by child labor and truancy laws may have played some role. Joseph Kett, in this volume, notes that educators claimed the costs of "immaturity" were too high for employers to risk hiring young people.

27. On why the expansion occurred, see Braverman, *Labor*; Alfred D. Chandler, Jr., *The Visible Hand: The Managerial Revolution in American Business* (Cambridge, Mass., 1977); and Nelson, *Managers and Workers.*

28. The evidence on the returns to schooling is sparse, but there is circumstantial evidence that women who attended public or private commercial schools were able to translate their schooling into office jobs and higher earnings. See Janice Weiss, "Education for Clerical Work: A History of Commercial Education in the United States Since 1850," doctoral diss. (Harvard Graduate School of Education, 1978); and Miriam Cohen, "Changing Education Strategies Among Migrant Generations: New York Italians in Comparative Perspective," unpublished.

29. *Historical Statistics of the United States,* Series D-182 and D-184.

30. Robert S. and Helen M. Lynd, *Middletown* (New York, 1929), pp. 194–96.

31. See for example Henry Perkinson, *The Imperfect Panacea: American Faith in Education, 1865–1965* (New York, 1968); and Grubb, "Phoenix of Vocationalism."

32. See Miriam Cohen, "Changing Education Strategies," on the decision of Italian families to keep their daughters in school to gain access to office work. See also Weiss, "Education For Clerical Work."

33. On this conception of equal opportunity, see Sol Cohen, "The Industrial Education Movement, 1906–1915," *American Quarterly,* 20 (1968): 95–110; and Lazerson and Grubb, *American Education,* pp. 24–26, and documents 13 and 14.

34. The literature on credentialing and related models—such as the signaling theories, in which years of schooling measure an individual's innate ability—is by now large and complex. For a review of different models and some evidence supporting various credentialing theories, see W. Norton Grubb, "Signaling, Credentialing, and Variation in the Return to Schooling," unpublished draft, March 1978; Collins, *Credential Society*; and Hogan's essay in this volume.

35. The showing that educational attainments have outrun educational requirements is a favorite within the literature on credentialing. See, for example, Rawlins and Ulman, "Utilization," and Ivar Berg, *Education and Jobs: The Great Training Robbery* (New York, 1970), ch. 3.

36. For a similar argument, see Richard de Lone, *Small Futures* (New York, 1979).

37. See for example the court decision in *Griggs v. Duke Power Company*. See also David White and Richard Francis, "Title VII and the Masters of Reality: Eliminating Credentialism in the American Labor Market," *Georgetown Law Journal* (July 1976); and Collins, *Credential Society*.

Hogan: Work, Education, and Social Structure

1. Robert S. Lynd and Helen M. Lynd, *Middletown: A Study in Modern American Culture* (New York, 1929), pp. 194–95.

2. *Ibid.*, p. 188.

3. For general outlines of modernization theory, and the theory underlying it, see Neil Smelser, *Social Change in the Industrial Revolution* (Chicago, 1959); Alex Inkeles and David H. Smith, *Becoming Modern: Individual Change in Six Developing Countries* (Cambridge, Mass., 1974); Richard D. Brown, *Modernization: The Transformation of American Life, 1600–1865* (New York, 1976); Talcott Parsons, *The Social System* (Glencoe, Ill., 1951); Parsons, *Societies: Evolutionary and Comparative Perspectives* (Englewood Cliffs, N.J., 1966); and Ernest W.

Burgess and Harvey J. Locke, *The Family: From Institution to Companionship*, 2d ed. (New York, 1953).

4. Robert Dreeben, *On What is Learned in School* (Reading, Mass., 1968); Talcott Parsons, "The School Class as a Social System," *Harvard Educational Review*, 29 (1959): 297–318.

5. Richard Jensen, *The Winning of the Midwest* (Chicago, 1971); Jensen, *Illinois: A History* (New York, 1978); Timothy Smith, "Immigrant Social Aspirations and American Education, 1880–1930," *American Quarterly*, 21 (1969): 523–43; Selwyn K. Troen, *The Public and the Schools: Shaping the St. Louis System, 1838–1920* (Columbia, Mo., 1975).

6. Douglas S. North, "Capital Formation in the United States During the Early Period of Industrialization," in Robert W. Fogel and Stanley L. Engerman, eds., *The Reinterpretation of American Economic History* (New York, 1971); Don Adams and Gerald Reagan, *Schooling and Social Change in Modern America* (New York, 1972); H. J. Habakkuk, *American and British Technology in the Nineteenth Century* (Cambridge, Mass., 1962); Martin Trow, "The Second Transformation of American Secondary Education," in Reinhard Bendix and Seymour M. Lipset, eds., *Class, Status, and Power: A Reader in Social Stratification* (London, 1967), pp. 437–49.

7. North, "Capital," p. 277.

8. Habakkuk, *American and British Technology*, p. 21.

9. Trow, "Transformation," pp. 438–39.

10. Lynds, *Middletown*, pp. 39–40, 44.

11. *Ibid.*, pp. 73, 74.

12. *Ibid.*, pp. 74–75.

13. *Ibid.*, pp. 74, 56–67.

14. Randall Collins, "Functional and Conflict Theories of Educational Stratification," *American Sociological Review*, 36 (1971): 1002–19; Alexander Field, *Skill Requirements in Early Industrialization: The Case of Massachusetts* (Berkeley, Calif., 1973); John Folger and Charles B. Nam, *Education of the American Population* (Washington, D.C., 1967).

15. Walter E. Weyl and A. M. Sakolski, *Conditions of Entrance to the Principal Trades*, Bureau of Labor Bulletin no. 67 (Washington, D.C., 1906); Paul Douglas, *American Apprenticeship and Industrial Education* (New York, 1921); Clyde and Sally Griffen, *Natives and Newcomers: The Ordering of Opportunity in Mid-Nineteenth-Century Poughkeepsie* (Cambridge, Mass., 1977); Alan Dawley, *Class and Community: The Industrial Revolution in Lynn* (Cambridge, Mass., 1976); David Brody, *Steelworkers in America* (New York, 1960); Eugene Ericksen and William Yancey, "Immigrants and Their Opportunities: Philadelphia, 1850–

1936," Philadelphia Social History Project, 1976; David Hogan, "Capitalism and Schooling: The Political Economy of Education in Chicago, 1880–1930," Ph.D. diss. (Univ. of Ill., 1978); Harry Braverman, *Labor and Monopoly Capital: The Degradation of Work in the Twentieth Century* (New York, 1974).

16. Folger and Nam, *Education.*

17. Ivar Berg, *Education and Jobs: The Great Training Robbery* (Boston, 1971); Collins, "Functional"; Dorothy K. Newman et al., *Protest, Politics, and Prosperity* (New York, 1978), ch. 3.

18. Cited in Braverman, *Monopoly Capital,* p. 220.

19. Kingsley Davis and William E. Moore, "Some Principles of Stratification," *American Sociological Review,* 10 (1945): 242–49; Talcott Parsons, "Equality and Inequality in Modern Society, or Social Stratification Revisited," *Sociological Inquiry,* 40 (1970); Richard Hernstein, *IQ in the Meritocracy* (Boston, 1971); W. Lloyd Warner, Robert J. Havinghurt, and Martin B. Loeb, *Who Shall Be Educated?* (Chicago, 1944).

20. Democratic capitalism of course goes by many other names: equality of opportunity, the Lincoln ideal, liberal capitalism, and so on. See Louis Hartz, *The Liberal Tradition in America* (New York, 1955).

21. Peter M. Blau and Otis Dudley Duncan, *The American Occupational Structure* (New York, 1967), pp. 429–30. See also Seymour M. Lipset and Reinhard Bendix, *Social Mobility in Industrial Society* (Berkeley, Calif., 1964).

22. Thus in a study of Hamilton, Ontario, during its early industrialization between 1851 and 1871, Katz and Davey discovered that educational behavior progressively followed class lines, and that ethnicity mattered less over time. Jensen and Friedberger, in a study of Iowa at the turn of the century, concluded that despite substantial "openness," family background did matter. Bowles and Gintis argue that in the recent past, educational achievement has been strongly dependent on social background, even for people of similar childhood IQ; indeed, they conclude that contrary to the hypothesis of expanding universalism, "the number of years of school attained by a child depends upon family background as much in the recent period as it did fifty years ago." On the other hand, Blau, Duncan, Sewell, and Hauser argue that socioeconomic factors by themselves do not explain very much of the variance in educational achievement, and that ability or intelligence is probably the primary determinant. See Michael Katz and Ian Davey, "Youth and Early Industrialization in a Canadian City," in John Demos and Sarane S. Boocock, eds., *Turning Points* (Chicago, 1978), p. 103; Richard Jensen and Mark Freidberger, *Education and Social Structure: An Historical*

Study of Iowa, 1870–1930 (Chicago, 1976); Samuel Bowles and Herbert Gintis, *Schooling in Capitalist America: Educational Reform and the Contradictions of Economic Life* (New York, 1976), pp. 30–33; Blau and Duncan, *American Occupational Structure*, pp. 401–3; and William H. Sewell and Robert M. Hauser, "Causes and Consequences of Higher Education: Models of the Status Attainment Process," in William H. Sewell, Robert M. Hauser, and David Featherman, eds., *Schooling and Achievement in American Society* (New York, 1976), ch. 1.

23. Blau and Duncan, *American Occupational Structure*, pp. 402–3.

24. Christopher Jencks, *Inequality* (New York, 1973). For reviews of Jencks, see the symposium in *American Educational Research Journal* (Spring 1974), *Harvard Educational Review* (1973), and *Sociology of Education* (Winter 1973).

25. Raymond Boudon, "La sociologie des inégalities dans l'impasse?," *Analyse et Prévision*, 17 (1974): 83–95, cited in Jerome Karabel and A. H. Halsey, eds., *Power and Ideology in Education* (New York, 1977), p. 24.

26. Bowles and Gintis, *Schooling*, pp. 111–13, 120; Sewell and Hauser, "Causes," ch. 1.

27. Bowles and Gintis, *Schooling*, p. 34.

28. Lester Thurow, "Education and Economic Inequality," in Karabel and Halsey, *Power and Ideology*, pp. 326–27.

29. Barry Chiswick and Jacob Mincer, "Time Series Changes in Personal Income Inequality in the U.S.," *Journal of Political Economy*, 80, 3, pt. 2 (1972), cited in Bowles and Gintis, *Schooling*.

30. Gary Becker, *The Economics of Discrimination* (Chicago, 1959).

31. Lynds, *Middletown*, pp. 25–27, 39.

32. Michael Reich, "The Evolution of the U.S. Labor Force," in Richard C. Edwards, Michael Reich, and Thomas Weisskopf, eds., *The Capitalist System* (Englewood Cliffs, N.J., 1972), p. 175. See also Braverman, *Labor*, p. 379. For a general discussion of the expansion of markets in labor in the context of Western capitalism, see Karl Polanyi, *The Great Transformation* (Boston, 1957); Karl Marx, *Capital* (New York, 1972), vol. 1, pt. 7; and Maurice Dobb, *Studies in the Development of Capitalism* (New York, 1947).

33. The best introduction to the class analysis of the structures of capitalist societies is Robert W. Connell and Terry Irving, *Class Structure in Australian History* (Melbourne, 1980), ch. 1.

34. Nicos Poulantzas, *Classes in Contemporary Capitalism* (London, 1975), p. 17.

35. See Anthony Giddens, *New Rules of Sociological Methods* (New York, 1976), ch. 3; Giddens, *Central Problems in Social Theory* (Berke-

ley, Calif., 1979), chs. 2 and 3; and Connell and Irving, *Class Structure,* ch. 1.

36. In 1880 only 12.8 percent of all women worked in nonagricultural jobs; by 1900 the figure had climbed to 17.3 percent, and by 1910 to 20.7 percent. For the labor force as a whole, the percentage of women grew from 18.2 percent in 1890, to 30 percent in 1950, and to slightly over 41 percent by 1970. For general discussion of female labor force participation, see Michael Gordon, ed., *The American Family: Past, Present, and Future* (New York, 1978), ch. 14; Alice Kessler-Harris, "Stratifying by Sex: Understanding the History of Working Women," in Richard C. Edwards, Michael Reich, and David Gordon, *Labor Market Segmentation* (Lexington, Mass., 1975); A. Miller, "Changing Life Patterns: A Twenty-Five Year Review," *Annals of the American Academy of Political and Social Science,* 435 (1978): 82–101; Elyce Rotella, "Women's Participation in the U.S. Paid Labor Force, 1870–1930: The Decline of the Family Economy and the Rise of the Clerical Sector," Memo, Dept. of Economics, San Diego State Univ., 1977; and Jeremy Brecher and Tom Costello, *Common Sense for Hard Times* (New York, 1976), ch. 12. For blacks, see Hal Baron, "The Demand for Black Labor: Historical Notes on the Political Economy of Racism," *Radical America*, 5 (1971): 1–46.

37. There is no good introduction to the "structures" of American capitalism, or to their development over time. Short of this, see Edwards et al., *Capitalist System*; Gabriel Kolko, *Main Currents in Modern American History* (New York, 1976); and Michael Katz, Michael Doucet, and Mark Stern, *The Social Organization of Industrial Capitalism* (Cambridge, Mass., forthcoming 1982).

38. See Connell and Irving, *Class Structure*, ch. 1; Perry Anderson, *Debates Within English Marxism* (London, 1980), ch. 2.

39. Collins, "Functional"; Berg, *Education*; Thurow, "Education."

40. Bowles and Gintis, *Schooling,* ch. 5. The distinction between technical efficiency and productivity is discussed in Marglin, "What Do Bosses Do?" and Herbert Gintis, "Nature of Labor Exchange and the Theory of Capitalist Production," *Review of Radical Political Economics*, 8 (1976): 36–54. This argument is also supported by a wealth of sociological research on the organization of work.

41. Richard C. Edwards, *Contested Terrain: The Transformation of the Workplace in America* (New York, 1980), chs. 2, 4, 7–9.

42. *Ibid.*, p. 178.

43. *Ibid.*, p. 179.

44. *Ibid.*, p. 180.

45. See my *Education and Progressive Reform in Chicago*, forthcoming.

46. Peter Doeringer and Michael Piore, *Internal Labor Markets and Manpower Analysis* (Lexington, Mass., 1971).

47. Magali S. Larson, *The Rise of Professionalism: A Sociological Analysis* (Berkeley, Calif., 1977), pt. 1; Joseph F. Kett, *Rites of Passage: Adolescence in America, 1790 to the Present* (New York, 1977), pp. 153–57.

48. Raymond Boudon, "Education and Social Mobility: A Structural Model," in Karabel and Halsey, *Power*, pp. 187, 194. See also Boudon, *Education, Opportunity, and Social Inequality: Changing Prospects in Western Society* (New York, 1974).

49. Robert M. Hauser, "Review Essay: On Boudon's Model of Social Mobility," *American Journal of Sociology*, 81 (1974): 911–27.

50. Collins, "Functional."

51. Berg, *Education*.

52. Thurow, "Education," pp. 326, 328, 330.

53. *Ibid.*, p. 326.

54. Labor market segmentation theory is surveyed in Gordon, *Theories*, and Edwards, *Contested Terrain*, ch. 9.

55. Edwards, *Contested Terrain*, ch. 9; Robert Buchele, "Jobs and Workers: A Labor Market Segmentation Perspective on the Work Experience of Middle-Aged Men," cited by Edwards, pp. 170, 173, 175; Paul Osterman, "An Empirical Study of Labor-Market Segmentation," *Journal of Industrial and Labor Relations* (1975); David Gordon, *Theories of Poverty and Underemployment* (Lexington, Mass., 1973), ch. 7; Martin Carnoy and Russell Rumberger, *Segmented Labor Markets: Some Empirical Forays* (Palo Alto, Calif., 1975).

56. Edwards, *Contested Terrain*, pp. 194–97.

57. For a review of the evidence on return to education for blacks, see Gordon, *Theories*, pp. 118–19.

58. Robert Merton, "Bureaucratic Structure and Personality," in *Social Theory and Social Structure*, rev. ed. (New York, 1957); Raymond Callahan, *Education and the Cult of Efficiency* (Chicago, 1962); Michael Katz, *Class Bureaucracy and Schools* (New York, 1971); Joseph M. Cronin, *The Control of Urban Schools* (New York, 1973).

59. David B. Tyack, *The One Best System* (Cambridge, Mass., 1974), pts. 2 and 3.

60. Robert Dreeben, "American Schooling: Patterns and Processes of Stability and Change," in Bernard Barber and Alex Inkeles, eds., *Stability and Social Change* (Boston, 1971), p. 113; Dreeben, *On What is Learned*, chs. 4, 5, 6; Talcott Parsons, "The Social Class as a Social System," *Harvard Educational Review*, 29 (1959): 297–318; Inkeles, "Social Structure and the Socialization of Competence," *ibid.*, 36 (1966):

265–83; Arthur Stinchcombe, "Social Structure and Organizations," in James G. March, *Handbook of Organizations* (Chicago, 1965).

61. Dreeben, "American Schooling," p. 113.

62. Bowles and Gintis, *Schooling*, p. 131, 132–33.

63. *Ibid.*, p. 265.

64. Basil Bernstein, *Class Codes and Control*, vol. 3 (London, 1977).

65. Pierre Bourdieu and Jean-Claude Passeron, *Reproductions* (Beverly Hills, Calif., 1977).

66. Bowles and Gintis, *Schooling*, pp. 131, 139.

67. Paul Willis, *Learning to Labor* (London, 1977), p. 171.

68. For a useful discussion see Michael Apple, "The New Sociology of Education: Analyzing Cultural and Economic Reproduction," *Harvard Educational Review*, 48 (1978): 495–503.

69. David Kamens, "Legitimating Myths and Educational Organization: The Relationship Between Organizational Ideology and Formal Structure," *American Sociological Review*, 41 (1977): 208–19; John W. Meyer, "The Effects of Education as an Institution," *American Journal of Sociology*, 83 (1977).

70. Jencks, *Inequality*, p. 135.

71. Ronald Corwin, "Education and the Sociology of Complex Organizations," in Charles A. Hansen and Gordon E. Gerstle, eds., *On Education: Sociological Perspectives* (New York, 1967); Charles E. Bidwell, "The School as a Formal Organization," in March, *Handbook*, ch. 23; Dan C. Lortie, "The Balance of Control and Autonomy in Elementary School Training," in Amitai Etzioni, ed., *The Semi-Professions and Their Organizations* (New York, 1969).

72. See for example Wolf Heydebrand, "Organizational Contradictions in Public Bureaucracies: Toward a Marxist Theory of Organization," *Sociological Quarterly*, 18 (1977): 83–107; and J. Kenneth Benson, "Organizations: A Dialectical View," *Administrative Science Quarterly*, 22 (1977): 1–21.

73. Bowles and Gintis, *Schooling*, pp. 236–39.

74. Ira Katznelson, "Class Ethnicity and Urban School Politics, 1870–1930," National Opinion Research Center, Univ. of Chicago, 1979, p. 64. Yet despite the fact that it is exactly this kind of argument that Bowles and Gintis make in their book, their critics, from both the left and the right, have asserted that Bowles and Gintis are guilty of "functionalism."

75. See for example Robert Dahl, *Who Governs?* (New Haven, Conn., 1961); Henry S. Kariel, ed., *Frontiers of Democratic Theory* (New York, 1970); Nelson W. Polsby, *Community Power and Political Theory* (New Haven, Conn., 1963); G. William Domhoff and Harold

Ballard, *C. Wright Mills and the Power Elite* (Boston, 1968); Michael P. Rogin, *The Intellectuals and McCarthy* (Cambridge, Mass., 1967); Ronald P. Swierenga, "Ethnocultural Political Analysis: A New Approach to American Ethnic Studies," *American Studies*, 5 (1971): 59–71; and David E. Wright, "The Ethnocultural Model of Voting," *American Behavioral Scientist*, 16 (1973): 653–84.

76. See my "Education and Class Formation: The Peculiarities of the Americans," in Michael Apple, ed., *Education and Social Reproduction* (London, 1981).

77. Hogan, *School and Society*, chs. 6, 8; Paul Violas, *The Training of the Urban Working Class* (Chicago, 1978); Marvin Lazerson and W. Norton Grubb, *American Education and Vocationalism: A Documentary History, 1870–1970* (New York, 1977).

78. See Dawley, *Class*; Gordon Wood, *The Creation of the American Republic* (New York, 1972); J. G. A. Pocock, *The Machiavellian Movement* (Princeton, N.J., 1975); David Montgomery, *Beyond Equality* (New York, 1967); Daniel T. Rodgers, *The Work Ethic in Industrial America, 1850–1920* (Chicago, 1978), esp. chs. 1, 2, 5; John Cawelti, *Apostles of the Self-Made Man* (Chicago, 1965), chs. 1, 2, 3; Donald Meyer, *The Positive Thinkers* (New York, 1965); Eric Foner, *Free Soil, Free Labor, Free Men* (New York, 1970), ch. 1; Irvin G. Wyllie, *The Self-Made Man in America*, rev. ed. (New York, 1966); Stephan Thernstrom, *Poverty and Progress: Social Mobility in a Nineteenth-Century City* (New York, 1969), ch. 3; Griffens, *Natives*, ch. 2; and Theodore Hershberg, ed., *Philadelphia* (New York, 1981).

79. Pocock, *Machiavellian Movement*, chs. 14, 15; Albert O. Hirschman, *The Passions and the Interests* (Princeton, 1977), esp. pt. 1; Max Weber, *The Protestant Ethic and the Spirit of Capitalism* (New York, 1958); C. B. McPherson, *The Political Theory of Possessive Individualism* (London, 1962); Alexis de Tocqueville, *Democracy in America*, ed. J. P. Mayer (New York, 1969), vol. 2; Hartz, *Liberal Tradition*; Herbert Croly, *The Promise of American Life* (Indianapolis, 1965, orig. ed. 1909); Peter Steinfels, *The Neo-Conservatives* (New York, 1979); Peter Bachrach, *The Theory of Democratic Elitism* (Boston, 1967); Edward A. Purcell, *The Crisis of Democratic Theory* (Lexington, Ky., 1973); J. H. Schaar, "Equality of Opportunity and Beyond," in J. Roland Pennock and John W. Chapman, eds., *Equality* (New York, 1967); R. H. Turner, "Modes of Social Ascent Through Education: Sponsored and Contest Mobility," in Bendix and Lipset, *Class*, pp. 449–58; Alvin W. Gouldner, *The Coming Crisis of Western Sociology* (London, 1970), esp. ch. 3; Clarence J. Karier, ed., *Shaping the American Educational State: 1900 to the Present* (New York, 1975); Godfrey Hodgson, *America in Our*

Time: From World War II to Nixon—What Happened and Why (New York, 1978), esp. chs. 4, 13, 24.

Anderson: Black Vocational Education

1. Benjamin Brawley, *Early Efforts for Industrial Education*, John F. Slater Fund, Occasional Papers, no. 22 (1923): 1–3; William Louis Lang, "Black Bootstraps: The Abolition Educators' Ideology and the Education of the Northern Free Negro, 1828–1860," Ph.D. diss. (Univ. of Delaware, 1974), pp. 90–92.

2. *Ibid.*

3. Frederick Douglass, "A Few Words More About Learning Trades," *Frederick Douglass Paper,* March 11, 1853; Brawley, *Early Efforts,* pp. 10–11.

4. Clyde W. Hall, *Black Vocational, Technical, and Industrial Arts Education: Development and History* (Chicago, 1973), pp. 7–12.

5. *Ibid.*, p. 17; Allen W. Jones, "The Role of Tuskegee Institute in the Education of Black Farmers," *Journal of Negro History* 60 (1975): 252; Donnie D. Bellamy, "Henry A. Hunt and Black Agricultural Leadership in the New South," *ibid.*, p. 464; August Meier, *Negro Thought in America: 1880–1915* (Ann Arbor, Mich., 1968 ed.), p. 93.

6. Samuel C. Armstrong, *Twenty-Two Years' Work of the Hampton Normal and Agricultural Institute* (Hampton, Va., 1893), p. 293; *Catalogue of the Hampton Normal and Agricultural Institute* (Hampton, Va., 1900), pp. 109, 114; James D. Anderson, "The Hampton Model of Normal School Industrial Education, 1868–1900," in Vincent Franklin and James D. Anderson, eds., *New Perspectives in Black Educational History* (Boston, 1978), pp. 61–96.

7. Anderson, "Hampton Model," p. 70; Donald Spivey, *Schooling for the New Slavery: Black Industrial Education, 1868–1915* (Westport, Conn., 1978), p. 19.

8. Samuel Armstrong, "Nothing to Do," *Southern Workman,* 3 (1874): 26; *Southern Workman,* 6 (1877): 94; and 10 (1881): 91.

9. *Southern Workman*, 21 (1893): 93 and 9 (1880): 112; Samuel Armstrong, *Principal's Annual Report of Hampton Institute* (Hampton, Va., 1887), p. 3.

10. Samuel Armstrong, "Industries," *Southern Workman*, 19 (1890): 71–73; *Southern Workman*, 21 (1893): 93.

11. W. E. B. DuBois, *The Negro American Artisan* (Atlanta, 1912), pp. 42, 119–22; Anderson, "Hampton Model," pp. 66–68.

12. James D. Anderson, "Northern Foundations and the Shaping of

Southern Black Rural Education, 1902–1935," *History of Education Quarterly,* 18 (1978): 371–96.

13. Hall, *Black Vocational, Technical, and Industrial Arts,* pp. 92–98.

14. Samuel Henry Shannon, "Agricultural and Industrial Education at Tennessee State University During the Normal School Phase, 1912–1922: A Case Study," Ph.D. diss. (George Peabody College for Teachers, 1974), pp. 141, 154, 235.

15. *Ibid.,* pp. 242–44.

16. DuBois, *Negro American Artisan,* pp. 79–83, 115; black artisan quoted in Shannon, "Tennessee State," pp. 243–44.

17. *Ibid.,* pp. 161, 227–29; B. D. Mayberry, ed., *Development of Research at Historically Black Land-Grant Institutions* (Tuskegee, Ala., 1976), pp. iv–v.

18. Shannon, "Tennessee State," pp. 240–44; DuBois, *Negro American Artisan,* p. 121.

19. Shannon, "Tennessee State," pp. 141–42, 149. Edward Danforth Eddy, *Colleges for Our Land and Time* (New York, 1957), pp. 57–59, 85, 148, 259; Leedell W. Neyland and John W. Riley, *The History of Florida Agricultural and Mechanical University* (Gainesville, Fla., 1913), p. 63; Charles W. Florence, "The Federally-Aided Program of Vocational Teacher-Training in Negro Schools," *Journal of Negro Education,* 7 (1938): 292.

20. Elizabeth H. Pleck, *Black Migration and Poverty: Boston, 1865–1900* (New York, 1979), pp. 127–29.

21. David M. Katzman, *Before the Ghetto: Black Detroit in the Nineteenth Century* (Urbana, Ill., 1975), pp. 104–6; Kenneth L. Kusmer, *A Ghetto Takes Shape: Black Cleveland, 1870–1930* (Urbana, Ill., 1976), pp. 66–68.

22. David B. Tyack, *The One Best System: A History of American Urban Education* (Cambridge, Mass., 1974), pp. 221–22.

23. E. Franklin Frazier, "The Occupational Differentiation of the Negro in Cities," *Southern Workman,* 59 (1930); Charles S. Johnson, *The Economic Status of Negroes* (Nashville, Tenn., 1933); Ira De A. Reid, "Vocational Guidance for Negroes," *Occupations,* 12 (1934); Alain Locke, "The Negro in Times Like These," *The Survey,* 69 (1933); Rayford W. Logan, "Educational Segregation in the North," *Journal of Negro Education,* 2 (1933); Charles H. Thompson, "The Federal Program of Vocational Education in Negro Schools of Less than College Grade," *ibid.,* 7 (1938); Doxey A. Wilkerson, "The Participation of Negroes in the Federally-Aided Program of Civilian Vocational Rehabilitation," *ibid.*; Benjamin E. Mays, "After College What? for the Negro," *The Crisis,* 37 (1930); Ralph W. Bullock, "A Study of the Occupational

Choices of Negro High School Boys," *ibid.*; Robert C. Weaver, "Training Negroes for Occupational Opportunities," *Journal of Negro Education,* 7 (1938); Ambrose Caliver, "Negro Education in the Depression," *School Life*, 18 (1933); W. E. B. DuBois, "Education and Work," *Howard University Bulletin*, 9 (1931); Robert Sutherland, "Planning for Negro Youth," *Journal of Educational Sociology*, 15 (1942); George Zook, "The National Conference on Negro Education," *Journal of Negro Education,* 3 (1934); T. J. Woofter, *A Study of the Economic Status of the Negro* (New York, 1930); Allison Davis and John Dollard, *Children of Bondage* (Washington, D.C., 1940); W. Lloyd Warner et al., *Color and Human Nature: Negro Personality Development in a Northern City* (Washington, D.C., 1941).

24. U.S. Department of Commerce, Bureau of the Census, *Negroes in the United States, 1920–1932* (Washington, D.C., 1935), pp. 48, 49, 144–45; Paul K. Edwards, *The Southern Urban Negro as a Consumer* (College Park, Md., 1969; orig. ed. 1932), pp. 1–4; U.S. Department of Commerce, Bureau of the Census, *Fifteenth Census of the United States: 1930 Population*, vol. 3, pt. 1 (Washington, D.C., 1932), p. 98.

25. *Negroes in the United States*, pp. 123–33. Robert C. Weaver, "The Economic Status of the Negro in the United States," *Journal of Negro Education*, 19 (1950): 235–37; Lester B. Granger, "Problems and Needs of Negro Adolescent Workers," *ibid.*, 9 (1940): 321–31; Mary Anderson, "The Plight of Negro Domestic Labor," *ibid.*, 5 (1936): 66–67; Raymond Wolters, *Negroes and the Great Depression: The Problem of Economic Recovery* (Westport, Conn., 1970); Charles S. Johnson, *The Economic Status of Negroes* (Nashville, Tenn., 1933); Robert C. Weaver, *Male Negro Skilled Workers in the United States, 1930–1936* (Washington, D.C., 1939), p. 17; Richard Sterner, *The Negro's Share* (New York, 1943), pp. 41–43.

26. Bullock, "Occupational Choices," pp. 301–3; Mays, "After College What?," pp. 408–10.

27. *Ibid.*

28. *Ibid.*

29. *Ibid.*

30. Melvin Reuben Maskin, "Black Education and the New Deal: The Urban Experience," Ph.D. diss. (New York University, 1973), pp. 60–63.

31. Harold Ickes, "Why a National Conference on the Education of Negroes," *Journal of Negro Education*, 3 (1934): 577; George F. Zook, "The National Conference on Negro Education," *ibid.*, pp. 581–85; in the same issue see T. Arnold Hill's report, "Vocations," p. 653.

32. "The Vocational Guidance of Negroes," *Journal of Negro Education*, 4 (1935): 1–4.

33. Ira De A. Reid, "Vocational Guidance for Negroes," *Occupations*, 12 (1934): 25, 28; Logan, "Educational Segregation," p. 15; Weaver, "Training Negroes," p. 495; Lucius Smith, "Education and Vocational Guidance in Schools for Negroes," *Journal of Business Education*, 15 (1940): 17.

34. Maskin, "Black Education," pp. 47–50, 137, 144.

35. *Ibid.*, pp. 48–49, 228.

36. Bullock, "Occupational Choices," p. 303; Mays, "After College What?," p. 408; T. Arnold Hill, "Educating and Guiding Negro Youth for Occupational Efficiency," *Journal of Negro Education*, 4 (1935): 23–24.

37. Robert C. Weaver, "Economic Status," pp. 236, 239–40; Weaver, *Male Negro Skilled Workers*, p. 17; Hill, "Educating," p. 28.

38. Ambrose Caliver, *Vocational Education and Guidance of Negroes: Report of a Survey Conducted by the U.S. Office of Education* (Washington, D.C., 1937), pp. 1–3, 8–10, 59–60.

39. Maskin, "Black Education," p. 98.

40. Ira De A. Reid, *In a Minor Key: Negro Youth in Story and Fact* (Washington, D.C., 1940); Charles S. Johnson, *Growing Up in the Black Belt: Negro Youth in the Rural South* (Washington, D.C., 1941); Allison Davis and John Dollard, *Children of Bondage: The Personality Development of Negro Youth in the Urban South* (Washington, D.C., 1940); Warner et al., *Color and Human Nature;* E. Franklin Frazier, *Negro Youth At the Crossways: Their Personality Development in the Middle States* (Washington, D.C., 1940); J. Howell Atwood et al., *Thus Be Their Destiny: The Personality Development of Negro Youth in Three Communities* (Washington, D.C., 1941); Robert L. Sutherland, *Color, Class, and Personality* (Washington, D.C., 1942).

41. Johnson, *Growing Up*, p. 134; Davis and Dollard, *Children of Bondage*, p. 285; Frazier, *Negro Youth*, p. 266.

42. Sutherland, quoted in Atwood, *Thus Be Their Destiny*, p. 93; Frazier, *Negro Youth*, pp. 134, 166; Johnson, *Growing Up*, pp. 195–98.

43. John P. Davis, "A Survey of the Problems of the Negro Under the New Deal," *Journal of Negro Education*, 5 (1936): 10; *idem*, "A Black Inventory of the New Deal," *The Crisis*, 42 (1935): 142; George Schuyler, "New Job Frontiers for Negro Youth," *ibid.*, 43 (1936): 328; Ralph J. Bunche, "Education in Black and White," *Journal of Negro Education*, 5 (1936): 351–58; E. Franklin Frazier, "A Critical Summary of Articles Contributed to Symposium on Negro Education," *ibid.*, p. 533.

44. Walter G. Daniel and Carroll L. Miller, "The Participation of the Negro in the National Youth Administration Program," *ibid.*, 7 (1938): 357–65; Howard W. Oxley, "The Civilian Conservation Corps and the Education of the Negro," *ibid.*, pp. 375–82; Maskin, "Black Education," pp. 116–18; "The WPA and After," *Opportunity*, 16 (1939): 322.

45. Weaver, "Economic Status," p. 238.

46. Ira De A. Reid, *The Urban Negro Worker in the United States, 1935–36*, vol. 1 (Washington, D.C., 1938), p. 7; Robert C. Weaver, *ibid.*, vol. 2 (Washington, D.C., 1939), p. 25; Ambrose Caliver, *Negro High School Graduates and Non-Graduates* (Washington, D.C., 1940); T. Edwards Davis, "Vocational Education and Guidance in the Negro Secondary School," *Journal of Negro Education*, 9 (1940): 498–503.

47. Bullock, "Occupational Choices," pp. 301–3; Mays, "After College What?," pp. 408–10; Elizabeth McDougal, "Negro Youth Plans Its Future," *Journal of Negro Education*, 10 (1941): 229; George Wright, "Vocational Choices of a Selected Sample of Negro Pupils," *Educational Research Bulletin*, 21 (1942); Paul F. Lawrence, "Vocational Aspirations of Negro Youth of California," *Journal of Negro Education*, 19 (1950): 47–56. Johnson, *Growing Up in the Black Belt*, pp. 194–98; B. A. Turner, *Occupational Choices of High School Seniors in the Space Age* (Houston, 1964); for a view of the "reach for talent" climate, see Horace Mann Bond, *The Search for Talent* (Cambridge, Mass., 1959).

48. Dorothy K. Newman et al., *Protest, Politics, and Prosperity: Black Americans and White Institutions, 1940–75* (New York, 1978), pp. 79–82; Faustine Jones, "Effects of Schooling," *Crisis*, Aug.–Sept. 1975, pp. 236–37; U.S. Bureau of the Census, Current Population Reports, *The Social and Economic Status of the Black Population in the United States, 1974*, Series P–23, no. 54 (Washington, D.C., 1975), pp. 93, 96–97; U.S. Commission on Civil Rights, *Social Indicators of Equality for Minorities and Women* (Washington, D.C., 1978).

49. "Blacks Attending College up 275%," *Chicago Sun-Times*, June 10, 1978, p. 1; U.S. Bureau of the Census, Current Population Reports, *Population Characteristics*, Series P–20, no. 321 (Washington, D.C., 1978), pp. 1–4; U.S. Department of Health, Education, and Welfare, National Center for Education Statistics, *The Condition of Education, 1978* (Washington, D.C., 1978), p. 170; *Social Indicators*, p. 26; Jones, "Effects of Schooling," p. 236; Vernon Jordan, "Black College Gains an Illusion," *Springfield, Ill., State Journal Register*, May 18, 1979, p. 11.

50. Newman, *Protest*, pp. 64, 72.

51. F. Ray Marshall and Vernon M. Briggs, Jr., *The Negro and Apprenticeship* (Baltimore, 1967), pp. 27–29.

52. Newman, *Protest*, p. 42; Alfred L. Malabre, Jr., "Through Good Times and Bad, Joblessness Among Young Blacks Keeps Right on Rising," *Wall Street Journal*, Feb. 1, 1979, p. 36; Michael Ruby and Henry McGee, "Blacks on a New Plateau," *Newsweek*, Oct. 4, 1976, pp. 73–74; Alfred L. Malabre, Jr., "After Shrinking, the Gap Widens Again Between Black and White Family Income," *Wall Street Journal*, March 6, 1979, p. 40; "U.S. Figures Low on Black Jobless Rate, Says National

Urban League," *The Daily Illini* (University of Illinois), July 26, 1979.

53. *Ibid.* Robert B. Hill, "Discrimination and Minority Youth Employment," in Vice-President's Task Force on Youth Employment, *A Review of Youth Employment Problems, Programs, and Policies: Volume II* (Washington, D.C.: U.S. Department of Labor, 1980).

54. *Proceedings of the First Annual Convention of the National Association for the Advancement of Black Americans in Vocational Education* (Prairie View, Tex., 1978), pp. iv–v; DuBois, *Negro American Artisan*, pp. 122, 129.

55. Newman, *Protest, p. 73.*

56. William Julius Wilson, *The Declining Significance of Race: Blacks and Changing American Institutions* (Chicago, 1978), p. 2; Nathan Glazer, *Affirmative Discrimination: Ethnic Inequality and Public Policy* (New York, 1975), p. 46; Irwin Garfinkel and Robert H. Haveman, *Earnings Capacity, Poverty, and Inequality* (New York, 1977), p. 90; Stanley Masters, *Black-White Income Differentials* (New York, 1975).

Clifford: Educating Women for Work

1. Caroline Healey Dall (1822–1912), *The College, the Market, and the Court; or, On Women's Relation to Education, Labor, and Law* (Boston, 1867), p. 208. For Dall's earlier years, see Barbara Welter, "The Merchant's Daughter: A Tale from Life," *New England Quarterly*, 42 (1969): 3–22.

2. Carrie M. White Diary, July 18, 1884; May 13, 1884; and Feb. 9, 1883; White MSS (Univ. of Wash. Library, by permission).

3. Alice Beal Parsons, *Woman's Dilemma* (New York, 1926), p. 108.

4. Daniel T. Rodgers, *The Work Ethic in Industrial America, 1850–1920* (Chicago, 1978), pp. 206–7.

5. Reported figures vary somewhat. These are from W. Elliott Brownlee and Mary M. Brownlee, eds., *Women in the American Economy: A Documentary History, 1675–1929* (New Haven, Conn., 1976), p. 3; Alice Kessler-Harris, "Women's Wage Work as Myth and History," *Labor History*, 19 (1978): 289.

6. Mary P. Ryan, *Womanhood in America: From Colonial Times to the Present* (New York, 1975), p. 327.

7. U.S. Dept of Labor, *Handbook on Women Workers, 1975* (Washington, D.C., 1975), p. 191.

8. Paul H. Douglas, *American Apprenticeship and Industrial Education* (New York, 1921), p. 139.

9. Joseph F. Kett observes that "the plowboy with few prospects might stay around the district school till eighteen or nineteen. Older

students in college might include those who got a late start and those uncertain about their occupational direction." Kett, *Rites of Passage: Adolescence in America, 1790 to the Present* (New York, 1977), pp. 21, 32–33. For the reliance on the clerkship as the preferred means of acquiring business skills, see Lewis E. Atherton, "Mercantile Education in the Ante-Bellum South," *Mississippi Valley Historical Review*, 39 (1953): 623–40.

10. *A Home in the Woods: Oliver Johnson's Reminiscences of Early Marion County* (Indianapolis, 1951), p. 184.

11. Jean S. Pond and Dale Mitchell, *Bradford, A New England Academy* (Bradford, Mass., 1954); Kathryn Babb Vossler, "Women and Education in West Virginia, 1810–1909," *West Virginia History*, 36 (1975): 278.

12. Sarah D. Stow, *History of Mount Holyoke Seminary, South Hadley, Mass., During Its First Half Century, 1837–1887* (South Hadley, 1887), p. 6.

13. *Good Behavior: Phelps' Elementary Reader for Public Schools*, 6th ed. (Brattleboro, Vt., 1881), p. 51. Maris A. Vinovskis and Richard M. Bernard, "Beyond Catharine Beecher: Female Education in the Antebellum Period," *Signs*, 3 (1978): 864, acknowledge that "in practice it was not always possible to separate the girls from the boys; nevertheless, segregation remained the ideal." My research indicates that segregation did not operate very effectively, and fails to confirm that it was even the "ideal" of practicing pedagogues.

14. A useful, if partisan, history is Arthur Beverly Mays, *The Concept of Vocational Education in the Thinking of the General Educator, 1845 to 1945* (Urbana, Ill., 1946).

15. In Helen Campbell, *Prisoners of Poverty: Women Wage Workers, Their Trades and Their Lives* (Boston, 1900), p. 247.

16. Marvin Lazerson and W. Norton Grubb, eds., *American Education and Vocationalism: A Documentary History, 1870–1970* (New York, 1974), p. 32; Arthur G. Wirth, *Education in the Technological Society: The Vocational-Liberal Studies Controversy in the Early Twentieth Century* (Scranton, Pa., 1972).

17. Heidi Hartmann, "Capitalism, Patriarchy, and Job Segregation by Sex," in Martha Blaxall and Barbara Reagan, eds., *Women and the Workplace: The Implications of Occupational Segregation* (Chicago, 1976), p. 159; Joan W. Scott and Louise A. Tilly, "Women's Work and the Family in Nineteenth-Century Europe," *Comparative Studies in Society and History*, 17 (1975), esp. pp. 44–46; Ann Oakley, *Woman's Work: The Housewife, Past and Present* (New York, 1974).

18. Peggy Johnson to "Dear Mother," Oct. 10, 1813. Margaret Yundt

Kostmayer MSS (Special Collections Division, Tulane Univ. Library, by permission).

19. Julia Ellen Rogers, "A Long Look Backward," Rogers Family Papers (Courtesy of Peggy Thompson Shoenhair, Cupertino, Calif.).

20. Rogers, "Autobiography of Ruth Dodd Luellen Rogers," *ibid.,* p. 174.

21. Florence Colby Peck Diary, April 12, 1901 (emphasis in original). Peck MSS (Rare Books and Manuscripts Division, New York Public Library, Astor, Lenox and Tilden Foundations, by permission).

22. John Ise, *Sod and Stubble: The Story of a Kansas Homestead* (New York, 1936).

23. Alan Dawley, *Class and Community: The Industrial Revolution in Lynn* (Cambridge, Mass., 1976), p. 29.

24. Indenture of Sarah Carpenter, Aug. 1, 1803, in "Footnotes to Vermont History," *Vermont Quarterly*, 20 (1952): 306. Sewing was of course an early candidate for inclusion in the public school curriculum. See Marvin Lazerson, *Origins of the Urban School: Public Education in Massachusetts, 1870–1915* (Cambridge, Mass., 1971).

25. Nancy Barnard Batchelder, "Growing Up in Peru (1815–1840)," *Vermont History*, 11 (1953): 5.

26. Donald E. Baker, ed., "The Conine Family Letters, 1849–1851: Employed in Honest Business and Doing the Best We Can," *Indiana Magazine of History*, 69 (1973): 341.

27. Kathryn Kish Sklar, "The Founding of Mount Holyoke Female Seminary: A Look at Causation and Change in Female Education in Massachusetts, 1776–1837" (Paper presented at Mount Holyoke College and South Hadley Joint Bicentennial Celebrations, Feb. 13, 1976). A shorter version appears in Mary Beth Norton and Carol Berkin, eds., *Women of America* (Boston, 1979).

28. Rosalyn Baxandall, Linda Gordon, and Susan Reverby, eds., *America's Working Women: A Documentary History, 1600 to the Present* (New York, 1976), p. 38; Ansley J. Coale and Melvin Selnick, *New Estimates of Fertility and Population in the United States* (Princeton, N.J., 1963). For an example of the working out of these general trends see Mary P. Ryan, "A Woman's Awakening: Evangelical Religion and the Families of Utica, N.Y., 1800–1840," *American Quarterly,* 30 (1978): 602–23.

29. Sally Rice to Hazelton and Rhoda Rice, 1839, in Nell W. Kull, "I Can Never Be Happy There in Among So Many Mountains—The Letters of Sally Rice," *Vermont History*, 38 (1970): 52.

30. George M. Woytanowitz, "Educating 'Watch City': The Transformation of Education in Waltham, Massachusetts, 1840–1880," *Journal of the Midwest History of Education Society*, 6 (1978): 19.

31. Sally Rice to Hazelton Rice, Feb. 23, 1845. In Kull, "I Can Never Be Happy," p. 53.

32. Caroline F. Ware, *The Early New England Cotton Manufacture: A Study in Industrial Beginnings* (Boston, 1931), pp. 200–203, 291.

33. On the short-term employment of early women factory employees see Hannah Josephson, *The Golden Threads: New England's Mill Girls and Magnates* (New York, 1949); and Thomas Dublin, "Women Workers and the Study of Social Mobility," *Journal of Interdisciplinary History*, 9 (1979): 654–55. The situation did not change greatly for the Scottish women workers studied in Ray Ginger, "Labor in a Massachusetts Cotton Mill, 1853–60," *Business History Review*, 28 (1954): 67–91.

34. From "My Experience as a Factory Operative," in Philip S. Foner, ed., *The Factory Girls* (Urbana, Ill., 1977), p. 341. See also Lucy Larcom, *A New England Girlhood* (Boston, 1889).

35. Lucy Ann to Cousin Charlotte, June 29, 1851, in "An Independent Voice: A Mill Girl from Vermont Speaks Her Mind," *Vermont History*, 41 (1972): 144.

36. Mary C. Todd to Lucy Chase, Dec. 3, 1837, Chase Family Papers (American Antiquarian Society, by permission).

37. Mary to Ellen Bartlett, Oct. 9, 1870, Ellen [Helen L.] Bartlett MSS (Manuscript Department, William R. Perkins Library, Duke University, by permission).

38. In Foner, *Factory Girls*, p. 336.

39. In Zylpha S. Morton, "Harriet Bishop, Frontier Teacher," *Minnesota History*, 28 (1947): 134, 139 (emphasis added).

40. Richard M. Bernard and Maris A. Vinovskis, "The Female School Teacher in Ante-Bellum Massachusetts," *Journal of Social History*, 10 (1977): 333.

41. Francis Merritt Quick Diary, May 14, 1855, Quick Diary (Radcliffe College, by permission).

42. Charles A. Harper, *Development of the Teachers College in the United States, With Special Reference to the Illinois State Normal University* (Bloomington, Ill., 1935), pp. 102–3.

43. Caroline Prescott, "Female Education," October 9, 1817. Prescott was a student in the Augusta (Maine) Female Academy at this writing. In Quick MSS.

44. See the survey of curricula in female seminaries from 1749 to 1871, with the comparison of earlier (1749–1829) and later (1830–1871) offerings, in Thomas Woody, *A History of Women's Education in the United States* (New York, 1929), 1: 563. The interpretation of the role of female seminaries seems exaggerated and anachronistic in Keith Melder, "Mask of Oppression: The Female Seminary Movement in the United States," *New York History*, 55 (1974): 261–79. Also, the famous academies like

Mount Holyoke and the many obscure ones appear to have been more important in educating women for work like teaching and in reaching below the "upper crust" than is suggested in Vinovskis and Bernard, "Beyond Catharine Beecher," p. 860. Cf. Michael Flusche, "Antislavery and Spiritualism: Myrtilla Miner and Her School," *New York Historical Society Quarterly*, 59 (1975), esp. pp. 154–55, on the Clinton Female Seminary; Forest C. Ensign, "The Era of Private Academies," *Palimpsest*, 27 (March 1946): 75–85, on Iowa seminaries and academies; and Timothy L. Smith, "Uncommon Schools: Christian Colleges and Social Idealism in Midwestern America, 1820–1950," in *The History of Education in the Middle West: Indiana Historical Society Lectures, 1976–1977* (Indianapolis, 1978), esp. p. 30.

45. See the interesting brief biographies, some of them of Mount Holyoke women, in Ethel McMillan, "Women Teachers in Oklahoma, 1820–1860," *Chronicles of Oklahoma*, 27 (1949): 2–32.

46. William L. Hiemstra, "Presbyterian Mission Schools Among the Chocktaws and Chickasaws, 1845–1861," *ibid.*, p. 36.

47. Women teachers who either lived at home or boarded with another family lived overwhelmingly in male-headed households: 60.8 percent with the father present and 27.9 percent in other male-headed families. Ann Weingarten, "Women Common School Teachers in Michigan, 1836–1860: A Study of Their Economic, Social, and Occupational Characteristics," Senior honors thesis (Univ. of Mich., 1976), p. 87, Mich. Historical Collections (Bentley Historical Library, Univ. of Mich.).

48. Melder incorrectly contends that after 1830 informal networks were replaced by formal means of communication and certification; see his "Woman's High Calling: The Teaching Profession in America, 1830–1860," *American Studies*, 13 (1972): 26. On family influence in factory life, see Rosabeth M. Kanter, "Families, Family Processes, and Economic Life: Toward Systematic Analysis of Social Historical Research," in John Demos and Sarane Spence Boocock, eds., *Turning Points: Historical and Sociological Essays on the Family* (Chicago, 1978), pp. 316–39.

49. Kenneth W. Porter, ed., "A Little Girl on an Iowa Forty, 1873–1880—Catherine Wiggins Porter" and "School Days in Coin, Iowa, 1880–1885—Catherine Wiggins Porter," *Iowa Journal of History and Politics*, 51 (1953): 131–55 and 301–28.

50. Millard Fillmore Kennedy, *Schoolmaster of Yesterday: A Three-Generation Family* (New York, 1940). The Applegate Papers are in the Univ. of Oregon Library and the Andrew Funkhouser Papers in the Duke Univ. Library.

51. Joseph W. Snell, ed., "Roughing It on Her Kansas Claim: The

Diary of Abbie Bright, 1870–71," *Kansas Historical Quarterly*, 37 (1971): 234.

52. Jabez Brown MSS (State Historical Society of Wisconsin).

53. Robert Jameson Jones, ed., "An Oakland Girlhood: Lydia Murdoch Jones," *Western Pennsylvania Historical Magazine*, 57 (1974): 463–73.

54. In John Sutherland MSS (Barker Texas History Center Archives, Univ. of Texas, by permission).

55. Johnson, *Home in the Woods*, p. 175.

56. Redding S. Sugg, Jr., *Motherteacher: The Feminization of American Education* (Charlottesville, Va., 1978); Richard G. Boone, *Education in the United States* (New York, 1912), pp. 381–82; U.S. Office of Education, *Report of the Commissioner of Education*, 1 (1899–1900): lxxii; San Francisco Board of Education, *Annual Report* (June 1898), p. 66; Los Angeles Board of Education, *Annual Report of the Board of Education* (1899–1900), pp. 48–50; *Report of the United States Commissioner of Education for 1907–1908*, for cities of 8,000 inhabitants and over, cited in Marion Talbot, *The Education of Women* (Chicago, 1910), p. 23.

57. In Jacob A. Swisher, "Iowa Schools in 1846," *Palimpsest*, 27 (March 1946): 66.

58. Travel Reports, ca. 1913, p. 4, Amanda Stoltzfus MSS (Barker Texas History Center Archives, Univ. of Texas, by permission).

59. Albert H. Leake, *The Vocational Education of Girls and Women* (New York, 1918), p. 152.

60. Elson is quoted in Talbot, *Education of Women*, p. 154. See also James F. Barker, "The Separate Technical High School," in Chester Parker, ed., *Industrial Education: Typical Experiments Described and Interpreted*, 11th Yearbook of the National Society for the Study of Education, pt. 1 (Chicago, 1912), pp. 56–57. The Cleveland Technical High School also offered vocational education to those already at work who wished to acquire skills. That it approached a comprehensive high school may be inferred from the fact that it promised those wishing further schooling "the opportunity to prepare for entrance to technical schools of college rank" (p. 57).

61. A detailed survey of curricular differentiation prior to the Smith-Hughes Act is John Elbert Stout, *The Development of High-School Curricula in the North Central States from 1860 to 1918* (Chicago, 1921). Stout was optimistic that adjustments and reorganization, which were most evident in the years 1910–18, gave "abundant evidence that this movement would continue (p. 259). Cf. Mays, *Concept of Vocational Education*.

62. Charles A. Prosser, *A Study of the Boston Mechanic Arts High School; Being a Report to the Boston School Committee* (New York, 1915), esp. pp. 8, 69.

63. Edward L. Thorndike, "A Neglected Aspect of the American High School," *Educational Review*, 33 (March 1907): 245–55. There were 7,174 high schools reported in America in 1904; of these, 2,175 were one-teacher schools. Often a high school was nothing more than a year or so tacked onto a rural eight-grade elementary school.

64. T. S. Rosen, "Curriculum Opportunities in the Small Six-Year High School," *School Review*, 41 (Feb. 1933): 123–28; F. T. Spaulding, "Can the Small High School Improve Its Curriculum?," *ibid.*, 39 (June 1931): 423–38.

65. Alan Peshkin, *Growing Up American: Schooling and the Survival of Community* (Chicago, 1978), pp. 3, 200. By 1970 school systems like hers, with under 600 students, enrolled only 2.3 percent of the nation's public school students.

66. Yoshi Kasuya, *A Comparative Study of the Secondary Education of Girls in England, Germany, and the United States, with a Consideration of the Secondary Education of Girls in Japan* (New York, 1933), pp. 131, 134.

67. Franklin J. Keller and Morris S. Viteles, *Vocational Guidance Throughout the World: A Comparative Survey* (New York, 1937).

68. Dorothy Canfield Fisher, *Our Young Folks* (New York, 1943), p. 69; Sister M. Teresa Gertrude Murray, *Vocational Guidance in Catholic Secondary Schools: A Study of Development and Present Status* (New York, 1938), pp. 121–22.

69. Selwyn K. Troen, *The Public and the Schools: Shaping the St. Louis System, 1838–1920* (Columbia, Mo., 1975), p. 192.

70. Herbert A. Toops, *Trade Tests in Education* (New York, 1921), pp. 76–79.

71. E. W. Weaver, *Vocations for Girls* (New York, 1913), p. 8.

72. Howard M. Bell, *Youth Tell Their Story: A Study of the Conditions and Attitudes of Young People in Maryland Between the Ages of 16 and 24* (Washington, D.C., 1938), pp. 72–79.

73. Emma H. Minesinger (1866–?), "Montana Memories," typescript in Ida S. Patterson MSS (Univ. of Montana Library).

74. Joseph A. Hill, *Women in Gainful Occupations, 1870 to 1920*, Census Monographs no. 9 (Washington, D.C., 1929), p. 109. For a comparison of black male and female occupations in one city see John W. Blassingame, "Before the Ghetto: The Making of the Black Community in Savannah, Georgia, 1865–1880," *Journal of Social History*, 6 (1973): 466–67. Useful contrasts between white and black women in the labor

force, in the context of the sociology of the family, appear in Bonnie Thorton Dill, "The Dialectics of Black Womanhood," *Signs* 4 (1979): 548–50.

75. In John Burnett, ed., *The Annals of Labour: Autobiographies of British Working Class People, 1820–1920* (Bloomington, Ind., 1947), p. 235.

76. Katherine Anthony, *Mothers Who Must Earn* (New York, 1914), pp. 60–61. As a result of the rejection of domestic work by girls of immigrant parentage, the proportion of native white girls among domestic workers approached 50 percent in 1900. See also Mary Trueblood, "Housework vs. Shop and Factories" (1902), in Baxandal et al., *America's Working Woman*, pp. 156–59; Lucy Maynard Salmon, *Domestic Service* (New York, 1901); Susan M. Strasser, "Mistress and Maid, Employer and Employee: Domestic Service Reform in the United States, 1897–1920," *Marxist Perspectives*, 1 (Winter 1978)): 52–67. For the difference between groups in their patterns of employment see Laurence A. Glasco, "The Life Cycles and Household Structure of American Ethnic Groups: Irish, Germans, and Native-born Whites in Buffalo, New York, 1855," *Journal of Urban History*, 1 (1975): 339–64; Virginia Yans-McLaughlin, *Family and Community: Italian Immigrants in Buffalo, 1880–1930* (Ithaca, N.Y., 1977), esp. pp. 203–10; Maxine S. Seller, "Beyond the Stereotype: A New Look at the Immigrant Woman, 1880–1924," *Journal of Ethnic Studies*, 3 (1975), 59–70.

77. E. W. Weaver, *Vocations for Girls* (New York, 1913), p. 58.

78. Ralph M. Lyon, *The Basis for Constructing Curricular Materials in Adult Education for Carolina Cotton Mill Workers* (New York, 1937), pp. 20, 51.

79. Herbert G. Gutman, *Work, Culture and Society in Industrializing America* (New York, 1977), p. 240; M. Ryan, *Womanhood in America*, p. 201. Though women averaged about 24 percent of all manufacturing employees in 1920, they dominated production in only a few industrial fields. See Douglas, *American Apprenticeship*, pp. 142–62.

80. Porter, "School Days," p. 327.

81. Andria Taylor Hourwich and Gladys L. Palmer, eds., *I Am A Woman Worker: A Scrapbook of Autobiographies* (New York, 1936); Eli Ginzberg and Hyman Berman, *The American Worker in the Twentieth Century: A History Through Autobiographies* (New York, 1963); Helen M. Todd, "Why Children Work: The Children's Answer," *McClures Magazine*, 40 (April 1913): 68–79. Studies of school leavers are surveyed in Meyer Bloomfield, *Youth, School, and Vocation* (Boston, 1915), ch. 2; Bloomfield, ed., *Readings in Vocational Guidance* (Boston, 1915), pp. 396–453; and Will Carson Ryan, Jr., *Vocational Guidance and the Public*

Schools, Bureau of Education Bulletin, 1918, no. 24 (Washington, D.C., 1919).

82. Franklin J. Keller, *Day Schools for Young Workers* (New York, 1924), p. 248; J. Edward Mayman, "The Evolution of the Continuation School in New York City," *School Review*, 41 (1933): 193–205; Willystine Goodsell, *The Education of Women: Its Social Background and Its Problems* (New York, 1923), p. 178.

83. Troen, *Public and the Schools,* p. 191; Talbot, *Education of Women*, p. 24.

84. Bessie Van Vorst and Marie Van Vorst, *The Woman Who Toils; Being the Experiences of Two Gentlewomen as Factory Girls* (New York, 1903), p. 91.

85. Ginzberg and Berman, *American Worker,* pp. 125–26.

86. In southern Italy fathers had received the wages of daughters working in the northern silk mills. Judith Smith, "City and Family: Italians and Jews in Industrial Rhode Island" (Paper presented at the American Historical Association Annual Meeting, Washington, D.C., Dec. 1976), p. 4. On Cohoes, see Daniel J. Walkowitz, "The Alienation of Working-Class Women in the Gilded Age: Factory, Community and Family Life Among Cohoes, New York, Cotton Workers (unpub. paper), pp. 7, 10. On Manchester, see Tamara K. Hareven, "Family Time and Industrial Time: Family and Work in a Planned Corporation Town, 1900–1924," in Hareven, ed., *Family and Kin in Urban Communities, 1700–1930* (New York, 1977), esp. p. 198. On Scranton, see John Bodnar, "Materialism and Morality: Slavic-American Immigrants and Education, 1890–1940," *Journal of Ethnic Studies*, 3 (1976): 1–19. In the 1850's it was estimated that at some time in the family cycle children in the Lowell mills contributed up to 75 percent of family incomes. Thomas Dublin, "Women, Work, and the Family: Female Operatives in the Lowell Mills, 1830–1860," *Feminist Studies*, 3 (1975): 37.

87. Yans-McLaughlin, *Family and Community*, p. 203.

88. Miriam Cohen, *Changing Education Strategies among Migrant Generations: New York Italians in Comparative Perspective* (Paper presented at the American Historical Association Annual Meeting, San Francisco, Dec. 1978), p. 10.

89. Henry Lester Smith, *A Survey of A Public School System* [Bloomington, Ind.] (New York, 1917), pp. 88, 108.

90. David Hogan, "Education and the Making of the Chicago Working Class, 1880–1930," *History of Education Quarterly*, 18 (1978), esp. pp. 238–42; John Modell and Tamara K. Hareven, "Urbanization and the Malleable Household: An Examination of Boarding and Lodging in American Families," in Hareven, *Family and Kin*, pp. 164–86.

91. Robert Smuts, *Women and Work in America* (New York, 1971),

pp. 15–16. On "out-work" in England before 1850, see Ivy Pinchbeck, *Women Workers and the Industrial Revolution, 1750–1850* (New York, 1969), pp. 202–39.

92. Cohen, *Changing Education Strategies*; Selma C. Berrol, *Down from the Pedestal: The High School Experience of Women in New York City, 1900–1920* (Paper presented at the American Educational Research Association Annual Meeting, San Francisco, April 1979).

93. Holman Hamilton and Gayle Thornbrough, eds., *Indianapolis in the "Gay Nineties": High School Diaries of Claude G. Bowers* (Indianapolis, 1964), p. 115. Bowers's mother was a widow who supported herself and her only child as a dressmaker; he did not attend college.

94. Olive Schreiner, *Woman and Labor* (1911), quoted in Rodgers, *Work Ethic*, p. 182.

95. M. Ryan, *Womanhood*, p. 234. A survey of the work available only to boys in a mining community will help explain the two-to-one dominance by girls of the town's high school; see Ivan C. Crawford, "School Days in Leadville," *Colorado Magazine*, 36 (1959): 223–30.

96. Grace Elizabeth Laleger, *The Vocational Interests of High School Girls, as Inventoried by the Strong and Mason Blanks* (New York, 1942), pp. 39–42.

97. Joseph King Van Denburg, *Causes of the Elimination of Students in Public Secondary Schools of New York City* (New York, 1911), p. 185. To the question "Is a high school education necessary for your plans for the future?" the boys answered "yes" more often than the girls (56 to 41 percent) and "no" less often (27 to 37 percent); see p. 71.

98. Elizabeth Woodbridge, "The Unknown Quantity in the Woman Problem," *Atlantic Monthly*, 113 (April 1914): 519.

99. John Moddell, "Suburbanization and Change in the American Family," *Journal of Interdisciplinary History*, 9 (1979): 630.

100. William O. Lynch, a teacher at Elkhart (Ind.) High School during the 1890's, attributed rapid increases in high school attendance to the long depression. In Lynch, "I Complete My Normal Training and Go to Elkhart" [Autobiography, installment 7], *Indiana Magazine of History*, 33 (1937): 355n.

101. Leake, *Vocational Education,* pp. 336, 341, 347.

102. Mary Grant to Elizabeth L. Grant (grandmother), Sept. 14, 1862, Grant Family MSS (Sophia Smith Collection, Women's History Archive, Smith College, by permission).

103. Mary A. Laselle and Katherine E. Wiley, *Vocations for Girls* (Boston, 1913), p. 79. Also see Marjery Davies, "Woman's Place Is at the Typewriter: The Feminization of the Clerical Labor Force," *Radical America*, 8 (July–Aug. 1974): 1–28.

104. Goodsell, *Education of Women*, p. 184; Baxandall et al., *Ameri-*

ca's Working Women, pp. 236, 407. Only one census, in 1950, found telephone operators among the ten leading occupations of women.

105. Berrol, *Down from the Pedestal*, p. 11; Cohen, *Changing Education Strategies*, pp. 33–34, 36, 37. The percentage of New York's Italian women employed in clerical occupations was 8 percent in the first generation and 40 percent in the second; it was 58 percent among those born between 1926 and 1936.

106. Howard N. Rabinowitz, "Half a Loaf: The Shift from White to Black Teachers in the Negro Schools of the Urban South, 1865–1890," *Journal of Southern History*, 40 (1974): 565–94.

107. Troen, *Public and the Schools*, pp. 91, 94.

108. Mary White Ovington, "On the Black Woman as Breadwinner" (1911), in Nancy F. Cott, ed., *Roots of Bitterness: Documents of the Social History of American Women* (New York, 1972), pp. 343–47.

109. Theodore C. Blegen, ed., *Land of Their Choice: The Immigrants Write Home* (Minneapolis, 1955), pp. 388–418.

110. Lotus Delta Coffman, *The Social Composition of the Teaching Population* (New York, 1911), p. 55.

111. Marvin Lowenthal, *Henrietta Szold: Life and Letters* (New York, 1942).

112. Ruth Hill to Kate I. Hansen, June 7, 1896; June ?, 1896; July 12, 1896; July 26, 1896; Hansen-Bales Family MSS (Spencer Research Library, Univ. of Kansas).

113. Kay H. Kamin, *The Woman Peril in American Public Schools: How Perilous?* (Paper presented at the Berkshire Conference on the History of Women, Bryn Mawr College, June 1976.)

114. Garlin Hill to Nell Hill Denlinger, Sept. 4, 1897, Hill Family MSS (Univ. of Oregon Library, by permission).

115. Ernest O. Holland, *The Pennsylvania State Normal Schools and Public School System* (New York, 1912), p. 56.

116. Van Denburg, *Causes of the Elimination of Students*, p. 56.

117. James S. Coleman, *The Adolescent Society* (New York, 1961).

118. Parsons, *Woman's Dilemma*, pp. 274–75. See also Kett, *Rites of Passage*, pp. 95–96.

119. Laura V. Clark, *A Study of Occupations, Other than Homemaking, Open to Women Trained in Home Economics*, Homemaking Education Series no. 1, Leaflet no. 5 (Berkeley, Calif., April 1927), p. 4.

120. Stow, *History of Mount Holyoke Seminary*, p. 127.

121. The proportions of all women in the professions declined between 1930 (15 percent) and 1960 (11 percent); and the percentage and sometimes even the absolute number of professionals *other than teachers* slipped steadily. See Barbara J. Harris, *Beyond Her Sphere: Women and*

the Professions (Westport, Conn., 1978), p. 156. Black women have come to constitute a greater proportion of black professionals than is the case with white professionals; see Cynthia Fuchs Epstein, "Positive Effects of the Multiple Negative: Explaining the Success of Black Professional Women," *American Journal of Sociology*, 78 (1973): 916.

122. Goodsell, *Education of Women*, pp. 153–54.

123. Mabel Louise Robinson, *The Curriculum of the Women's College*, Bureau of Education Bulletin, 1918, no. 6 (Washington, D.C., 1918), p. 120.

124. Parsons, *Woman's Dilemma*, pp. 277–78.

125. Dee Garrison, "The Tender Technicians: The Feminization of Public Librarianship, 1876–1905," in Mary S. Hartman and Lois Banner, eds., *Clio's Consciousness Raised: New Perspectives on the History of Women* (New York, 1974), pp. 158–78; Mary Elizabeth Downey, "Librarianship," in Doris E. Fleischman, ed., *An Outline of Careers for Women: A Practical Guide to Achievement* (Garden City, N.Y., 1928), p. 285.

126. Harris, *Beyond Her Sphere*, p. 118; Jane Addams, *Twenty Years at Hull House* (1910; repr. ed., New York, 1961), p. 93. See also Jill Conway, "Women Reformers and American Culture, 1870–1930," *Journal of Social History*, 5 (1971–72): 164–77; and the Epilogue to Susan P. Conrad, *Perish the Thought: Intellectual Women in Romantic America, 1830–1860* (New York, 1976).

127. *Reminiscences of Linda Richards: America's First Trained Nurse* (Boston, 1915), p. 4.

128. O. Latham Hatcher, ed., *Occupations for Women: A Study for the Southern Woman's Educational Alliance* (Atlanta, 1927), p. 329.

129. Florence Peck Diary, Jan. 23, 1901.

130. Troen, *Public and the Schools*, p. 189; Margery Stewart Gillson, *Developing a High School Chemistry Course Adapted to the Differentiated Needs of Boys and Girls* (New York, 1937), p. 7.

131. Charles Henry Keyes, *Progress Through the Grades of City Schools: A Study of Acceleration and Arrest* (New York, 1911), pp. 12, 57, 59.

132. Harriet Lane Levy, *920 O'Farrell Street* (Garden City, N.Y., 1947), pp. 123–24, 129.

133. Elizabeth Kemper Adams, *Women Professional Workers* (New York, 1921), p. 18.

134. Keith W. Olson, *The G.I. Bill, the Veterans, and the Colleges* (Lexington, Ky., 1974), p. 103.

135. Bell, *Youth Tell Their Story*, pp. 233, 236; Oppenheimer, *Female Labor Force*.

136. John Moddell, Frank E. Furstenberg, Jr., and Theodore Hersh-

berg, "Social Change and Transitions to Adulthood in Historical Perspective," *Journal of Family History* (1976): 29.

137. Grant Allen, "Women's Place in Nature," *Forum*, 7 (June 1889): 263.

138. Henrietta W. Calvin, "Principles and Policies in Home Economics Education," Bureau of Education Home Economics Circular no. 4 (Washington, D.C., April 1918), pp. 1, 7.

139. Clara Brown Arny, *The Effectiveness of the High School Program in Home Economics: A Report of a Five-Year Study in Twenty Minnesota Schools* (Minneapolis, 1952), p. 100.

140. L. J. West, "Business Education," in Robert L. Ebel, ed., *Encyclopedia of Educational Research* (New York, 1969).

141. Frank Sticker challenges the tendency of historians to attribute the decline of organized feminism to a retreat by women from the goal of economic independence and betterment through work; see Stricker, "Cookbooks and Law Books: The Hidden History of Career Women in Twentieth Century America," *Journal of Social History*, 10 (1976): 1–19. Cf. Patricia Albjerg Graham, "Expansion and Exclusion: A History of Women in American Higher Education," *Signs*, 3 (1978): 759–73; and Roberta Frankfort, *Collegiate Women: Domesticity and Career in Turn-of-the-Century America* (New York, 1977). The growing enrollment of women in professional and graduate schools leads Victor R. Fuchs to foresee less segregation in the labor market; see Fuchs, "A Note on Sex Segregation in Professional Occupations," *Explorations in Economic Research*, 2 (1975): 105–111. According to Edward Gross, however, a more likely reason for less segregation is that female-dominated careers admit more males, rather than the reverse. See Gross, "Plus ça change. . . ? The Sexual Structure of Occupations Over Time," *Social Problems*, 16 (1968): 198–208.

142. Annie Robinson Dyer, *The Administration of Home Economics in City Schools: A Study of Present and Desired Practices in the Organization of the Home Economics Program* (New York, 1928), p. 62.

143. Erich Fromm, *The Art of Loving* (New York, 1956), p. 62.

Rodgers and Tyack: Critical Research Areas

1. Our essay has benefited from the critical commentary of Elisabeth Hansot and Harvey Kantor, though they should, of course, not be blamed for our errors and idiosyncracies. Since the preceding essays contain extensive documentation, we have chosen here to cite only studies that supplement those footnotes.

2. *The New-England Primer Restored* (Trenton, N.J., 1845), p. 7;

Robert A. Gross, *The Minutemen and Their World* (New York, 1976), p. 75.

3. Ruth Miller Elson, *Guardians of Tradition: American Schoolbooks of the Nineteenth Century* (Lincoln, Neb., 1964).

4. Daniel T. Rodgers, "Socializing Middle-Class Children: Institutions, Fables, and Work Values in Nineteenth-Century America," *Journal of Social History*, 13 (1980): 354–67.

5. On the displacement of young workers by machines, see Selwyn K. Troen, "The Discovery of the Adolescent by American Educational Reformers, 1900–1920: An Economic Perspective," in Lawrence Stone, ed., *Schooling and Society: Studies in the History of Education* (Baltimore, 1976), pp. 241–43.

6. Leslie Woodcock Tentler, *Wage-Earning Women: Industrial Work and Family Life in the United States, 1900–1930* (New York, 1979), ch. 4; John Modell, "Patterns of Consumption, Acculturation, and Family-Income Strategies in Late-Nineteenth-Century America," in Tamara K. Hareven and Maris A. Vinovskis, eds., *Family and Population in Nineteenth-Century America* (Princeton, N.J., 1978); Miriam Cohen, "Italian-American Women in New York City, 1900–1950: Work and School," in Milton Cantor and Bruce Laurie, eds., *Class, Sex, and the Woman Worker* (Westport, Conn., 1977); David Hogan, "Education and the Making of the Chicago Working Class, 1880–1930," *History of Education Quarterly*, 18 (1978): 227–70; Tamara K. Hareven and Randolph Langenbach, *Amoskeag: Life and Work in An American Factory-City* (New York, 1978).

7. Daniel Nelson, *Managers and Workers: Origins of the New Factory System in the United States, 1880–1920* (Madison, Wis., 1975); Alfred D. Chandler, *The Visible Hand: The Managerial Revolution in American Business* (Cambridge, Mass., 1977).

8. David Brody, *Steelworkers in America: The Nonunion Era* (Cambridge, Mass., 1960); Harry Braverman, *Labor and Monopoly Capital: The Degradation of Work in the Twentieth Century* (New York, 1974).

9. Samuel Bowles and Herbert Gintis, *Schooling in Capitalist America: Educational Reform and the Contradictions of Economic Life* (New York, 1976).

10. Joseph M. Rice, *The Public-School System of the United States* (New York, 1893); David B. Tyack, *The One Best System: A History of American Urban Education* (Cambridge, Mass., 1974), pp. 49–56.

11. A useful study of ideology is Arthur Wirth, *Education in the Technological Society: The Vocational-Liberal Studies Controversy in the Early Twentieth Century* (Scranton, Pa., 1972).

12. An early lead in this direction was made by Berenice M. Fisher in

Industrial Education: American Ideals and Institutions (Madison, Wis., 1967), pp. 165–94.

13. Robert H. Wiebe, *The Search for Order, 1877–1920* (New York, 1967); James Weinstein, *The Corporate Ideal in the Liberal State, 1900–1918* (Boston, 1968), ch. 1; Samuel P. Hays, *American Political History as Social Analysis* (Knoxville, Tenn., 1980).

14. Randall Collins, *The Credential Society: An Historical Sociology of Education and Stratification* (New York, 1979).

15. Frances FitzGerald, *America Revised: History Schoolbooks in the Twentieth Century* (Boston, 1979).

16. See David Hogan's discussion of recent social science literature in this volume.

17. Paul H. Douglas, *American Apprenticeship and Industrial Education* (New York, 1921); John Dewey, "Education vs. Trade-Training," *New Republic*, 3 (May 15, 1915): 42–43.

18. David Cohen and Bella Rosenberg, "Functions and Fantasies: Understanding Schools in Capitalist America," *History of Education Quarterly,* 17 (1977): 113–37; David B. Tyack and Elisabeth Hansot, "Conflict and Consensus in American Public Education," *Daedalus,* 110 (1981): 1–25.

INDEX

INDEX